Hooray!
Anime version
coming!

空 知 英 秋

Hideaki Sorachi

I do believe in miracles!

VRRRRRR

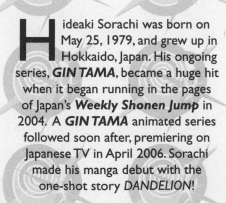

Hideaki Sorachi was born on May 25, 1979, and grew up in Hokkaido, Japan. His ongoing series, ***GIN TAMA***, became a huge hit when it began running in the pages of Japan's ***Weekly Shonen Jump*** in 2004. A ***GIN TAMA*** animated series followed soon after, premiering on Japanese TV in April 2006. Sorachi made his manga debut with the one-shot story *DANDELION*!

GIN TAMA VOL. 8
The SHONEN JUMP ADVANCED Manga Edition

STORY & ART BY HIDEAKI SORACHI

Translation/Matthew Rosin, Honyaku Center Inc.
English Adaptation/Gerard Jones
Touch-up Art & Lettering/Avril Averill
Cover & Interior Design/Sean Lee, Izumi Evers
Editor/Mike Montesa

Editor in Chief, Books/Alvin Lu
Editor in Chief, Magazines/Marc Weidenbaum
VP of Publishing Licensing/Rika Inouye
VP of Sales/Gonzalo Ferreyra
Sr. VP of Marketing/Liza Coppola
Publisher/Hyoe Narita

Printed in the U.S.A.

Published by VIZ Media, LLC
P.O. Box 77010
San Francisco, CA 94107

SHONEN JUMP ADVANCED Manga Edition
10 9 8 7 6 5 4 3 2 1
First printing, September 2008

RATED T+ FOR OLDER TEEN

PARENTAL ADVISORY
GIN TAMA is rated T+ for Older Teen and is recommended for ages 16 and up. It contains suggestive situations.

ratings.viz.com

www.viz.com

THE WORLD'S MOST CUTTING-EDGE MANGA
www.shonenjump.com

STORY & ART BY

HIDEAKI SORACHI

GIN TAMA

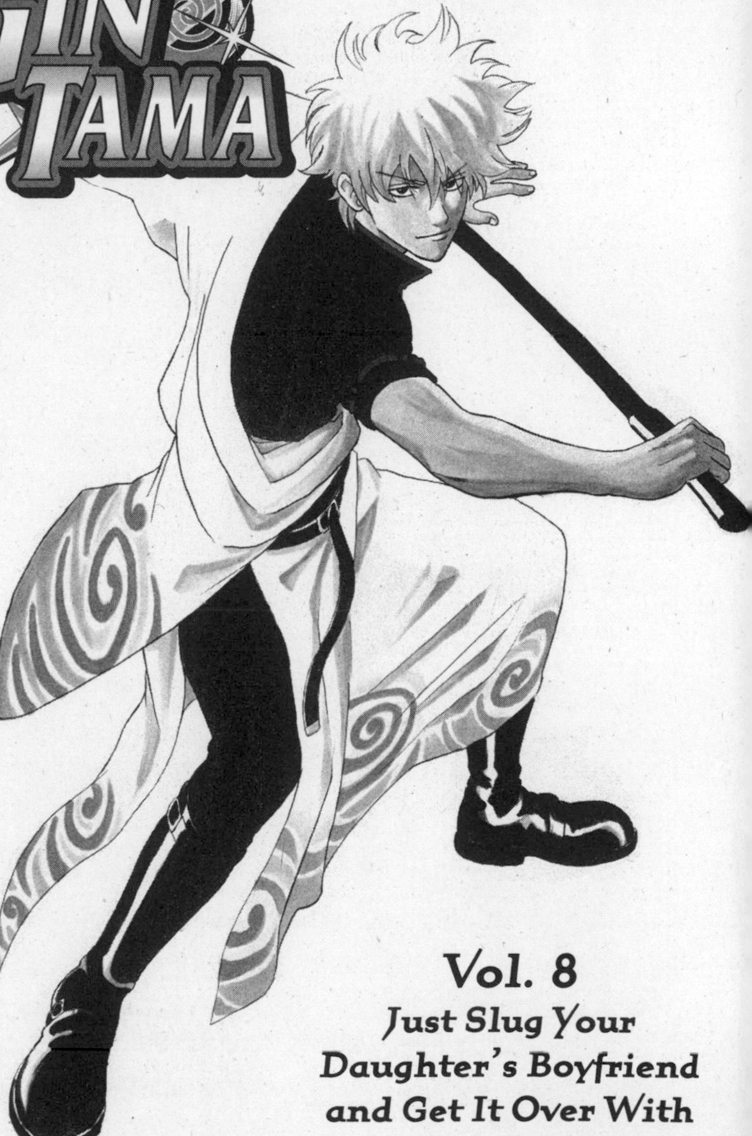

Vol. 8

Just Slug Your Daughter's Boyfriend and Get It Over With

Yorozuya Members

Shinpachi Shimura

Works under Gintoki in an attempt to learn about the samurai spirit, but has been regretting his decision recently. Also president of idol singer Tsu Terakado's fan club.

Gintoki Sakata

The hero of our story. He needs to eat something sweet periodically or he gets cranky. He commands a powerful sword arm but is one step away from diabetes. A former member of the exclusionist faction that seeks to eliminate the space aliens and protect the nation.

Kagura

A member of the "Yato Clan," the most powerful warrior race in the universe. Her voracious appetite and often inadvertent comic timing are unrivalled.

Sadaharu/animal

A giant space creature kept as a pet in the Yorozuya office. Likes to bite people (especially Gintoki).

Shinsengumi Soldiers

Okita

The most formidable swordsman in the Shinsengumi. His jovial attitude hides an utterly black heart. He wants to take over as the Vice-Chief.

Hijikata

Vice-Chief of the Shinsengumi, Edo's elite Delta Force police unit. His cool demeanor turns to rage the moment he draws his sword. The pupils of his eyes always seem a bit dilated.

Kondo

Chief of the Shinsengumi, and trusted by all its soldiers. Also stalking Shinpachi's elder sister Otae.

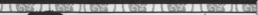

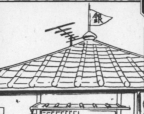

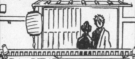

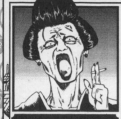

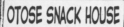

ODD JOBS GIN
OTOSE SNACK HOUSE

Other Characters

Otose-san

Proprietor of the pub below the Yorozuya hideout. She has a lot of difficulty collecting rent.

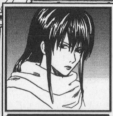

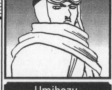

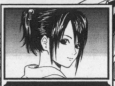

Otae

Shinpachi's elder sister. Appears demure, but is actually quite combative. Kondo's stalking has tipped her over the edge.

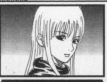

Ayame Sarutobi

A ninja assassin, called "Sachan" because of her last name. She likes Gin, and she likes to be pushed around.

Kotaro Katsura

The last living holdout among the exclusionist rebels, and Gintoki's pal. Nickname: "Zura."

Umibozu

Kagura's Dad. He travels the stars as the top alien-hunter in the galaxy.

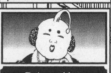

Prince Hata

An alien prince. Not too bright, but passionate about unusual animals.

The story thus far

In an alternate-universe Edo (Tokyo), extraterrestrials land in Japan and the new government issues an order outlawing swords. The samurai, who have reached the pinnacle of power and prosperity, fall into rapid decline.

Twenty years hence, only one samurai has managed to hold onto his fighting spirit: a somewhat eccentric fellow named Gintoki "Odd Jobs Gin" Sakata. A lover of sweets and near diabetic, our hero sets up shop as a *yorozuya*—an expert at managing trouble and handling the oddest jobs.

Joining "Gin" in his business is Shinpachi Shimura, whose sister Gintoki saved from the clutches of nefarious debt collectors. After a series of unexpected circumstances, the trio meets a powerful alien named Kagura, who becomes—after some arm-twisting—a part-time team member.

Then Gin-san gets amnesia from an accident, a spaceship crashes into the Yorozuya residence, a fierce battle erupts over who gets an issue of *JUMP*, and finally Kagura's father appears to say he's taking her home! Will she really leave them…?!

WHAT THIS MANGA'S FULL OF
vol. 8

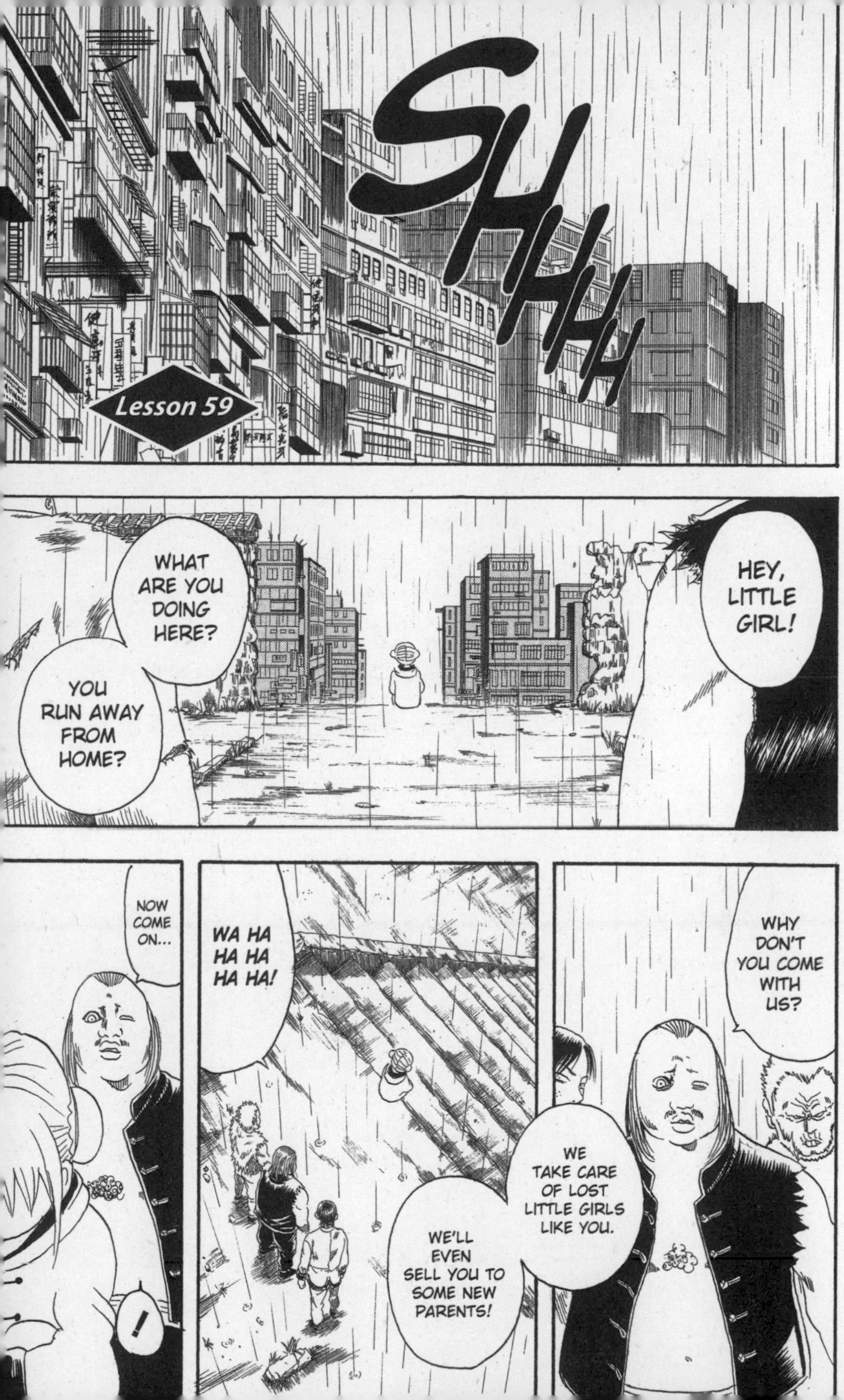
SHHHH
Lesson 59
HEY, LITTLE GIRL!
WHAT ARE YOU DOING HERE?
YOU RUN AWAY FROM HOME?
WHY DON'T YOU COME WITH US?
WE TAKE CARE OF LOST LITTLE GIRLS LIKE YOU.
WE'LL EVEN SELL YOU TO SOME NEW PARENTS!
WA HA HA HA HA HA!
NOW COME ON...
!

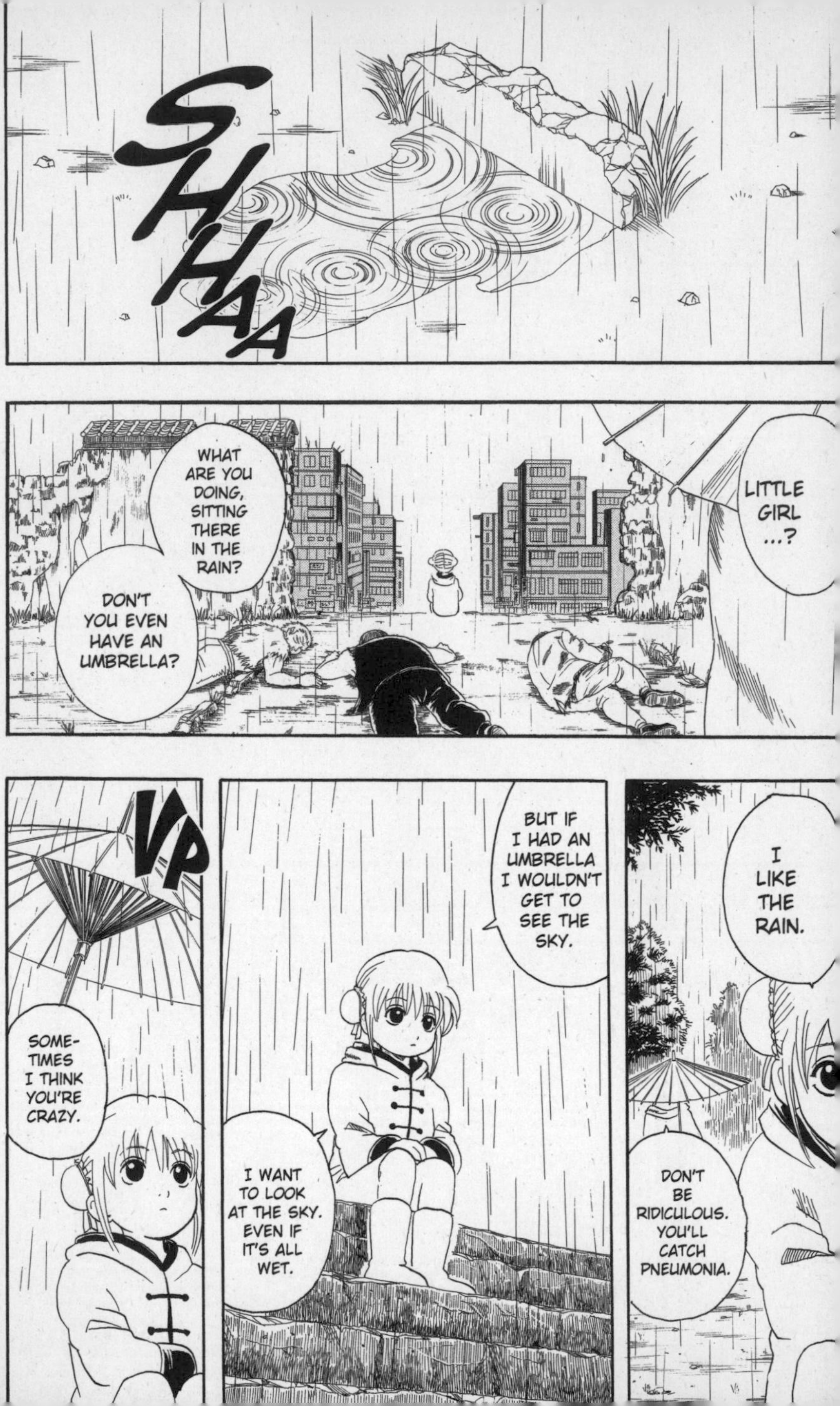
SHHAA
LITTLE GIRL ...?
WHAT ARE YOU DOING, SITTING THERE IN THE RAIN?
DON'T YOU EVEN HAVE AN UMBRELLA?
I LIKE THE RAIN.
DON'T BE RIDICULOUS. YOU'LL CATCH PNEUMONIA.
BUT IF I HAD AN UMBRELLA I WOULDN'T GET TO SEE THE SKY.
I WANT TO LOOK AT THE SKY. EVEN IF IT'S ALL WET.
VP
SOME-TIMES I THINK YOU'RE CRAZY.

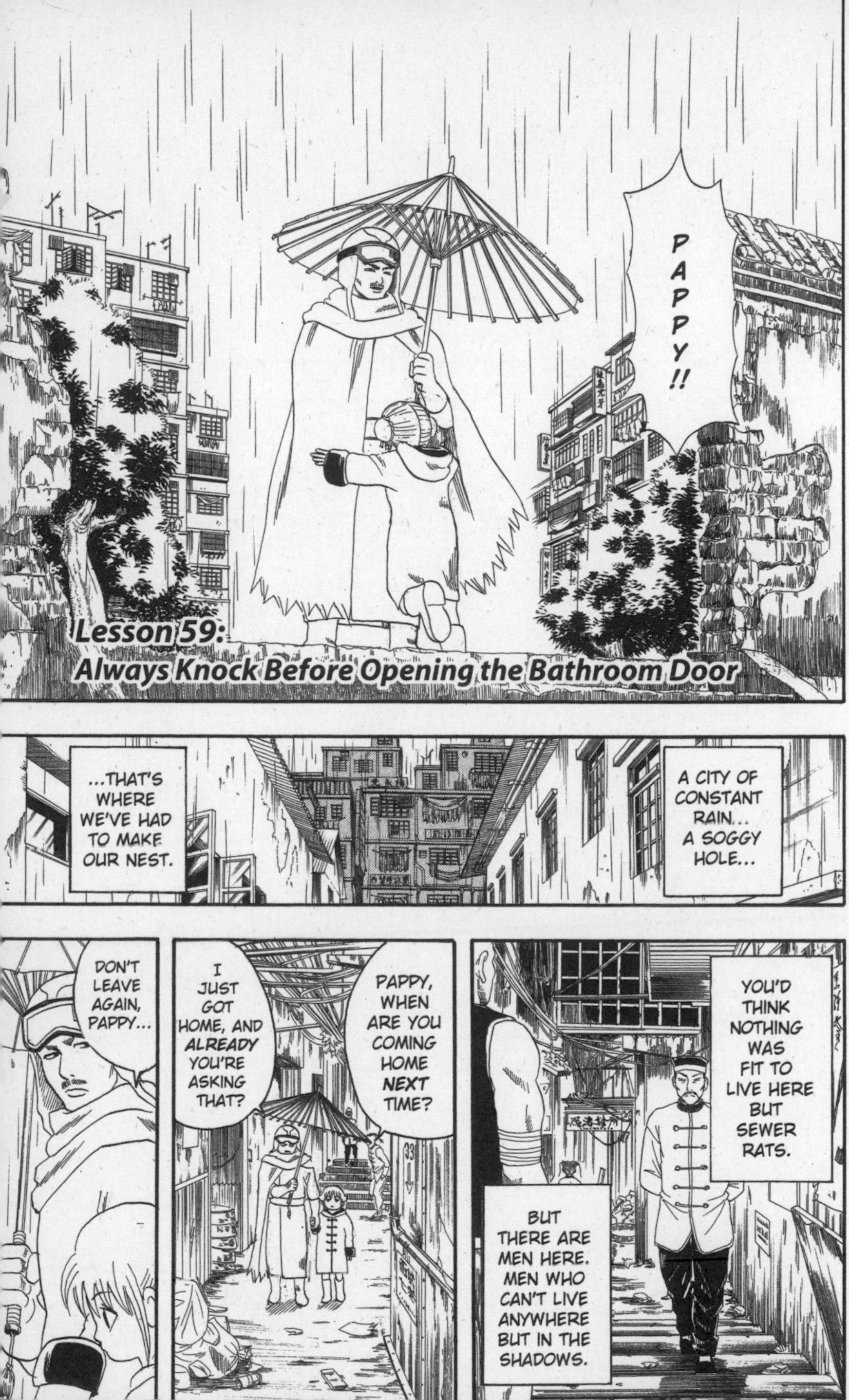
PAPPY!!
Lesson 59: Always Knock Before Opening the Bathroom Door
A CITY OF CONSTANT RAIN... A SOGGY HOLE...
...THAT'S WHERE WE'VE HAD TO MAKE OUR NEST.
YOU'D THINK NOTHING WAS FIT TO LIVE HERE BUT SEWER RATS.
BUT THERE ARE MEN HERE. MEN WHO CAN'T LIVE ANYWHERE BUT IN THE SHADOWS.
PAPPY, WHEN ARE YOU COMING HOME NEXT TIME?
I JUST GOT HOME, AND ALREADY YOU'RE ASKING THAT?
DON'T LEAVE AGAIN, PAPPY...

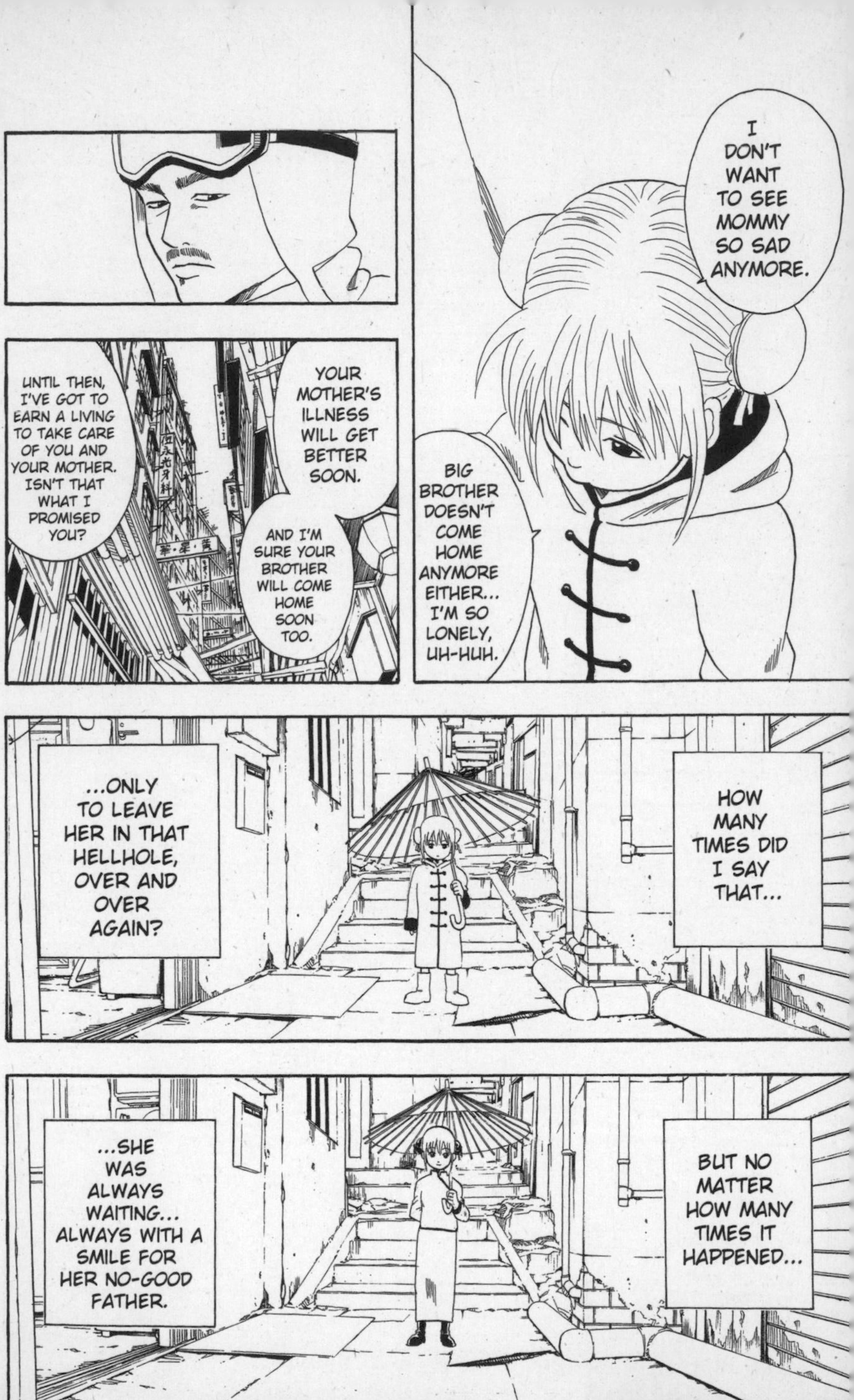
I DON'T WANT TO SEE MOMMY SO SAD ANYMORE.
BIG BROTHER DOESN'T COME HOME ANYMORE EITHER... I'M SO LONELY, UH-HUH.
YOUR MOTHER'S ILLNESS WILL GET BETTER SOON.
AND I'M SURE YOUR BROTHER WILL COME HOME SOON TOO.
UNTIL THEN, I'VE GOT TO EARN A LIVING TO TAKE CARE OF YOU AND YOUR MOTHER. ISN'T THAT WHAT I PROMISED YOU?
HOW MANY TIMES DID I SAY THAT...
...ONLY TO LEAVE HER IN THAT HELLHOLE, OVER AND OVER AGAIN?
BUT NO MATTER HOW MANY TIMES IT HAPPENED...
...SHE WAS ALWAYS WAITING... ALWAYS WITH A SMILE FOR HER NO-GOOD FATHER.

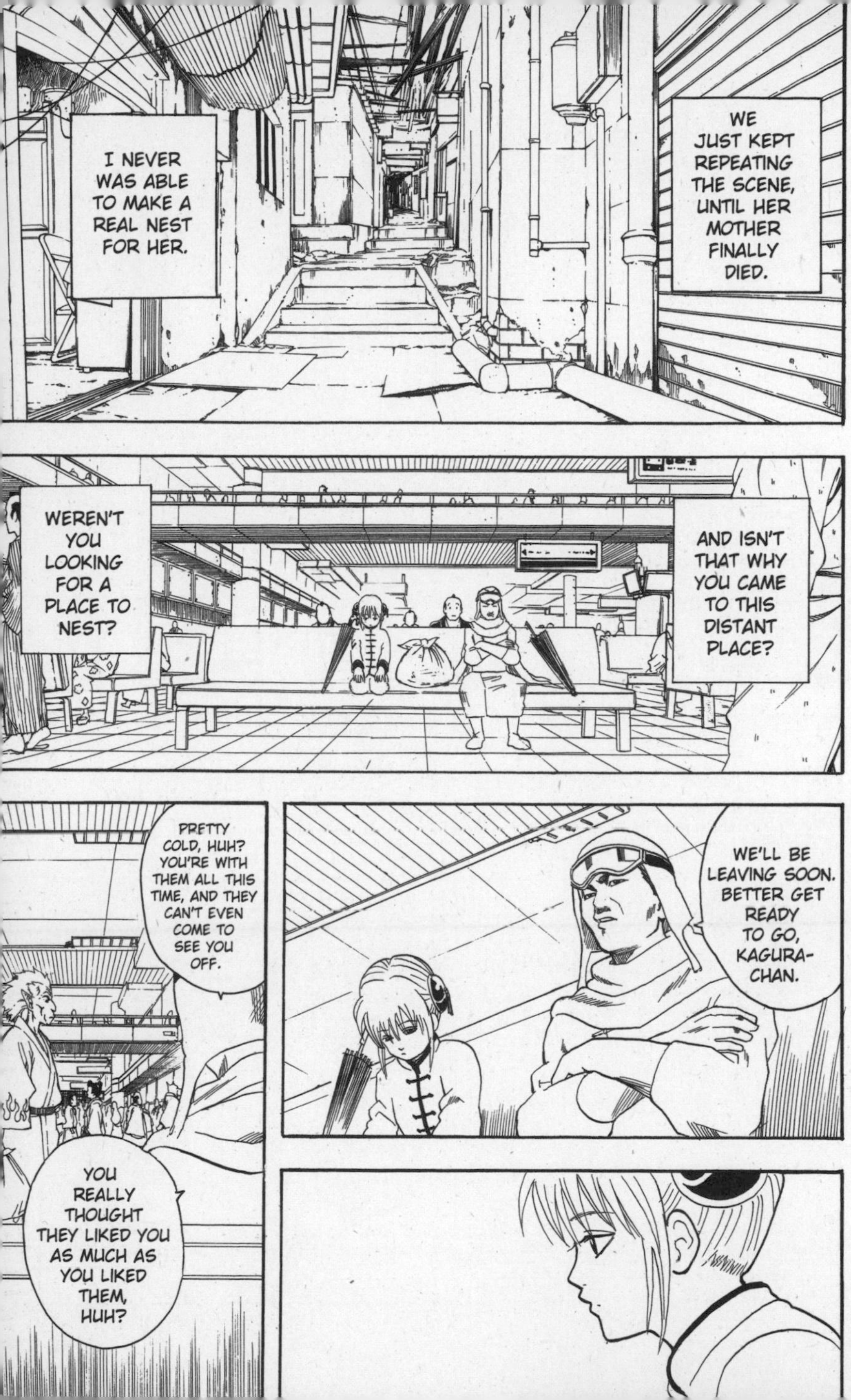
WE JUST KEPT REPEATING THE SCENE, UNTIL HER MOTHER FINALLY DIED.
I NEVER WAS ABLE TO MAKE A REAL NEST FOR HER.
AND ISN'T THAT WHY YOU CAME TO THIS DISTANT PLACE?
WEREN'T YOU LOOKING FOR A PLACE TO NEST?
WE'LL BE LEAVING SOON. BETTER GET READY TO GO, KAGURA-CHAN.
PRETTY COLD, HUH? YOU'RE WITH THEM ALL THIS TIME, AND THEY CAN'T EVEN COME TO SEE YOU OFF.
YOU REALLY THOUGHT THEY LIKED YOU AS MUCH AS YOU LIKED THEM, HUH?

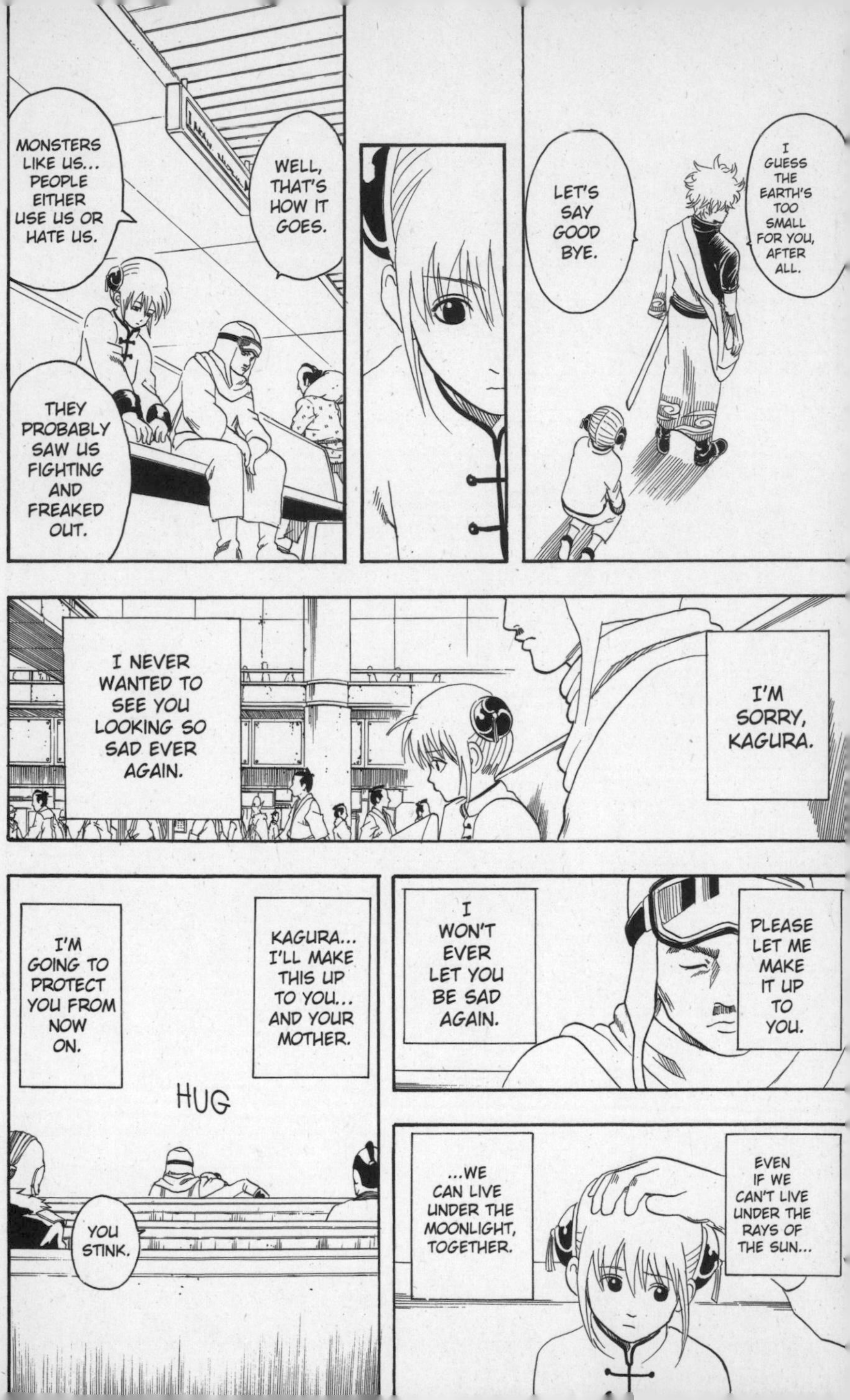
I GUESS THE EARTH'S TOO SMALL FOR YOU, AFTER ALL.
LET'S SAY GOOD BYE.
WELL, THAT'S HOW IT GOES.
MONSTERS LIKE US... PEOPLE EITHER USE US OR HATE US.
THEY PROBABLY SAW US FIGHTING AND FREAKED OUT.
I'M SORRY, KAGURA.
I NEVER WANTED TO SEE YOU LOOKING SO SAD EVER AGAIN.
PLEASE LET ME MAKE IT UP TO YOU.
I WON'T EVER LET YOU BE SAD AGAIN.
EVEN IF WE CAN'T LIVE UNDER THE RAYS OF THE SUN...
...WE CAN LIVE UNDER THE MOONLIGHT, TOGETHER.
KAGURA... I'LL MAKE THIS UP TO YOU... AND YOUR MOTHER.
I'M GOING TO PROTECT YOU FROM NOW ON.
HUG
YOU STINK.

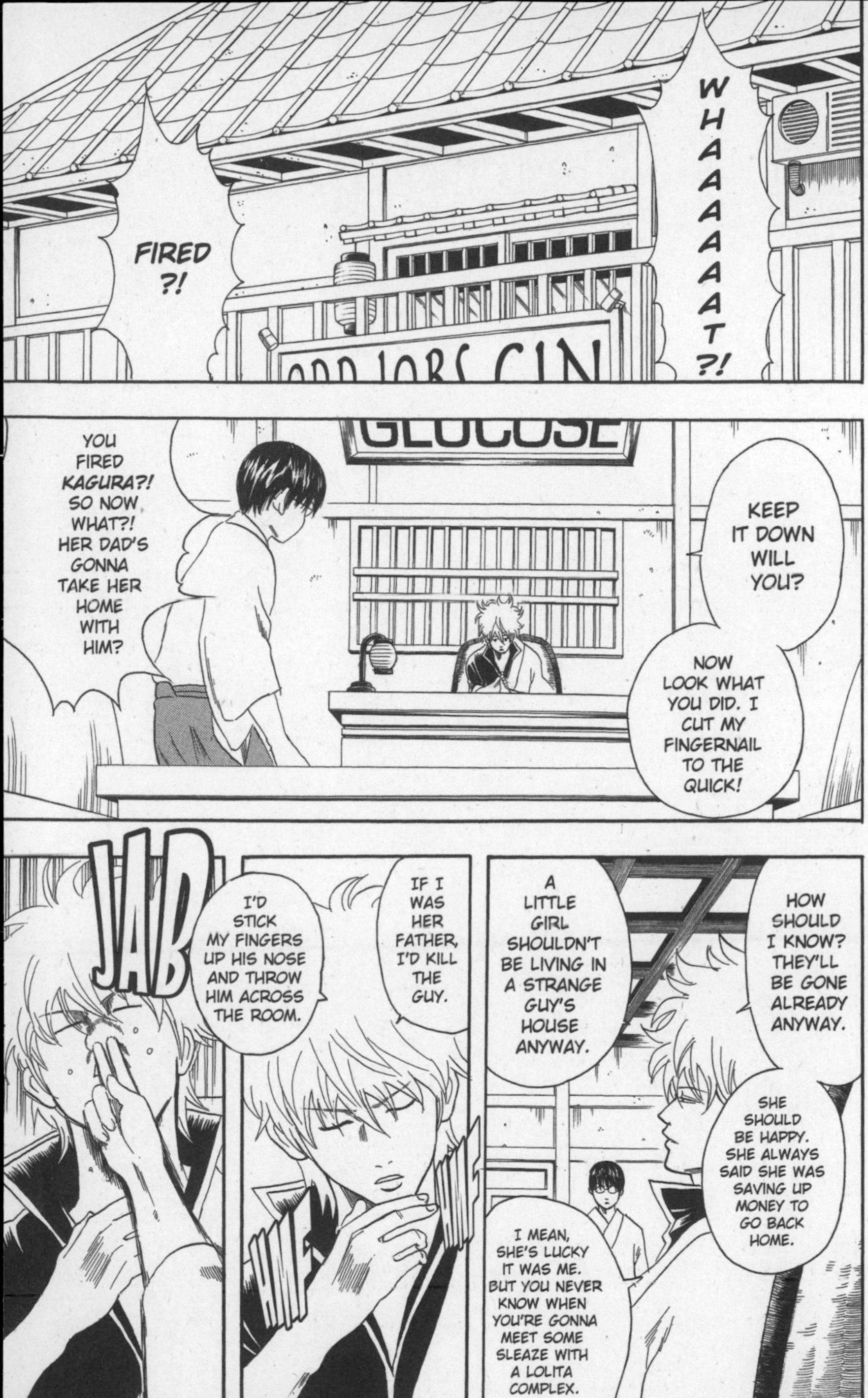

WHAAAAAAAT?!
FIRED ?!
GLUCOSE
YOU FIRED KAGURA?! SO NOW WHAT?! HER DAD'S GONNA TAKE HER HOME WITH HIM?
KEEP IT DOWN WILL YOU?
NOW LOOK WHAT YOU DID. I CUT MY FINGERNAIL TO THE QUICK!
HOW SHOULD I KNOW? THEY'LL BE GONE ALREADY ANYWAY.
A LITTLE GIRL SHOULDN'T BE LIVING IN A STRANGE GUY'S HOUSE ANYWAY.
SHE SHOULD BE HAPPY. SHE ALWAYS SAID SHE WAS SAVING UP MONEY TO GO BACK HOME.
I MEAN, SHE'S LUCKY IT WAS ME. BUT YOU NEVER KNOW WHEN YOU'RE GONNA MEET SOME SLEAZE WITH A LOLITA COMPLEX.
IF I WAS HER FATHER, I'D KILL THE GUY.
JAB
I'D STICK MY FINGERS UP HIS NOSE AND THROW HIM ACROSS THE ROOM.

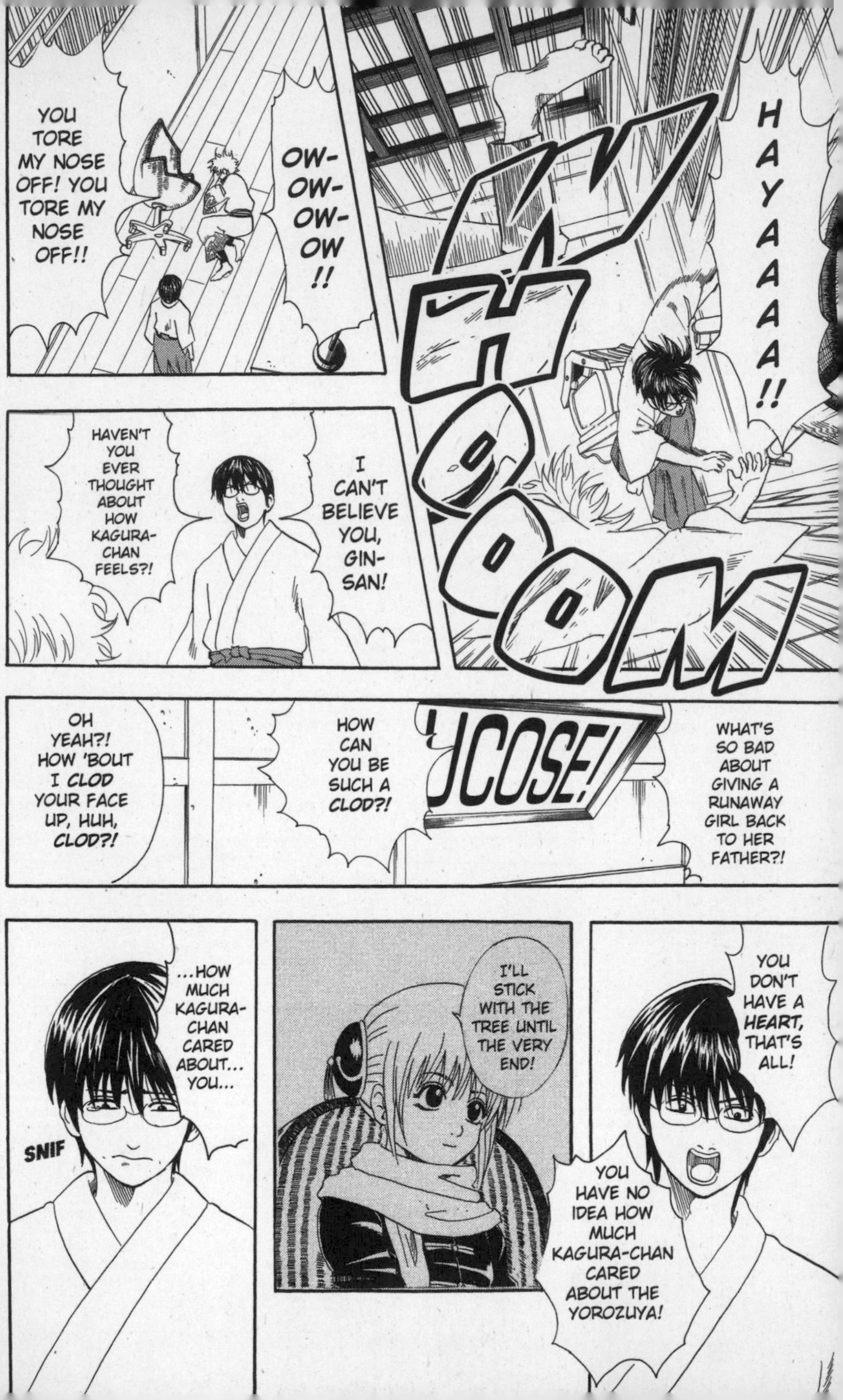
HAYAAAAA!!
WHOOOM
OW-OW-OW-OW!!
YOU TORE MY NOSE OFF! YOU TORE MY NOSE OFF!!
I CAN'T BELIEVE YOU, GIN-SAN!
HAVEN'T YOU EVER THOUGHT ABOUT HOW KAGURA-CHAN FEELS?!
WHAT'S SO BAD ABOUT GIVING A RUNAWAY GIRL BACK TO HER FATHER?!
JCOSE!
HOW CAN YOU BE SUCH A CLOD?!
OH YEAH?! HOW 'BOUT I CLOD YOUR FACE UP, HUH, CLOD?!
YOU DON'T HAVE A HEART, THAT'S ALL!
YOU HAVE NO IDEA HOW MUCH KAGURA-CHAN CARED ABOUT THE YOROZUYA!
I'LL STICK WITH THE TREE UNTIL THE VERY END!
...HOW MUCH KAGURA-CHAN CARED ABOUT... YOU...
SNIF

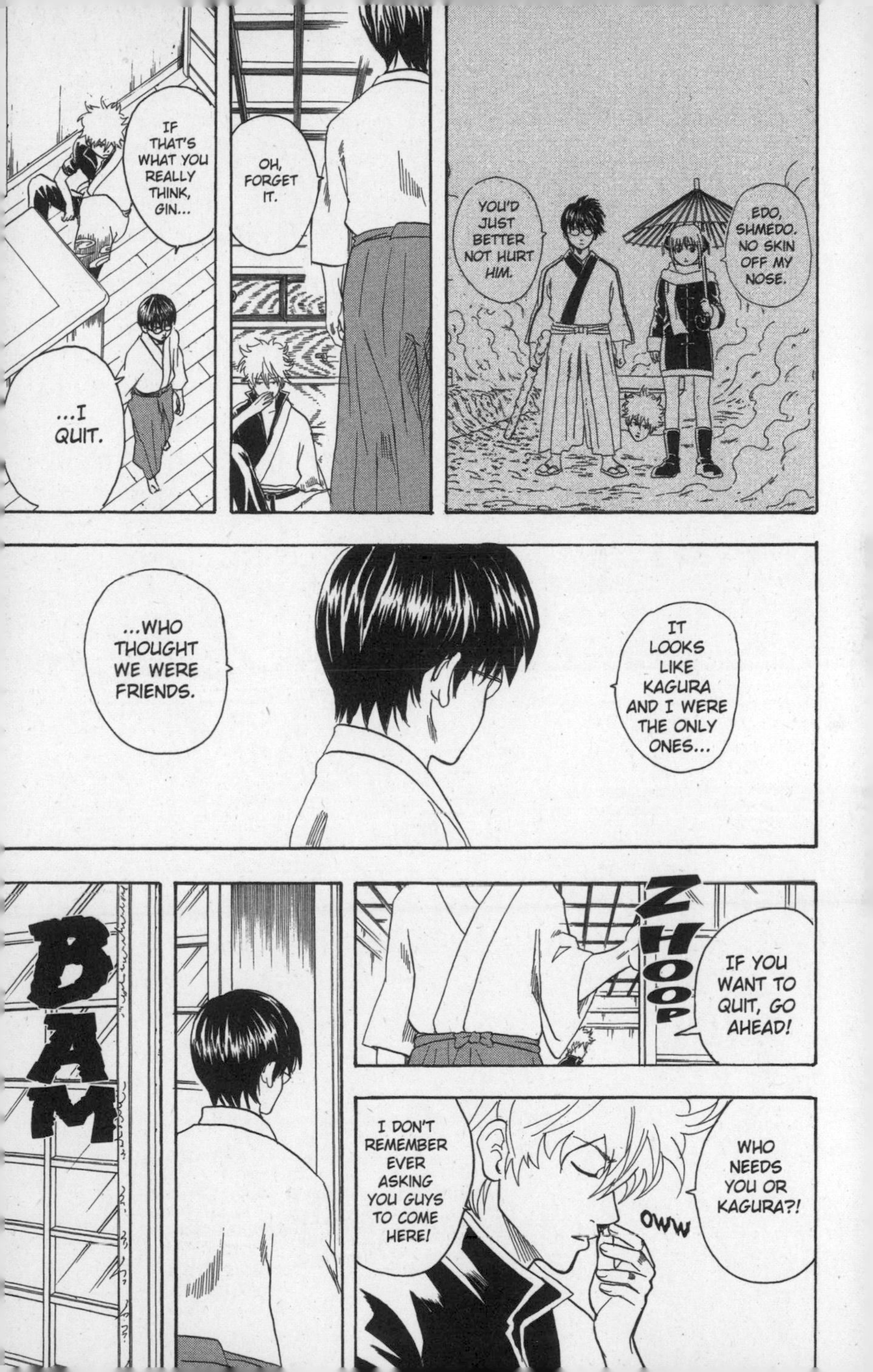
EDO, SHMEDO. NO SKIN OFF MY NOSE.
YOU'D JUST BETTER NOT HURT HIM.
OH, FORGET IT.
IF THAT'S WHAT YOU REALLY THINK, GIN...
...I QUIT.
IT LOOKS LIKE KAGURA AND I WERE THE ONLY ONES...
...WHO THOUGHT WE WERE FRIENDS.
IF YOU WANT TO QUIT, GO AHEAD!
ZHOOP
WHO NEEDS YOU OR KAGURA?!
OWW
I DON'T REMEMBER EVER ASKING YOU GUYS TO COME HERE!
BAM

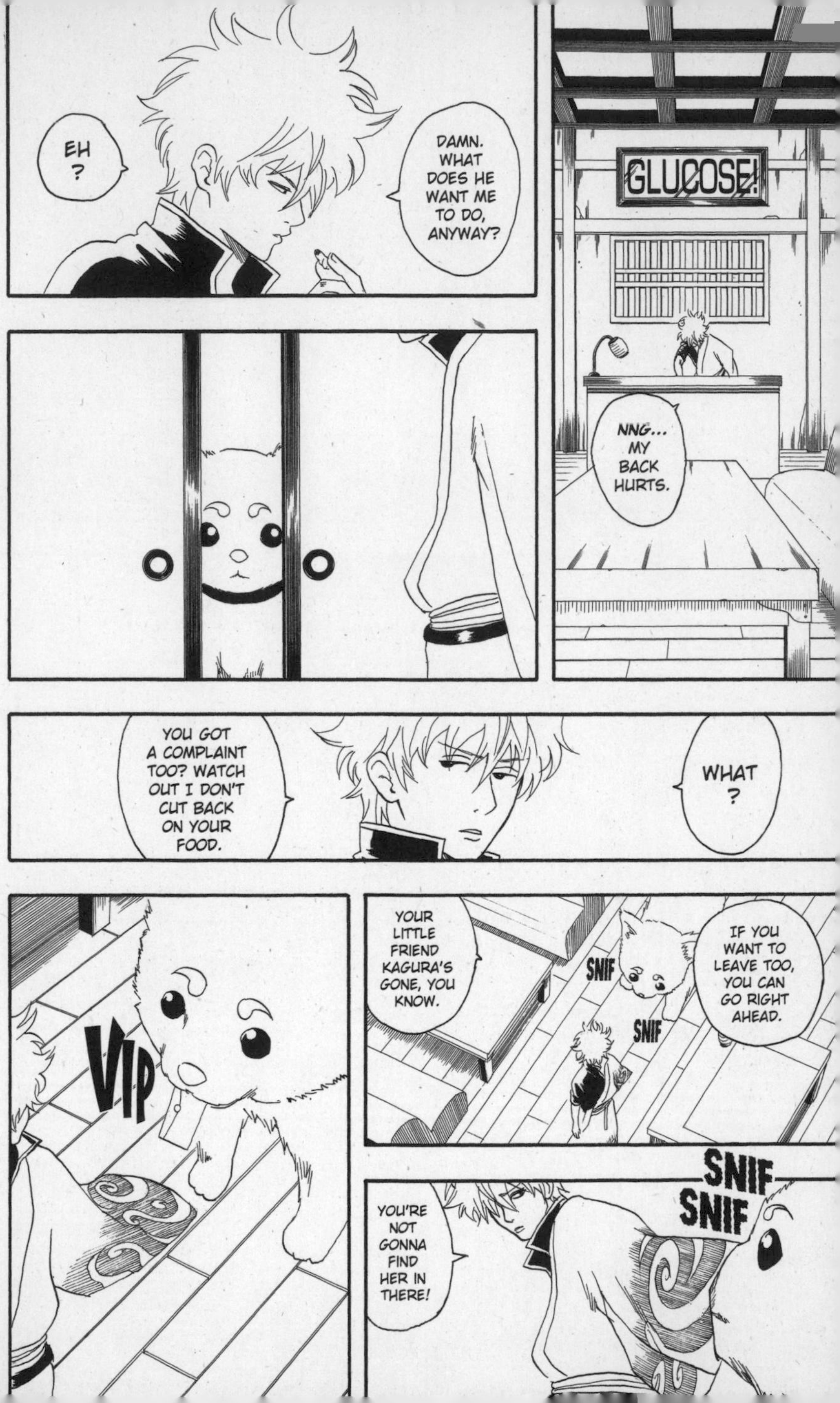
GLUCOSE!
NNG... MY BACK HURTS.
DAMN. WHAT DOES HE WANT ME TO DO, ANYWAY?
EH?
WHAT?
YOU GOT A COMPLAINT TOO? WATCH OUT I DON'T CUT BACK ON YOUR FOOD.
IF YOU WANT TO LEAVE TOO, YOU CAN GO RIGHT AHEAD.
SNIF
SNIF
YOUR LITTLE FRIEND KAGURA'S GONE, YOU KNOW.
SNIF SNIF
YOU'RE NOT GONNA FIND HER IN THERE!
VIP

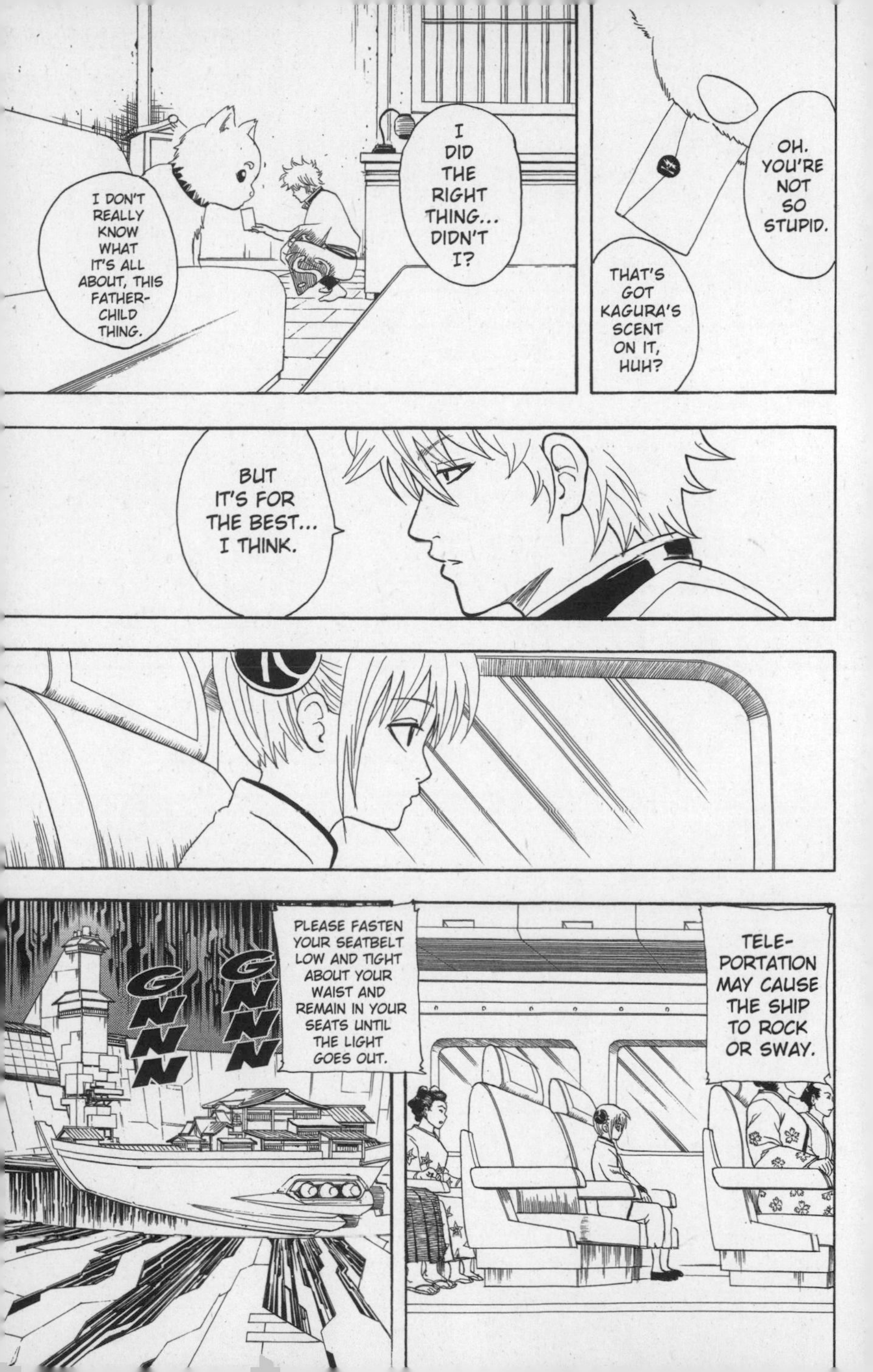
OH. YOU'RE NOT SO STUPID.
THAT'S GOT KAGURA'S SCENT ON IT, HUH?
I DID THE RIGHT THING... DIDN'T I?
I DON'T REALLY KNOW WHAT IT'S ALL ABOUT, THIS FATHER-CHILD THING.
BUT IT'S FOR THE BEST... I THINK.
TELE-PORTATION MAY CAUSE THE SHIP TO ROCK OR SWAY.
PLEASE FASTEN YOUR SEATBELT LOW AND TIGHT ABOUT YOUR WAIST AND REMAIN IN YOUR SEATS UNTIL THE LIGHT GOES OUT.
GNNN
GNNN

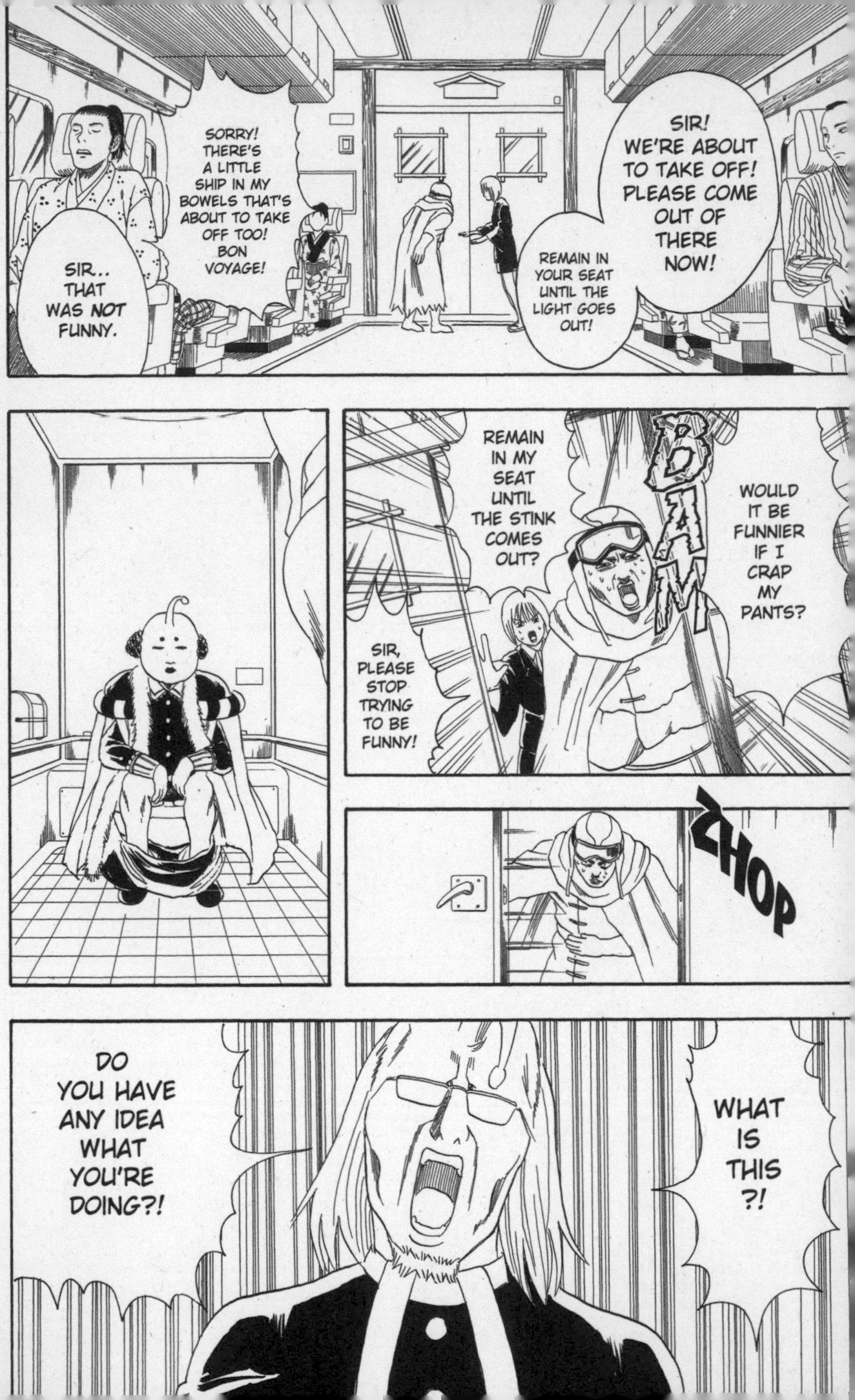
SIR! WE'RE ABOUT TO TAKE OFF! PLEASE COME OUT OF THERE NOW!
REMAIN IN YOUR SEAT UNTIL THE LIGHT GOES OUT!
SORRY! THERE'S A LITTLE SHIP IN MY BOWELS THAT'S ABOUT TO TAKE OFF TOO! BON VOYAGE!
SIR.. THAT WAS NOT FUNNY.
BAM
WOULD IT BE FUNNIER IF I CRAP MY PANTS?
REMAIN IN MY SEAT UNTIL THE STINK COMES OUT?
SIR, PLEASE STOP TRYING TO BE FUNNY!
CHOP
WHAT IS THIS ?!
DO YOU HAVE ANY IDEA WHAT YOU'RE DOING?!

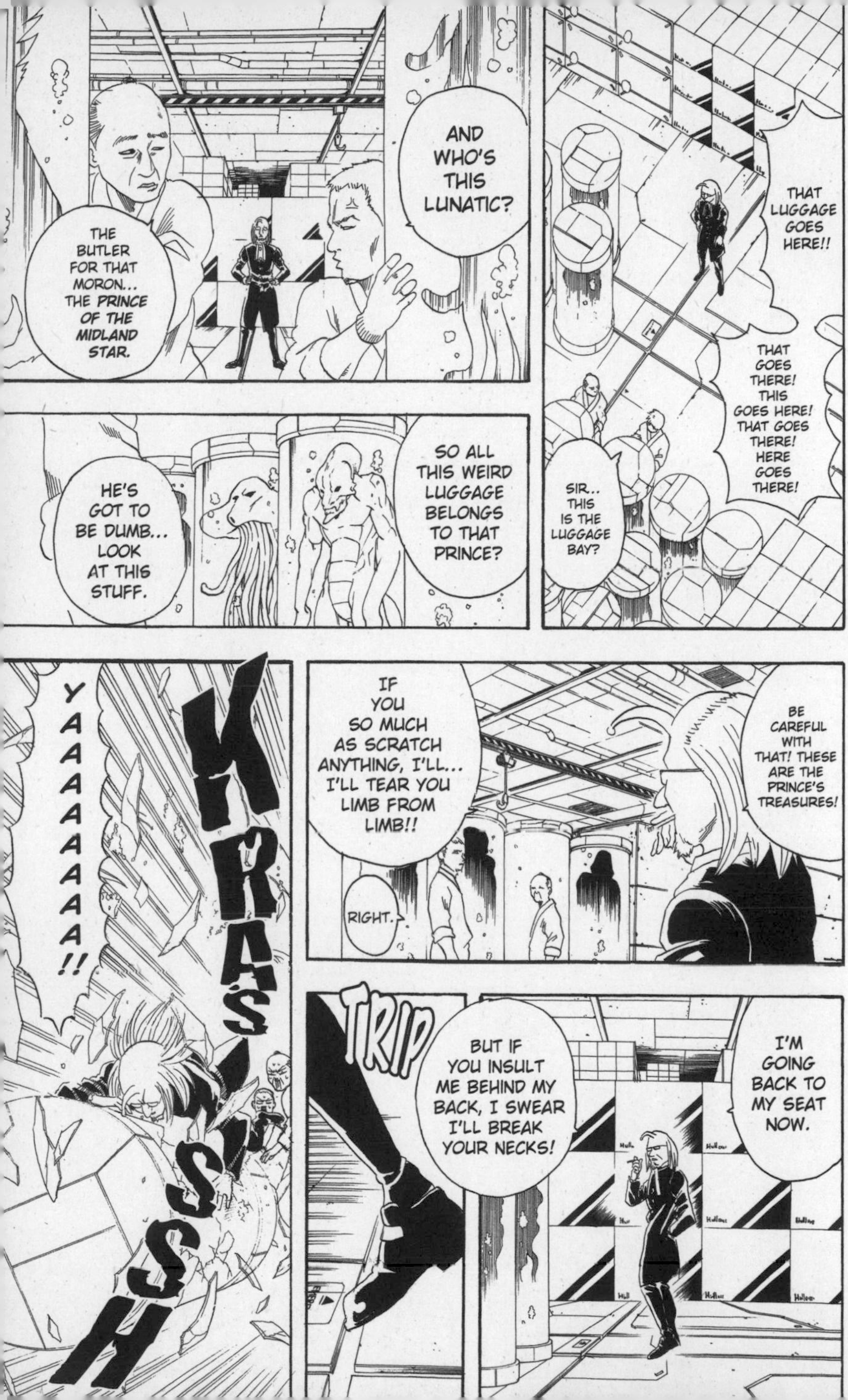
THAT LUGGAGE GOES HERE!!
THAT GOES THERE! THIS GOES HERE! THAT GOES THERE! HERE GOES THERE!
SIR... THIS IS THE LUGGAGE BAY?
AND WHO'S THIS LUNATIC?
THE BUTLER FOR THAT MORON... THE PRINCE OF THE MIDLAND STAR.
SO ALL THIS WEIRD LUGGAGE BELONGS TO THAT PRINCE?
HE'S GOT TO BE DUMB... LOOK AT THIS STUFF.
BE CAREFUL WITH THAT! THESE ARE THE PRINCE'S TREASURES!
IF YOU SO MUCH AS SCRATCH ANYTHING, I'LL... I'LL TEAR YOU LIMB FROM LIMB!!
RIGHT.
I'M GOING BACK TO MY SEAT NOW.
BUT IF YOU INSULT ME BEHIND MY BACK, I SWEAR I'LL BREAK YOUR NECKS!
TRIP
YAAAAAAAAAA!!
KRASSSH

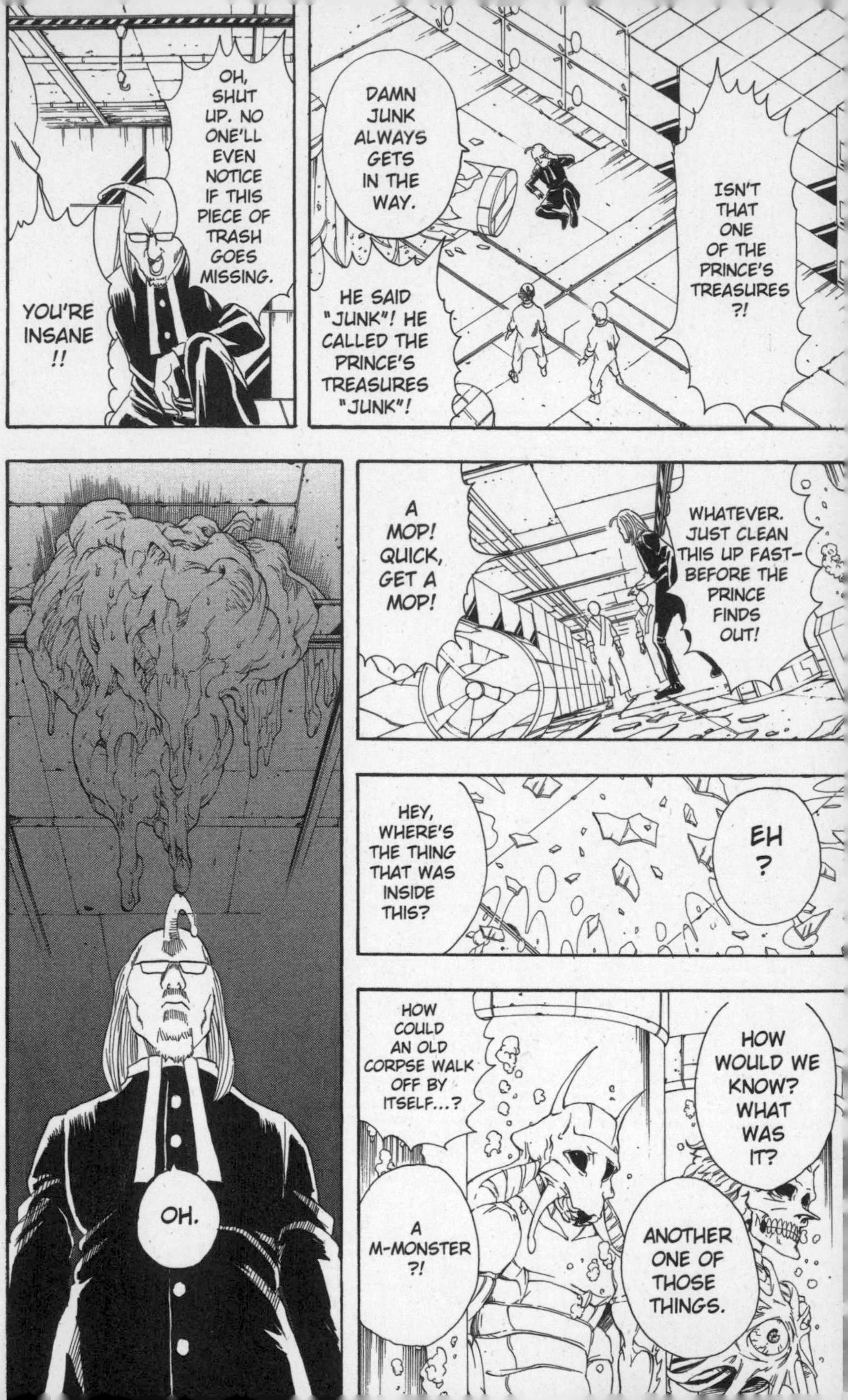
ISN'T THAT ONE OF THE PRINCE'S TREASURES ?!
DAMN JUNK ALWAYS GETS IN THE WAY.
HE SAID "JUNK"! HE CALLED THE PRINCE'S TREASURES "JUNK"!
OH, SHUT UP. NO ONE'LL EVEN NOTICE IF THIS PIECE OF TRASH GOES MISSING.
YOU'RE INSANE !!
WHATEVER. JUST CLEAN THIS UP FAST-BEFORE THE PRINCE FINDS OUT!
A MOP! QUICK, GET A MOP!
EH ?
HEY, WHERE'S THE THING THAT WAS INSIDE THIS?
HOW WOULD WE KNOW? WHAT WAS IT?
HOW COULD AN OLD CORPSE WALK OFF BY ITSELF...?
ANOTHER ONE OF THOSE THINGS.
A M-MONSTER ?!
OH.

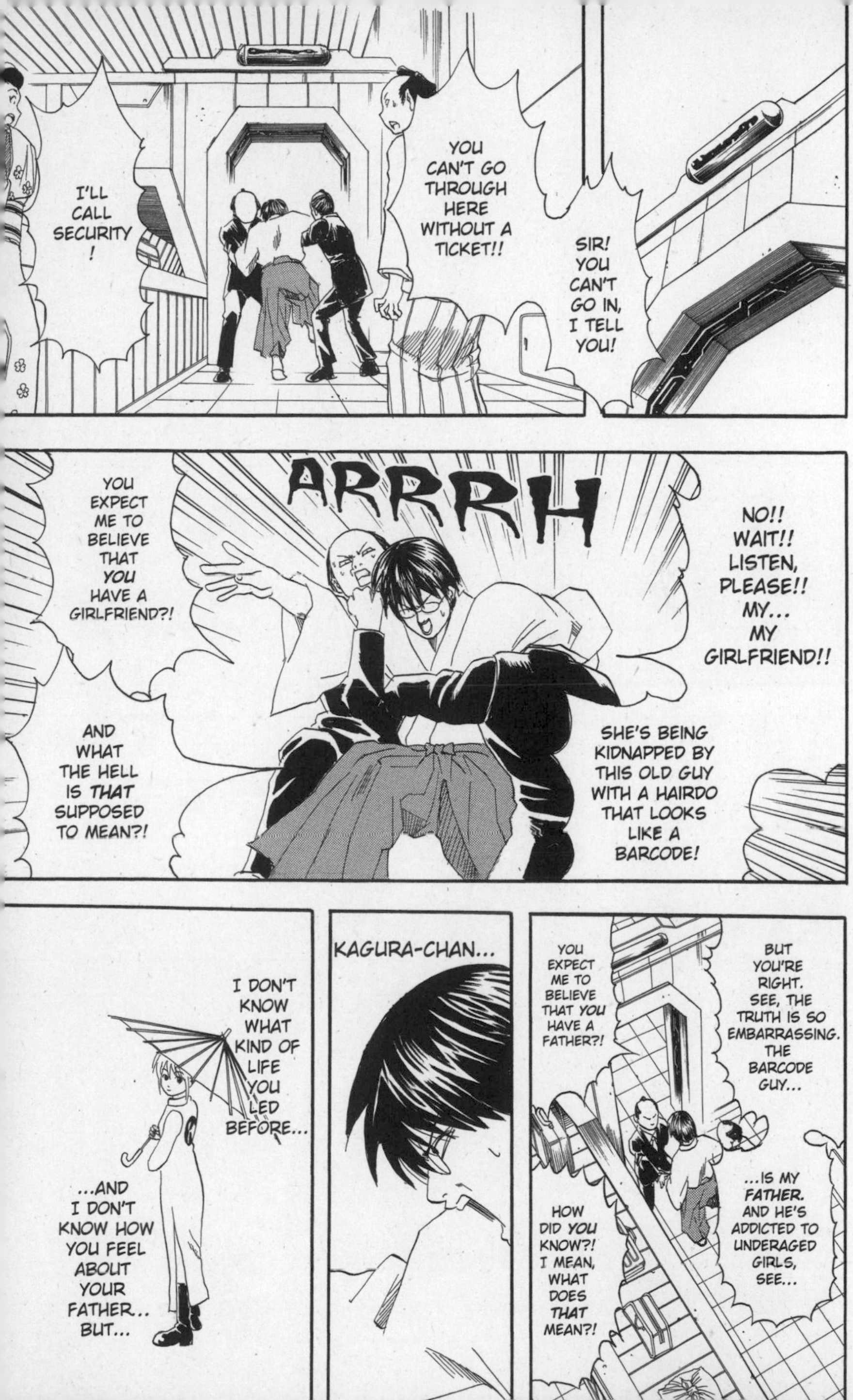
SIR! YOU CAN'T GO IN, I TELL YOU!
YOU CAN'T GO THROUGH HERE WITHOUT A TICKET!!
I'LL CALL SECURITY!
NO!! WAIT!! LISTEN, PLEASE!! MY... MY GIRLFRIEND!!
ARRRRH
YOU EXPECT ME TO BELIEVE THAT YOU HAVE A GIRLFRIEND?!
SHE'S BEING KIDNAPPED BY THIS OLD GUY WITH A HAIRDO THAT LOOKS LIKE A BARCODE!
AND WHAT THE HELL IS THAT SUPPOSED TO MEAN?!
BUT YOU'RE RIGHT. SEE, THE TRUTH IS SO EMBARRASSING. THE BARCODE GUY...
YOU EXPECT ME TO BELIEVE THAT YOU HAVE A FATHER?!
...IS MY FATHER. AND HE'S ADDICTED TO UNDERAGED GIRLS, SEE...
HOW DID YOU KNOW?! I MEAN, WHAT DOES THAT MEAN?!
KAGURA-CHAN...
I DON'T KNOW WHAT KIND OF LIFE YOU LED BEFORE...
...AND I DON'T KNOW HOW YOU FEEL ABOUT YOUR FATHER... BUT...

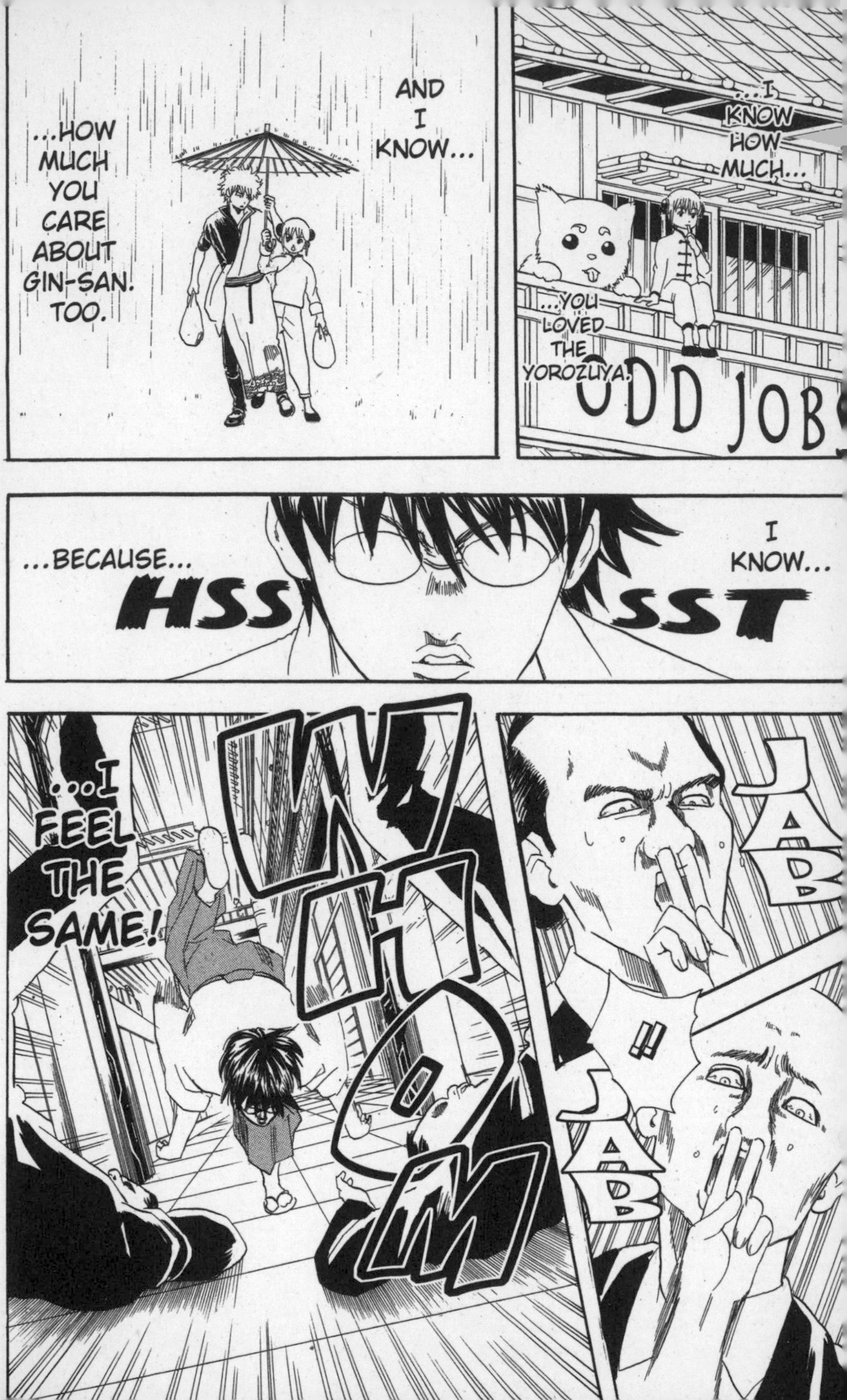
...I KNOW HOW MUCH...
...YOU LOVED THE YOROZUYA.
ODD JOB
AND I KNOW...
...HOW MUCH YOU CARE ABOUT GIN-SAN. TOO.
I KNOW...
...BECAUSE...
HSS
SST
JAB
!!
JAB
WHOOM
...I FEEL THE SAME!

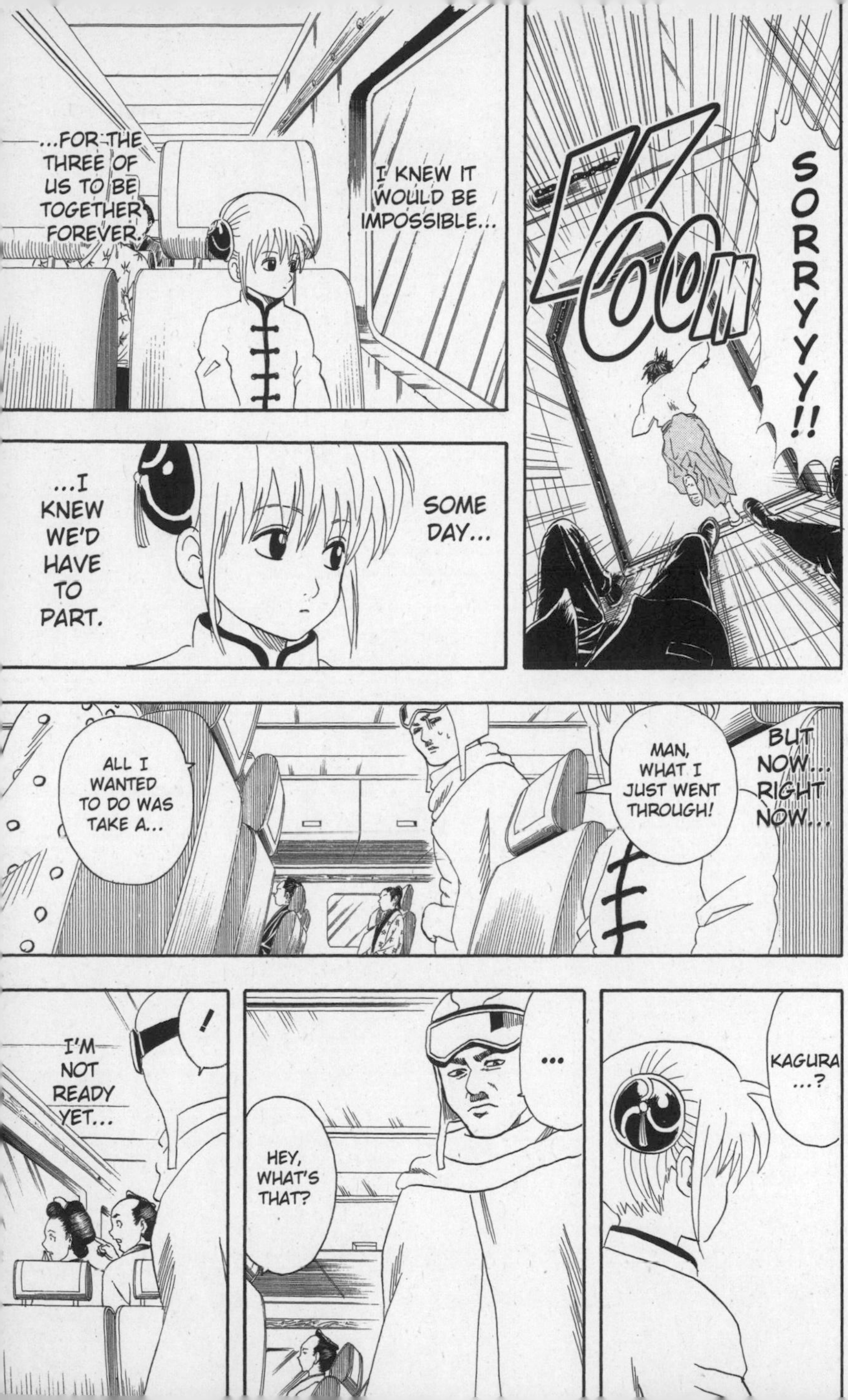
SORRYYY!!
ZOOM
I KNEW IT WOULD BE IMPOSSIBLE...
...FOR THE THREE OF US TO BE TOGETHER FOREVER.
SOME DAY...
...I KNEW WE'D HAVE TO PART.
BUT NOW... RIGHT NOW...
MAN, WHAT I JUST WENT THROUGH!
ALL I WANTED TO DO WAS TAKE A...
KAGURA ...?
...
HEY, WHAT'S THAT?
!
I'M NOT READY YET...

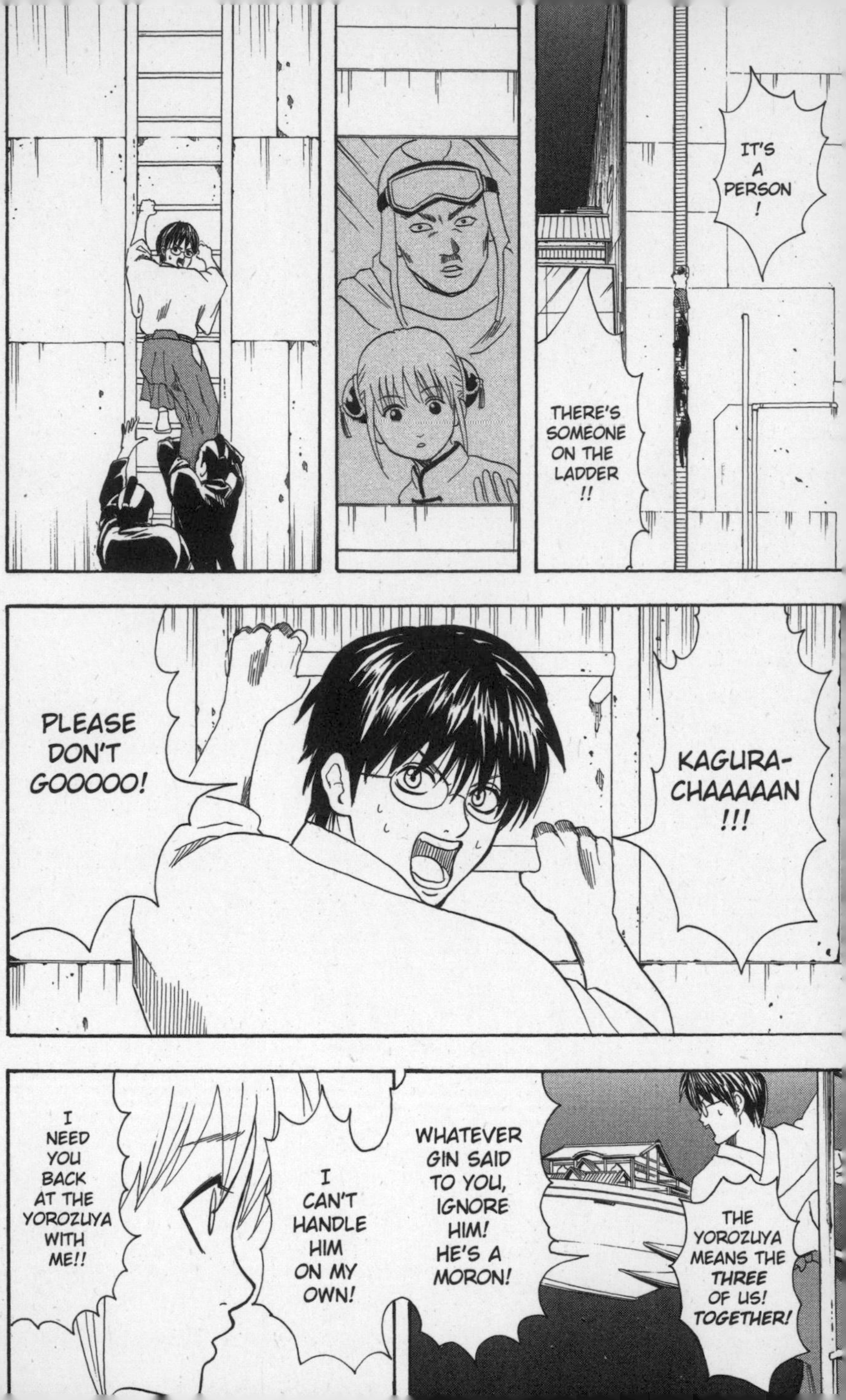
IT'S A PERSON!
THERE'S SOMEONE ON THE LADDER!!
KAGURA-CHAAAAAN!!!
PLEASE DON'T GOOOOO!
THE YOROZUYA MEANS THE THREE OF US! TOGETHER!
WHATEVER GIN SAID TO YOU, IGNORE HIM! HE'S A MORON!
I CAN'T HANDLE HIM ON MY OWN!
I NEED YOU BACK AT THE YOROZUYA WITH ME!!

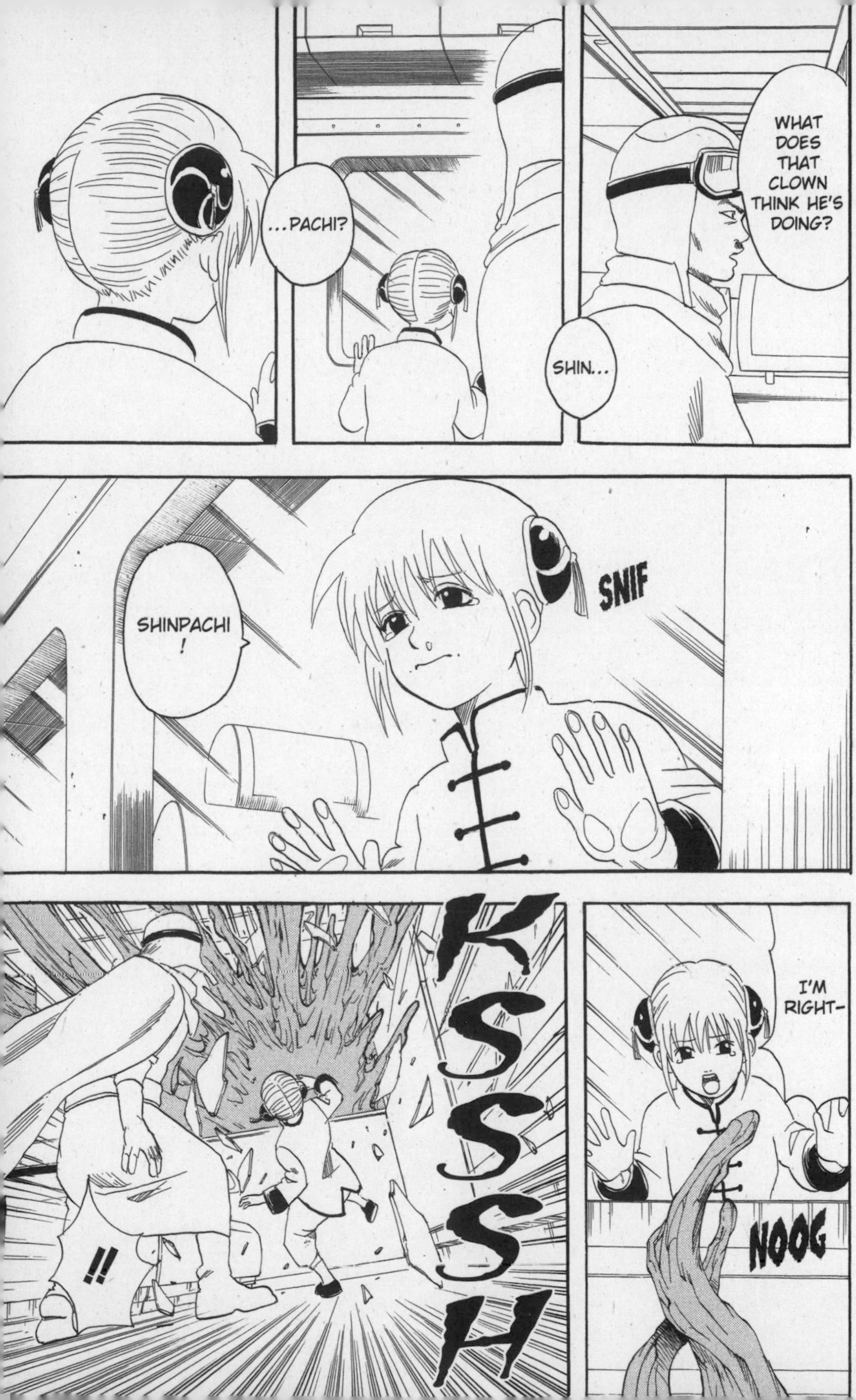
WHAT DOES THAT CLOWN THINK HE'S DOING?
SHIN...
...PACHI?
SNIF
SHINPACHI!
I'M RIGHT-
NOOG
KSSSH
!!

● **Cover illustration for Weekly**
   Shonen JUMP,
   Vol. 21/22 joint issue, 2005.

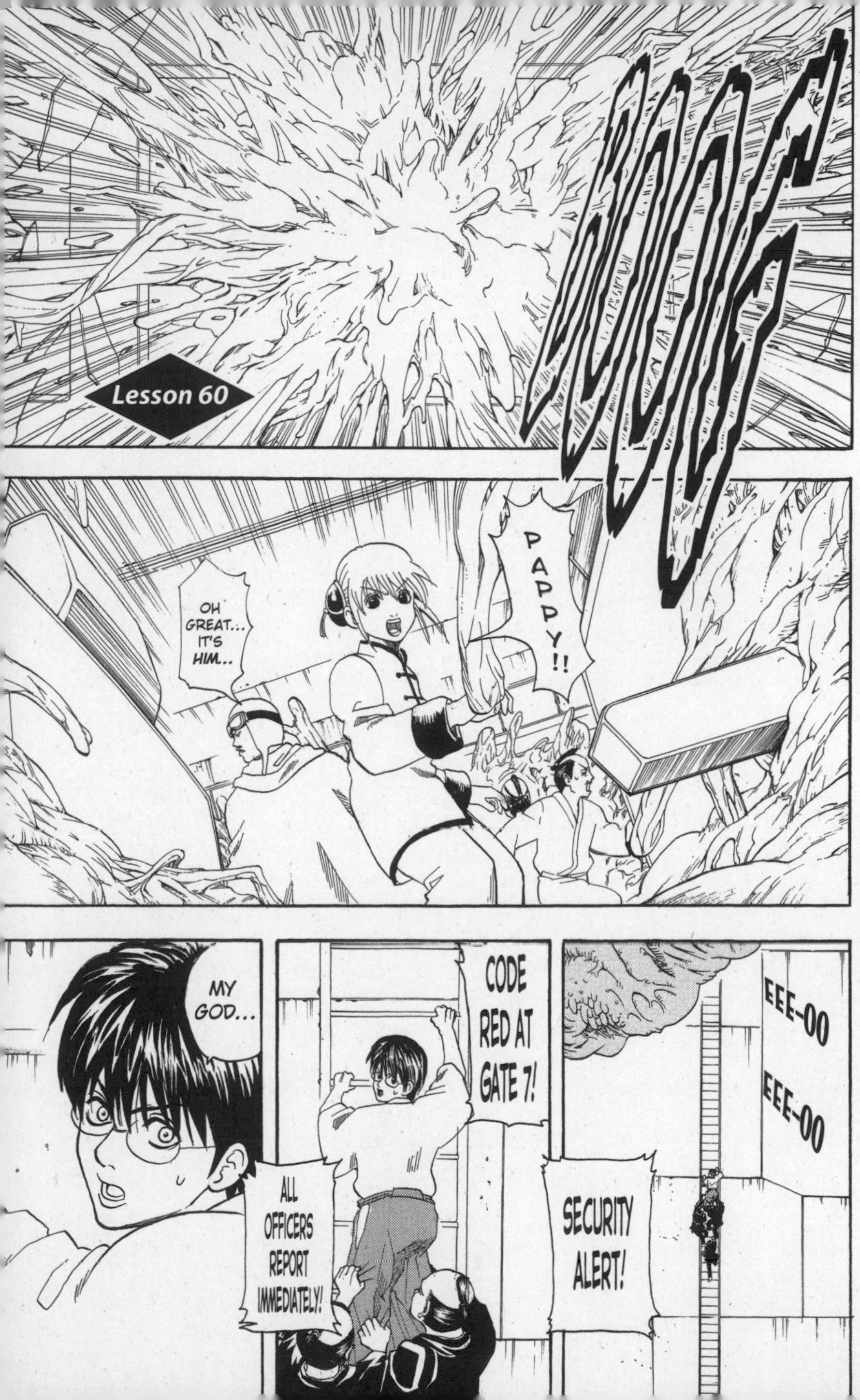
Lesson 60
PAPPY!!
OH GREAT... IT'S HIM...
EEE-OO
EEE-OO
SECURITY ALERT!
CODE RED AT GATE 7!
ALL OFFICERS REPORT IMMEDIATELY!
MY GOD...

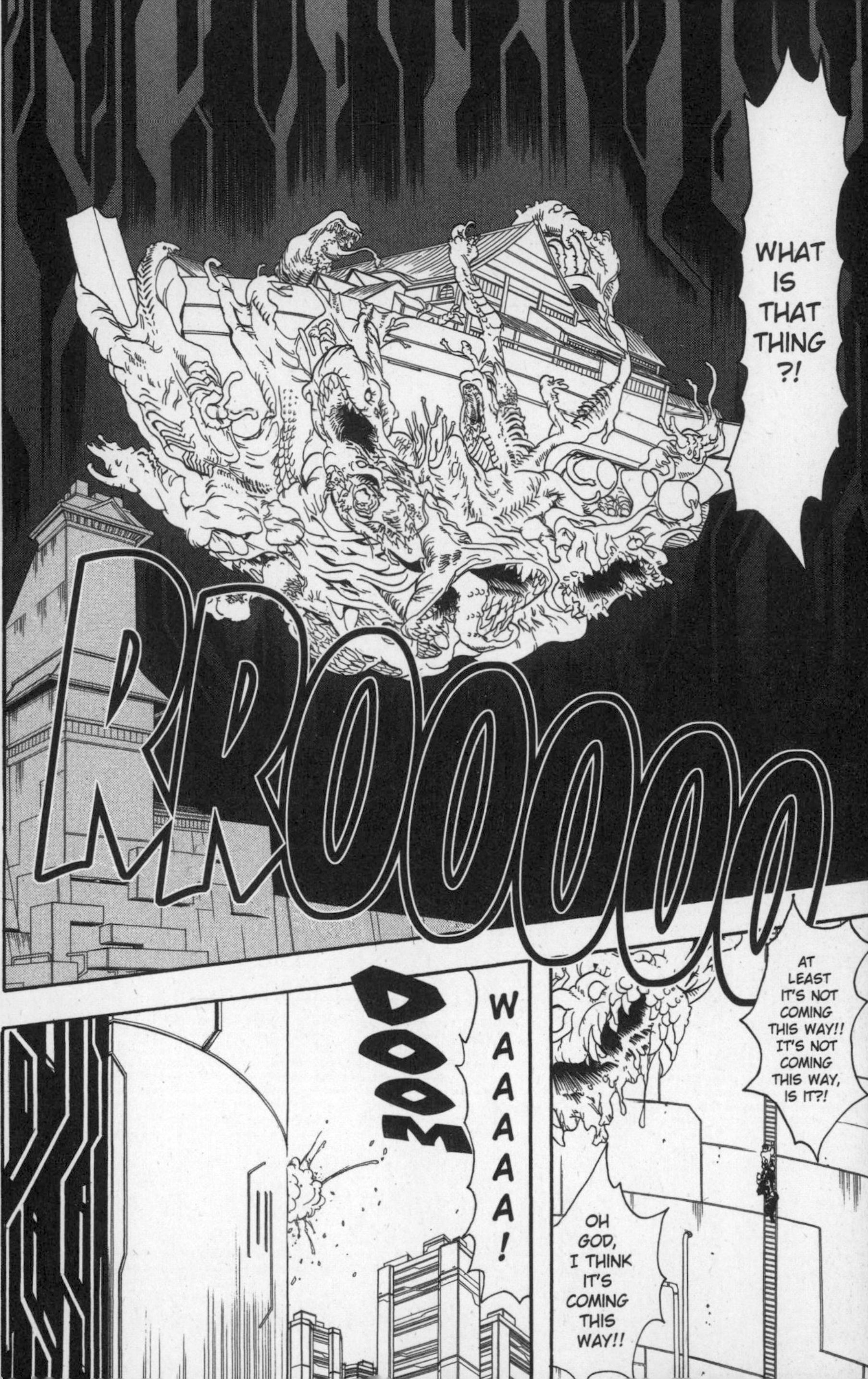
WHAT IS THAT THING?!
AT LEAST IT'S NOT COMING THIS WAY!! IT'S NOT COMING THIS WAY, IS IT?!
OH GOD, I THINK IT'S COMING THIS WAY!!
WAAAAAA!
DOOM

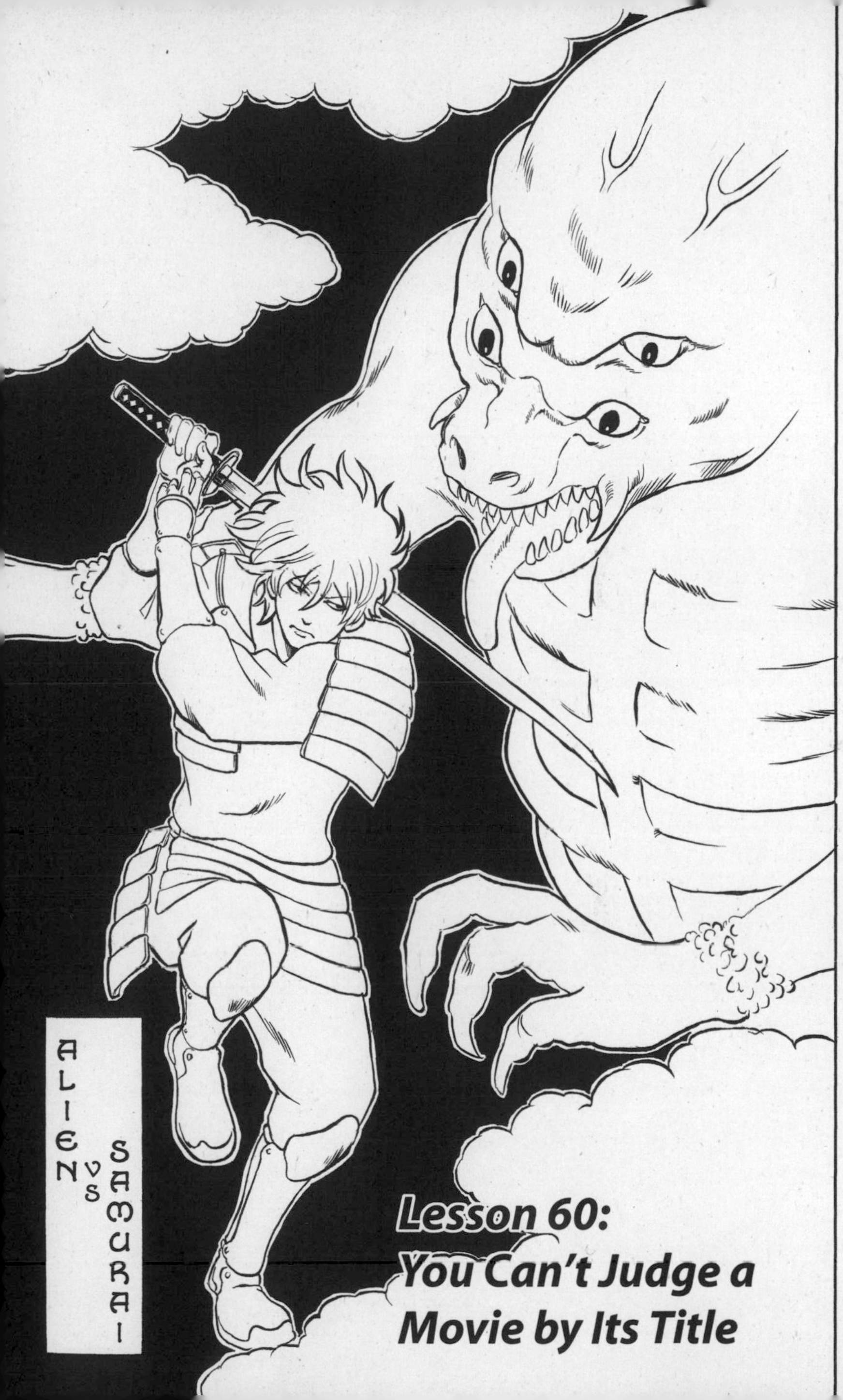
ALIEN VS SAMURAI
Lesson 60:
You Can't Judge a Movie by Its Title

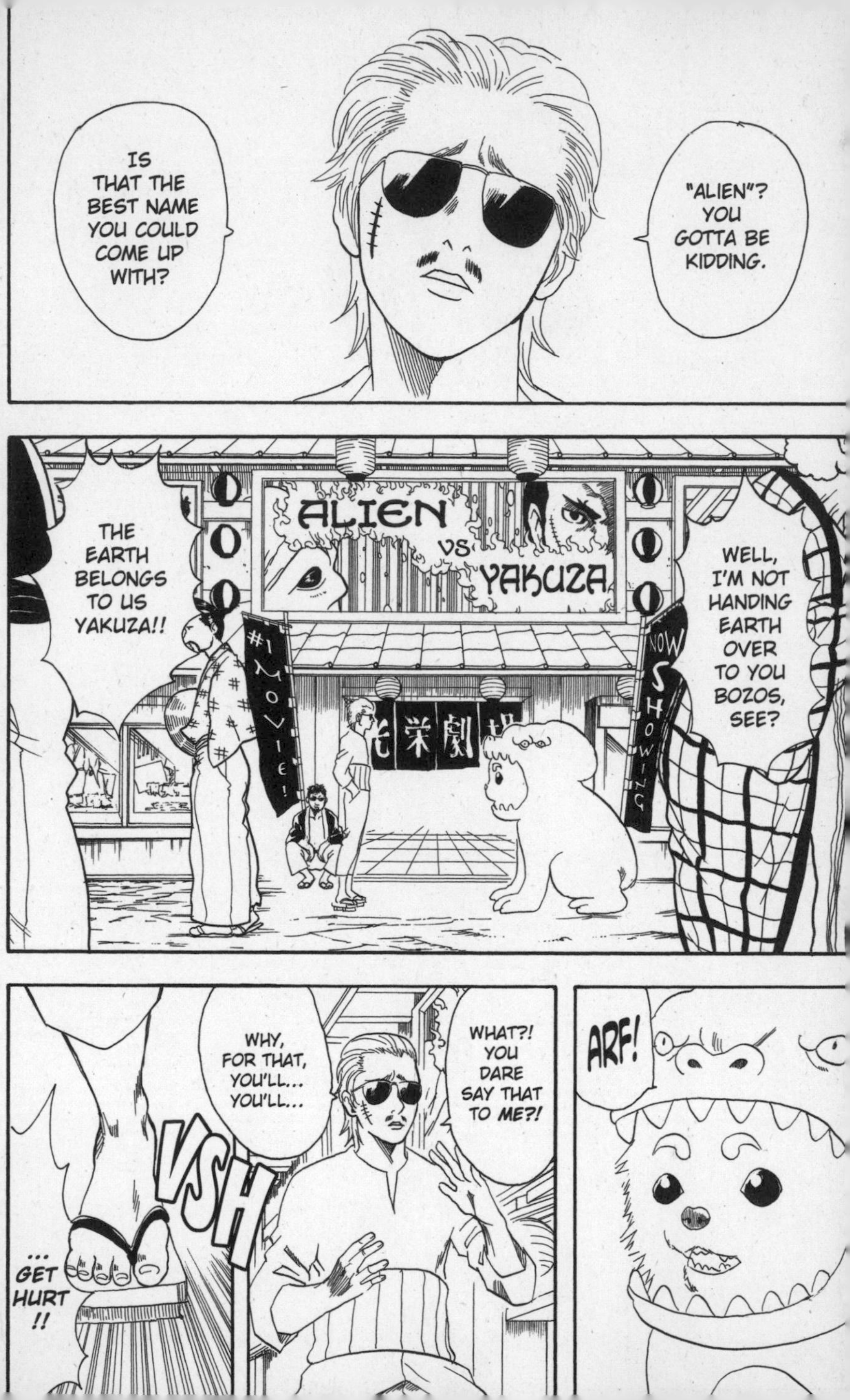
"ALIEN"? YOU GOTTA BE KIDDING.
IS THAT THE BEST NAME YOU COULD COME UP WITH?
ALIEN VS YAKUZA
NOW SHOWING
#1 MOVIE!
WELL, I'M NOT HANDING EARTH OVER TO YOU BOZOS, SEE?
THE EARTH BELONGS TO US YAKUZA!!
ARF!
WHAT?! YOU DARE SAY THAT TO *ME*?!
WHY, FOR THAT, YOU'LL... YOU'LL...
VSH
...GET HURT!!

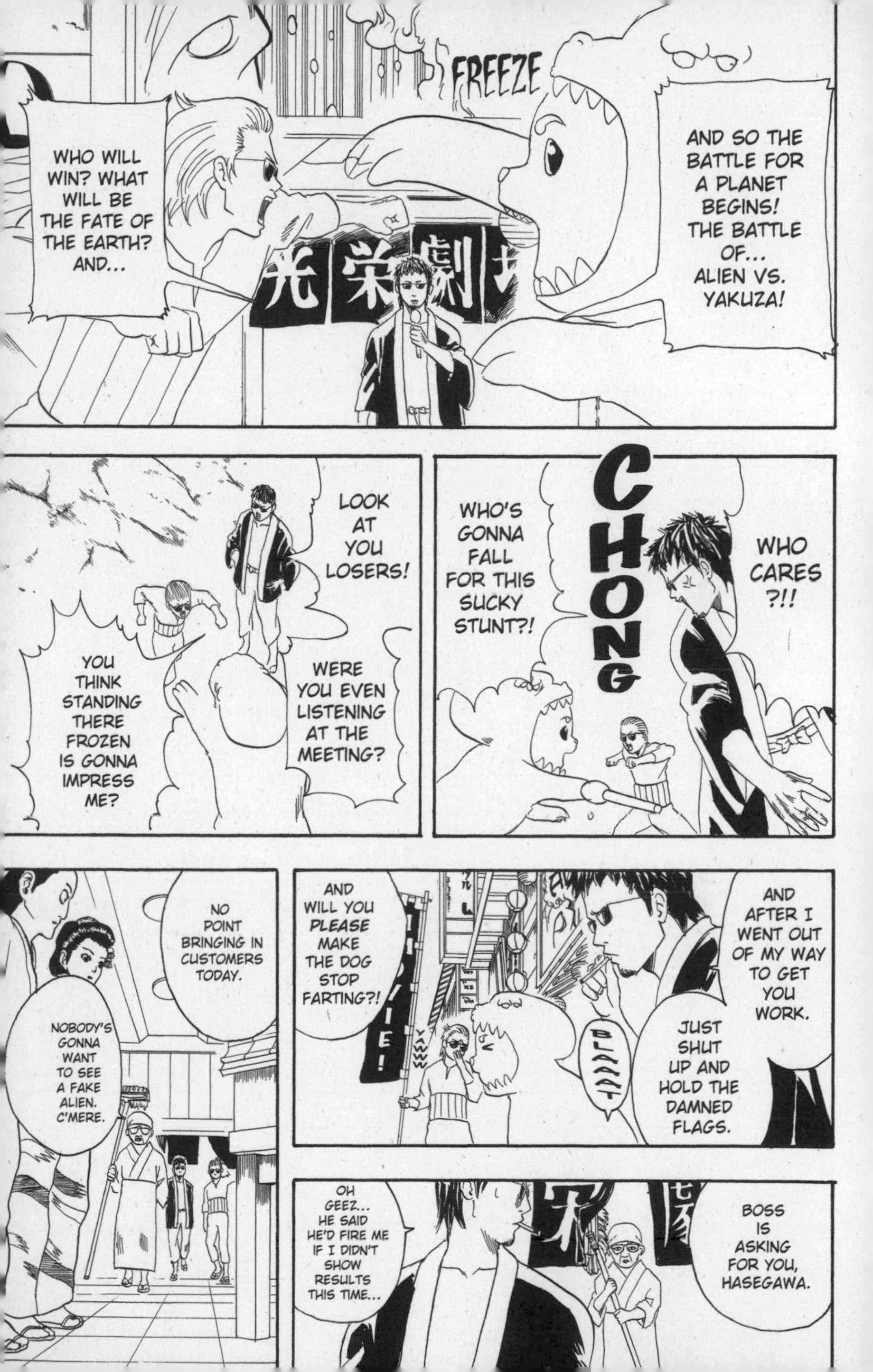
AND SO THE BATTLE FOR A PLANET BEGINS! THE BATTLE OF... ALIEN VS. YAKUZA!
FREEZE
WHO WILL WIN? WHAT WILL BE THE FATE OF THE EARTH? AND...
WHO CARES ?!!
CHONG
WHO'S GONNA FALL FOR THIS SUCKY STUNT?!
LOOK AT YOU LOSERS!
WERE YOU EVEN LISTENING AT THE MEETING?
YOU THINK STANDING THERE FROZEN IS GONNA IMPRESS ME?
AND AFTER I WENT OUT OF MY WAY TO GET YOU WORK.
JUST SHUT UP AND HOLD THE DAMNED FLAGS.
BLAAAT
AND WILL YOU PLEASE MAKE THE DOG STOP FARTING?!
YAWWN
BOSS IS ASKING FOR YOU, HASEGAWA.
OH GEEZ... HE SAID HE'D FIRE ME IF I DIDN'T SHOW RESULTS THIS TIME...
NO POINT BRINGING IN CUSTOMERS TODAY.
NOBODY'S GONNA WANT TO SEE A FAKE ALIEN. C'MERE.

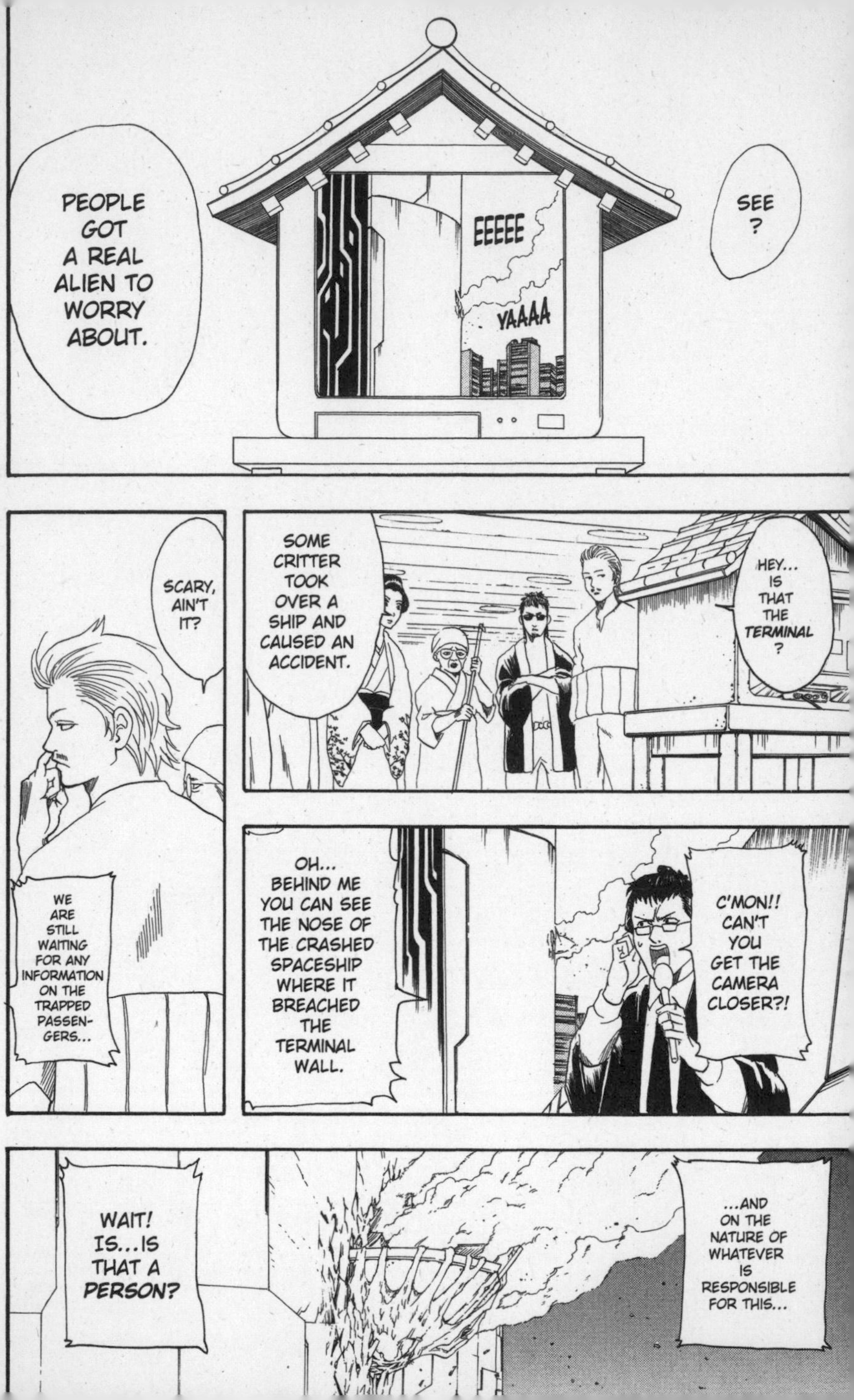
SEE?
EEEEE
YAAAA
PEOPLE GOT A REAL ALIEN TO WORRY ABOUT.
HEY... IS THAT THE TERMINAL?
SOME CRITTER TOOK OVER A SHIP AND CAUSED AN ACCIDENT.
C'MON!! CAN'T YOU GET THE CAMERA CLOSER?!
OH... BEHIND ME YOU CAN SEE THE NOSE OF THE CRASHED SPACESHIP WHERE IT BREACHED THE TERMINAL WALL.
SCARY, AIN'T IT?
WE ARE STILL WAITING FOR ANY INFORMATION ON THE TRAPPED PASSEN-GERS...
...AND ON THE NATURE OF WHATEVER IS RESPONSIBLE FOR THIS...
WAIT! IS...IS THAT A PERSON?

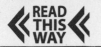

READ THIS WAY

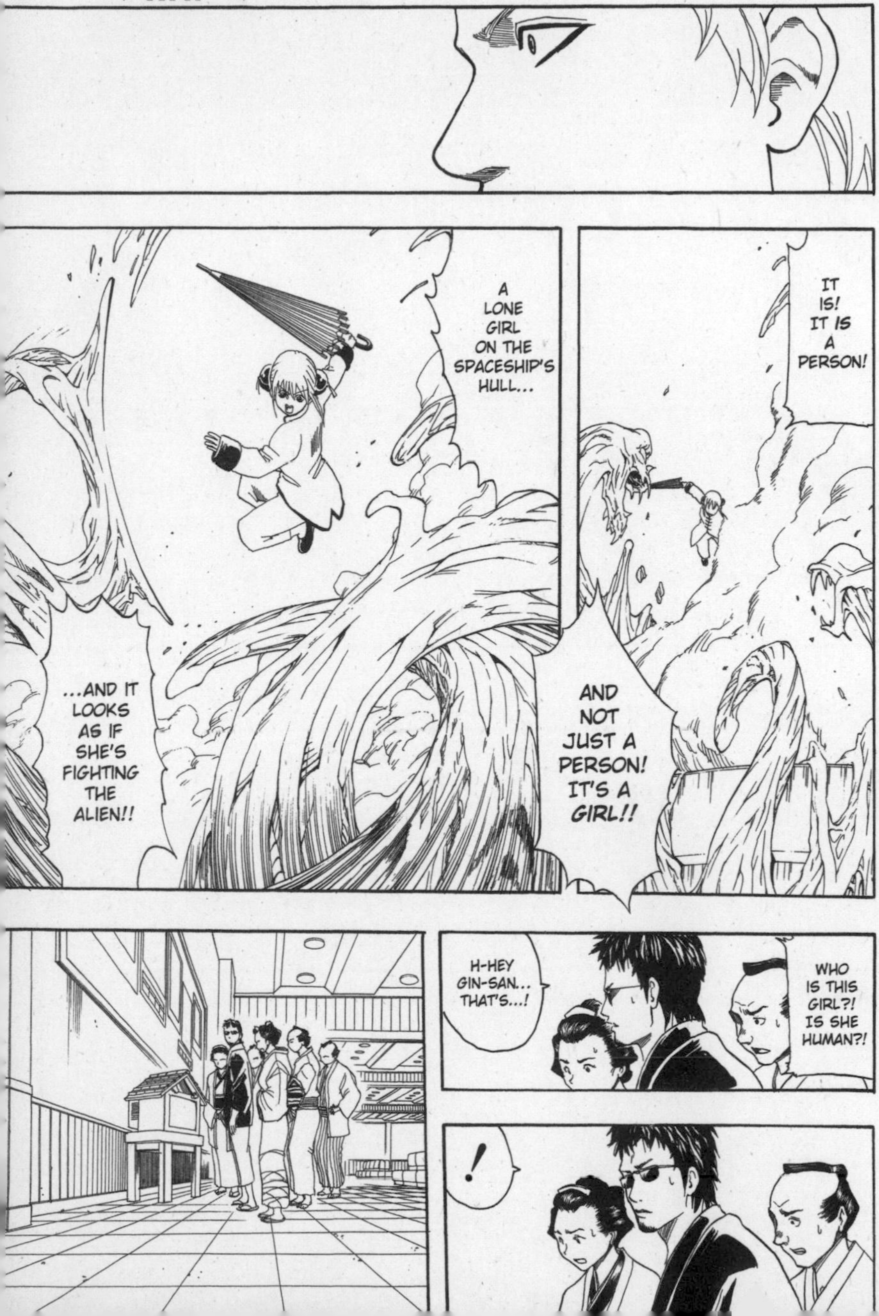
IT IS! IT IS A PERSON!
AND NOT JUST A PERSON! IT'S A GIRL!!
A LONE GIRL ON THE SPACESHIP'S HULL...
...AND IT LOOKS AS IF SHE'S FIGHTING THE ALIEN!!
WHO IS THIS GIRL?! IS SHE HUMAN?!
H-HEY GIN-SAN... THAT'S...!
!

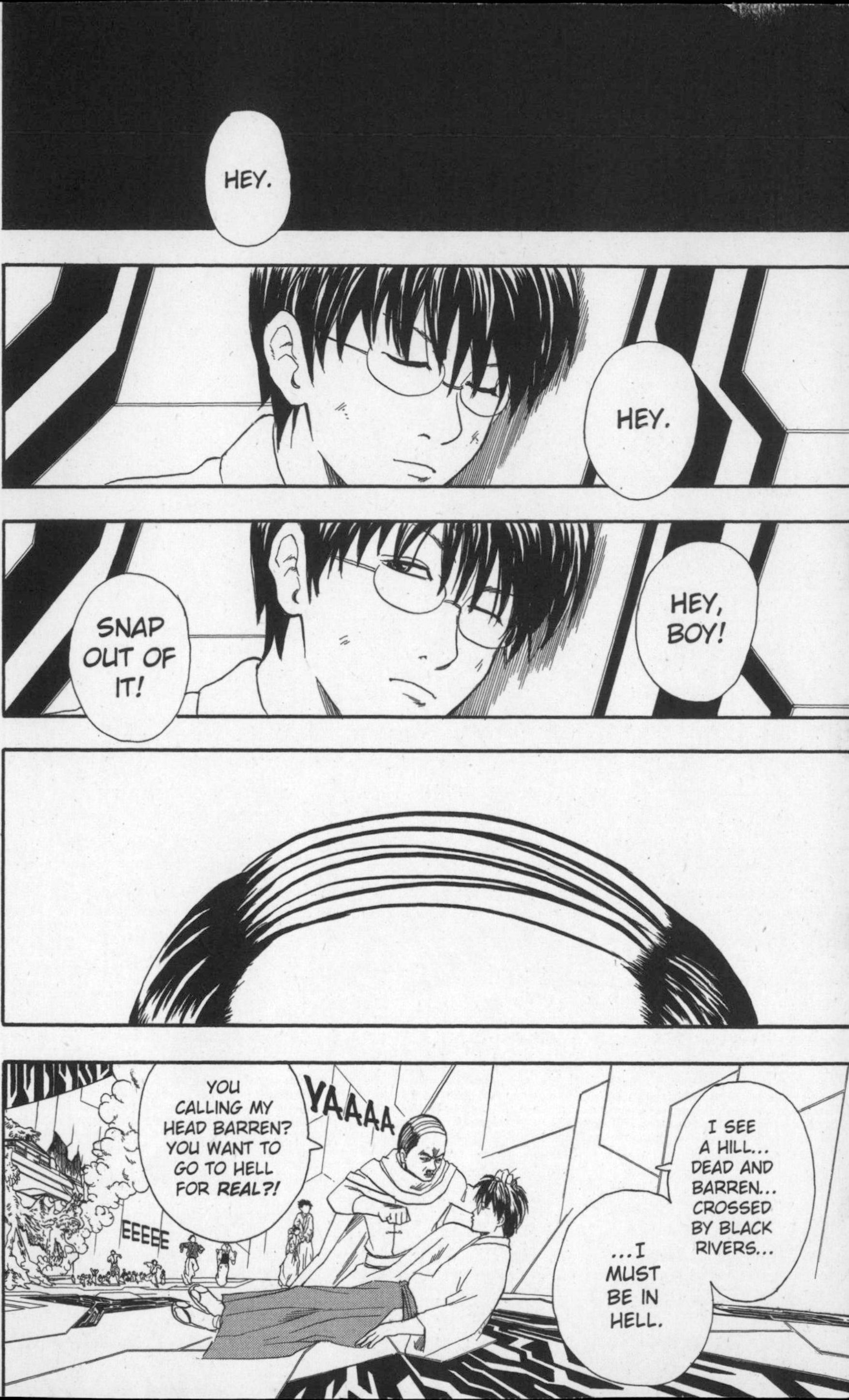
HEY.
HEY.
HEY, BOY!
SNAP OUT OF IT!
I SEE A HILL... DEAD AND BARREN... CROSSED BY BLACK RIVERS...
...I MUST BE IN HELL.
YAAAA
YOU CALLING MY HEAD BARREN? YOU WANT TO GO TO HELL FOR REAL?!
EEEEE

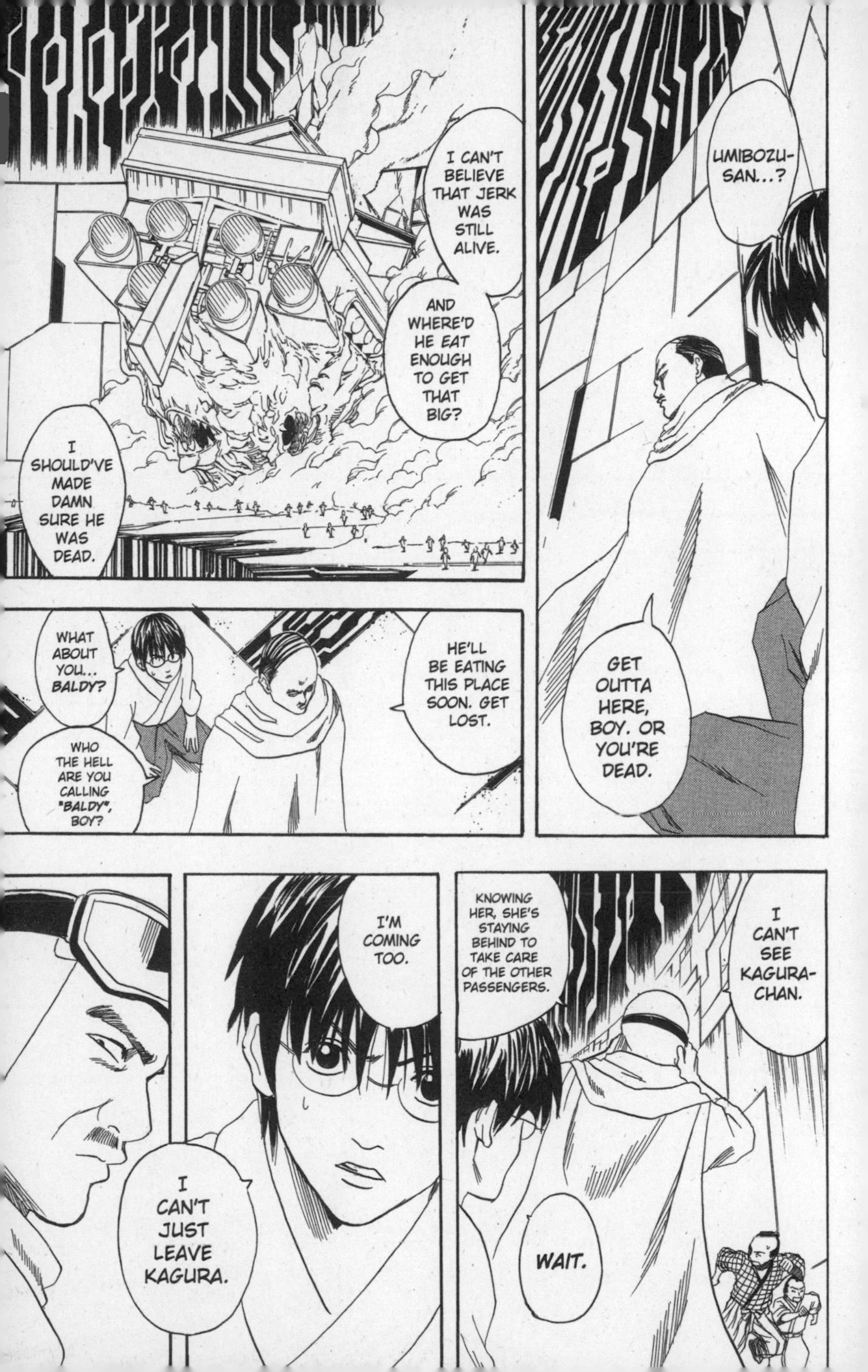
UMIBOZU-SAN...?
GET OUTTA HERE, BOY. OR YOU'RE DEAD.
I CAN'T BELIEVE THAT JERK WAS STILL ALIVE.
AND WHERE'D HE EAT ENOUGH TO GET THAT BIG?
I SHOULD'VE MADE DAMN SURE HE WAS DEAD.
HE'LL BE EATING THIS PLACE SOON. GET LOST.
WHAT ABOUT YOU... *BALDY?*
WHO THE HELL ARE YOU CALLING "BALDY", BOY?
I CAN'T SEE KAGURA-CHAN.
KNOWING HER, SHE'S STAYING BEHIND TO TAKE CARE OF THE OTHER PASSENGERS.
WAIT.
I'M COMING TOO.
I CAN'T JUST LEAVE KAGURA.

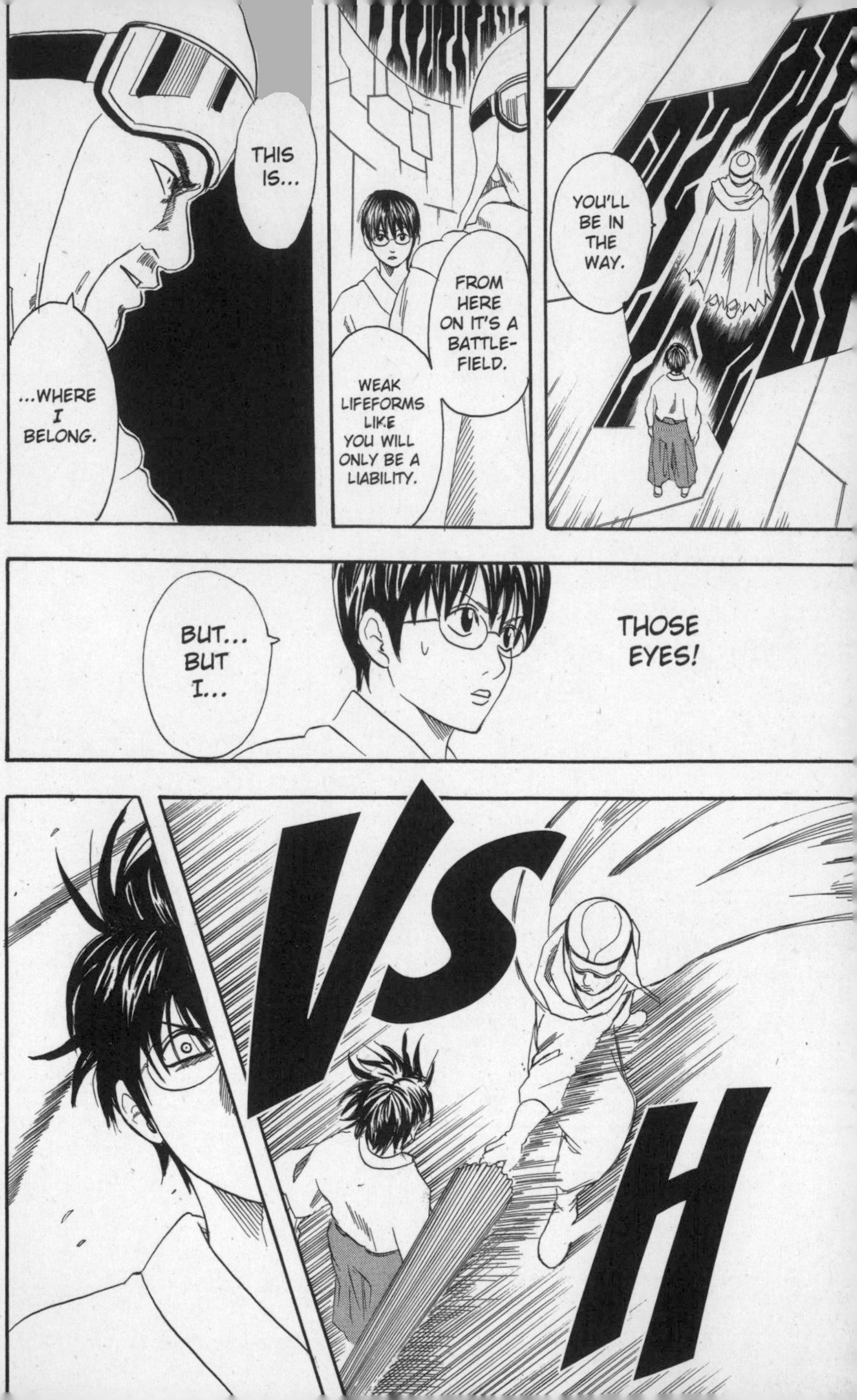
YOU'LL BE IN THE WAY.
FROM HERE ON IT'S A BATTLE-FIELD.
WEAK LIFEFORMS LIKE YOU WILL ONLY BE A LIABILITY.
THIS IS...
...WHERE I BELONG.
THOSE EYES!
BUT... BUT I...
VISH

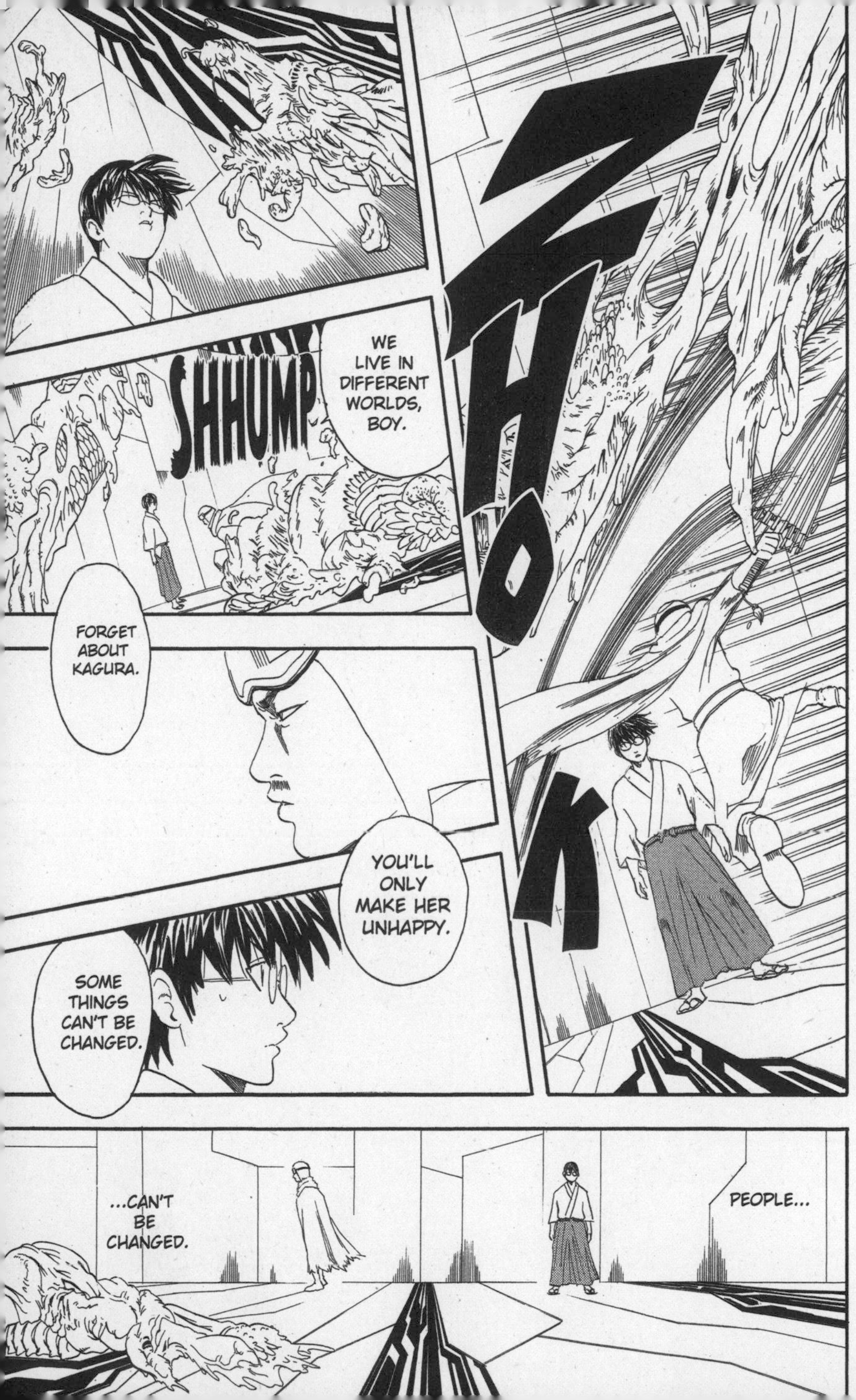
ZHOK
SHHUMP
WE LIVE IN DIFFERENT WORLDS, BOY.
FORGET ABOUT KAGURA.
YOU'LL ONLY MAKE HER UNHAPPY.
SOME THINGS CAN'T BE CHANGED.
PEOPLE...
...CAN'T BE CHANGED.

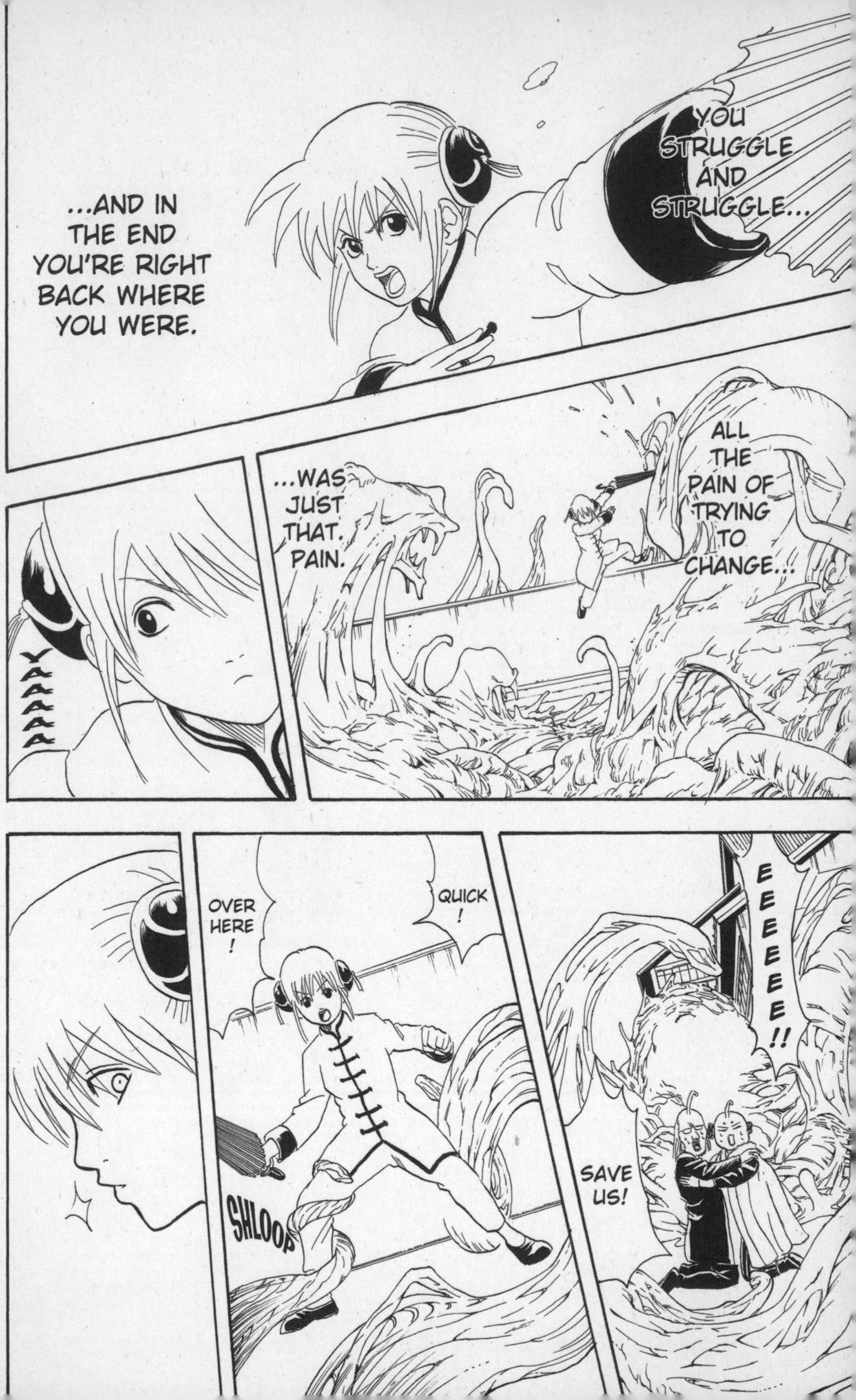
YOU STRUGGLE AND STRUGGLE...
...AND IN THE END YOU'RE RIGHT BACK WHERE YOU WERE.
ALL THE PAIN OF TRYING TO CHANGE...
...WAS JUST THAT. PAIN.
YAAAAA
EEEEEEE!!
SAVE US!
QUICK!
OVER HERE!
SHLOOP

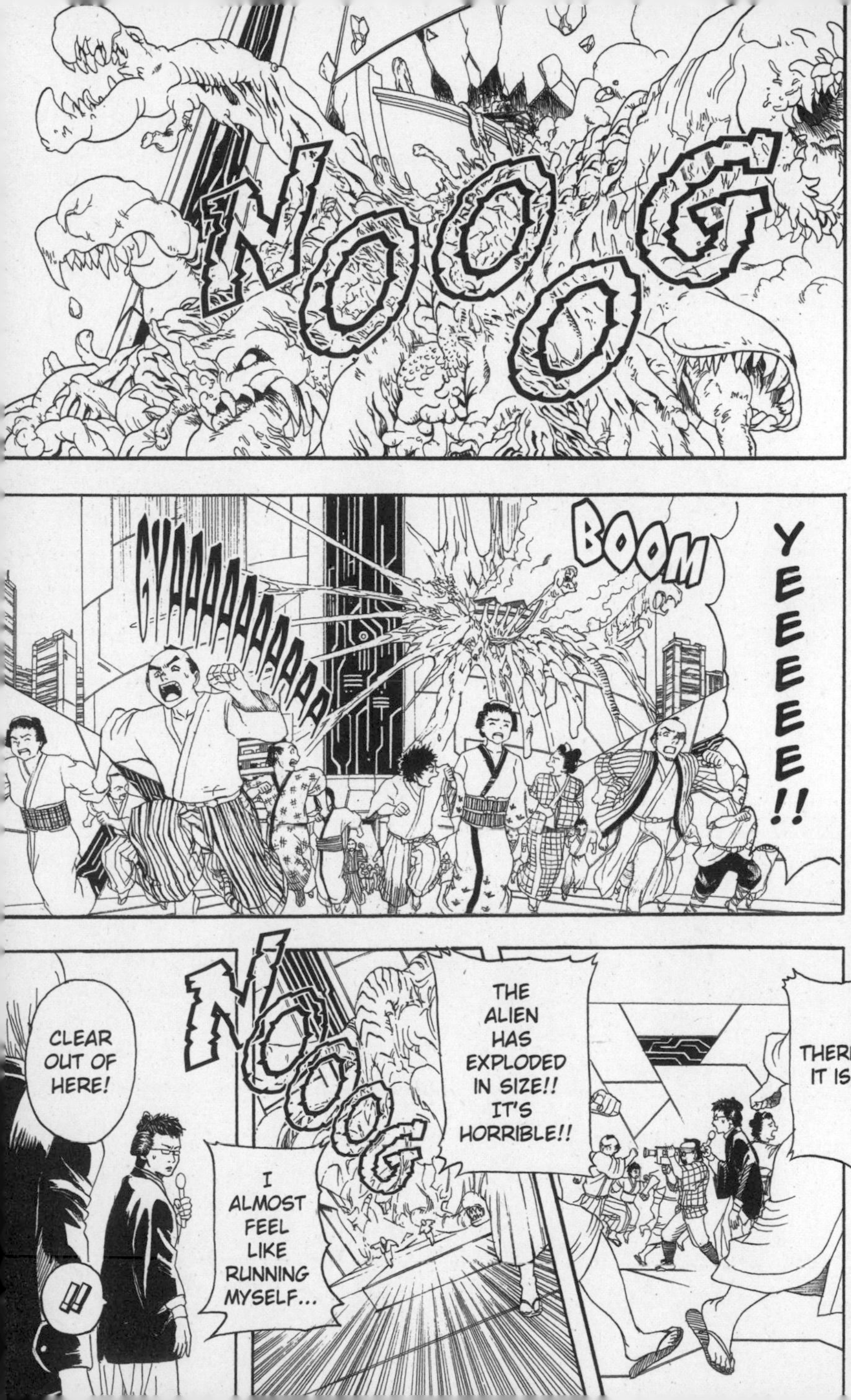
NOOOG
YEEEEEE!!
BOOM
GYAAAAAAAAAAAAAA
THERE IT IS!
THE ALIEN HAS EXPLODED IN SIZE!! IT'S HORRIBLE!!
NOOOG
I ALMOST FEEL LIKE RUNNING MYSELF...
CLEAR OUT OF HERE!
!!

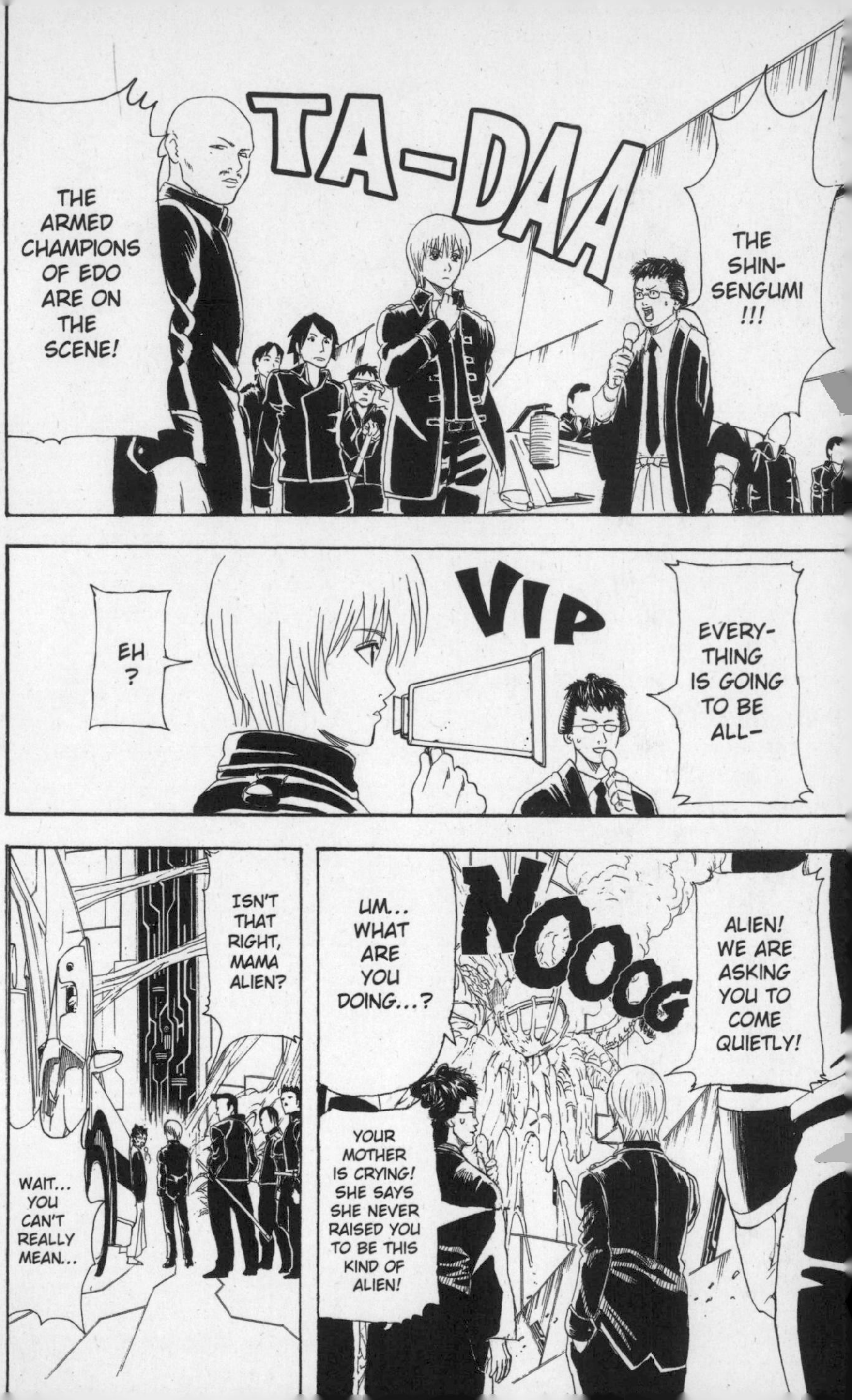
THE SHIN-SENGUMI!!!
TA-DAA
THE ARMED CHAMPIONS OF EDO ARE ON THE SCENE!
EVERY-THING IS GOING TO BE ALL-
VIP
EH?
ALIEN! WE ARE ASKING YOU TO COME QUIETLY!
NOOOG
UM... WHAT ARE YOU DOING...?
YOUR MOTHER IS CRYING! SHE SAYS SHE NEVER RAISED YOU TO BE THIS KIND OF ALIEN!
ISN'T THAT RIGHT, MAMA ALIEN?
WAIT... YOU CAN'T REALLY MEAN...

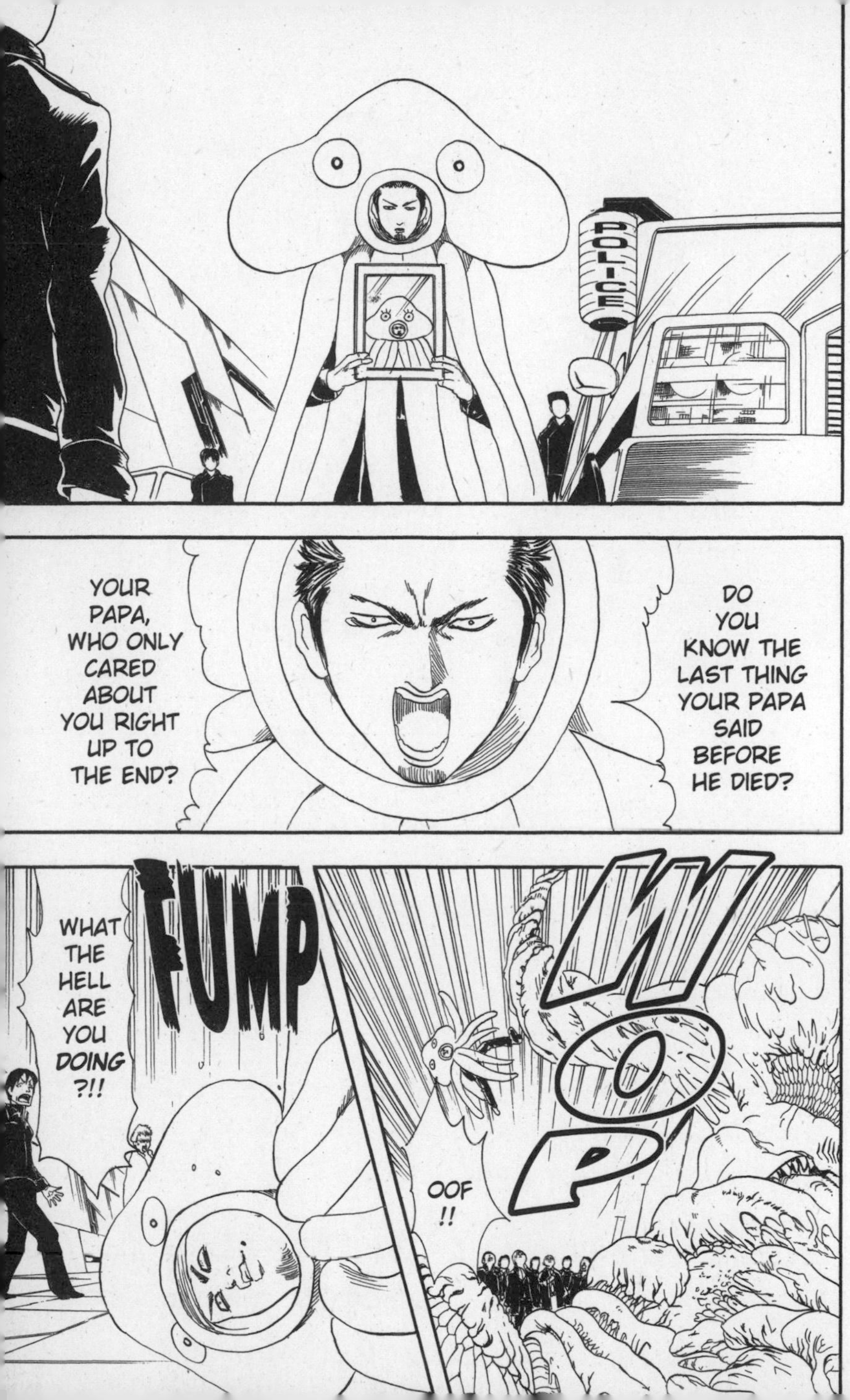
POLICE
DO YOU KNOW THE LAST THING YOUR PAPA SAID BEFORE HE DIED?
YOUR PAPA, WHO ONLY CARED ABOUT YOU RIGHT UP TO THE END?
WOP
FUMP
WHAT THE HELL ARE YOU DOING?!!
OOF!!

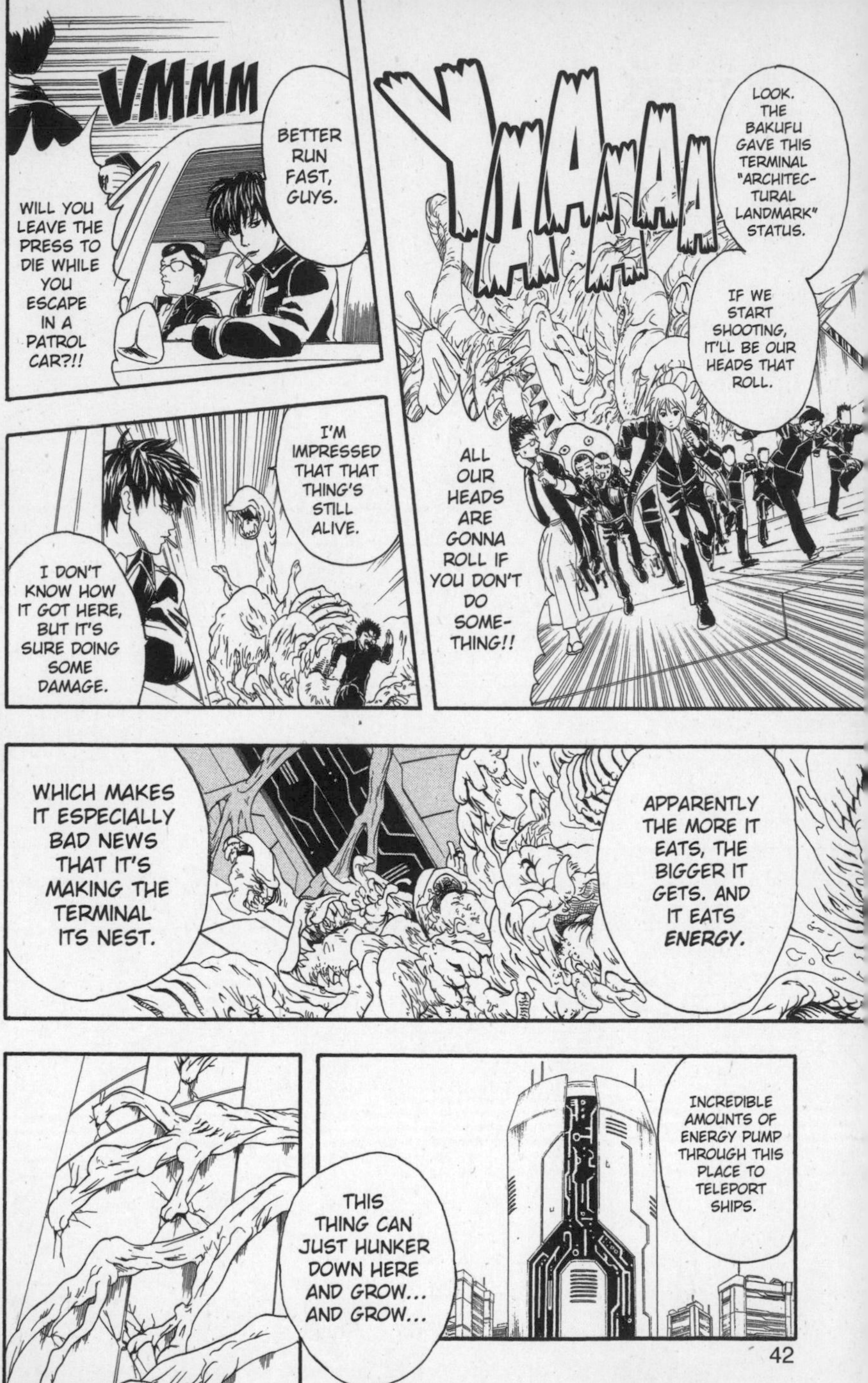
YAAAAA
LOOK. THE BAKUFU GAVE THIS TERMINAL "ARCHITECTURAL LANDMARK" STATUS.
IF WE START SHOOTING, IT'LL BE OUR HEADS THAT ROLL.
ALL OUR HEADS ARE GONNA ROLL IF YOU DON'T DO SOMETHING!!
VMMM
BETTER RUN FAST, GUYS.
WILL YOU LEAVE THE PRESS TO DIE WHILE YOU ESCAPE IN A PATROL CAR?!!
I'M IMPRESSED THAT THAT THING'S STILL ALIVE.
I DON'T KNOW HOW IT GOT HERE, BUT IT'S SURE DOING SOME DAMAGE.
APPARENTLY THE MORE IT EATS, THE BIGGER IT GETS. AND IT EATS ENERGY.
WHICH MAKES IT ESPECIALLY BAD NEWS THAT IT'S MAKING THE TERMINAL ITS NEST.
INCREDIBLE AMOUNTS OF ENERGY PUMP THROUGH THIS PLACE TO TELEPORT SHIPS.
THIS THING CAN JUST HUNKER DOWN HERE AND GROW... AND GROW...

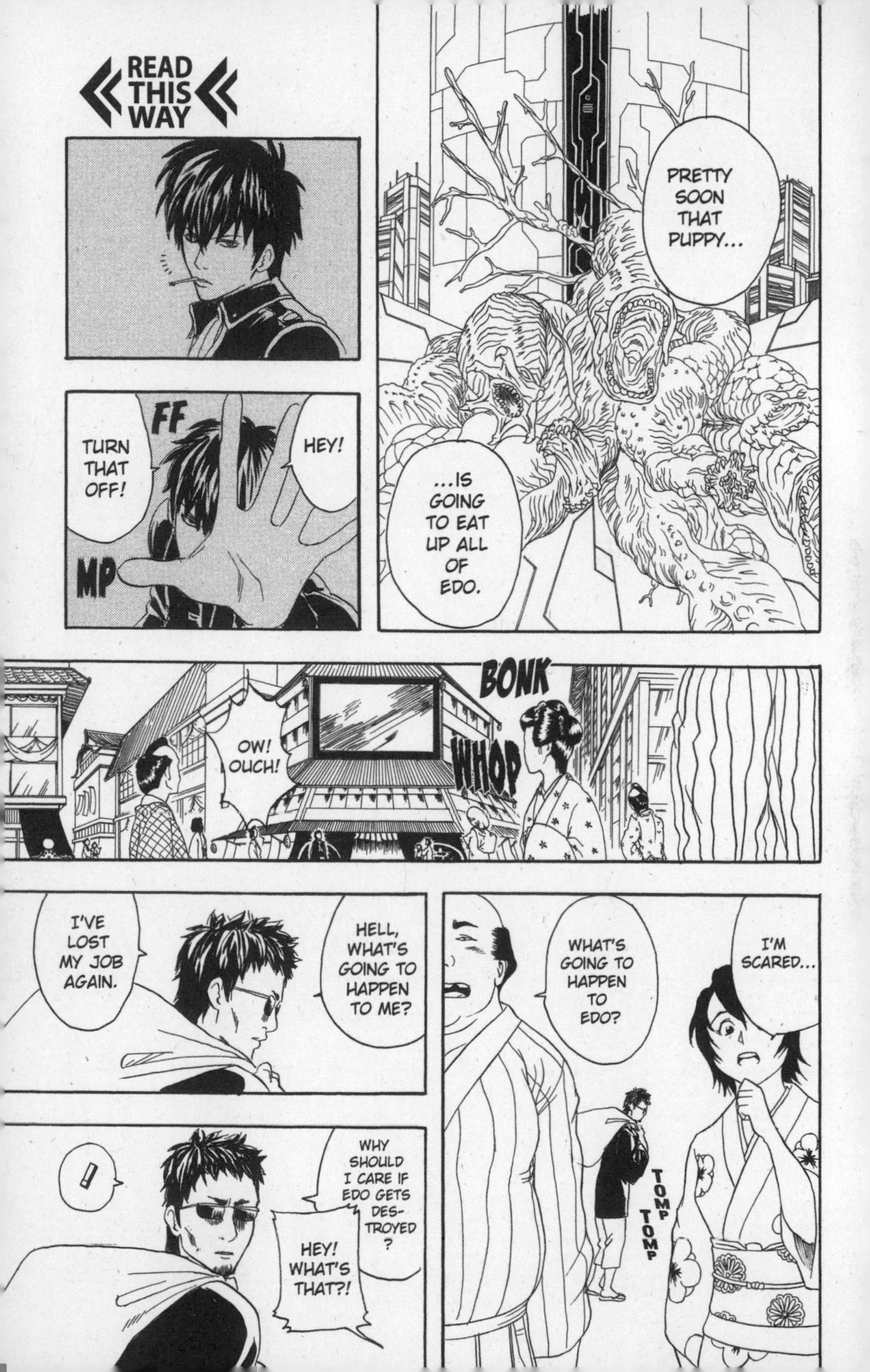
READ THIS WAY
PRETTY SOON THAT PUPPY...
...IS GOING TO EAT UP ALL OF EDO.
HEY!
FF
TURN THAT OFF!
MP
BONK
WHOP
OW! OUCH!
I'M SCARED...
WHAT'S GOING TO HAPPEN TO EDO?
TOMP TOMP
HELL, WHAT'S GOING TO HAPPEN TO ME?
I'VE LOST MY JOB AGAIN.
WHY SHOULD I CARE IF EDO GETS DES-TROYED?
HEY! WHAT'S THAT?!
!

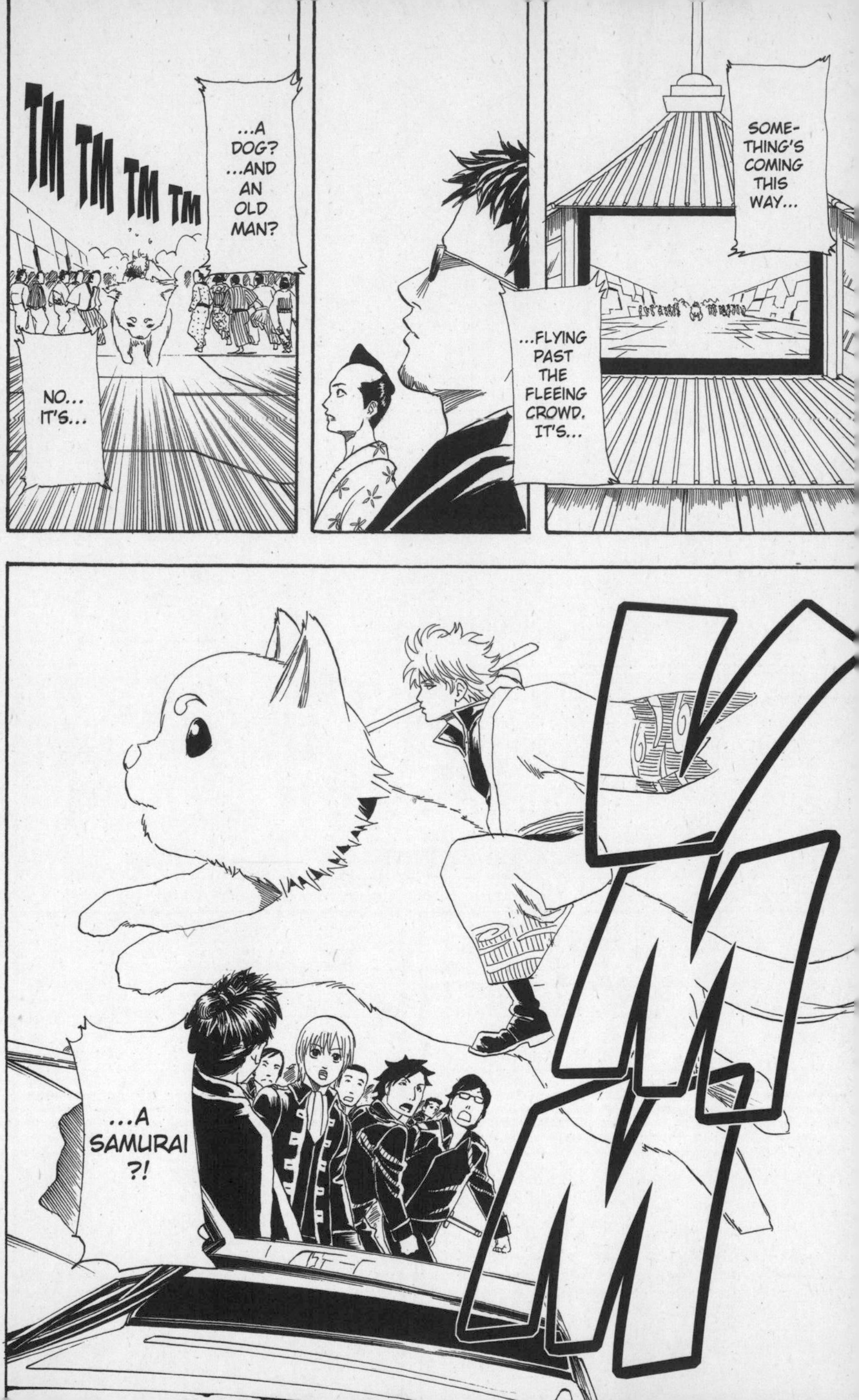
SOME-THING'S COMING THIS WAY...
...FLYING PAST THE FLEEING CROWD. IT'S...
...A DOG? ...AND AN OLD MAN?
TM TM TM TM
NO... IT'S...
MMM
...A SAMURAI ?!

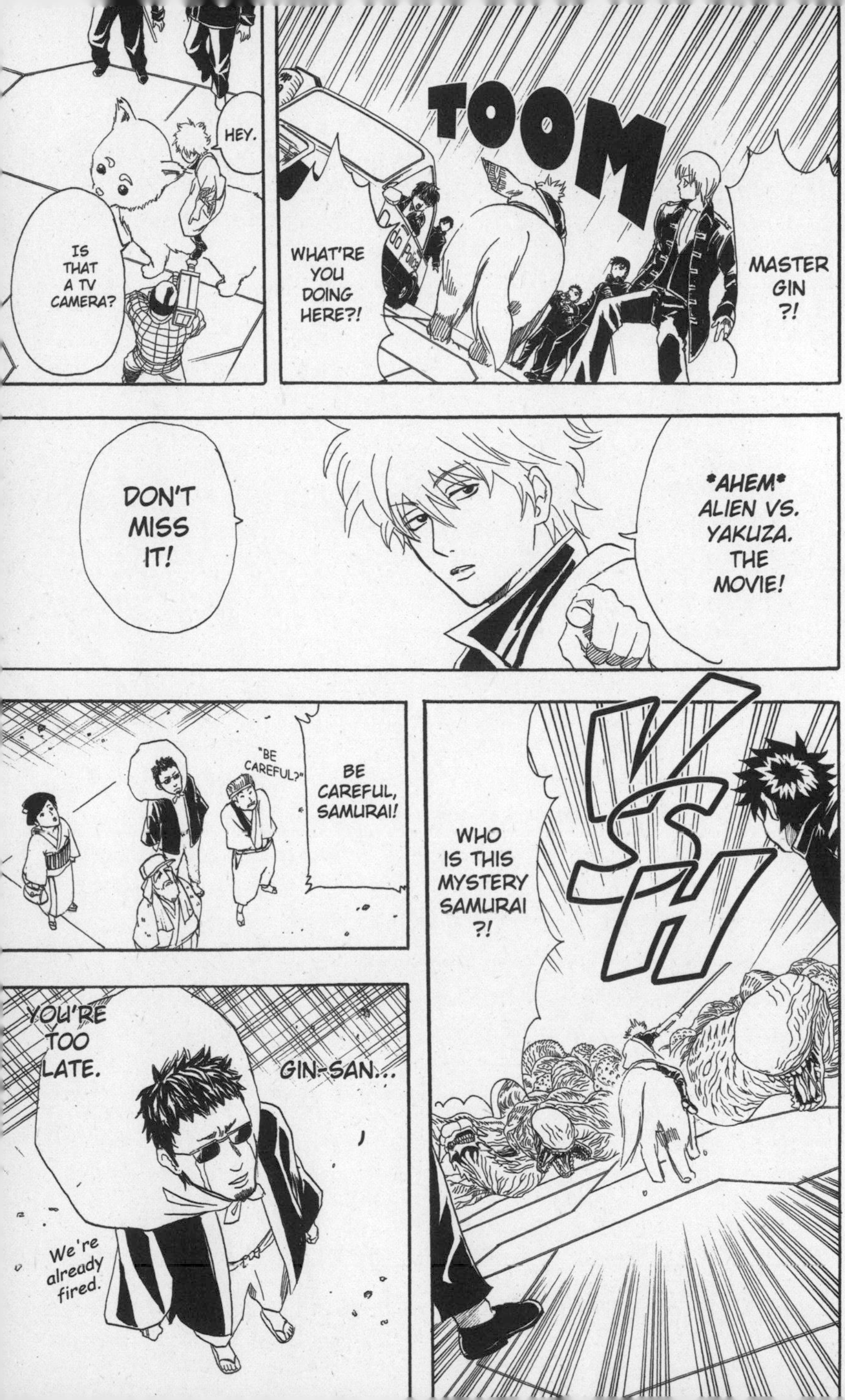
MASTER GIN ?!
TOOM
WHAT'RE YOU DOING HERE?!
HEY.
IS THAT A TV CAMERA?
AHEM ALIEN VS. YAKUZA. THE MOVIE!
DON'T MISS IT!
VSH
WHO IS THIS MYSTERY SAMURAI ?!
BE CAREFUL, SAMURAI!
"BE CAREFUL?"
GIN-SAN...
YOU'RE TOO LATE.
We're already fired.

Thank you so much for buying Gin Tama Volume 8!

It's been a while. Up to now, the bound edition has been coming out every two months, but this time it's been three months*. Well, a lot of things can happen in three months...

Heck, in three months, a lesser panda can stand up on his hind legs like a man! (It was in the news!)

In three months, a sumo wrestler can have a fight with his brother! (Also in the news!)

And in three months...Gin Tama can even turn into an anime!

...Yeah, you heard me! An animated version of Gin Tama is being made for JUMP Festa! Gin-san, Shinpachi and the whole gang are going to explode onto the screen...or so they say. And if it isn't an April Fools joke, the production's going to be by none other than Sunrise of Gundam fame. Let's hope the sun rises on Gin Tama! (Sorry!)

I guess I'm a little more excited than usual...but I've got to share this anime experience news with you! And I will, until you get sick of it!

So as they say on Gundam...sort of...
Here goes Sorachi!!

*Sorachi-sensei is referring to the Japanese edition. –Editor

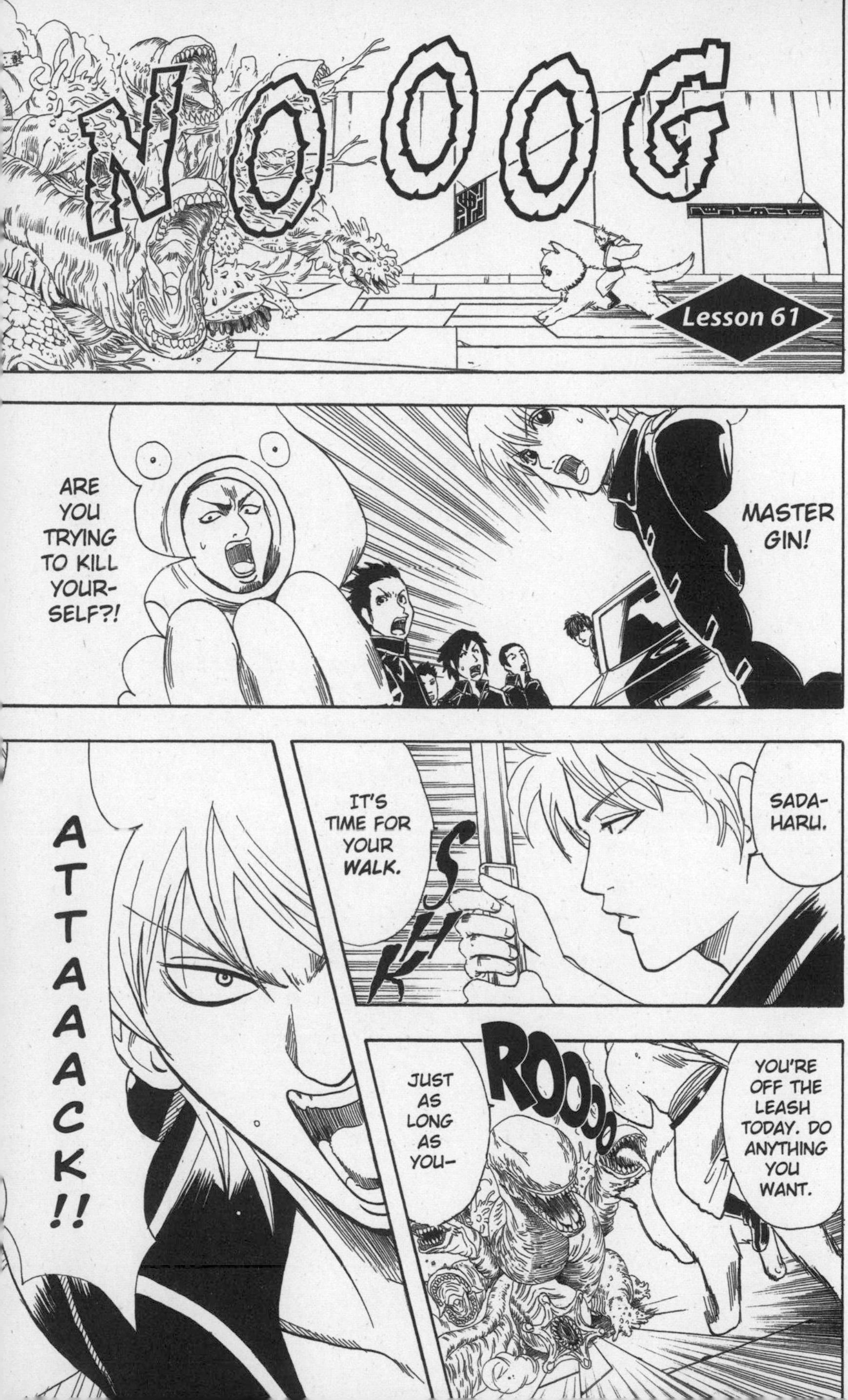
NOOOG
Lesson 61
MASTER GIN!
ARE YOU TRYING TO KILL YOURSELF?!
SADAHARU.
IT'S TIME FOR YOUR WALK.
SHK
YOU'RE OFF THE LEASH TODAY. DO ANYTHING YOU WANT.
ROOOO
JUST AS LONG AS YOU-
ATTAAAACK!!

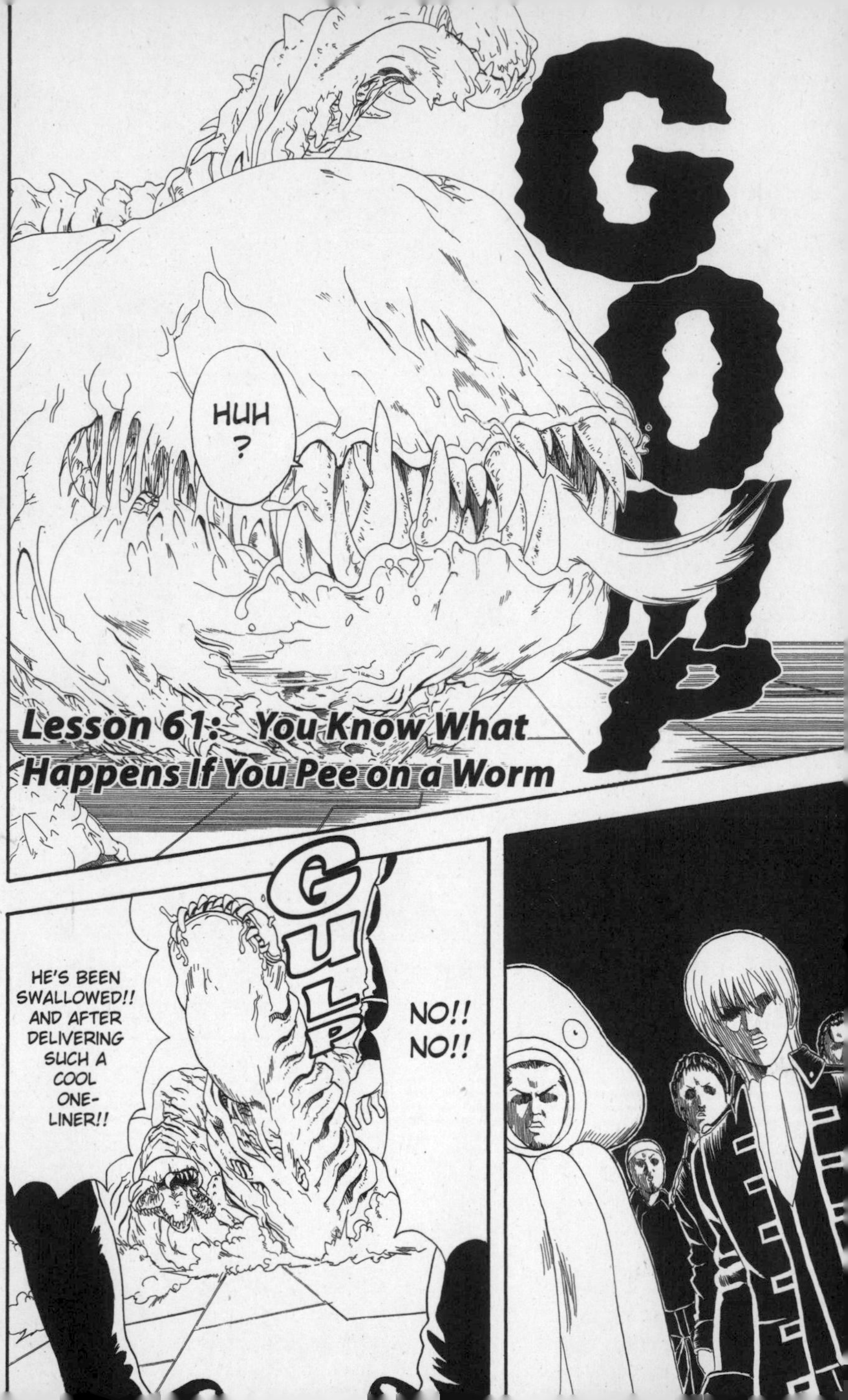
HUH ?
Lesson 61: You Know What Happens If You Pee on a Worm
GULP
NO!! NO!!
HE'S BEEN SWALLOWED!! AND AFTER DELIVERING SUCH A COOL ONE-LINER!!

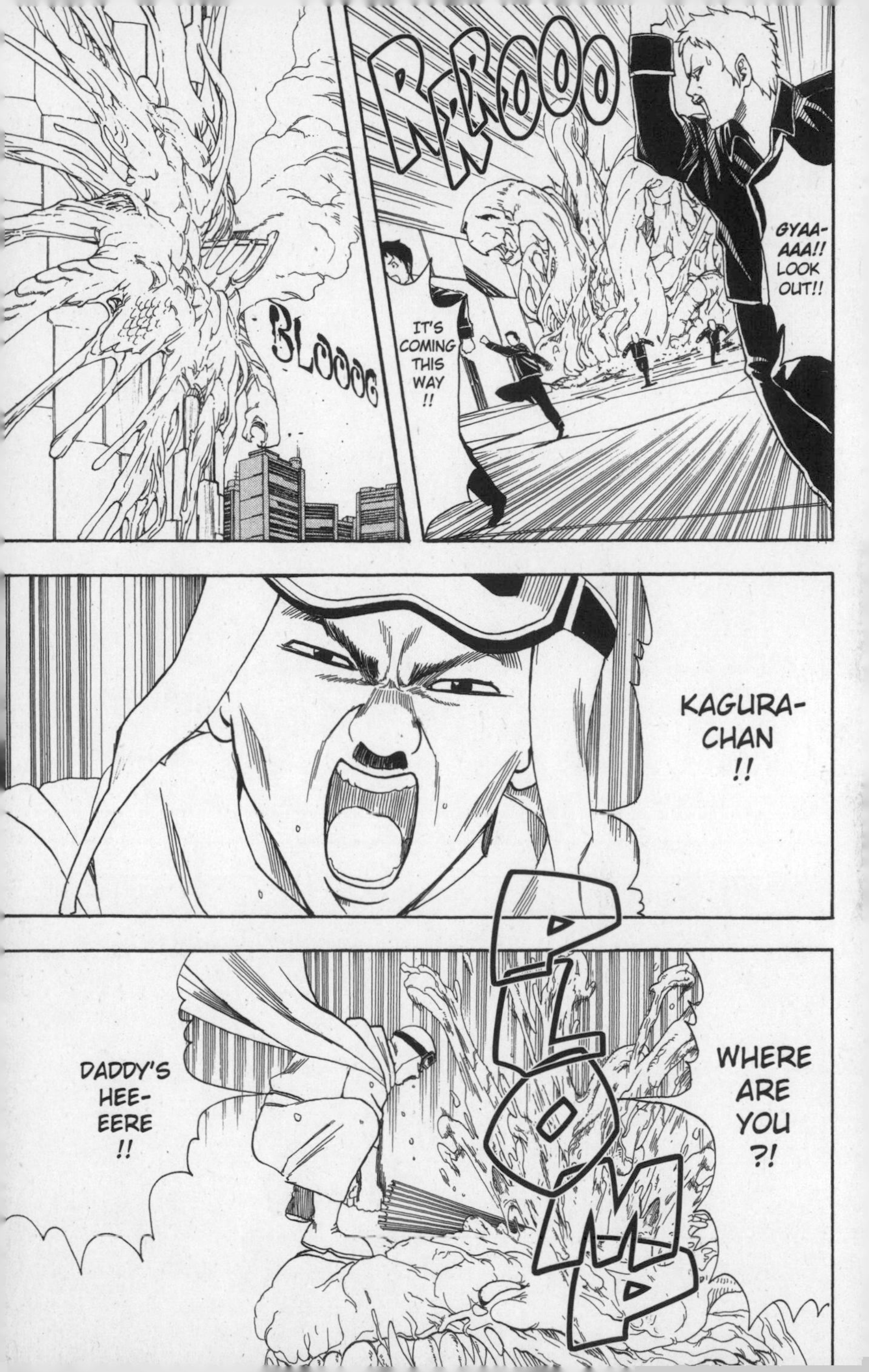
GYAA-AAA!! LOOK OUT!!
RRROOO
IT'S COMING THIS WAY!!
BLOOOG
KAGURA-CHAN!!
WHERE ARE YOU?!
PLOMP
DADDY'S HEE-EERE!!

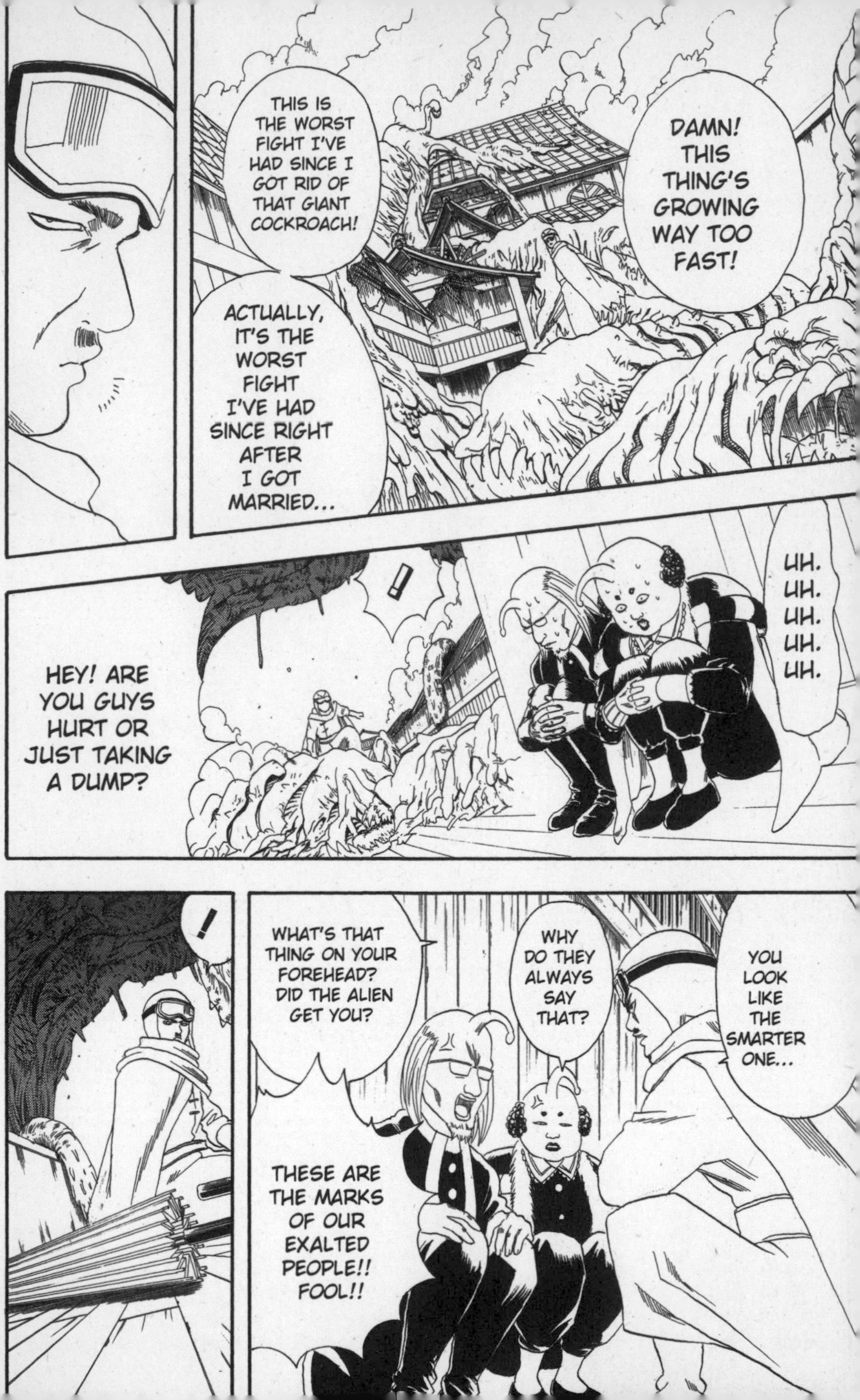
DAMN! THIS THING'S GROWING WAY TOO FAST!
THIS IS THE WORST FIGHT I'VE HAD SINCE I GOT RID OF THAT GIANT COCKROACH!
ACTUALLY, IT'S THE WORST FIGHT I'VE HAD SINCE RIGHT AFTER I GOT MARRIED...
UH. UH. UH. UH. UH.
!
HEY! ARE YOU GUYS HURT OR JUST TAKING A DUMP?
YOU LOOK LIKE THE SMARTER ONE...
WHY DO THEY ALWAYS SAY THAT?
WHAT'S THAT THING ON YOUR FOREHEAD? DID THE ALIEN GET YOU?
THESE ARE THE MARKS OF OUR EXALTED PEOPLE!! FOOL!!
!

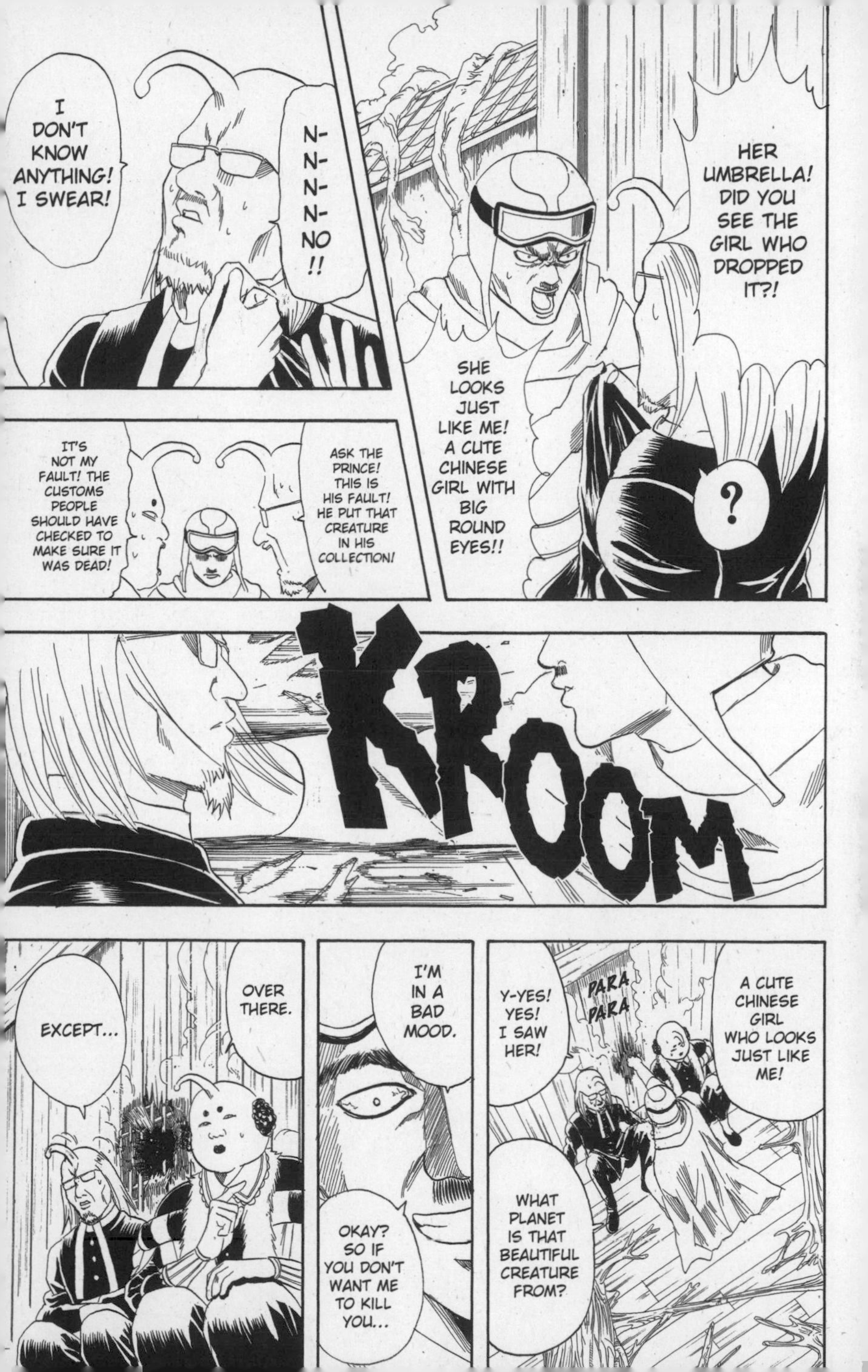
HER UMBRELLA! DID YOU SEE THE GIRL WHO DROPPED IT?!
SHE LOOKS JUST LIKE ME! A CUTE CHINESE GIRL WITH BIG ROUND EYES!!
?
N-N-N-N-NO!!
I DON'T KNOW ANYTHING! I SWEAR!
ASK THE PRINCE! THIS IS HIS FAULT! HE PUT THAT CREATURE IN HIS COLLECTION!
IT'S NOT MY FAULT! THE CUSTOMS PEOPLE SHOULD HAVE CHECKED TO MAKE SURE IT WAS DEAD!
KROOM
A CUTE CHINESE GIRL WHO LOOKS JUST LIKE ME!
PARA PARA
Y-YES! YES! I SAW HER!
WHAT PLANET IS THAT BEAUTIFUL CREATURE FROM?
I'M IN A BAD MOOD.
OKAY? SO IF YOU DON'T WANT ME TO KILL YOU...
OVER THERE.
EXCEPT...

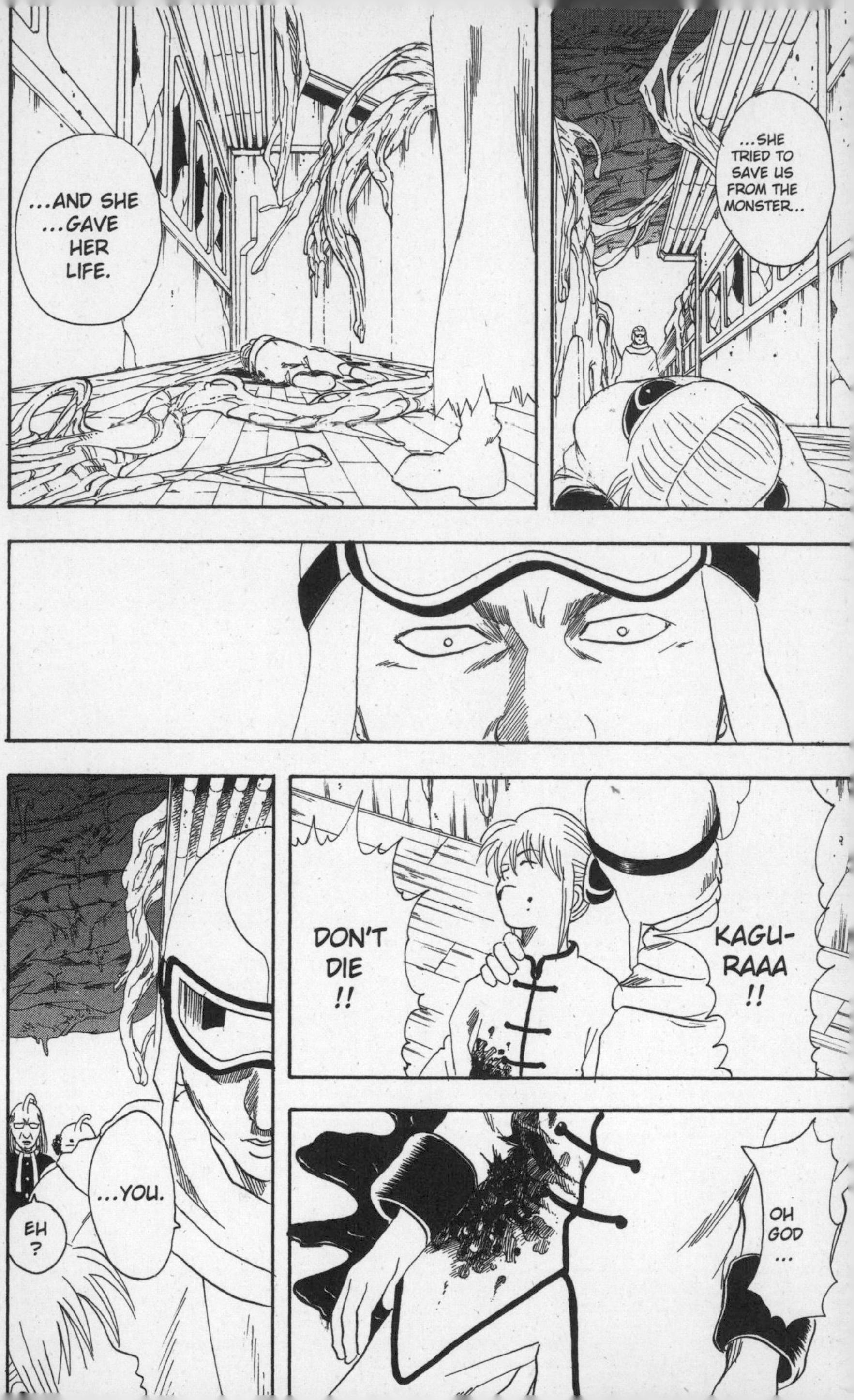
...SHE TRIED TO SAVE US FROM THE MONSTER...
...AND SHE ...GAVE HER LIFE.
KAGU-RAAA !!
DON'T DIE !!
OH GOD ...
...YOU.
EH ?

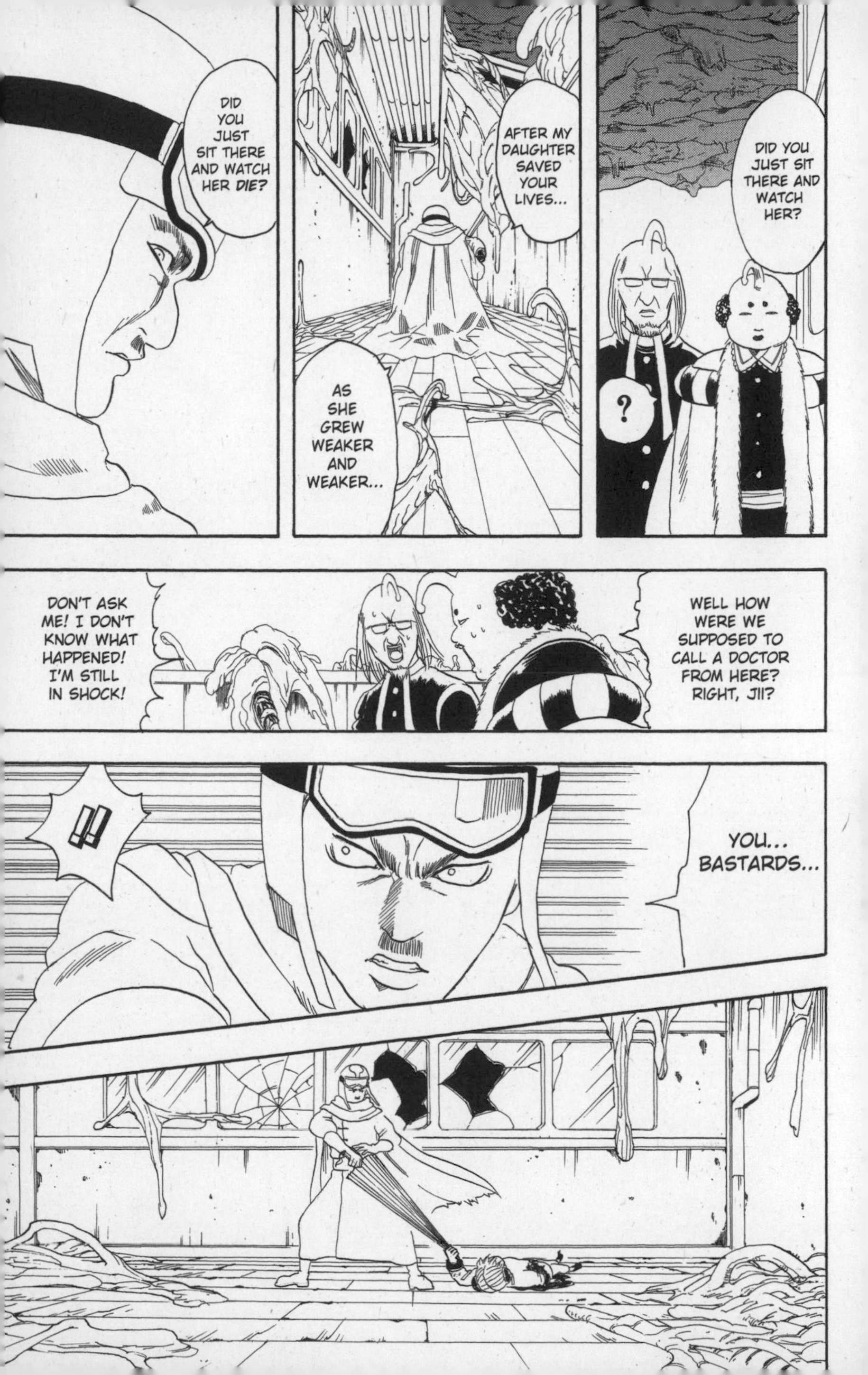
DID YOU JUST SIT THERE AND WATCH HER?
?
AFTER MY DAUGHTER SAVED YOUR LIVES...
AS SHE GREW WEAKER AND WEAKER...
DID YOU JUST SIT THERE AND WATCH HER *DIE*?
WELL HOW WERE WE SUPPOSED TO CALL A DOCTOR FROM HERE? RIGHT, JII?
DON'T ASK ME! I DON'T KNOW WHAT HAPPENED! I'M STILL IN SHOCK!
YOU... BASTARDS...
!!

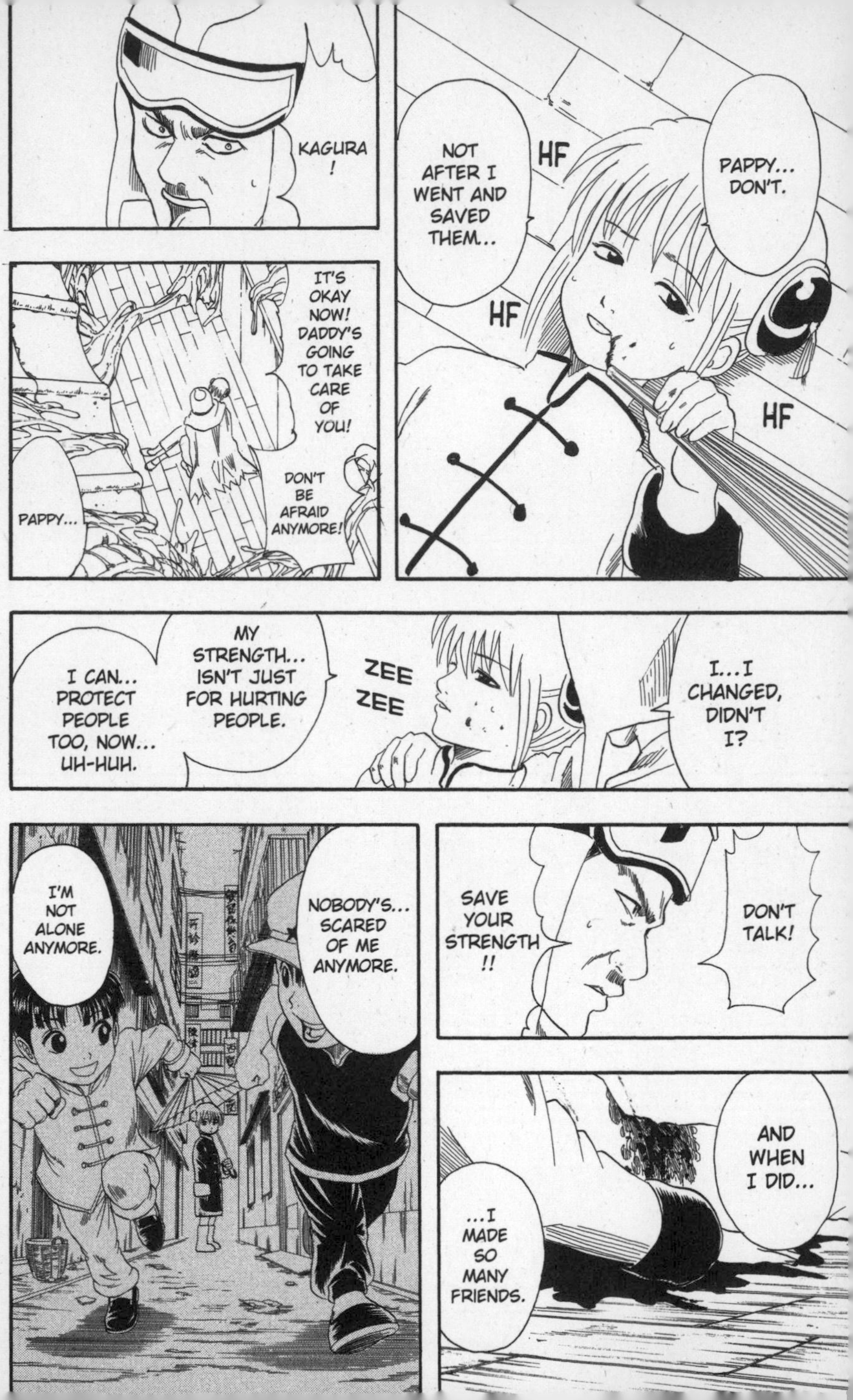
PAPPY... DON'T.
HF
NOT AFTER I WENT AND SAVED THEM...
HF
HF
KAGURA!
IT'S OKAY NOW! DADDY'S GOING TO TAKE CARE OF YOU!
DON'T BE AFRAID ANYMORE!
PAPPY...
I...I CHANGED, DIDN'T I?
ZEE ZEE
MY STRENGTH... ISN'T JUST FOR HURTING PEOPLE.
I CAN... PROTECT PEOPLE TOO, NOW... UH-HUH.
DON'T TALK!
SAVE YOUR STRENGTH!!
AND WHEN I DID...
...I MADE SO MANY FRIENDS.
NOBODY'S... SCARED OF ME ANYMORE.
I'M NOT ALONE ANYMORE.

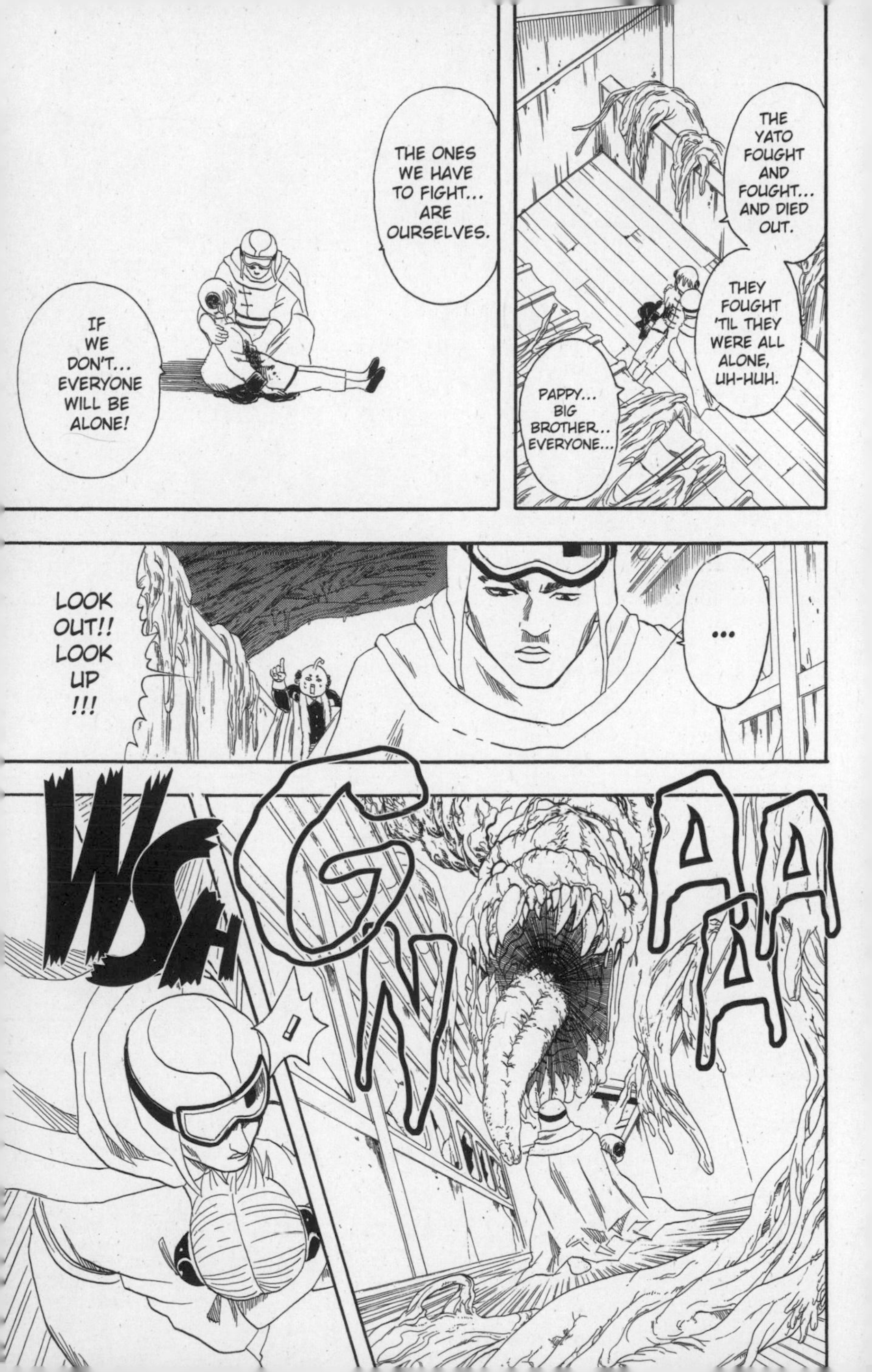
THE YATO FOUGHT AND FOUGHT... AND DIED OUT.
THEY FOUGHT 'TIL THEY WERE ALL ALONE, UH-HUH.
PAPPY... BIG BROTHER.. EVERYONE...
THE ONES WE HAVE TO FIGHT... ARE OURSELVES.
IF WE DON'T... EVERYONE WILL BE ALONE!
...
LOOK OUT!! LOOK UP!!!
GNAAAA
WSH
!

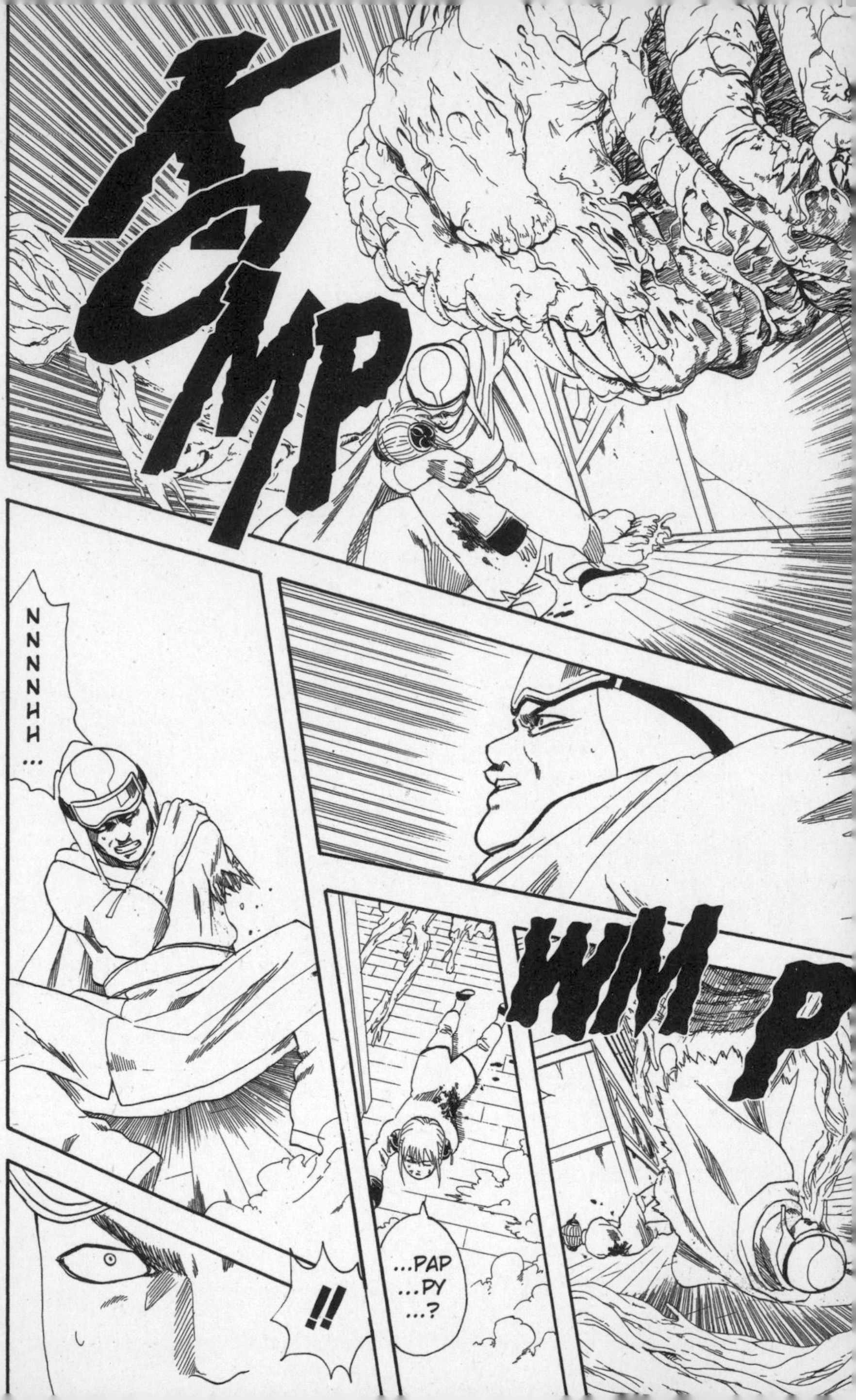
NNNNHH...
WMP
...PAP ...PY ...?
!!

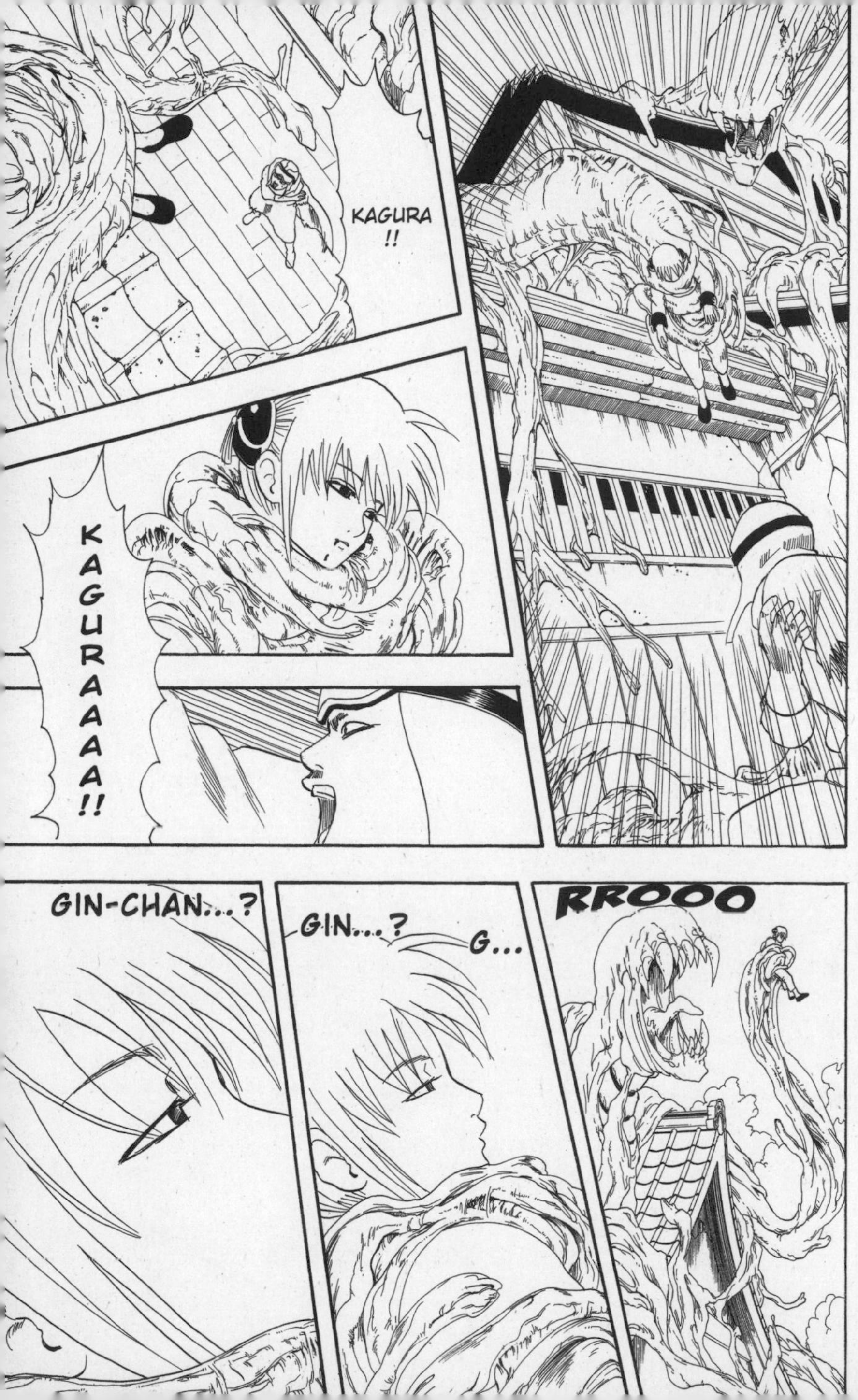
KAGURA !!
KAGURAAAAA!!
RROOO
GIN...?
G...
GIN-CHAN...?

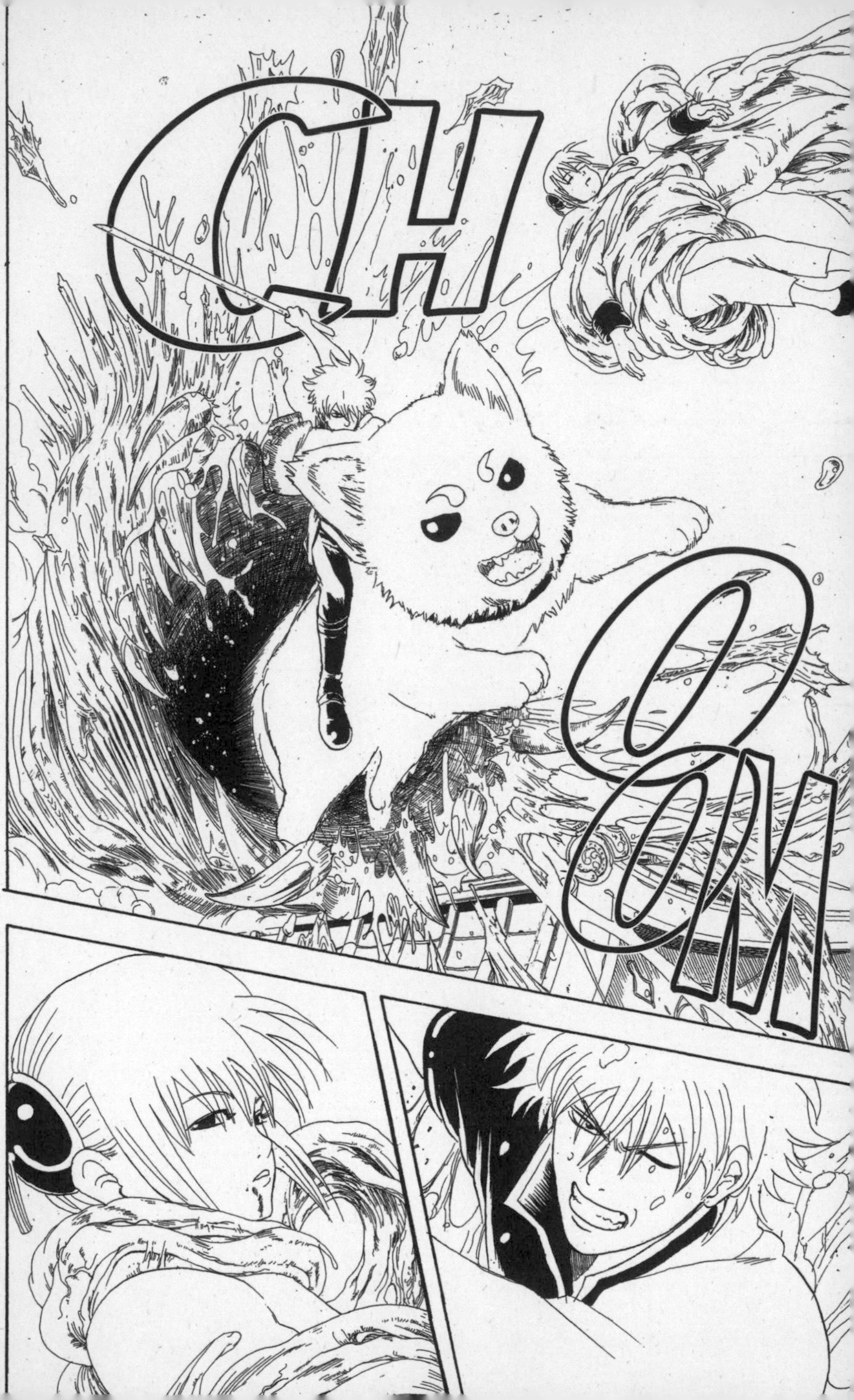
CHOOM

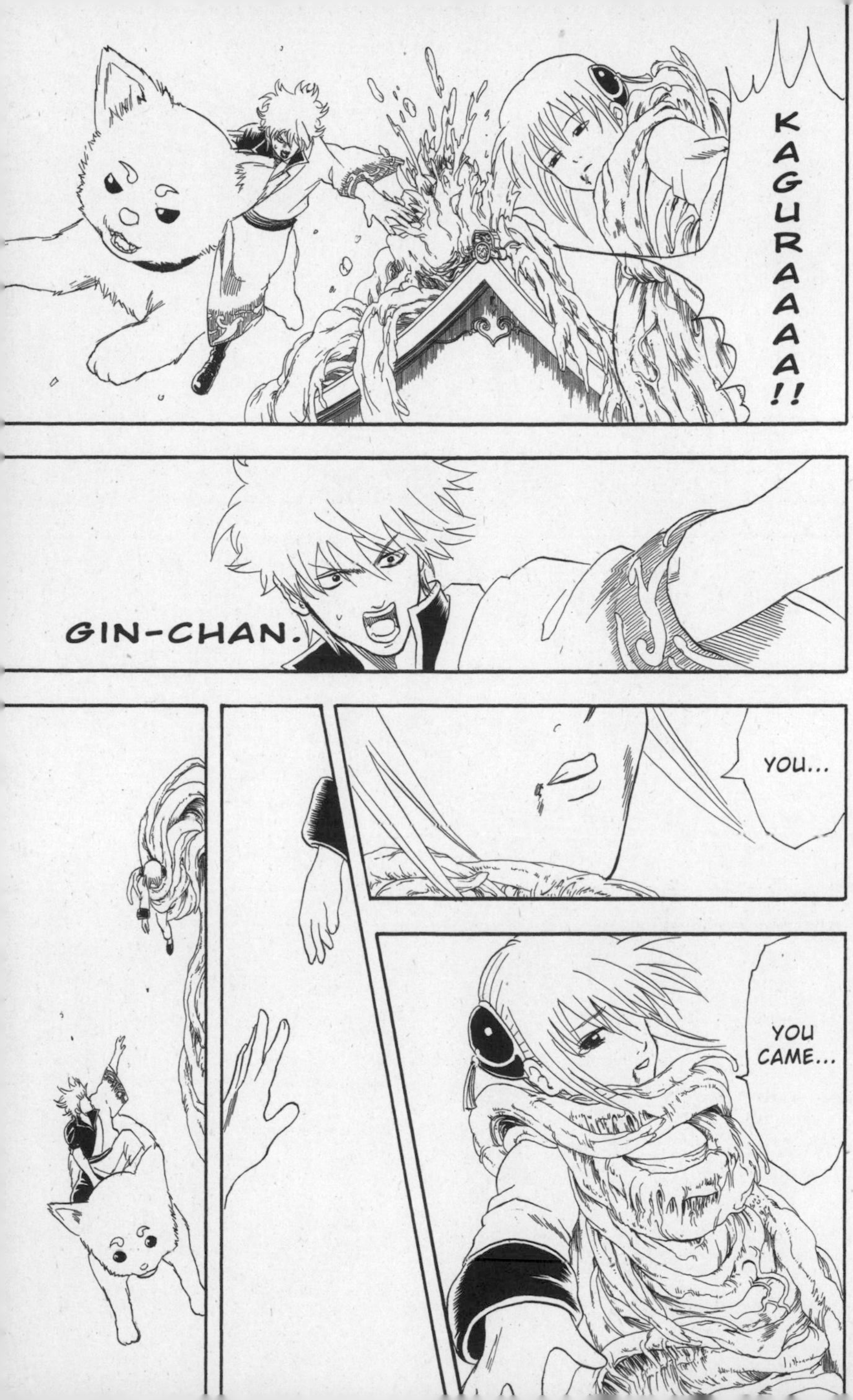
KAGURAAAAA!!
GIN-CHAN.
YOU...
YOU CAME...

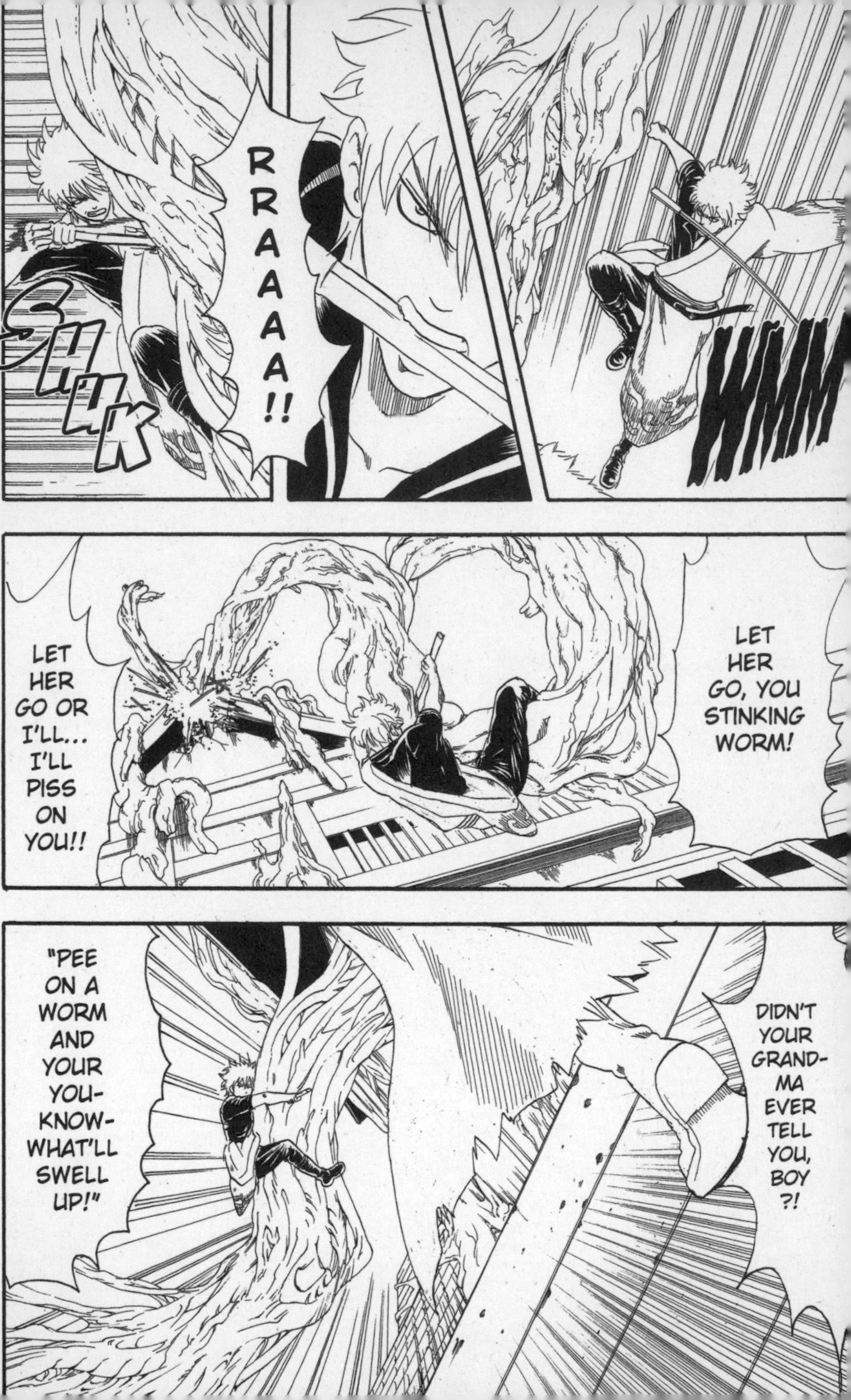
WHMM
RRAAAA!!
SHUK
LET HER GO, YOU STINKING WORM!
LET HER GO OR I'LL... I'LL PISS ON YOU!!
DIDN'T YOUR GRANDMA EVER TELL YOU, BOY?!
"PEE ON A WORM AND YOUR YOU-KNOW-WHAT'LL SWELL UP!"

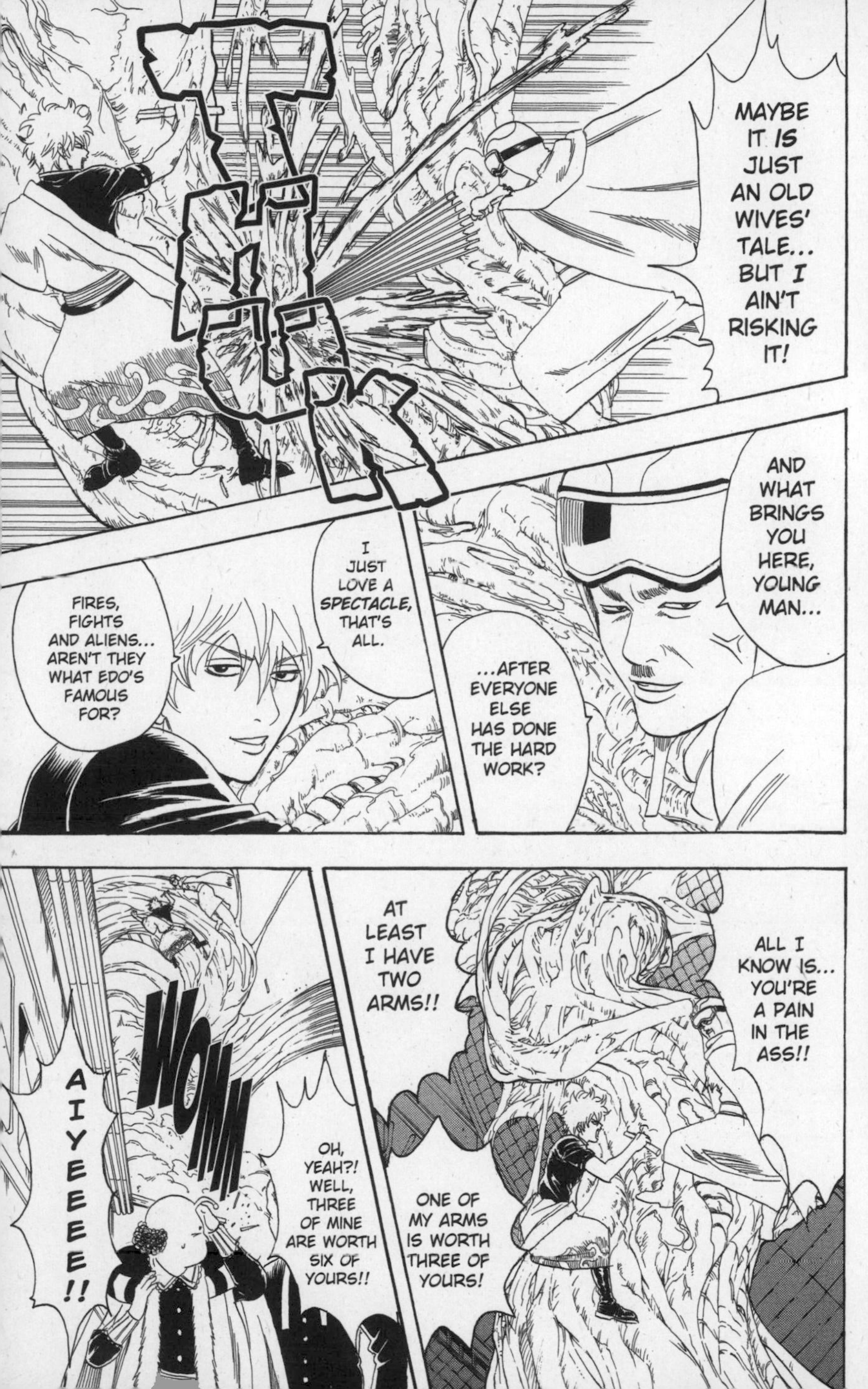
MAYBE IT IS JUST AN OLD WIVES' TALE... BUT I AIN'T RISKING IT!
AND WHAT BRINGS YOU HERE, YOUNG MAN...
...AFTER EVERYONE ELSE HAS DONE THE HARD WORK?
I JUST LOVE A SPECTACLE, THAT'S ALL.
FIRES, FIGHTS AND ALIENS... AREN'T THEY WHAT EDO'S FAMOUS FOR?
ALL I KNOW IS... YOU'RE A PAIN IN THE ASS!!
AT LEAST I HAVE TWO ARMS!!
ONE OF MY ARMS IS WORTH THREE OF YOURS!
OH, YEAH?! WELL, THREE OF MINE ARE WORTH SIX OF YOURS!!
WOMM
AIYEEEEE!!

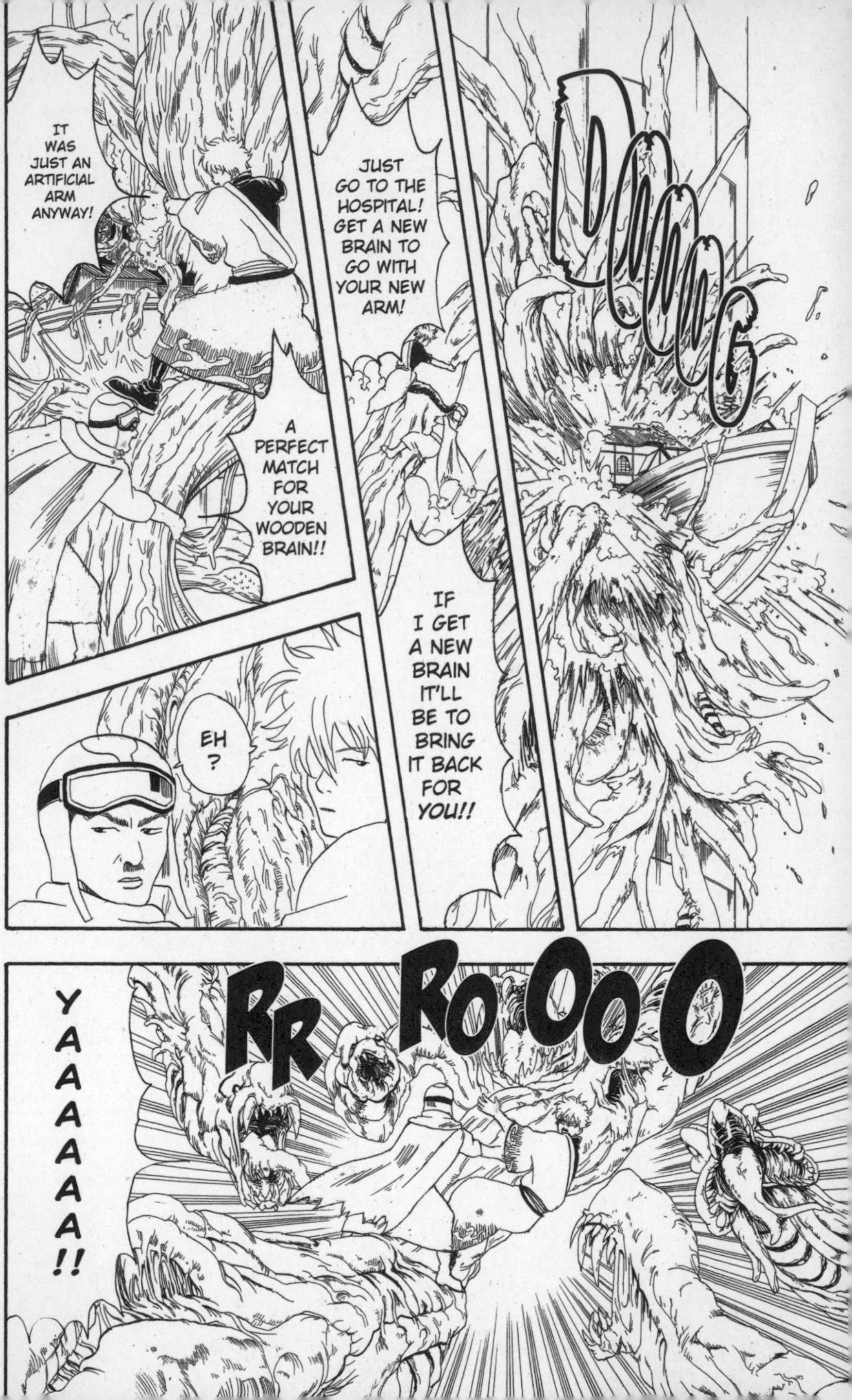
DOOOG
JUST GO TO THE HOSPITAL! GET A NEW BRAIN TO GO WITH YOUR NEW ARM!
IF I GET A NEW BRAIN IT'LL BE TO BRING IT BACK FOR *YOU!!*
IT WAS JUST AN ARTIFICIAL ARM ANYWAY!
A PERFECT MATCH FOR YOUR WOODEN BRAIN!!
EH?
RRROOOO
YAAAAAAA!!

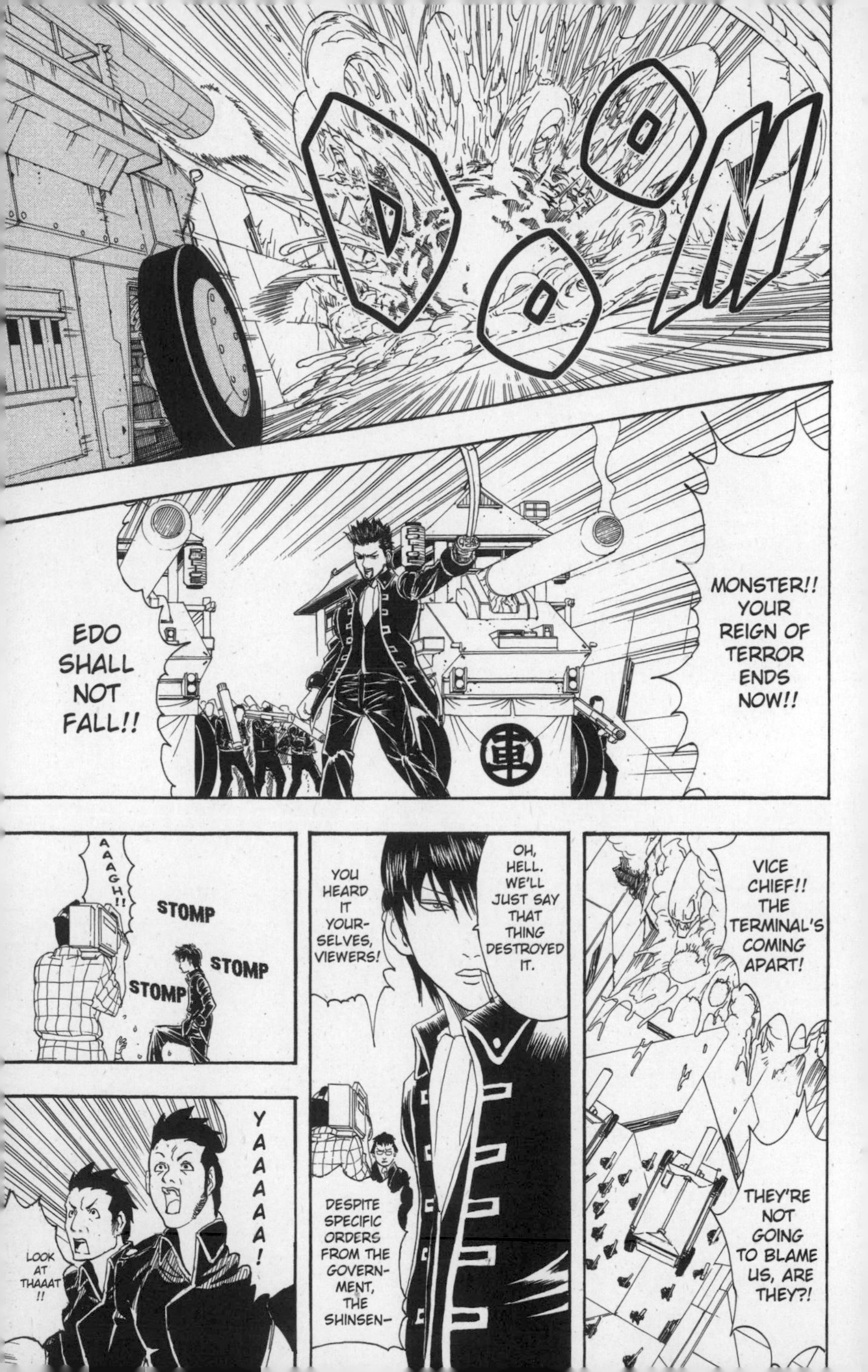
DOOM
MONSTER!! YOUR REIGN OF TERROR ENDS NOW!!
EDO SHALL NOT FALL!!
VICE CHIEF!! THE TERMINAL'S COMING APART!
THEY'RE NOT GOING TO BLAME US, ARE THEY?!
OH, HELL. WE'LL JUST SAY THAT THING DESTROYED IT.
YOU HEARD IT YOURSELVES, VIEWERS!
DESPITE SPECIFIC ORDERS FROM THE GOVERNMENT, THE SHINSEN-
AAAGH!!
STOMP
STOMP
STOMP
YAAAAAA!
LOOK AT THAAAT!!

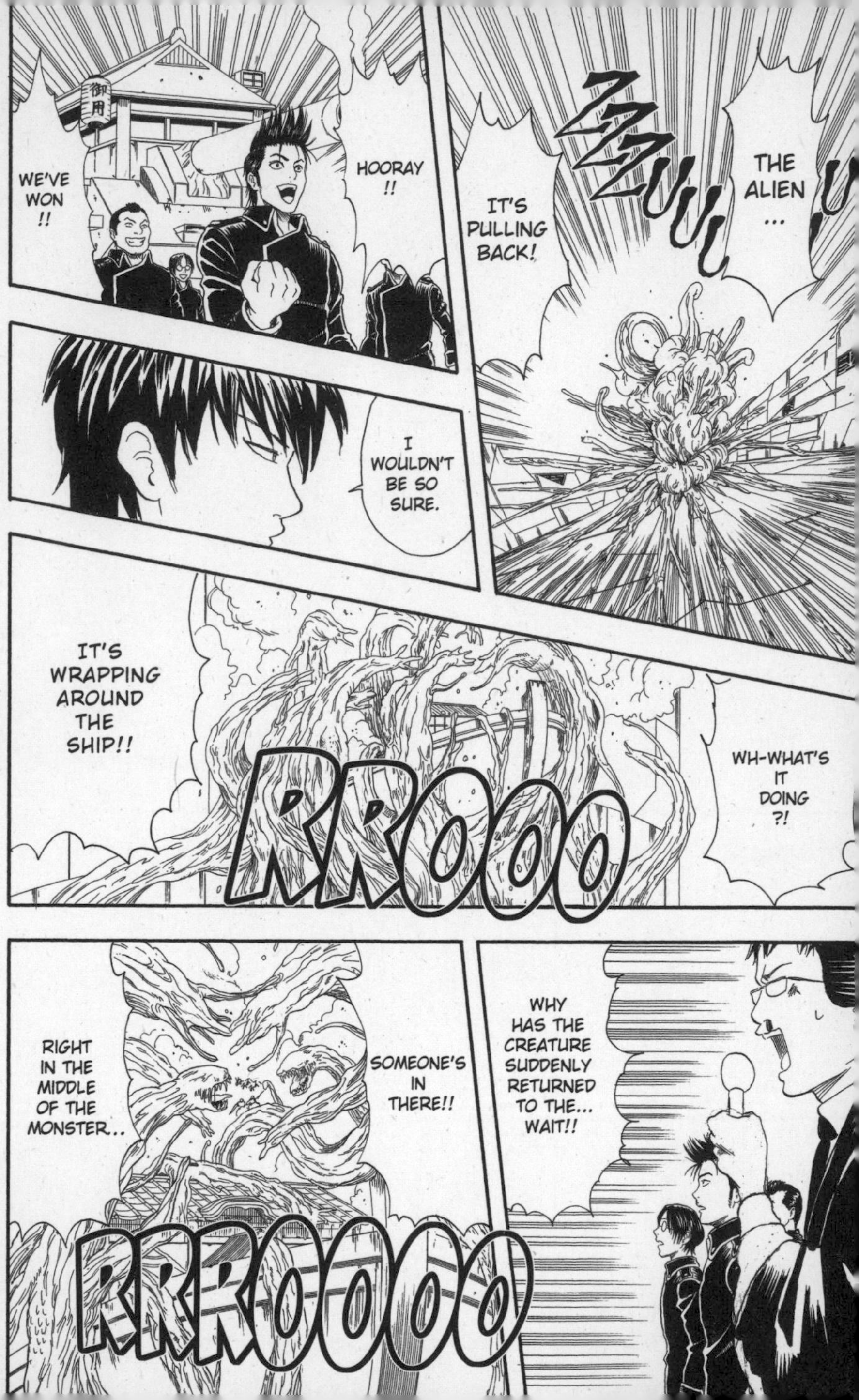
THE ALIEN ...
ZZZUUU
IT'S PULLING BACK!
御用
HOORAY !!
WE'VE WON !!
I WOULDN'T BE SO SURE.
WH-WHAT'S IT DOING ?!
RROOO
IT'S WRAPPING AROUND THE SHIP!!
WHY HAS THE CREATURE SUDDENLY RETURNED TO THE... WAIT!!
SOMEONE'S IN THERE!!
RIGHT IN THE MIDDLE OF THE MONSTER...
RRROOOO

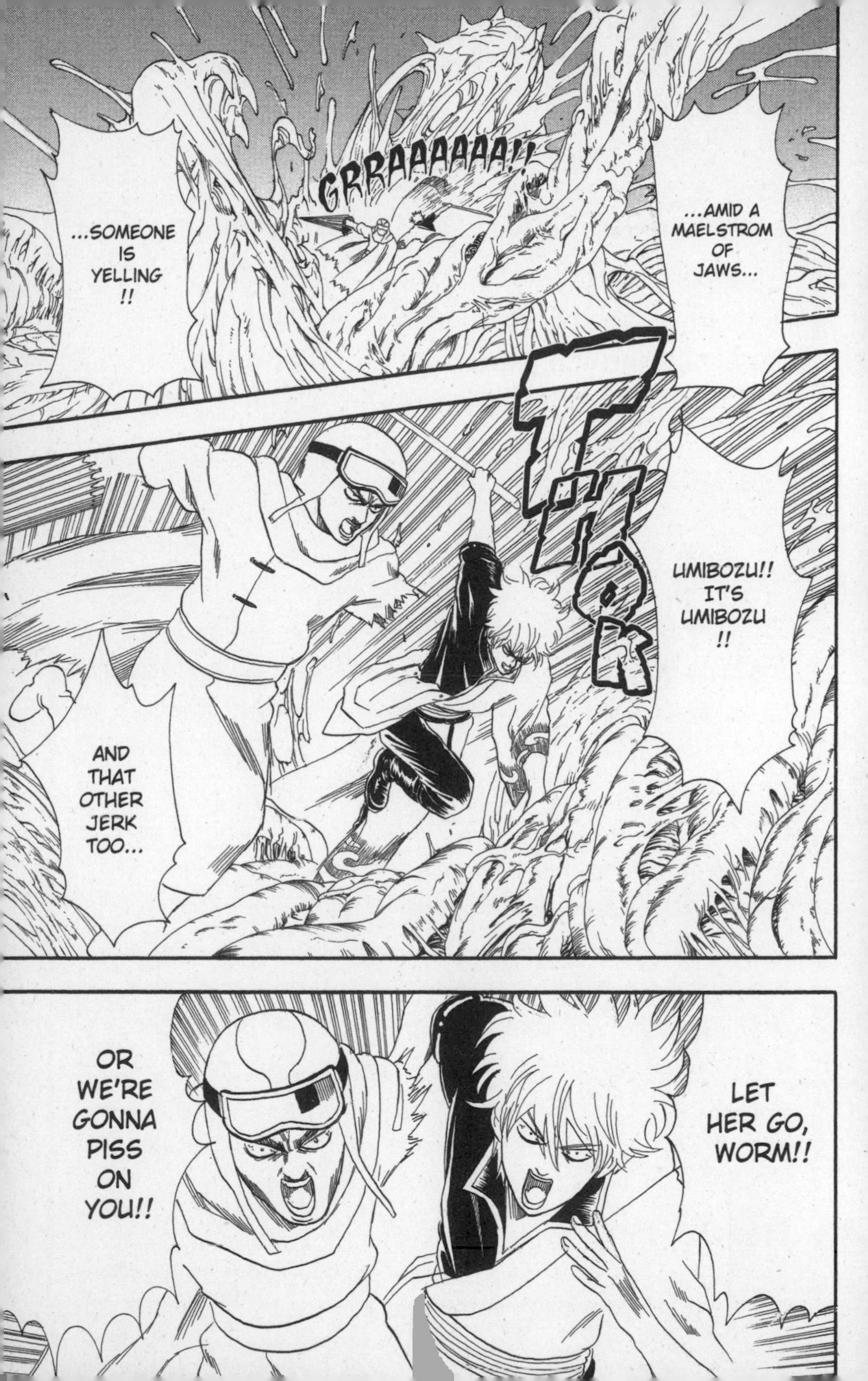
...AMID A MAELSTROM OF JAWS...
GRRAAAAAAA!!
...SOMEONE IS YELLING !!
THOK
UMIBOZU!! IT'S UMIBOZU !!
AND THAT OTHER JERK TOO...
LET HER GO, WORM!!
OR WE'RE GONNA PISS ON YOU!!

Sorachi's Q&A Corner #14

<From "Anonymous-san" of Tottori Prefecture>

Sorachi-sensei!
Among the anti-foreigner rebel factions we've seen the *Kaitento* (Vol. 3) and the *Moeru Tokon* (Vol. 4). But which anti-foreigner rebel faction does Katsura belong to (and Gin-san used to)?

<Answer>

It doesn't have any particular name. Incidentally, the organization that Katsura currently belongs to is different from the one Gin-san was a member of. When Gin was in it, it was much bigger. It was an age when the Kaitento and Moeru Kaito and everybody were all mixed up together, when all the young samurai were like, "Well, it's really cool so join up." After that the anti-foreigner movement faded due to the pressure from the Bakufu government and the Amanto, but the die-hards kept going of their own accord and each invented their own cliques. Some of them are still in existence, but barely. Like Katsura's.

(Q&A #15 is on page 86)

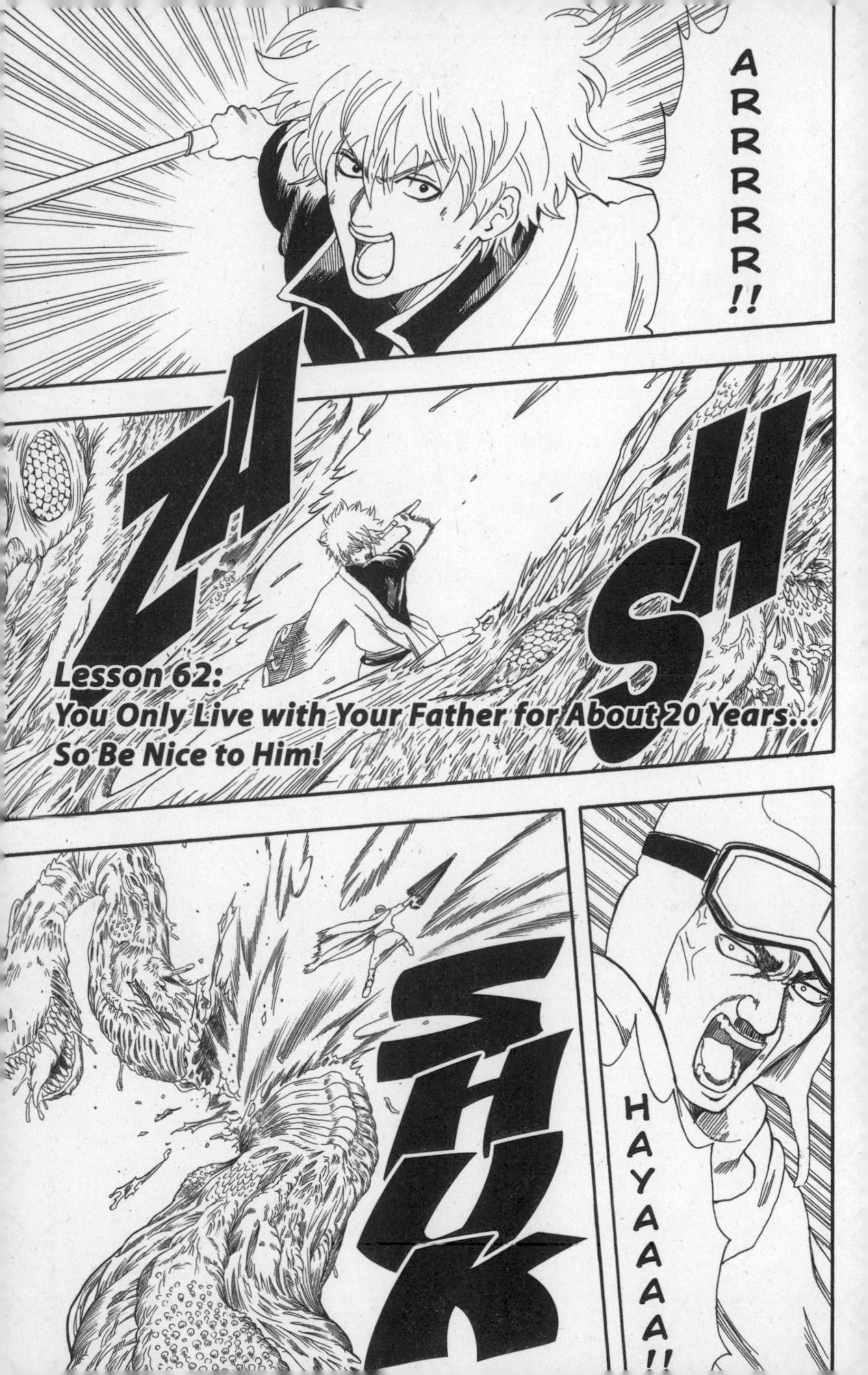
ARRRRR!!
ZASH
Lesson 62:
You Only Live with Your Father for About 20 Years...
So Be Nice to Him!
HAYAAAA!!
SHUK

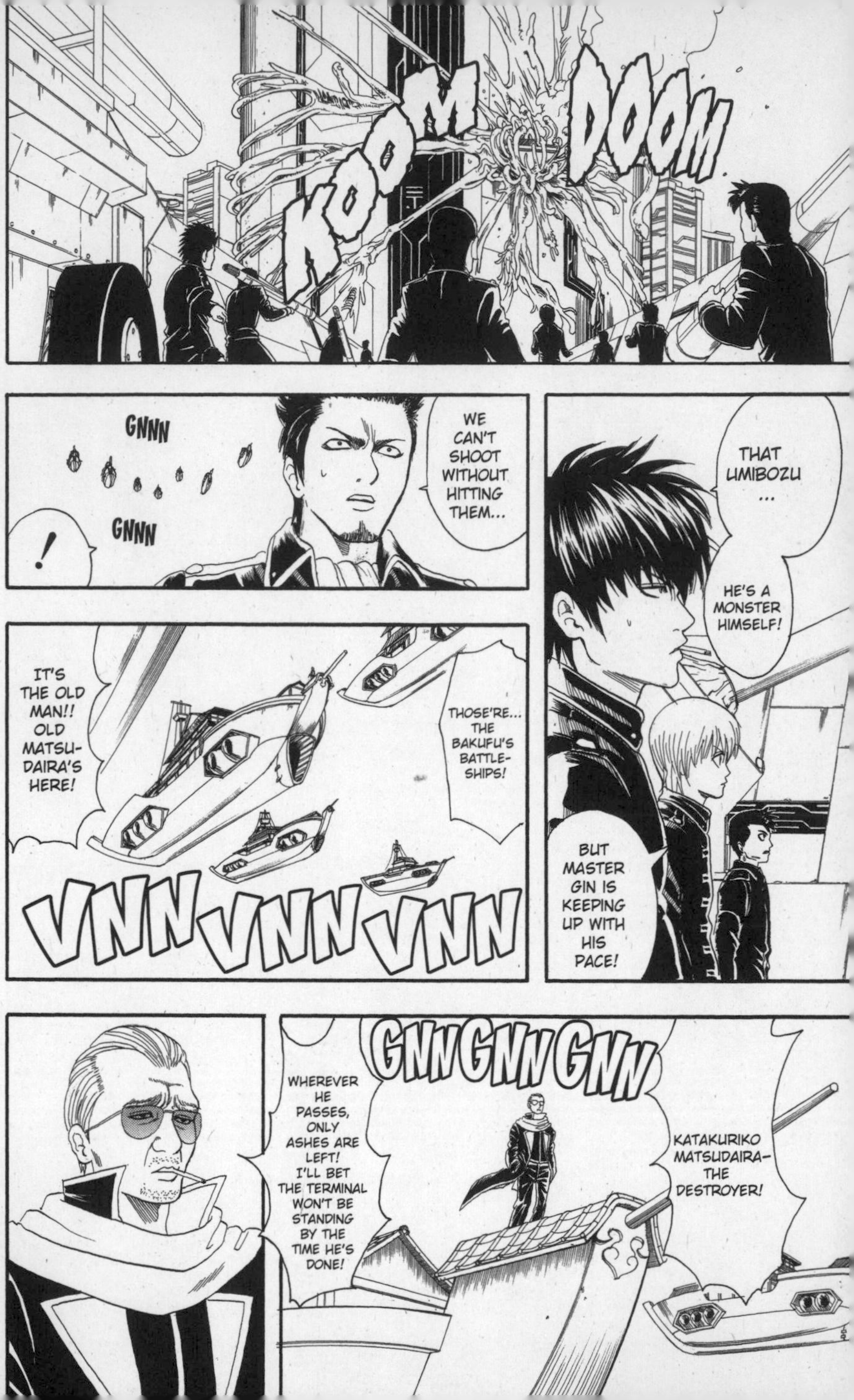
DOOM
KOOM
THAT UMIBOZU...
HE'S A MONSTER HIMSELF!
BUT MASTER GIN IS KEEPING UP WITH HIS PACE!
WE CAN'T SHOOT WITHOUT HITTING THEM...
GNNN
GNNN
!
THOSE'RE... THE BAKUFU'S BATTLESHIPS!
IT'S THE OLD MAN!! OLD MATSUDAIRA'S HERE!
VNN VNN VNN
GNNGNNGNN
KATAKURIKO MATSUDAIRA—THE DESTROYER!
WHEREVER HE PASSES, ONLY ASHES ARE LEFT! I'LL BET THE TERMINAL WON'T BE STANDING BY THE TIME HE'S DONE!

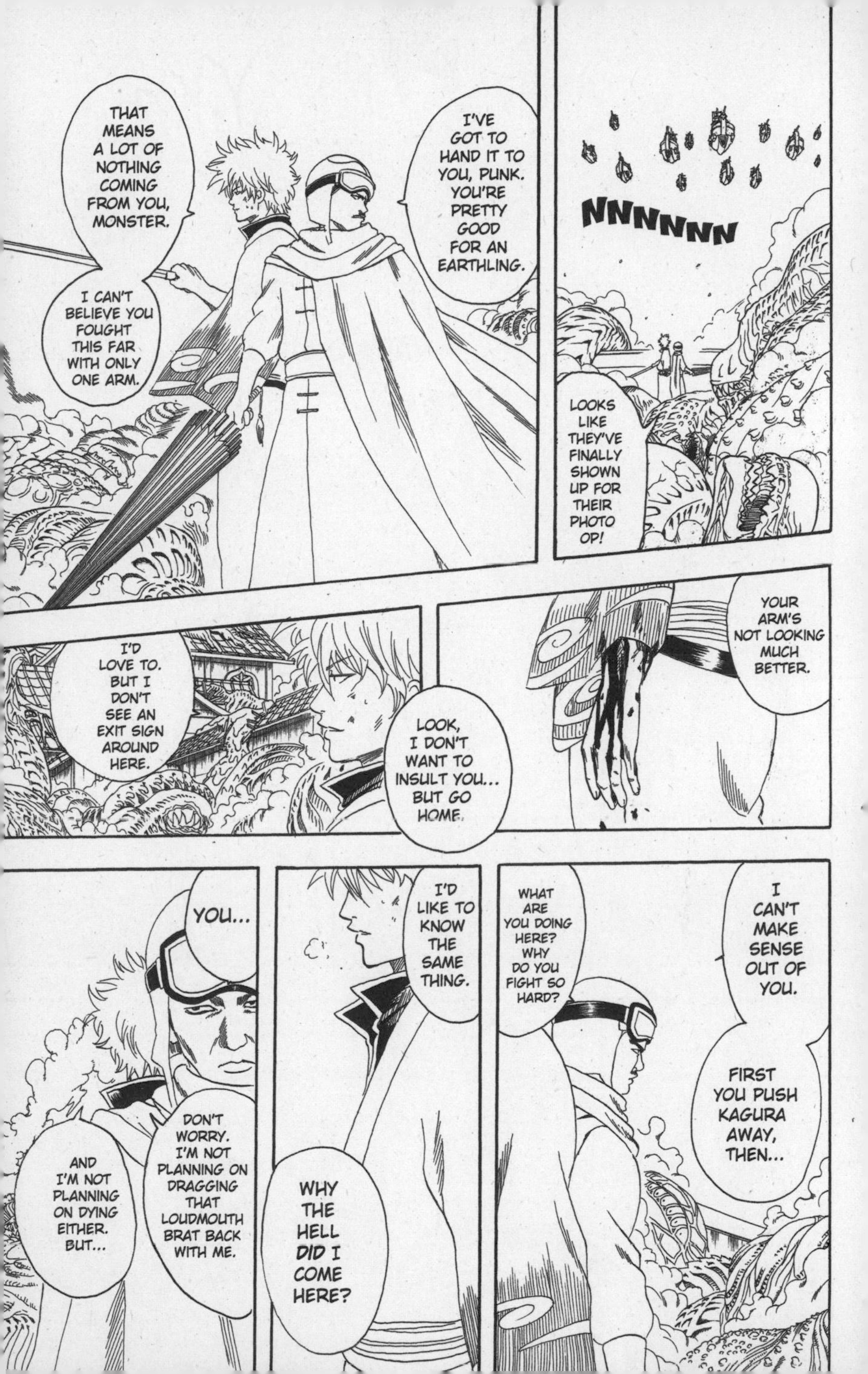
NNNNNN
LOOKS LIKE THEY'VE FINALLY SHOWN UP FOR THEIR PHOTO OP!
I'VE GOT TO HAND IT TO YOU, PUNK. YOU'RE PRETTY GOOD FOR AN EARTHLING.
THAT MEANS A LOT OF NOTHING COMING FROM YOU, MONSTER.
I CAN'T BELIEVE YOU FOUGHT THIS FAR WITH ONLY ONE ARM.
YOUR ARM'S NOT LOOKING MUCH BETTER.
LOOK, I DON'T WANT TO INSULT YOU... BUT GO HOME.
I'D LOVE TO. BUT I DON'T SEE AN EXIT SIGN AROUND HERE.
I CAN'T MAKE SENSE OF YOU.
FIRST YOU PUSH KAGURA AWAY, THEN...
WHAT ARE YOU DOING HERE? WHY DO YOU FIGHT SO HARD?
I'D LIKE TO KNOW THE SAME THING.
WHY THE HELL *DID* I COME HERE?
YOU...
DON'T WORRY. I'M NOT PLANNING ON DRAGGING THAT LOUDMOUTH BRAT BACK WITH ME.
AND I'M NOT PLANNING ON DYING EITHER. BUT...

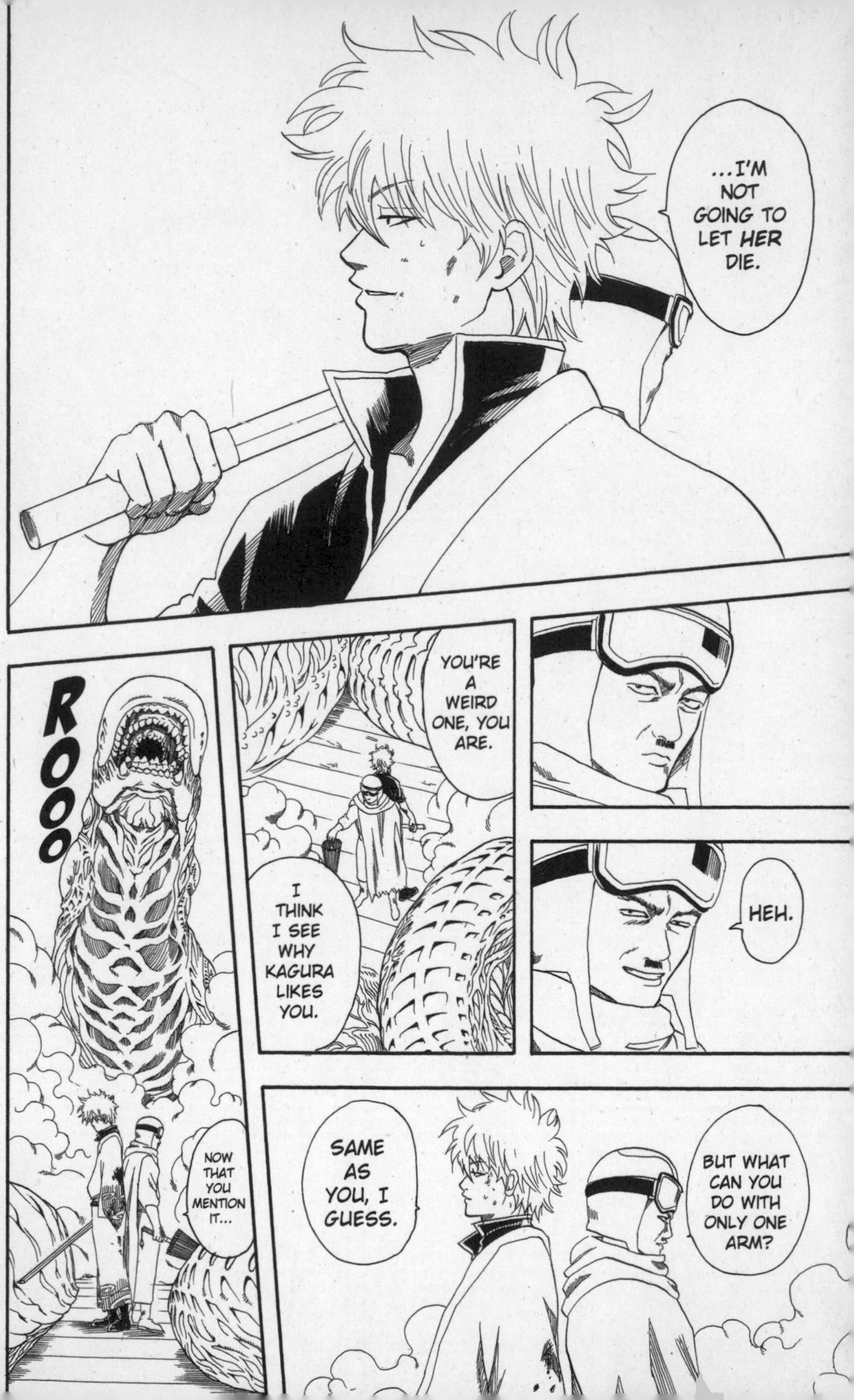
...I'M NOT GOING TO LET HER DIE.
HEH.
YOU'RE A WEIRD ONE, YOU ARE.
I THINK I SEE WHY KAGURA LIKES YOU.
BUT WHAT CAN YOU DO WITH ONLY ONE ARM?
SAME AS YOU, I GUESS.
ROOO
NOW THAT YOU MENTION IT...

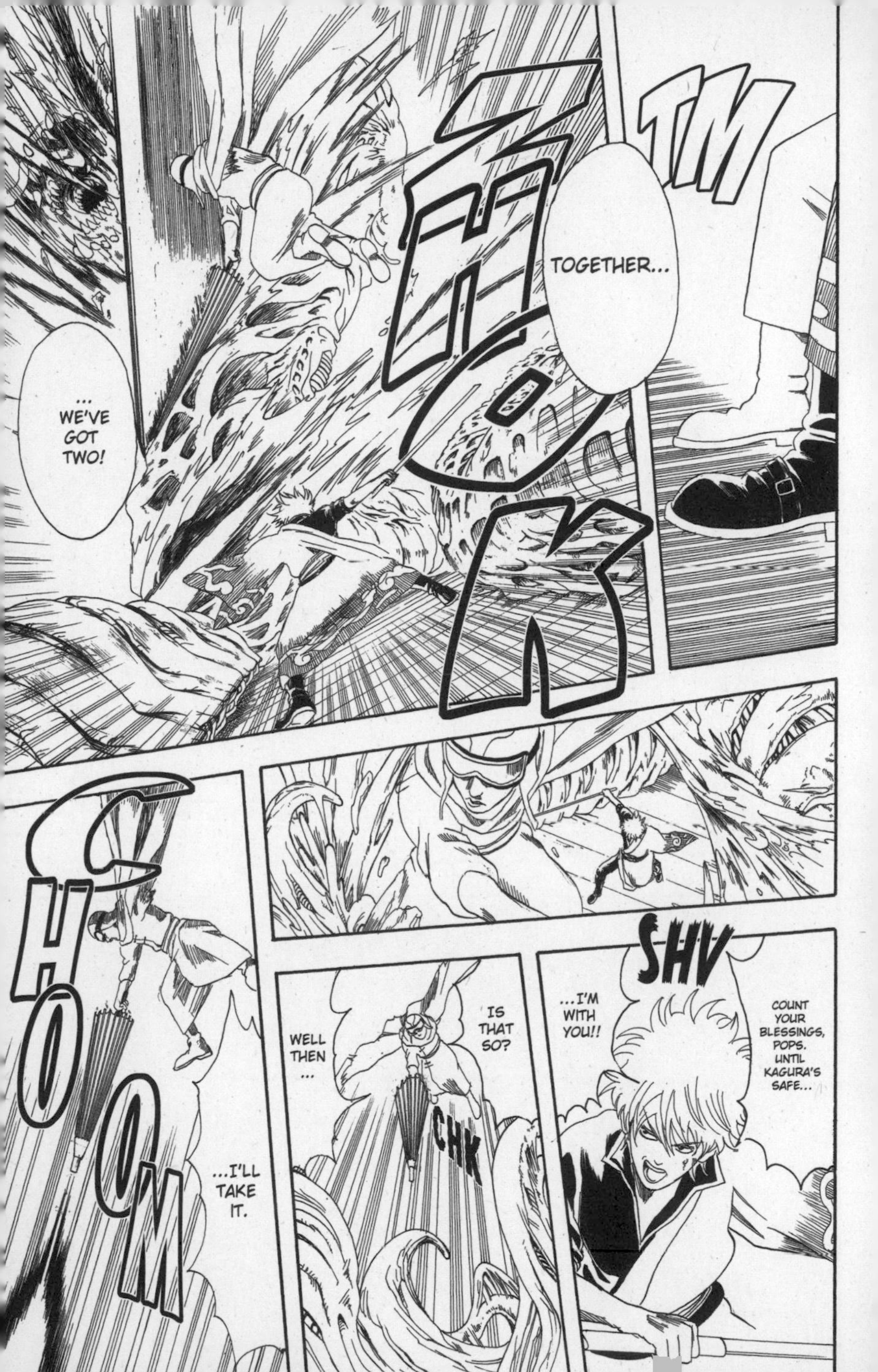
TM
TOGETHER...
...WE'VE GOT TWO!
SHV
COUNT YOUR BLESSINGS, POPS. UNTIL KAGURA'S SAFE...
...I'M WITH YOU!!
IS THAT SO?
WELL THEN ...
CHK
...I'LL TAKE IT.

THE BOTTOM OF THE SHIP BLEW OUT...

WHAT WAS THAT?!

BBBBB

DOOM

THAT'S...

H-HEY...

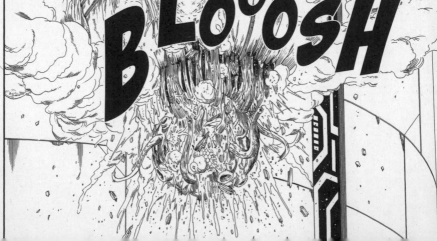

BLOOOSH

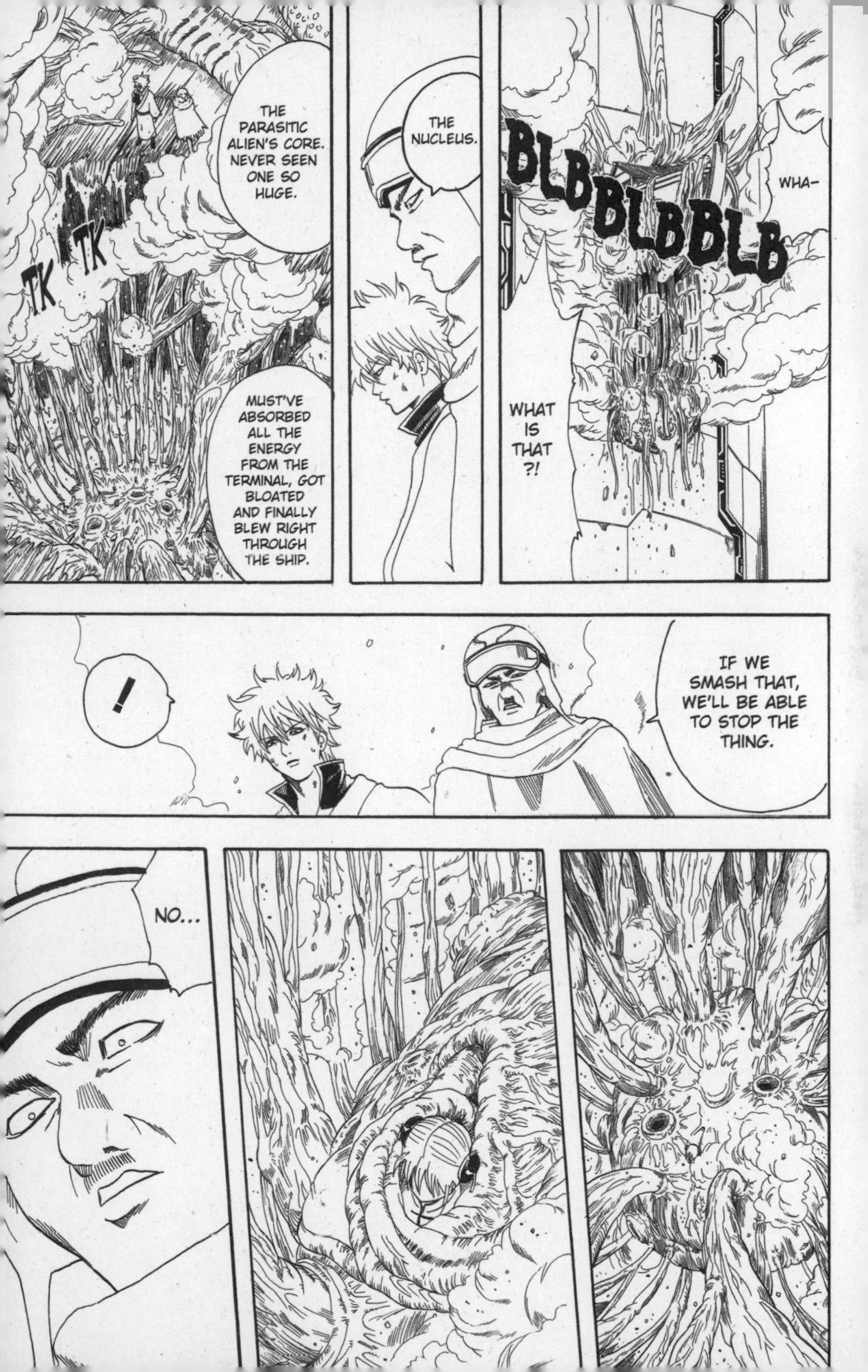
WHA-
BLBBLBBLB
WHAT IS THAT ?!
THE NUCLEUS.
THE PARASITIC ALIEN'S CORE. NEVER SEEN ONE SO HUGE.
TK TK
MUST'VE ABSORBED ALL THE ENERGY FROM THE TERMINAL, GOT BLOATED AND FINALLY BLEW RIGHT THROUGH THE SHIP.
IF WE SMASH THAT, WE'LL BE ABLE TO STOP THE THING.
!
NO...

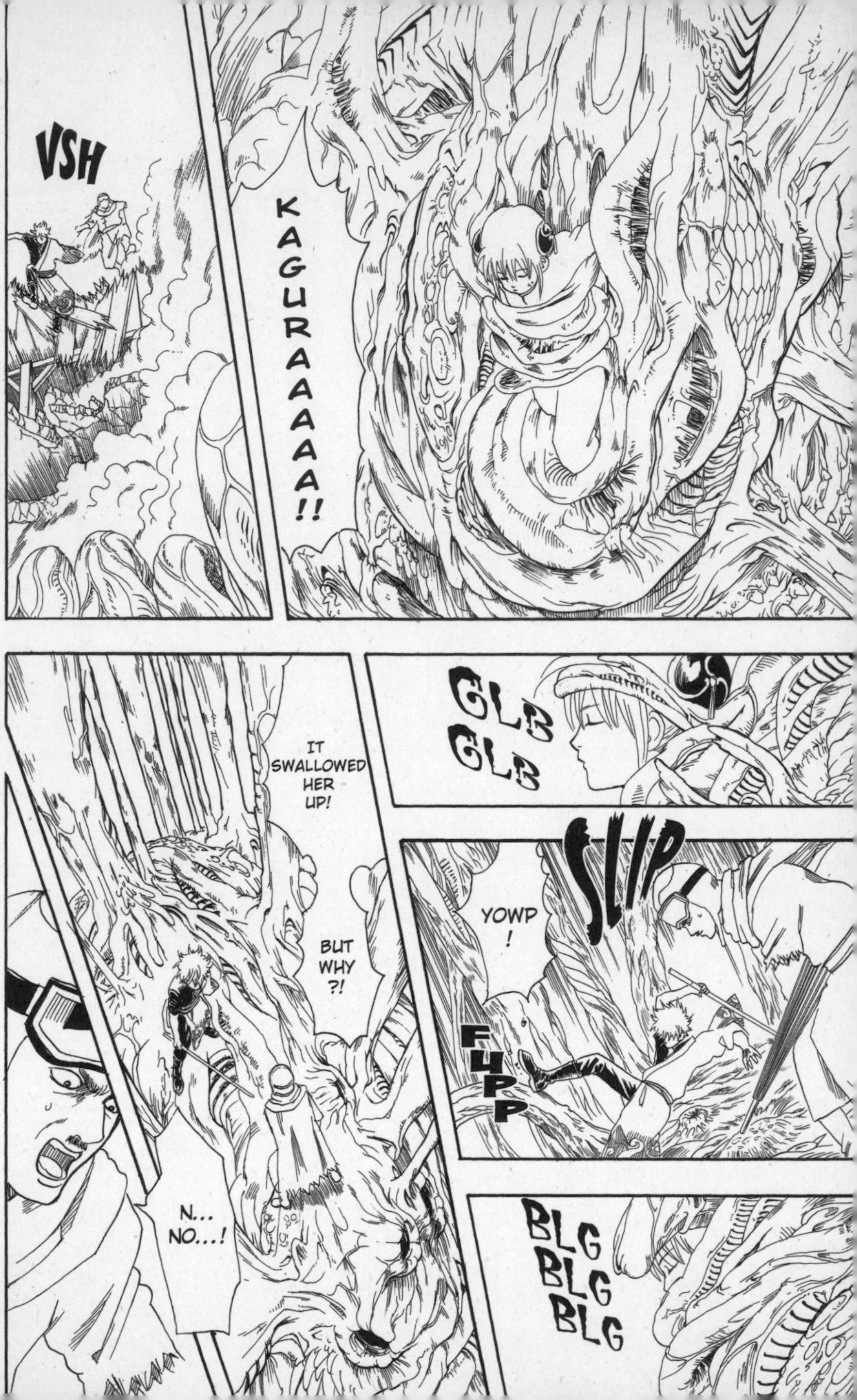
KAGURAAAAAA!!
VSH
GLB GLB
SLIP
YOWP!
FUPP
BLG BLG BLG
IT SWALLOWED HER UP!
BUT WHY?!
N... NO...!

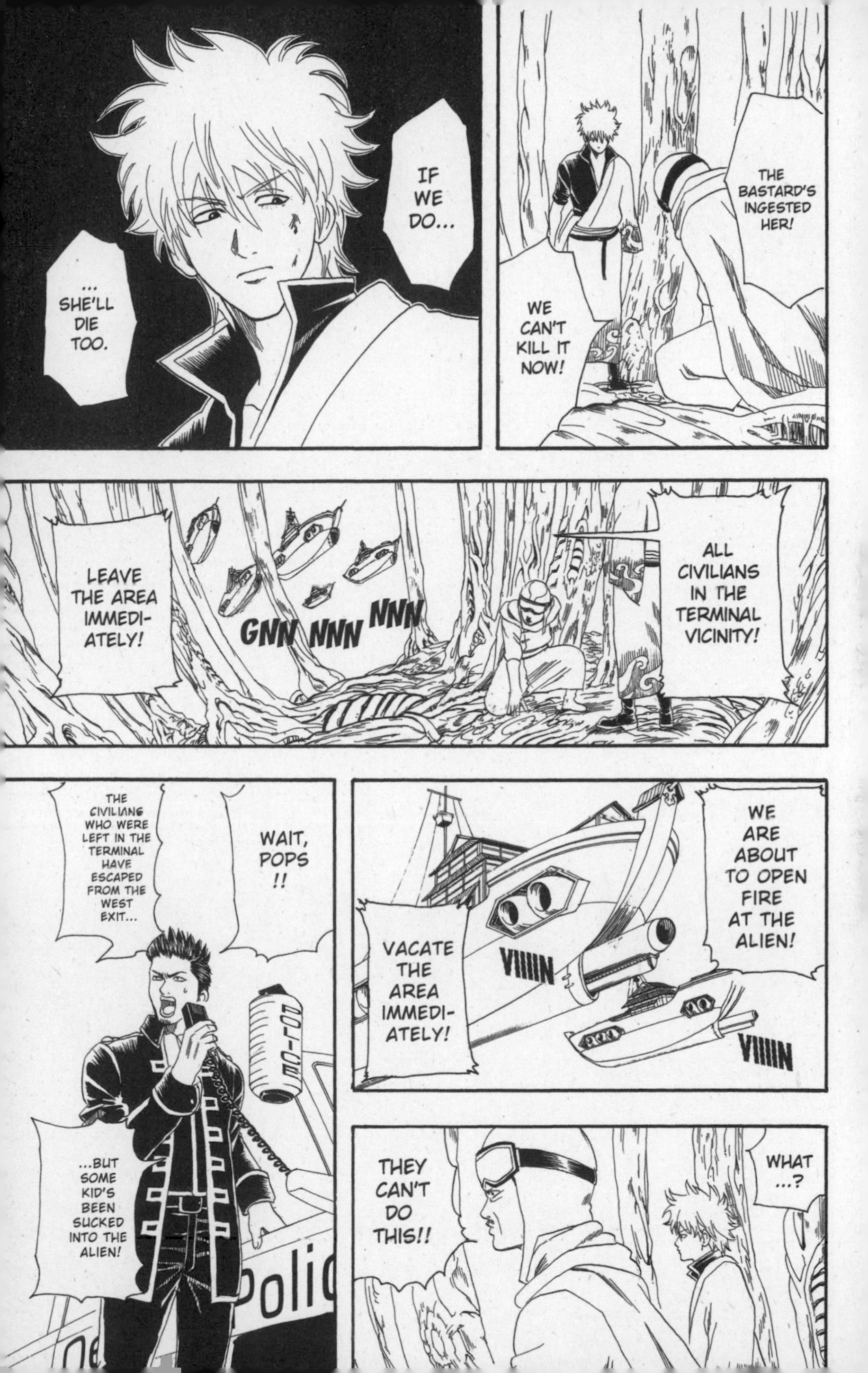
THE BASTARD'S INGESTED HER!
WE CAN'T KILL IT NOW!
IF WE DO...
... SHE'LL DIE TOO.
ALL CIVILIANS IN THE TERMINAL VICINITY!
GNN NNN NNN
LEAVE THE AREA IMMEDI-ATELY!
WE ARE ABOUT TO OPEN FIRE AT THE ALIEN!
VIIIIN
VACATE THE AREA IMMEDI-ATELY!
VIIIIN
WHAT ...?
THEY CAN'T DO THIS!!
WAIT, POPS!!
THE CIVILIANS WHO WERE LEFT IN THE TERMINAL HAVE ESCAPED FROM THE WEST EXIT...
...BUT SOME KID'S BEEN SUCKED INTO THE ALIEN!
POLICE

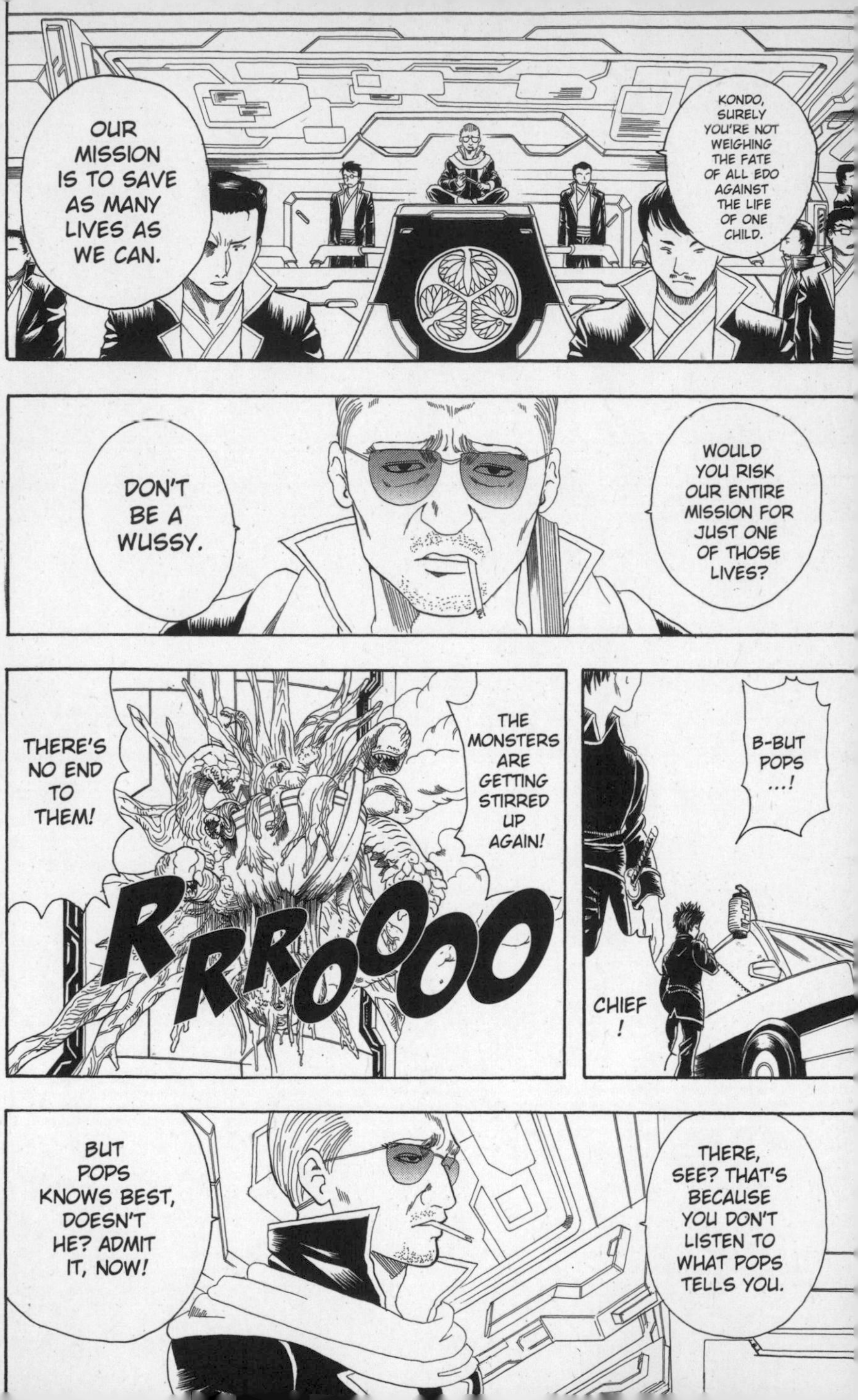
KONDO, SURELY YOU'RE NOT WEIGHING THE FATE OF ALL EDO AGAINST THE LIFE OF ONE CHILD.
OUR MISSION IS TO SAVE AS MANY LIVES AS WE CAN.
WOULD YOU RISK OUR ENTIRE MISSION FOR JUST ONE OF THOSE LIVES?
DON'T BE A WUSSY.
B-BUT POPS ...!
CHIEF !
THE MONSTERS ARE GETTING STIRRED UP AGAIN!
THERE'S NO END TO THEM!
RRROOOO
THERE, SEE? THAT'S BECAUSE YOU DON'T LISTEN TO WHAT POPS TELLS YOU.
BUT POPS KNOWS BEST, DOESN'T HE? ADMIT IT, NOW!

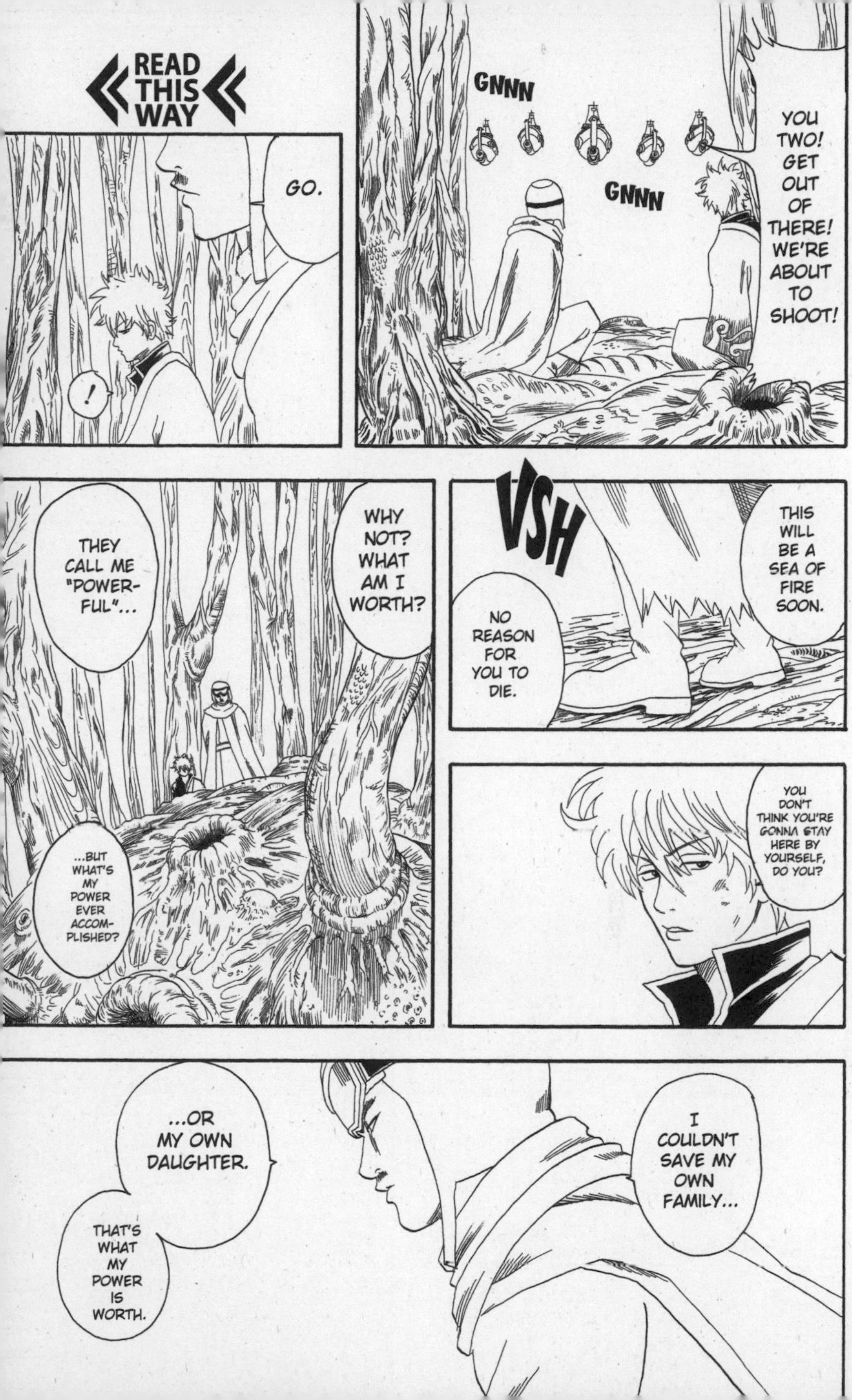
READ THIS WAY
GNNN
GNNN
YOU TWO! GET OUT OF THERE! WE'RE ABOUT TO SHOOT!
GO.
!
VSH
THIS WILL BE A SEA OF FIRE SOON.
NO REASON FOR YOU TO DIE.
YOU DON'T THINK YOU'RE GONNA STAY HERE BY YOURSELF, DO YOU?
WHY NOT? WHAT AM I WORTH?
THEY CALL ME "POWER-FUL"...
...BUT WHAT'S MY POWER EVER ACCOM-PLISHED?
I COULDN'T SAVE MY OWN FAMILY...
...OR MY OWN DAUGHTER.
THAT'S WHAT MY POWER IS WORTH.

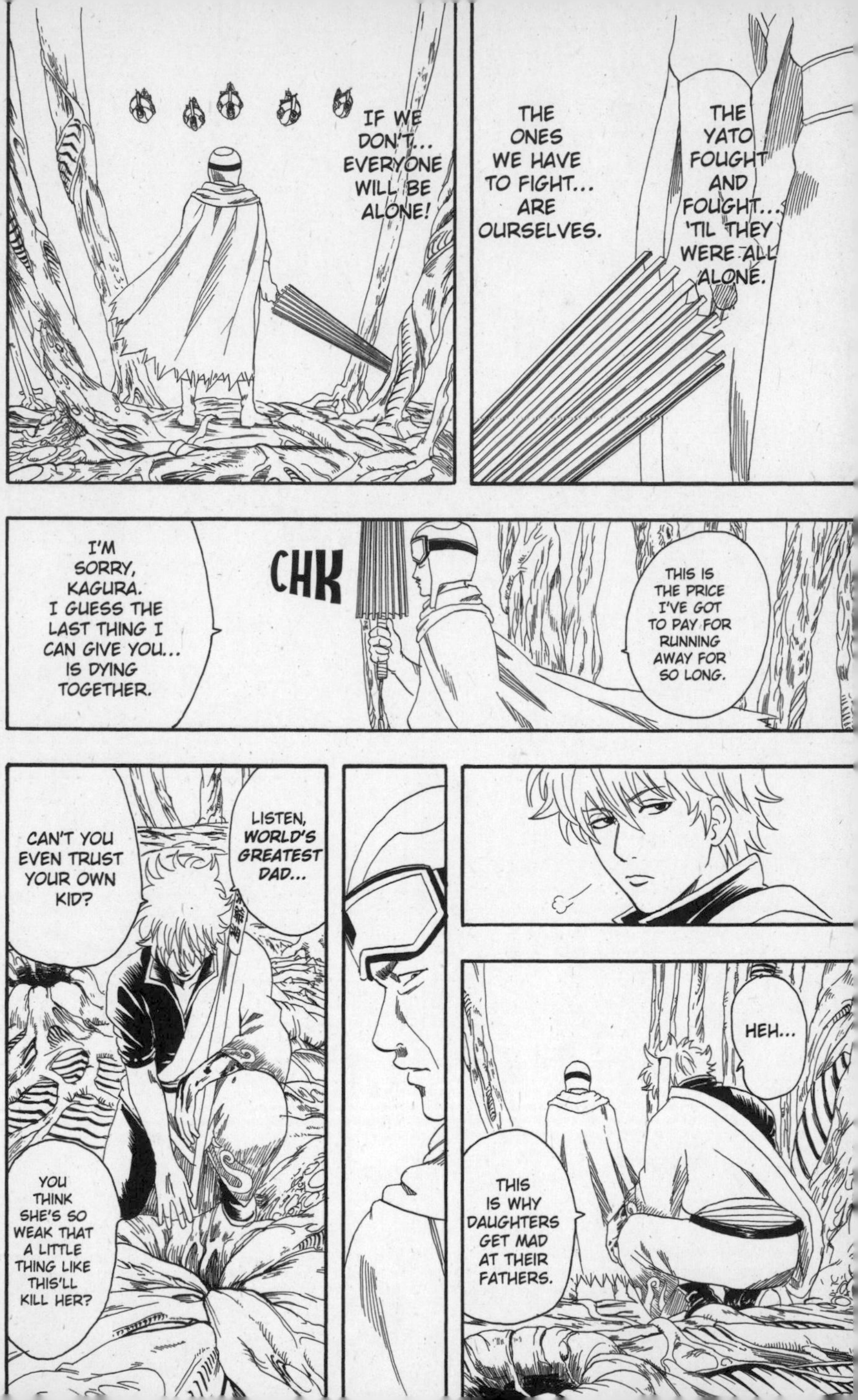
THE YATO FOUGHT AND FOUGHT... 'TIL THEY WERE ALL ALONE.
THE ONES WE HAVE TO FIGHT... ARE OURSELVES.
IF WE DON'T... EVERYONE WILL BE ALONE!
THIS IS THE PRICE I'VE GOT TO PAY FOR RUNNING AWAY FOR SO LONG.
CHK
I'M SORRY, KAGURA. I GUESS THE LAST THING I CAN GIVE YOU... IS DYING TOGETHER.
HEH...
THIS IS WHY DAUGHTERS GET MAD AT THEIR FATHERS.
LISTEN, WORLD'S GREATEST DAD...
CAN'T YOU EVEN TRUST YOUR OWN KID?
YOU THINK SHE'S SO WEAK THAT A LITTLE THING LIKE THIS'LL KILL HER?

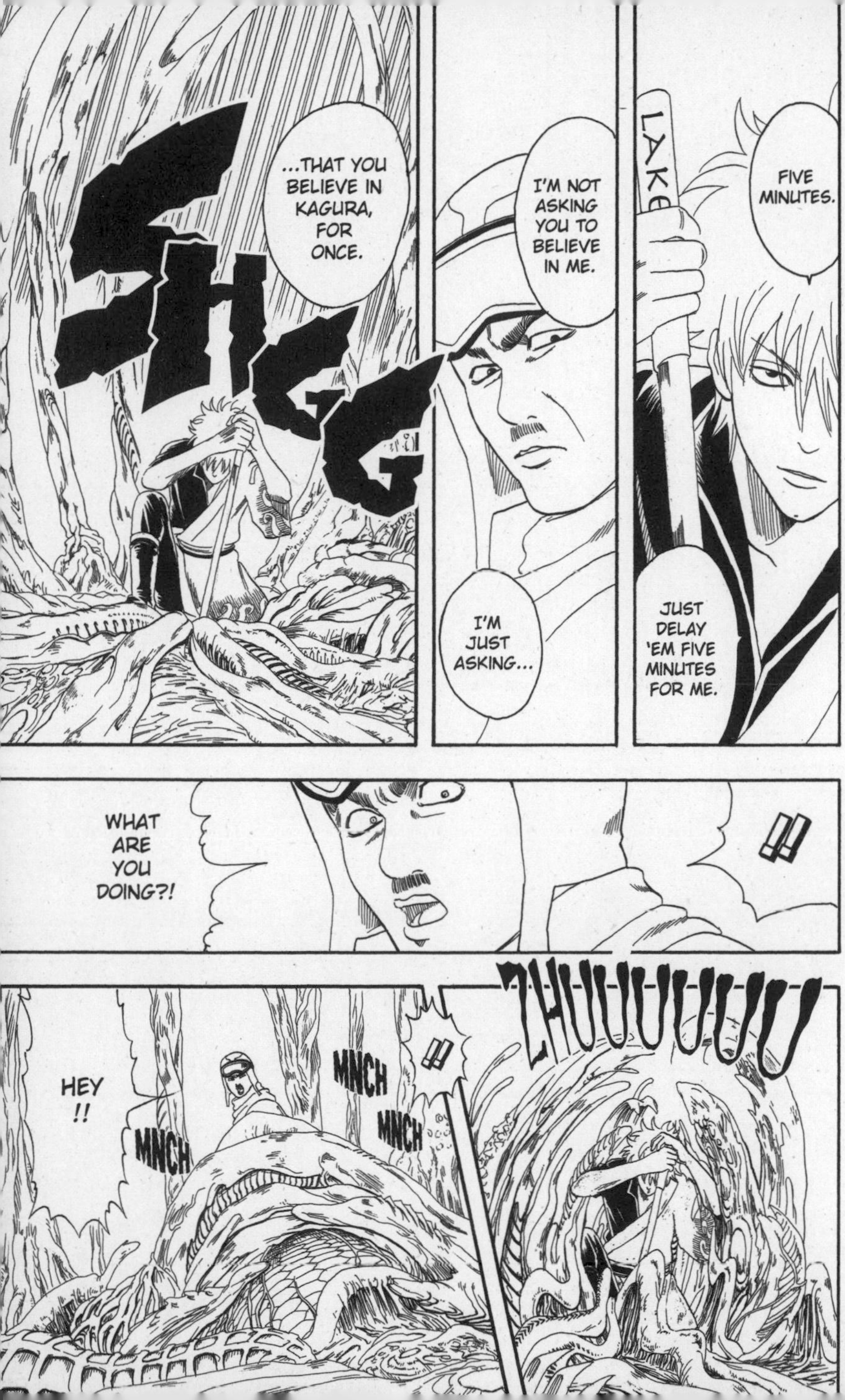
LAKE
FIVE MINUTES.
JUST DELAY 'EM FIVE MINUTES FOR ME.
I'M NOT ASKING YOU TO BELIEVE IN ME.
I'M JUST ASKING...
...THAT YOU BELIEVE IN KAGURA, FOR ONCE.
SHGG
!!
WHAT ARE YOU DOING?!
ZHUUUUUUU
!!
MNCH
MNCH
MNCH
HEY !!

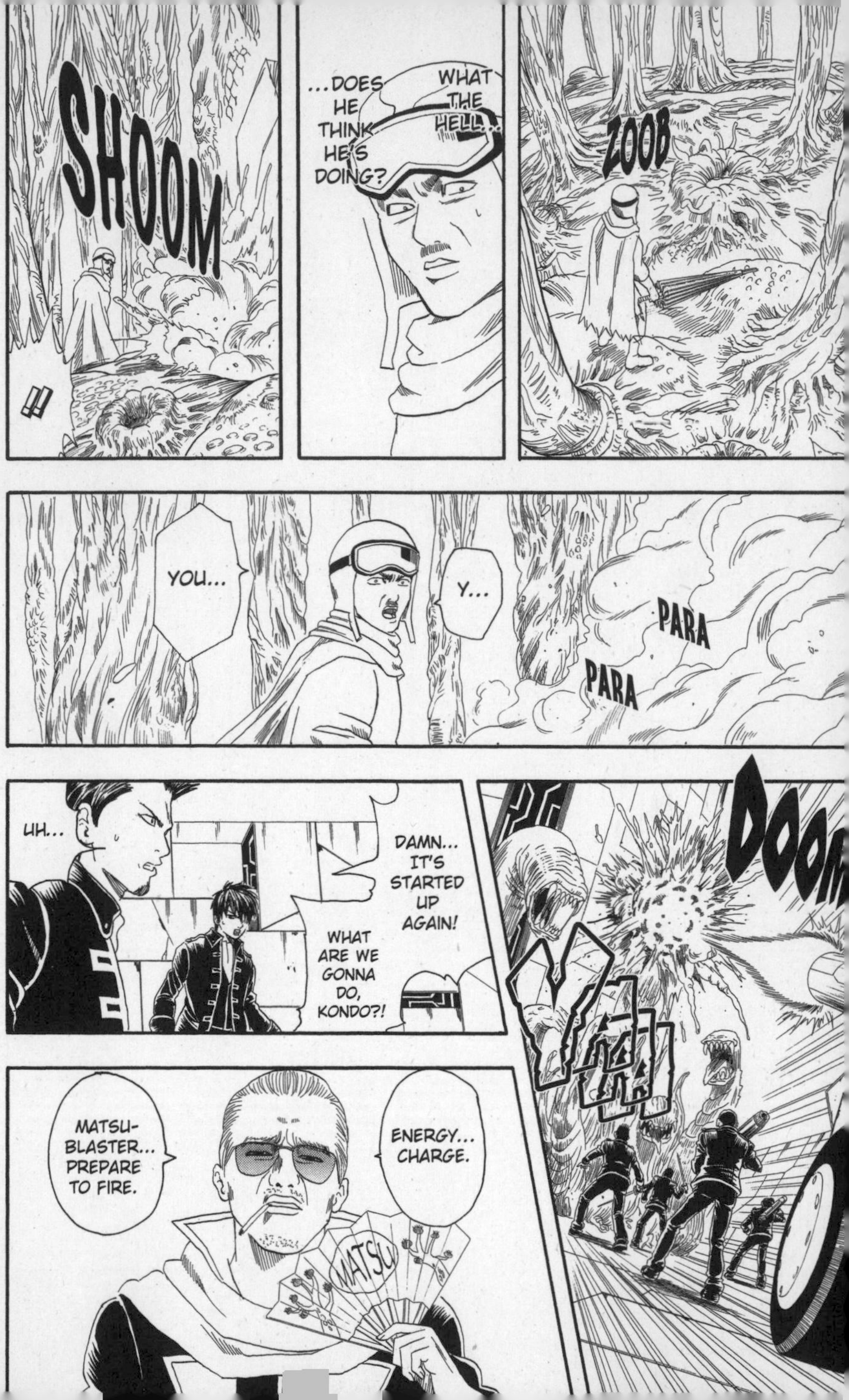
ZOOB
WHAT THE HELL...
...DOES HE THINK HE'S DOING?
SHOOM
!!
PARA
PARA
Y...
YOU...
DOOM
DAMN... IT'S STARTED UP AGAIN!
WHAT ARE WE GONNA DO, KONDO?!
UH...
ENERGY... CHARGE.
MATSU-BLASTER... PREPARE TO FIRE.
MATSU

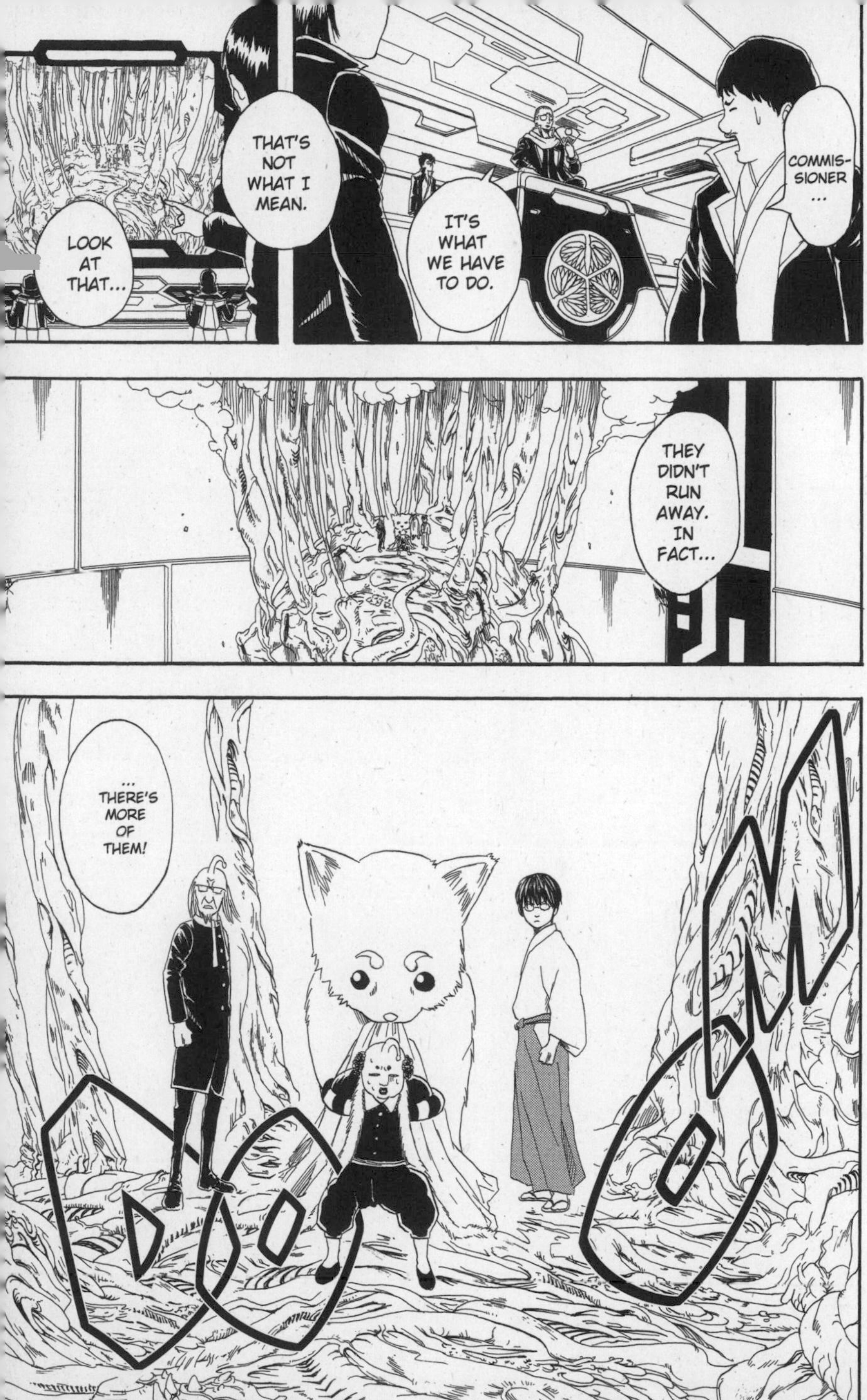
COMMIS-SIONER...
IT'S WHAT WE HAVE TO DO.
THAT'S NOT WHAT I MEAN.
LOOK AT THAT...
THEY DIDN'T RUN AWAY. IN FACT...
...THERE'S MORE OF THEM!
DOOM

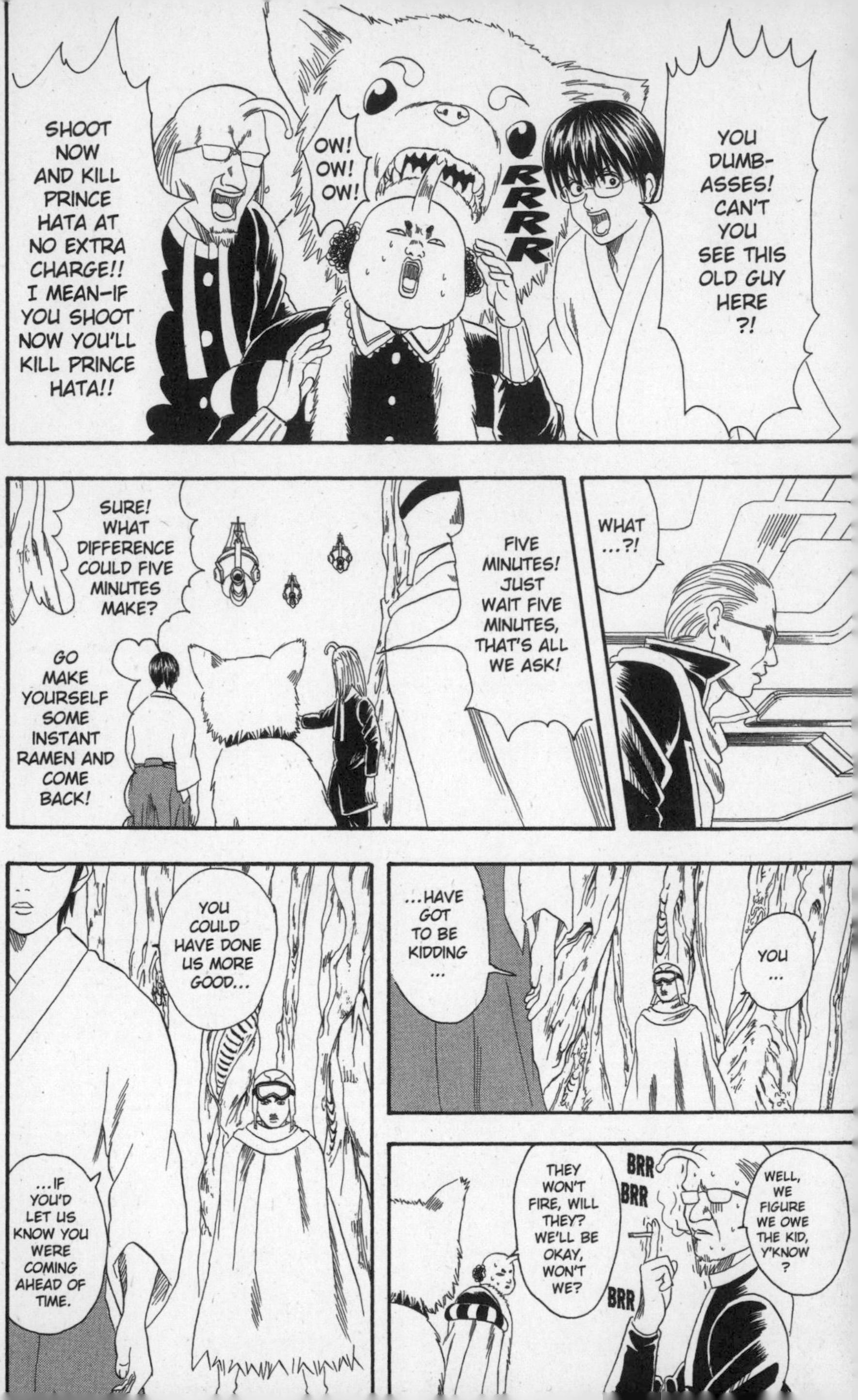
YOU DUMB-ASSES! CAN'T YOU SEE THIS OLD GUY HERE?!
RRRR
OW! OW! OW!
SHOOT NOW AND KILL PRINCE HATA AT NO EXTRA CHARGE!! I MEAN—IF YOU SHOOT NOW YOU'LL KILL PRINCE HATA!!
WHAT ...?!
FIVE MINUTES! JUST WAIT FIVE MINUTES, THAT'S ALL WE ASK!
SURE! WHAT DIFFERENCE COULD FIVE MINUTES MAKE?
GO MAKE YOURSELF SOME INSTANT RAMEN AND COME BACK!
YOU ...
...HAVE GOT TO BE KIDDING ...
WELL, WE FIGURE WE OWE THE KID, Y'KNOW?
BRR
BRR
THEY WON'T FIRE, WILL THEY? WE'LL BE OKAY, WON'T WE?
BRR
YOU COULD HAVE DONE US MORE GOOD...
...IF YOU'D LET US KNOW YOU WERE COMING AHEAD OF TIME.

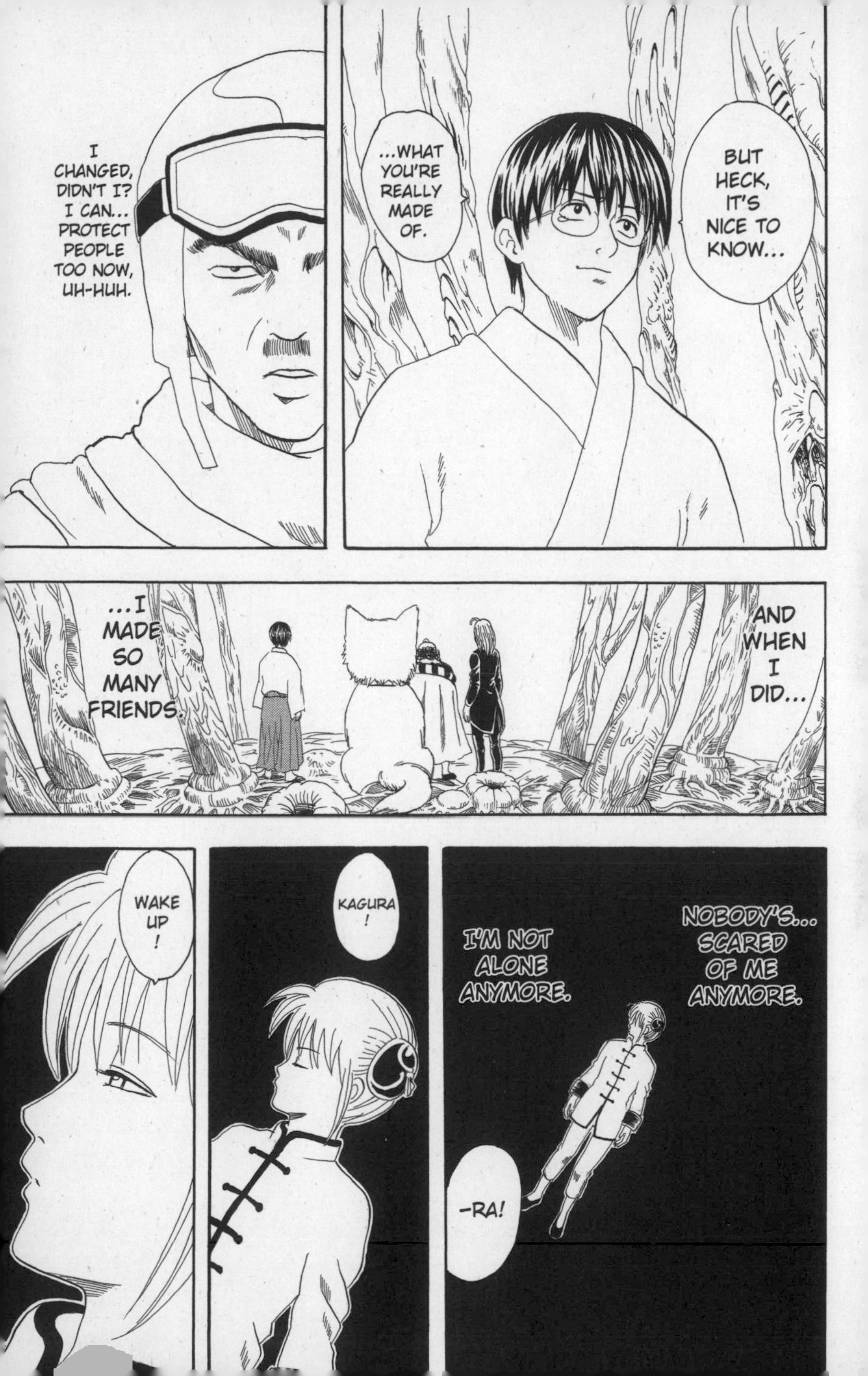
BUT HECK, IT'S NICE TO KNOW...
...WHAT YOU'RE REALLY MADE OF.
I CHANGED, DIDN'T I? I CAN... PROTECT PEOPLE TOO NOW, UH-HUH.
AND WHEN I DID...
...I MADE SO MANY FRIENDS.
NOBODY'S... SCARED OF ME ANYMORE.
I'M NOT ALONE ANYMORE.
-RA!
KAGURA!
WAKE UP!

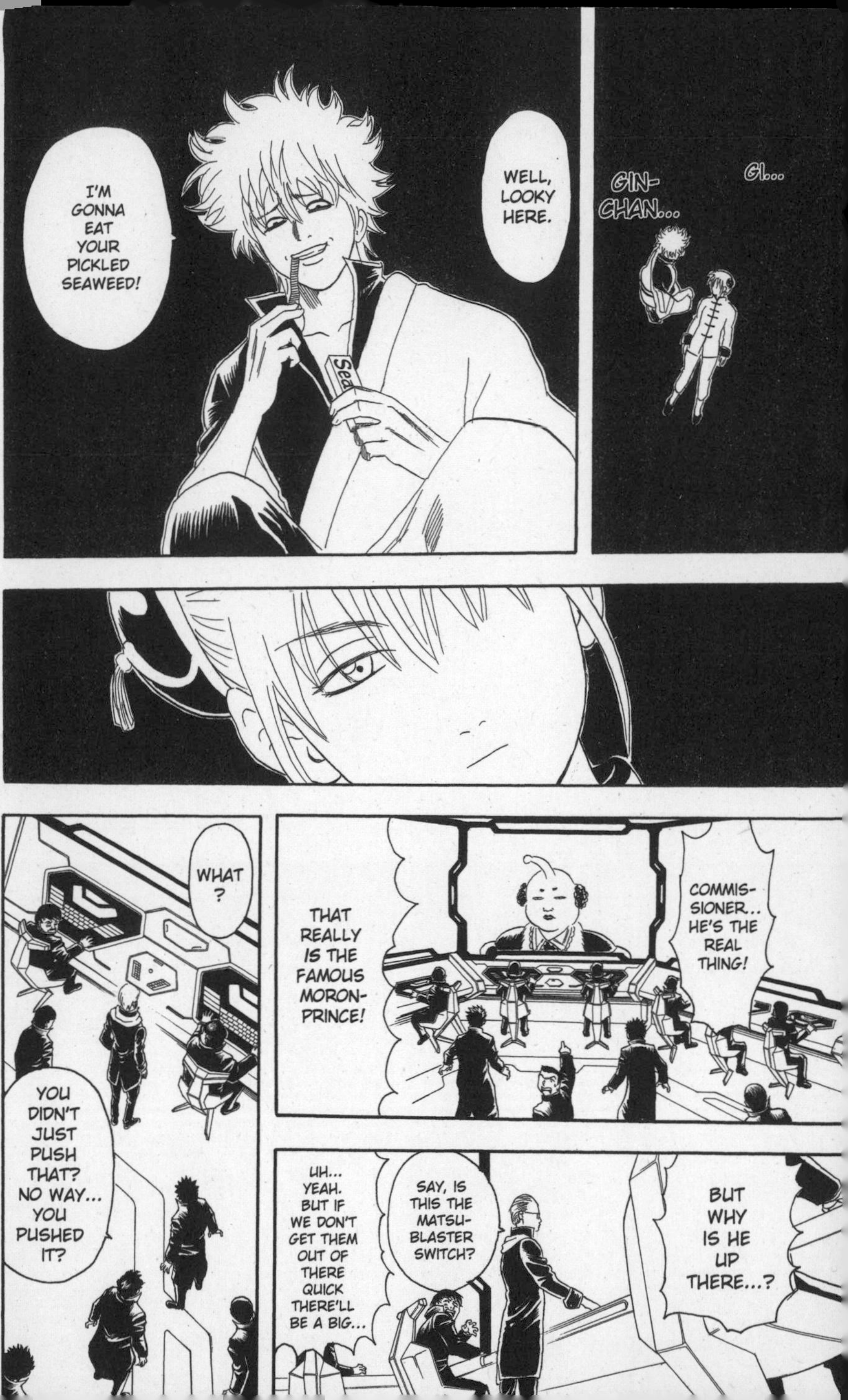
GI...
GIN-CHAN...
WELL, LOOKY HERE.
I'M GONNA EAT YOUR PICKLED SEAWEED!
COMMIS-SIONER... HE'S THE REAL THING!
THAT REALLY IS THE FAMOUS MORON-PRINCE!
BUT WHY IS HE UP THERE...?
SAY, IS THIS THE MATSU-BLASTER SWITCH?
UH... YEAH. BUT IF WE DON'T GET THEM OUT OF THERE QUICK THERE'LL BE A BIG...
WHAT?
YOU DIDN'T JUST PUSH THAT? NO WAY... YOU PUSHED IT?

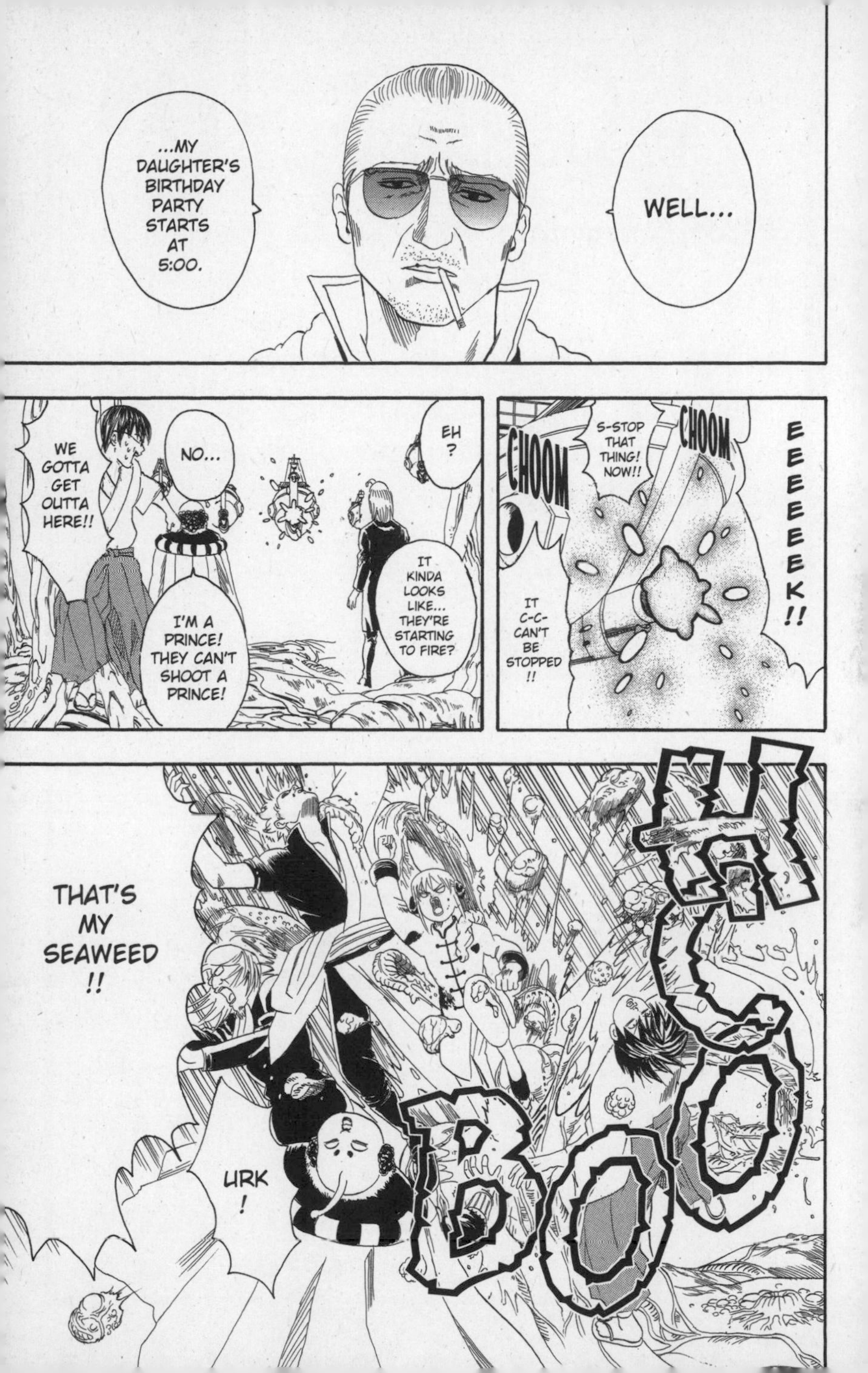
WELL...
...MY DAUGHTER'S BIRTHDAY PARTY STARTS AT 5:00.
EEEEEEK!!
CHOOM
S-STOP THAT THING! NOW!!
CHOOM
IT C-C-CAN'T BE STOPPED!!
EH?
IT KINDA LOOKS LIKE... THEY'RE STARTING TO FIRE?
NO...
WE GOTTA GET OUTTA HERE!!
I'M A PRINCE! THEY CAN'T SHOOT A PRINCE!
BOOM
THAT'S MY SEAWEED!!
URK!

Sorachi's Q&A Corner #15

<From "Anonymous-san" of Chiba Prefecture>

<Question>

In *Gin Tama*, Hasegawa and Kondo get called "Pops" but Gin-san and Hijikata, who are nearly the same age, don't. At what age do you get called "Pops"?

<Answer>

Once your pillow starts to smell like your Dad.

THAT'S WHAT YOU SMELL LIKE, IDIOT.

I CAN TELL BY THE SMELL !!

EWWW!! SOME OLD GUY'S BEEN USING MY PILLOW!!

(Q&A #16 is on page 108)

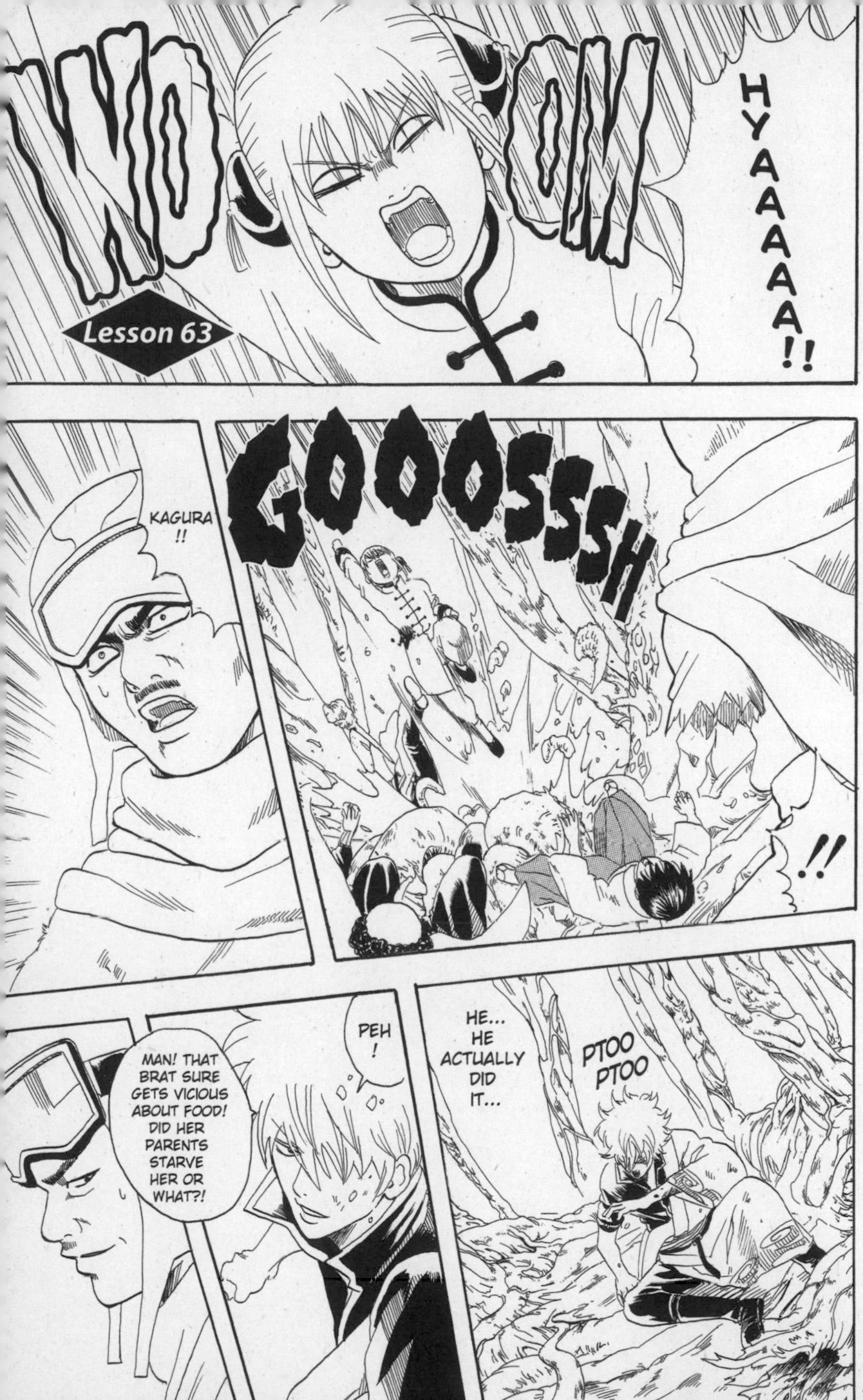
HYAAAAA!!
WO
OM
Lesson 63
GOOOSSSH
!!
KAGURA !!
PTOO PTOO
HE... HE ACTUALLY DID IT...
PEH!
MAN! THAT BRAT SURE GETS VICIOUS ABOUT FOOD! DID HER PARENTS STARVE HER OR WHAT?!

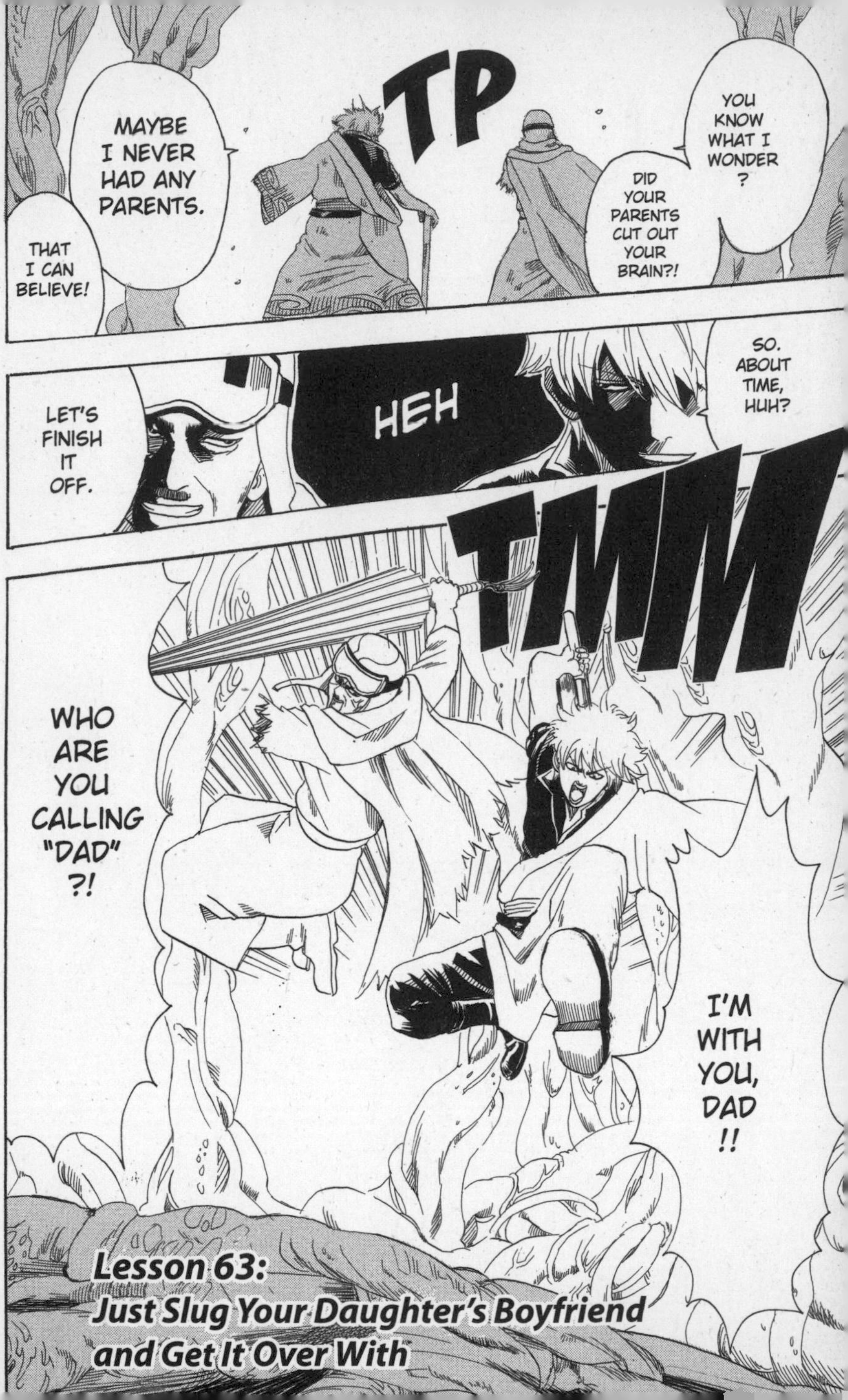
YOU KNOW WHAT I WONDER?
DID YOUR PARENTS CUT OUT YOUR BRAIN?!
TP
MAYBE I NEVER HAD ANY PARENTS.
THAT I CAN BELIEVE!
SO. ABOUT TIME, HUH?
HEH
LET'S FINISH IT OFF.
TMM
I'M WITH YOU, DAD!!
WHO ARE YOU CALLING "DAD"?!
Lesson 63:
Just Slug Your Daughter's Boyfriend and Get It Over With

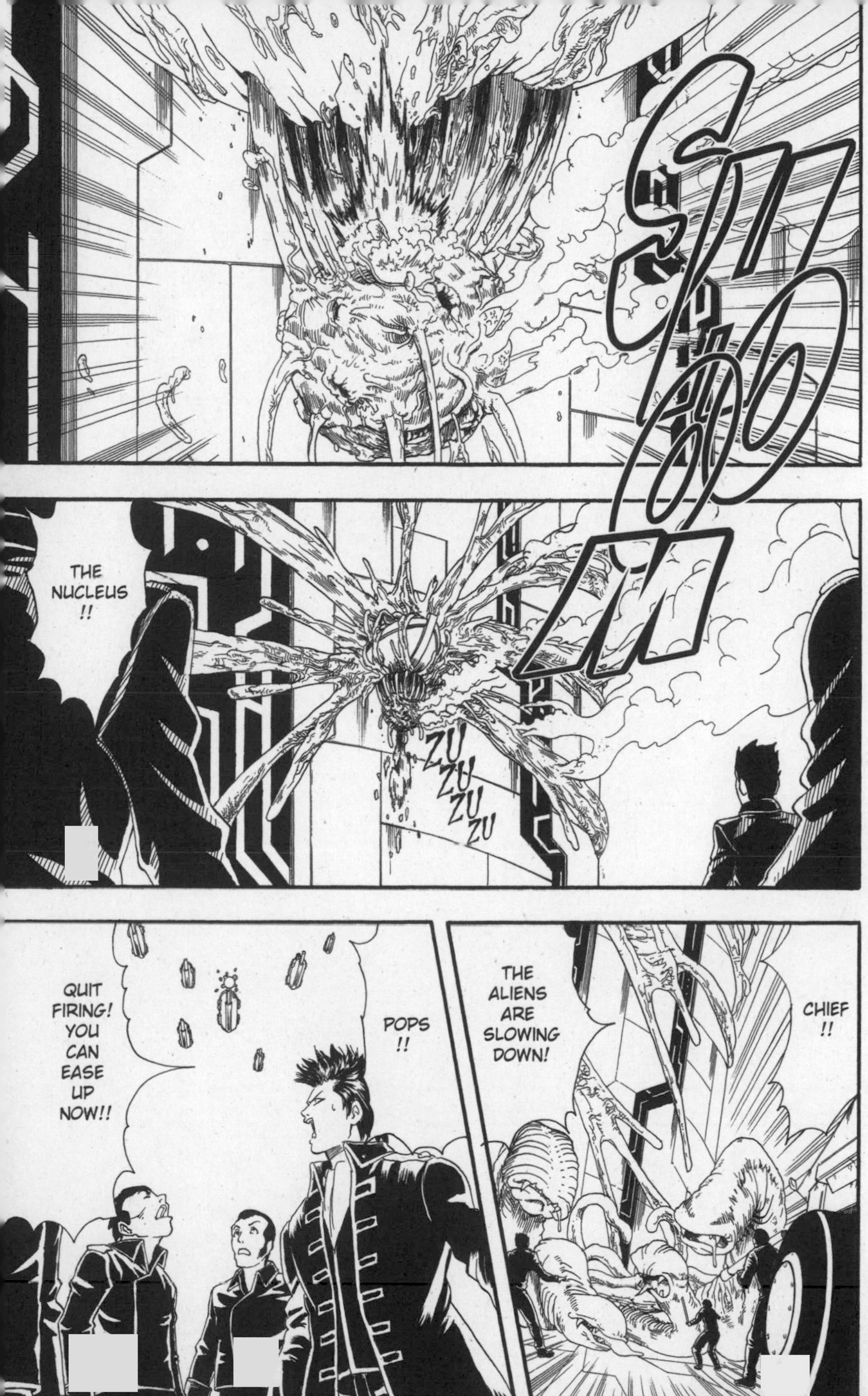
THE NUCLEUS !!
ZU ZU ZU ZU ZU
CHIEF !!
THE ALIENS ARE SLOWING DOWN!
POPS !!
QUIT FIRING! YOU CAN EASE UP NOW!!

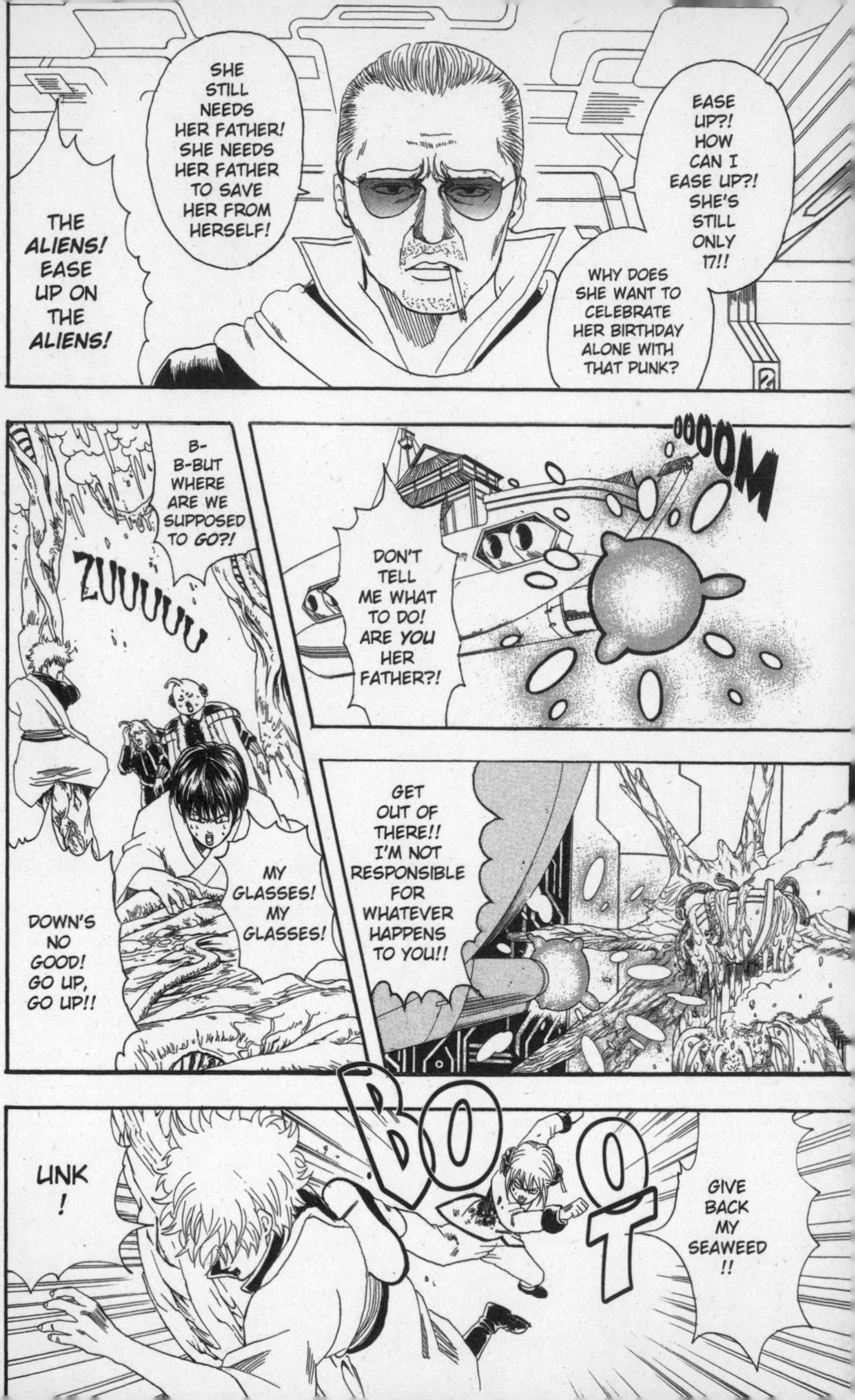
EASE UP?! HOW CAN I EASE UP?! SHE'S STILL ONLY 17!!
WHY DOES SHE WANT TO CELEBRATE HER BIRTHDAY ALONE WITH THAT PUNK?
SHE STILL NEEDS HER FATHER! SHE NEEDS HER FATHER TO SAVE HER FROM HERSELF!
THE ALIENS! EASE UP ON THE ALIENS!
OOOOM
DON'T TELL ME WHAT TO DO! ARE YOU HER FATHER?!
GET OUT OF THERE!! I'M NOT RESPONSIBLE FOR WHATEVER HAPPENS TO YOU!!
B-B-BUT WHERE ARE WE SUPPOSED TO GO?!
ZUUUUUU
MY GLASSES! MY GLASSES!
DOWN'S NO GOOD! GO UP, GO UP!!
GIVE BACK MY SEAWEED!!
BOOT
LINK!

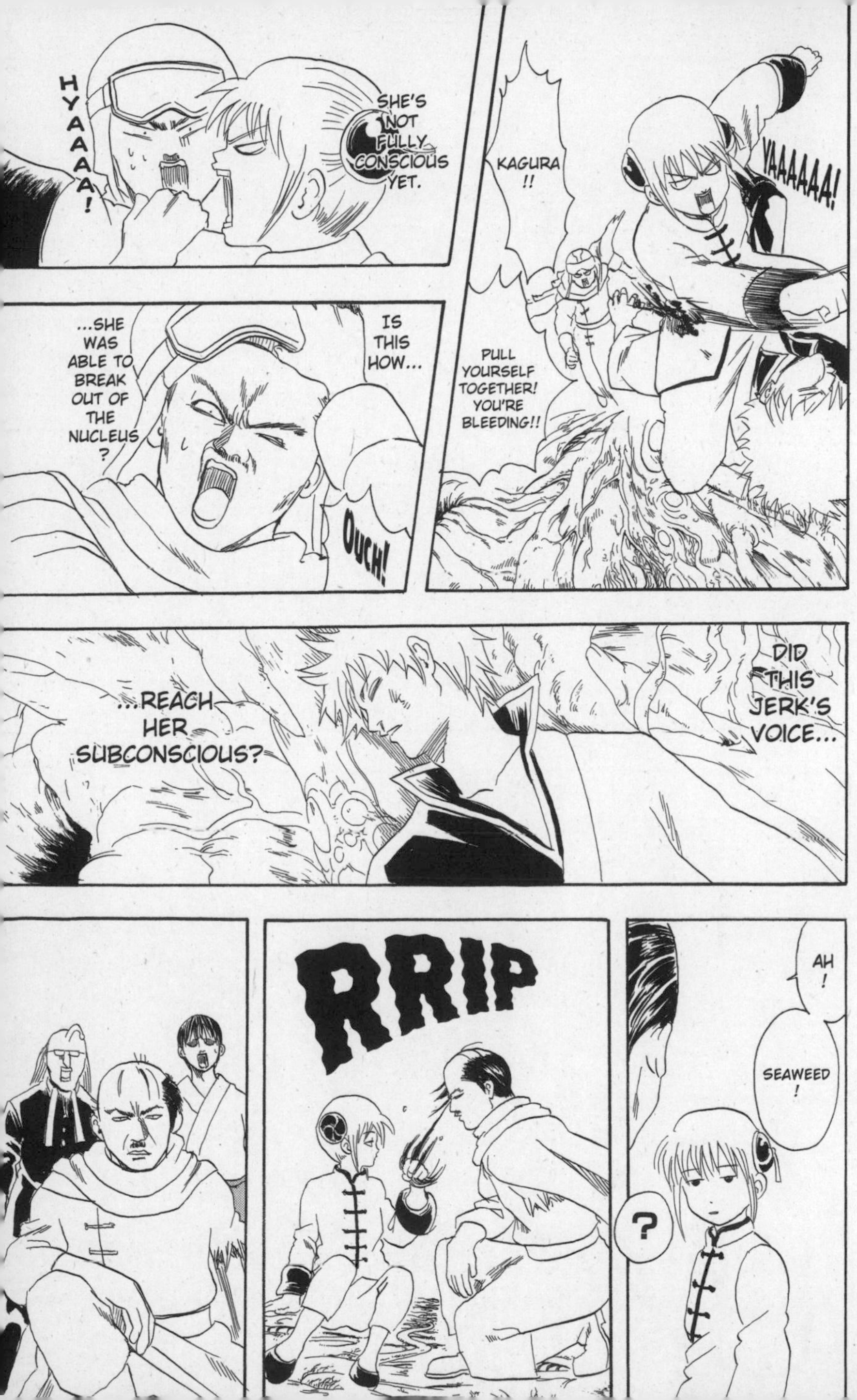
YAAAAAA!
KAGURA !!
PULL YOURSELF TOGETHER! YOU'RE BLEEDING!!
SHE'S NOT FULLY CONSCIOUS YET.
HYAAAA!
IS THIS HOW...
...SHE WAS ABLE TO BREAK OUT OF THE NUCLEUS?
OUCH!
DID THIS JERK'S VOICE...
...REACH HER SUBCONSCIOUS?
AH!
SEAWEED!
?
RRIP

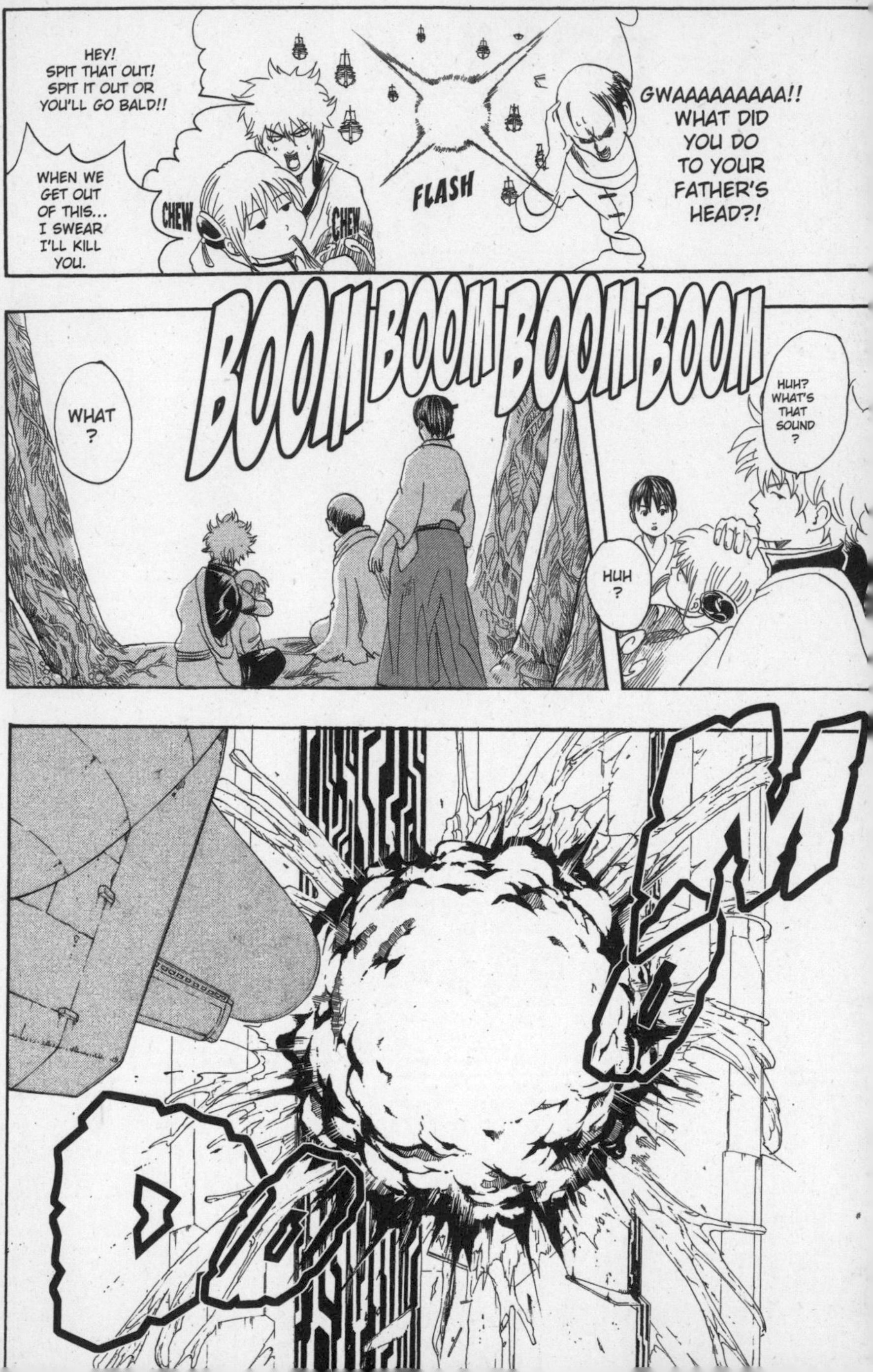
GWAAAAAAAAA!! WHAT DID YOU DO TO YOUR FATHER'S HEAD?!
FLASH
HEY! SPIT THAT OUT! SPIT IT OUT OR YOU'LL GO BALD!!
CHEW
CHEW
WHEN WE GET OUT OF THIS... I SWEAR I'LL KILL YOU.
BOOM BOOM BOOM BOOM
HUH? WHAT'S THAT SOUND?
HUH?
WHAT?
DOM

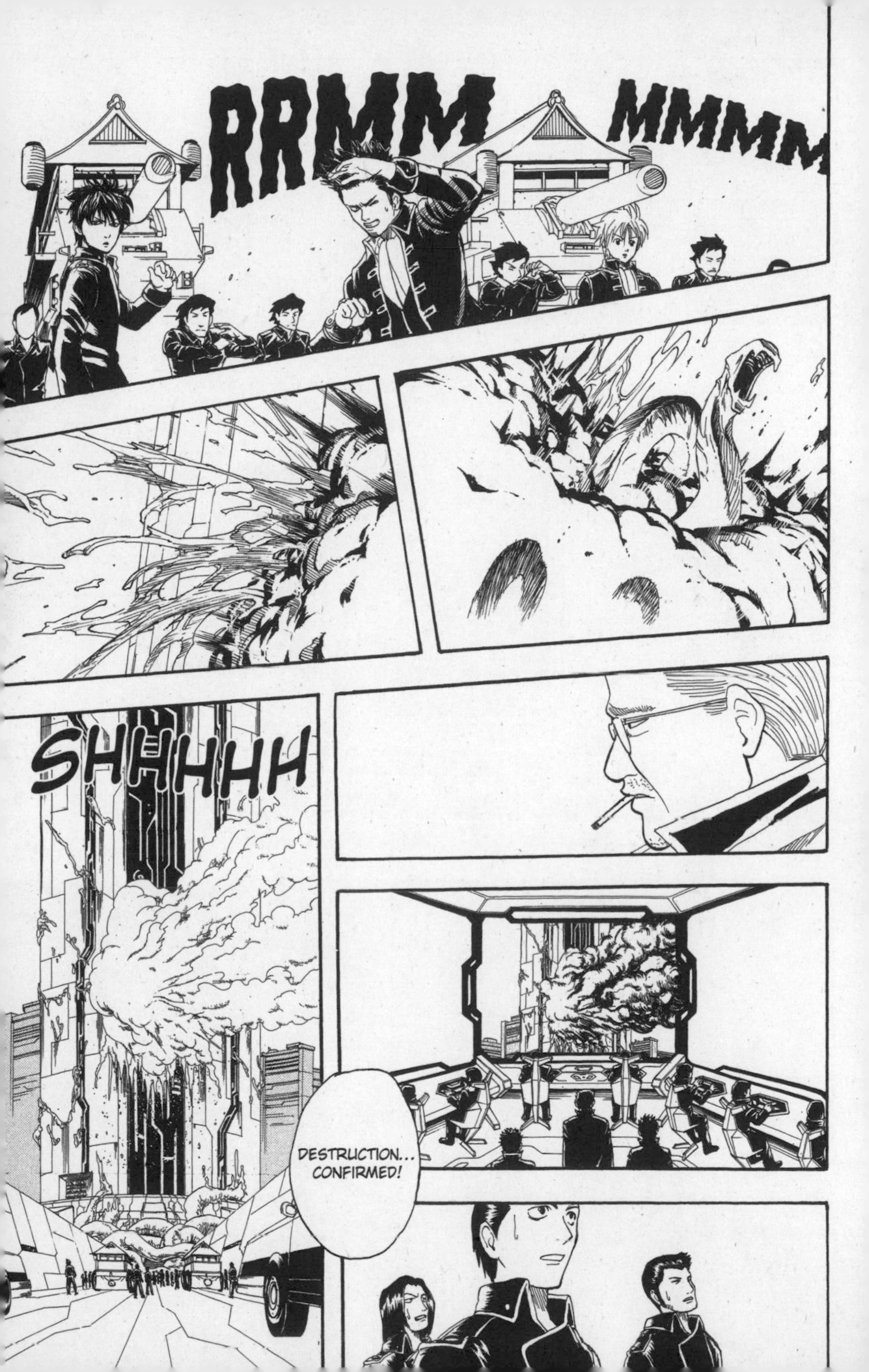
RRMM MMMMM
SHHHHH
DESTRUCTION... CONFIRMED!

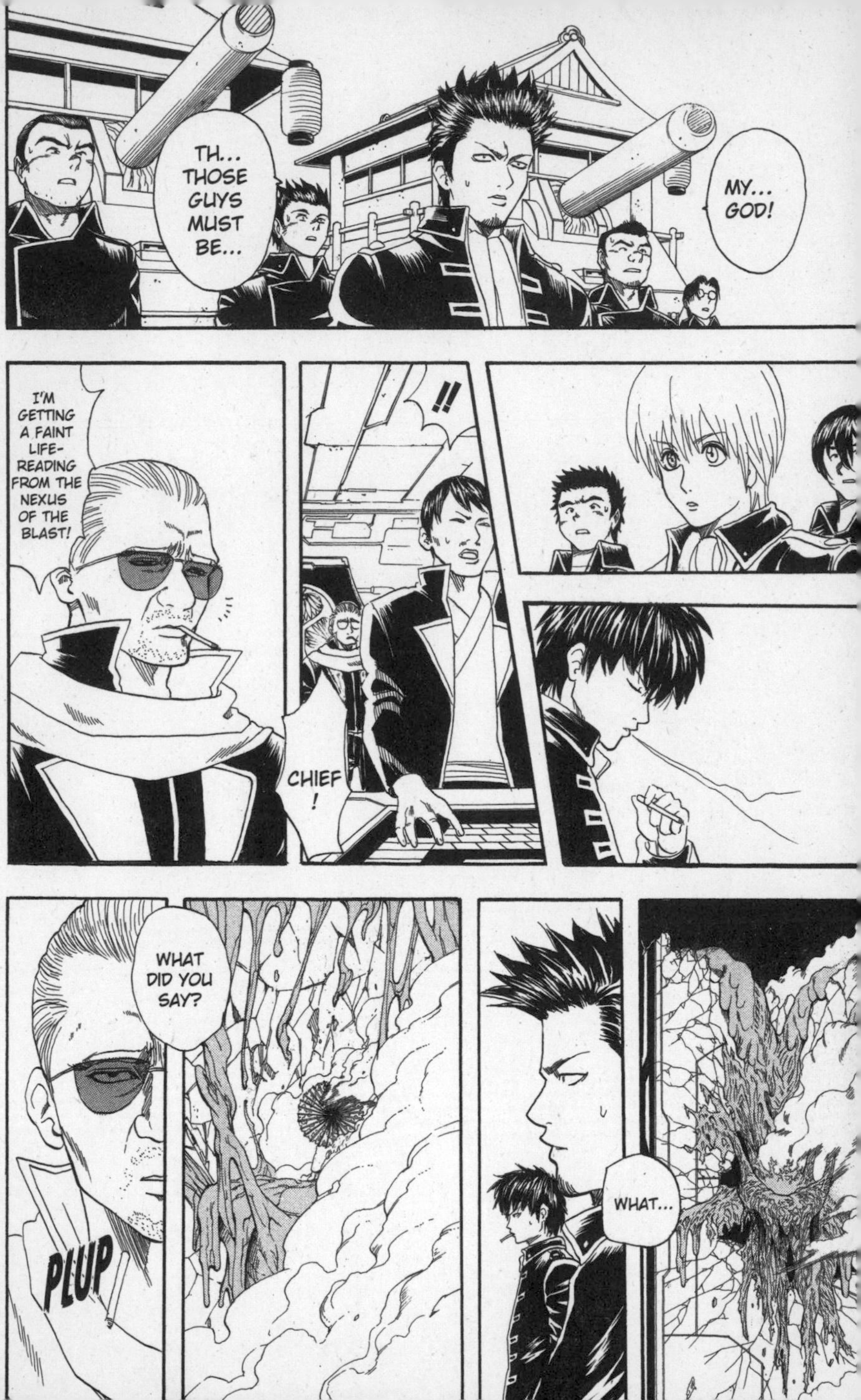
MY... GOD!
TH... THOSE GUYS MUST BE...
!!
CHIEF !
I'M GETTING A FAINT LIFE-READING FROM THE NEXUS OF THE BLAST!
WHAT...
WHAT DID YOU SAY?
PLUP

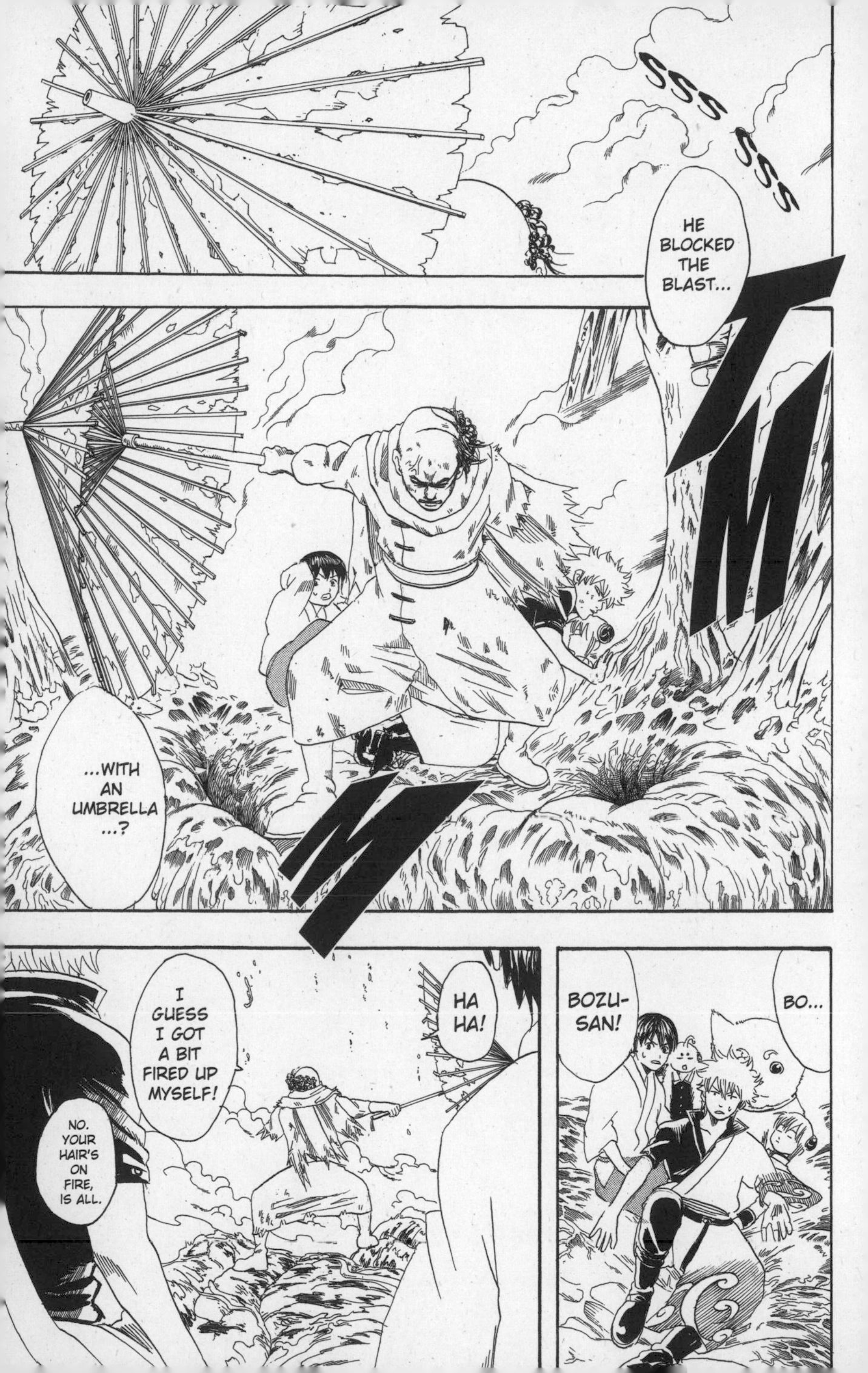
SSS SSS
HE BLOCKED THE BLAST...
TMM
...WITH AN UMBRELLA ...?
BO...
BOZU-SAN!
HA HA!
I GUESS I GOT A BIT FIRED UP MYSELF!
NO. YOUR HAIR'S ON FIRE, IS ALL.

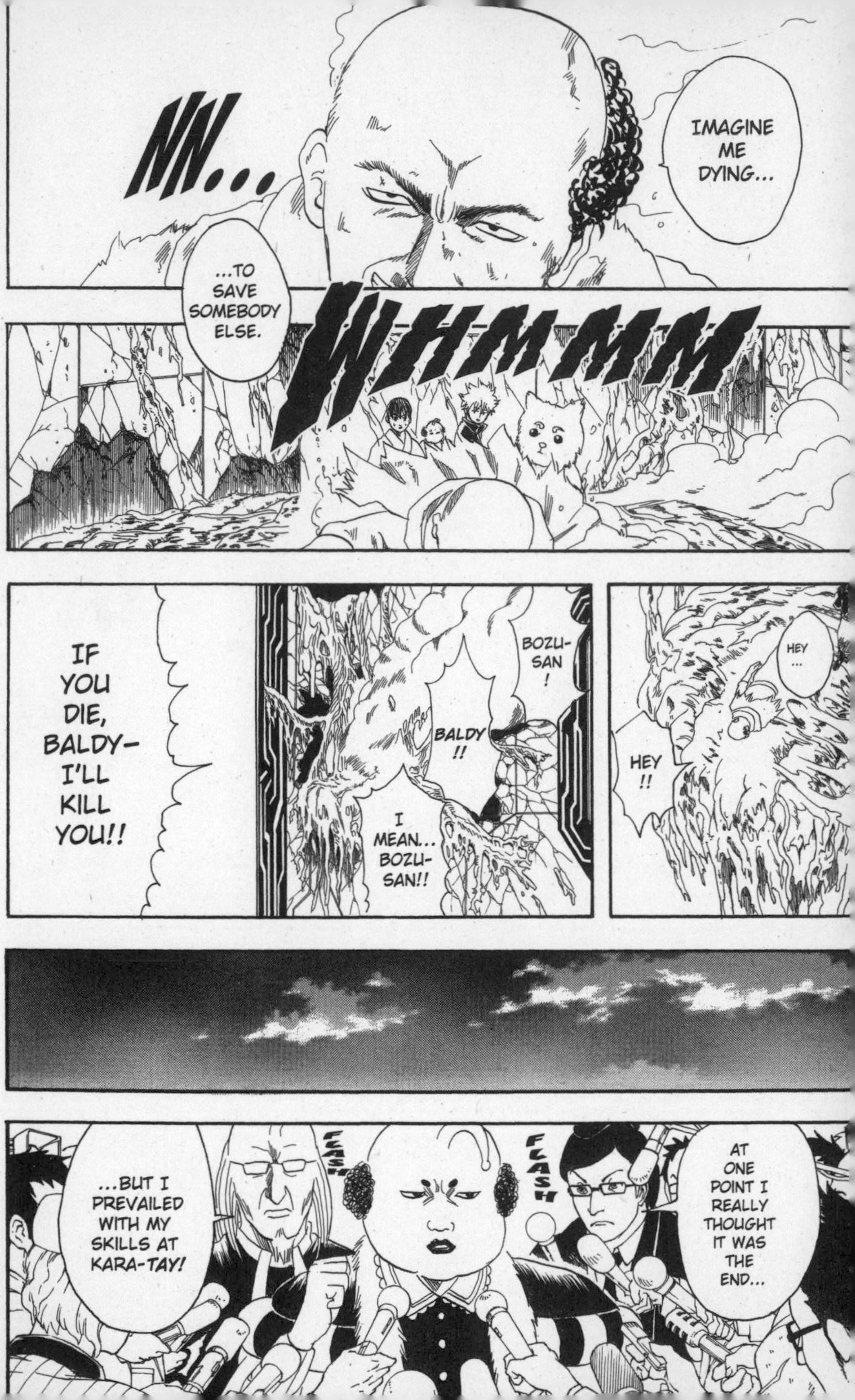
IMAGINE ME DYING...
NN...
...TO SAVE SOMEBODY ELSE.
WHMMM
HEY...
HEY!!
BOZU-SAN!
BALDY!!
I MEAN... BOZU-SAN!!
IF YOU DIE, BALDY– I'LL KILL YOU!!
AT ONE POINT I REALLY THOUGHT IT WAS THE END...
FLASH
FLASH
...BUT I PREVAILED WITH MY SKILLS AT KARA-TAY!

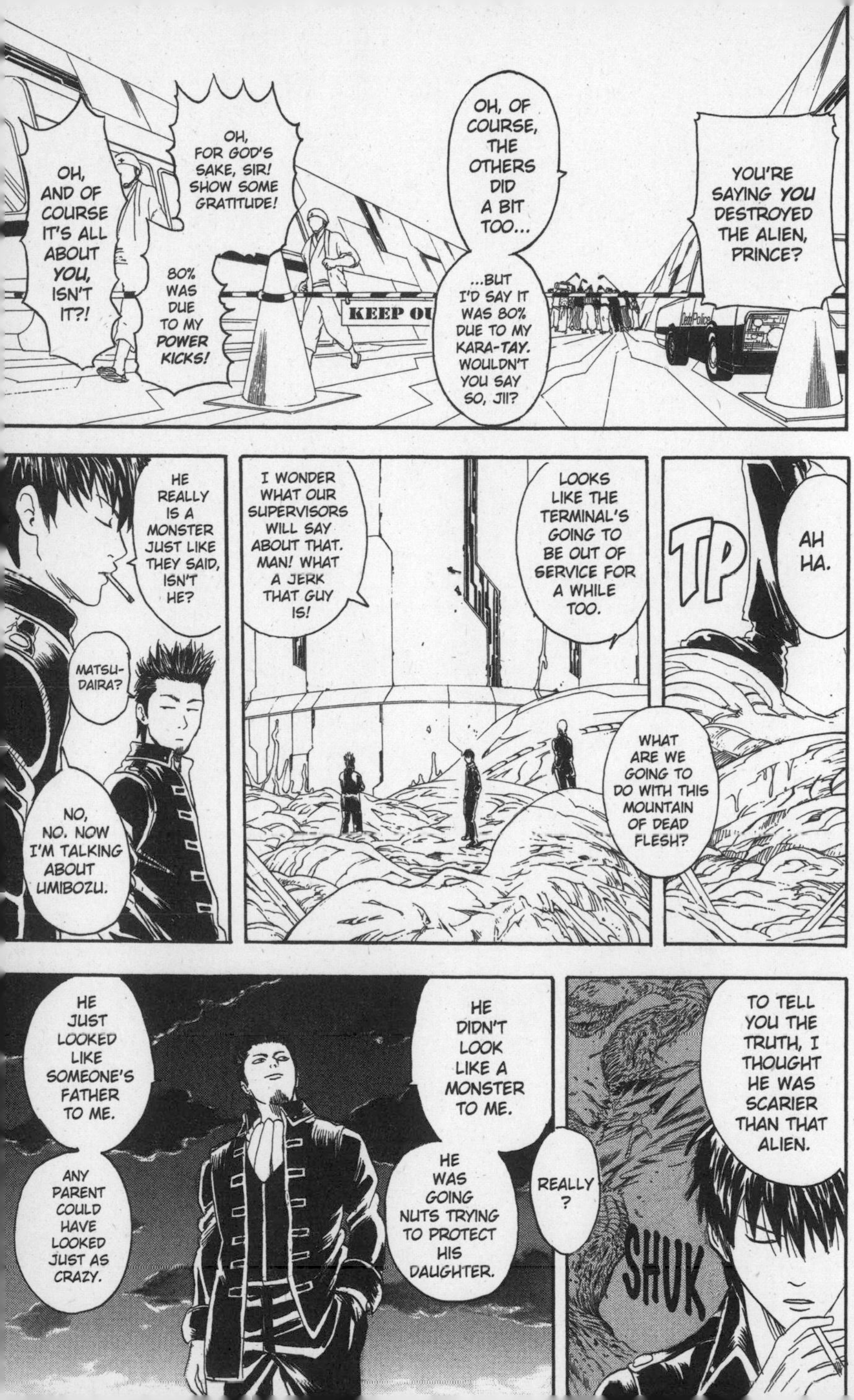
YOU'RE SAYING YOU DESTROYED THE ALIEN, PRINCE?
OH, OF COURSE, THE OTHERS DID A BIT TOO...
...BUT I'D SAY IT WAS 80% DUE TO MY KARA-TAY. WOULDN'T YOU SAY SO, JII?
OH, FOR GOD'S SAKE, SIR! SHOW SOME GRATITUDE!
80% WAS DUE TO MY POWER KICKS!
OH, AND OF COURSE IT'S ALL ABOUT YOU, ISN'T IT?!
KEEP OU
TP
AH HA.
LOOKS LIKE THE TERMINAL'S GOING TO BE OUT OF SERVICE FOR A WHILE TOO.
I WONDER WHAT OUR SUPERVISORS WILL SAY ABOUT THAT. MAN! WHAT A JERK THAT GUY IS!
WHAT ARE WE GOING TO DO WITH THIS MOUNTAIN OF DEAD FLESH?
HE REALLY IS A MONSTER JUST LIKE THEY SAID, ISN'T HE?
MATSU-DAIRA?
NO, NO. NOW I'M TALKING ABOUT UMIBOZU.
TO TELL YOU THE TRUTH, I THOUGHT HE WAS SCARIER THAN THAT ALIEN.
SHUK
REALLY?
HE DIDN'T LOOK LIKE A MONSTER TO ME.
HE WAS GOING NUTS TRYING TO PROTECT HIS DAUGHTER.
HE JUST LOOKED LIKE SOMEONE'S FATHER TO ME.
ANY PARENT COULD HAVE LOOKED JUST AS CRAZY.

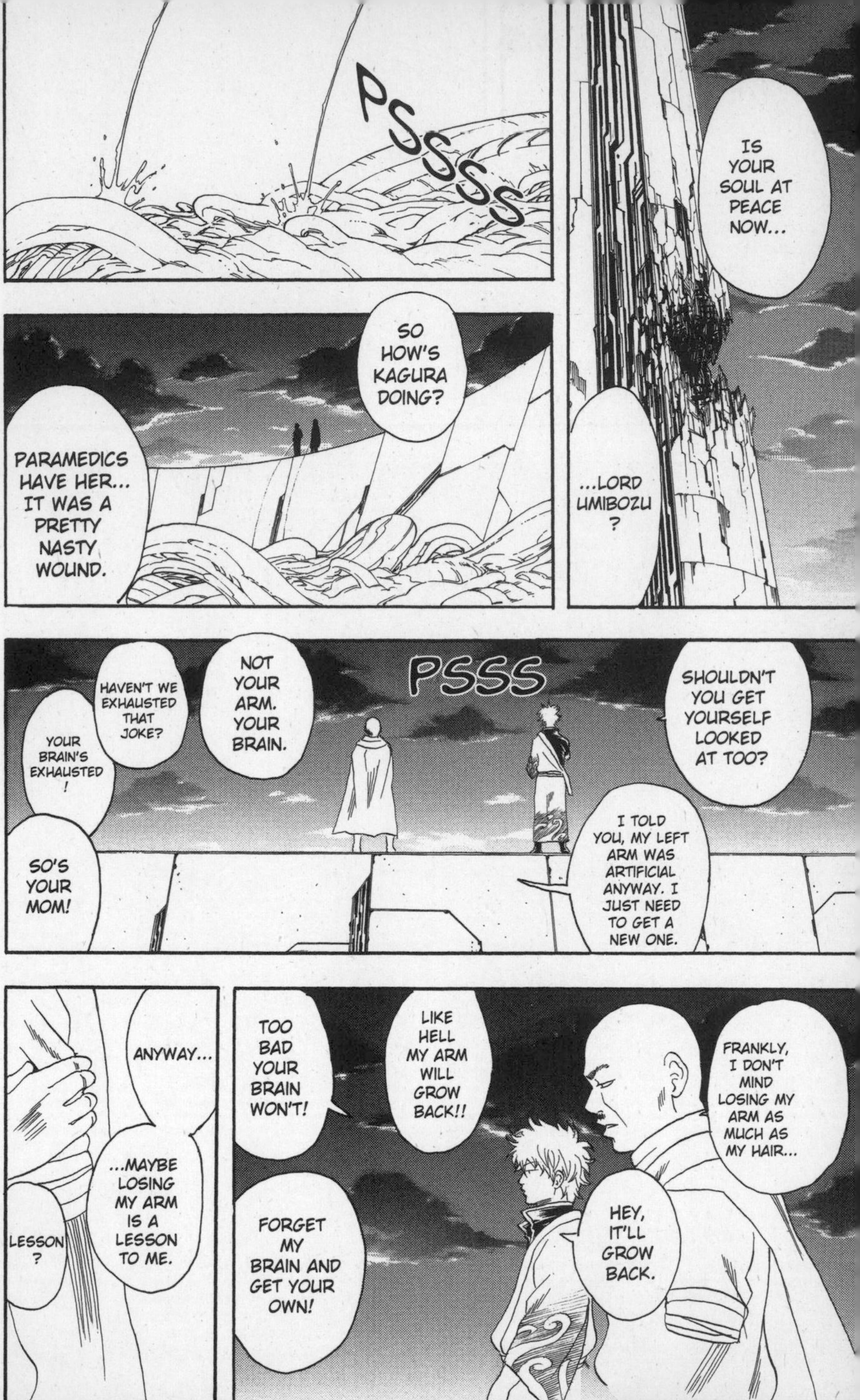
IS YOUR SOUL AT PEACE NOW...
...LORD UMIBOZU?
PSSSSS
SO HOW'S KAGURA DOING?
PARAMEDICS HAVE HER... IT WAS A PRETTY NASTY WOUND.
PSSSS
SHOULDN'T YOU GET YOURSELF LOOKED AT TOO?
I TOLD YOU, MY LEFT ARM WAS ARTIFICIAL ANYWAY. I JUST NEED TO GET A NEW ONE.
NOT YOUR ARM. YOUR BRAIN.
HAVEN'T WE EXHAUSTED THAT JOKE?
YOUR BRAIN'S EXHAUSTED!
SO'S YOUR MOM!
FRANKLY, I DON'T MIND LOSING MY ARM AS MUCH AS MY HAIR...
HEY, IT'LL GROW BACK.
LIKE HELL MY ARM WILL GROW BACK!!
TOO BAD YOUR BRAIN WON'T!
FORGET MY BRAIN AND GET YOUR OWN!
ANYWAY...
...MAYBE LOSING MY ARM IS A LESSON TO ME.
LESSON?

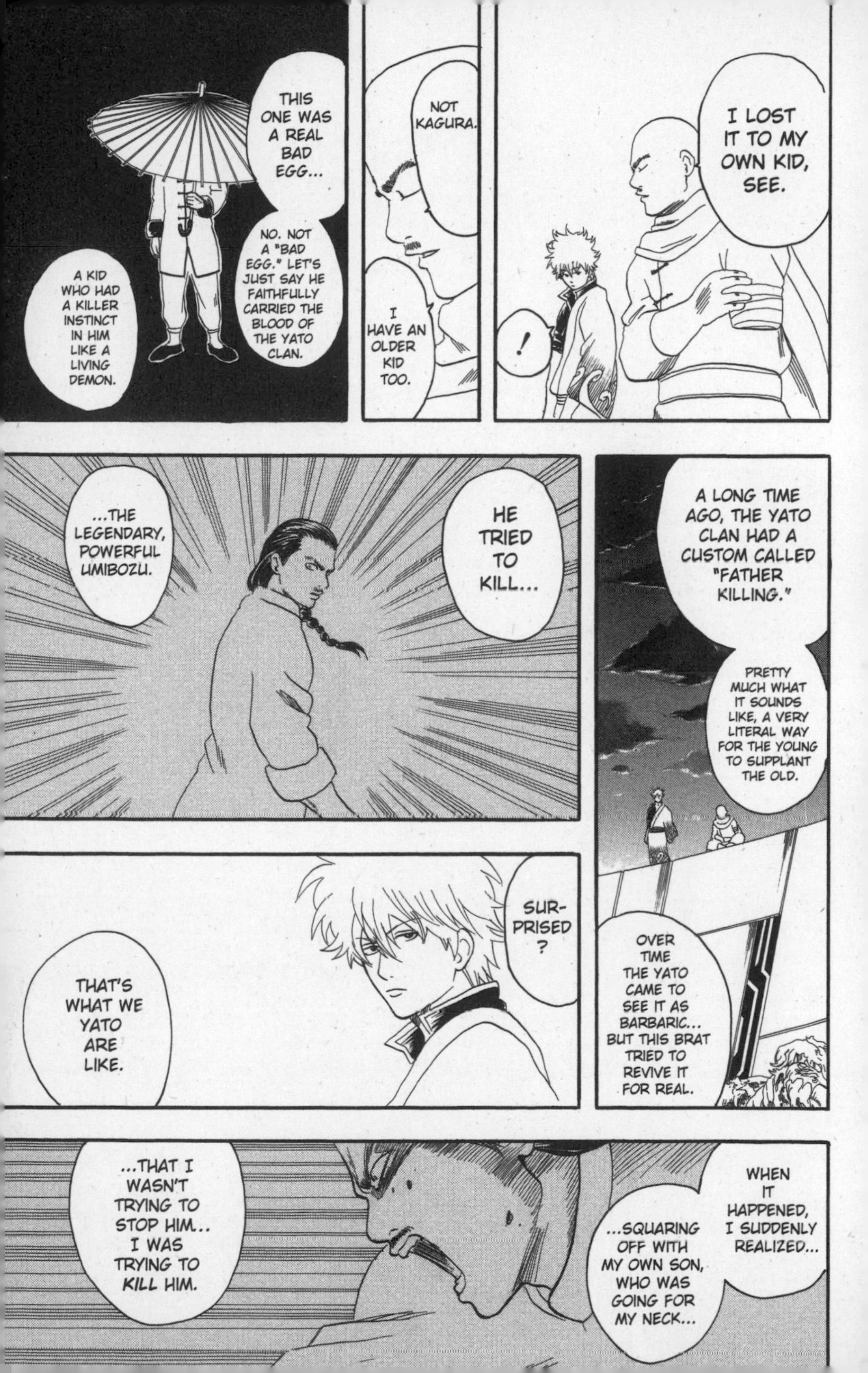
I LOST IT TO MY OWN KID, SEE.
!
NOT KAGURA.
I HAVE AN OLDER KID TOO.
THIS ONE WAS A REAL BAD EGG...
NO. NOT A "BAD EGG." LET'S JUST SAY HE FAITHFULLY CARRIED THE BLOOD OF THE YATO CLAN.
A KID WHO HAD A KILLER INSTINCT IN HIM LIKE A LIVING DEMON.
A LONG TIME AGO, THE YATO CLAN HAD A CUSTOM CALLED "FATHER KILLING."
PRETTY MUCH WHAT IT SOUNDS LIKE, A VERY LITERAL WAY FOR THE YOUNG TO SUPPLANT THE OLD.
OVER TIME THE YATO CAME TO SEE IT AS BARBARIC... BUT THIS BRAT TRIED TO REVIVE IT FOR REAL.
HE TRIED TO KILL...
...THE LEGENDARY, POWERFUL UMIBOZU.
SUR-PRISED?
THAT'S WHAT WE YATO ARE LIKE.
WHEN IT HAPPENED, I SUDDENLY REALIZED...
...SQUARING OFF WITH MY OWN SON, WHO WAS GOING FOR MY NECK...
...THAT I WASN'T TRYING TO STOP HIM.. I WAS TRYING TO KILL HIM.

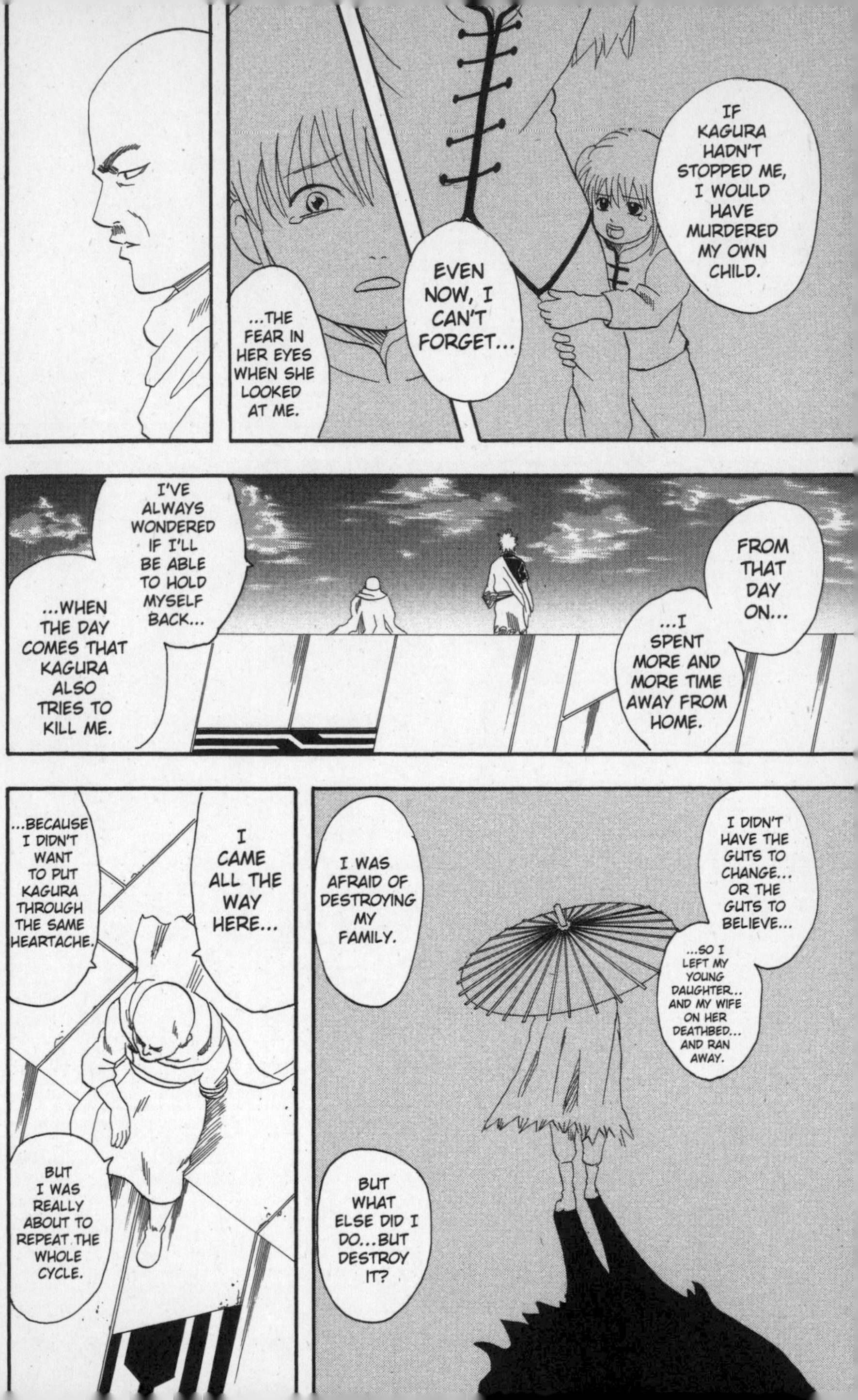
IF KAGURA HADN'T STOPPED ME, I WOULD HAVE MURDERED MY OWN CHILD.
EVEN NOW, I CAN'T FORGET...
...THE FEAR IN HER EYES WHEN SHE LOOKED AT ME.
FROM THAT DAY ON...
...I SPENT MORE AND MORE TIME AWAY FROM HOME.
I'VE ALWAYS WONDERED IF I'LL BE ABLE TO HOLD MYSELF BACK...
...WHEN THE DAY COMES THAT KAGURA ALSO TRIES TO KILL ME.
I DIDN'T HAVE THE GUTS TO CHANGE... OR THE GUTS TO BELIEVE...
...SO I LEFT MY YOUNG DAUGHTER... AND MY WIFE ON HER DEATHBED... AND RAN AWAY.
I WAS AFRAID OF DESTROYING MY FAMILY.
BUT WHAT ELSE DID I DO...BUT DESTROY IT?
I CAME ALL THE WAY HERE...
...BECAUSE I DIDN'T WANT TO PUT KAGURA THROUGH THE SAME HEARTACHE.
BUT I WAS REALLY ABOUT TO REPEAT THE WHOLE CYCLE.

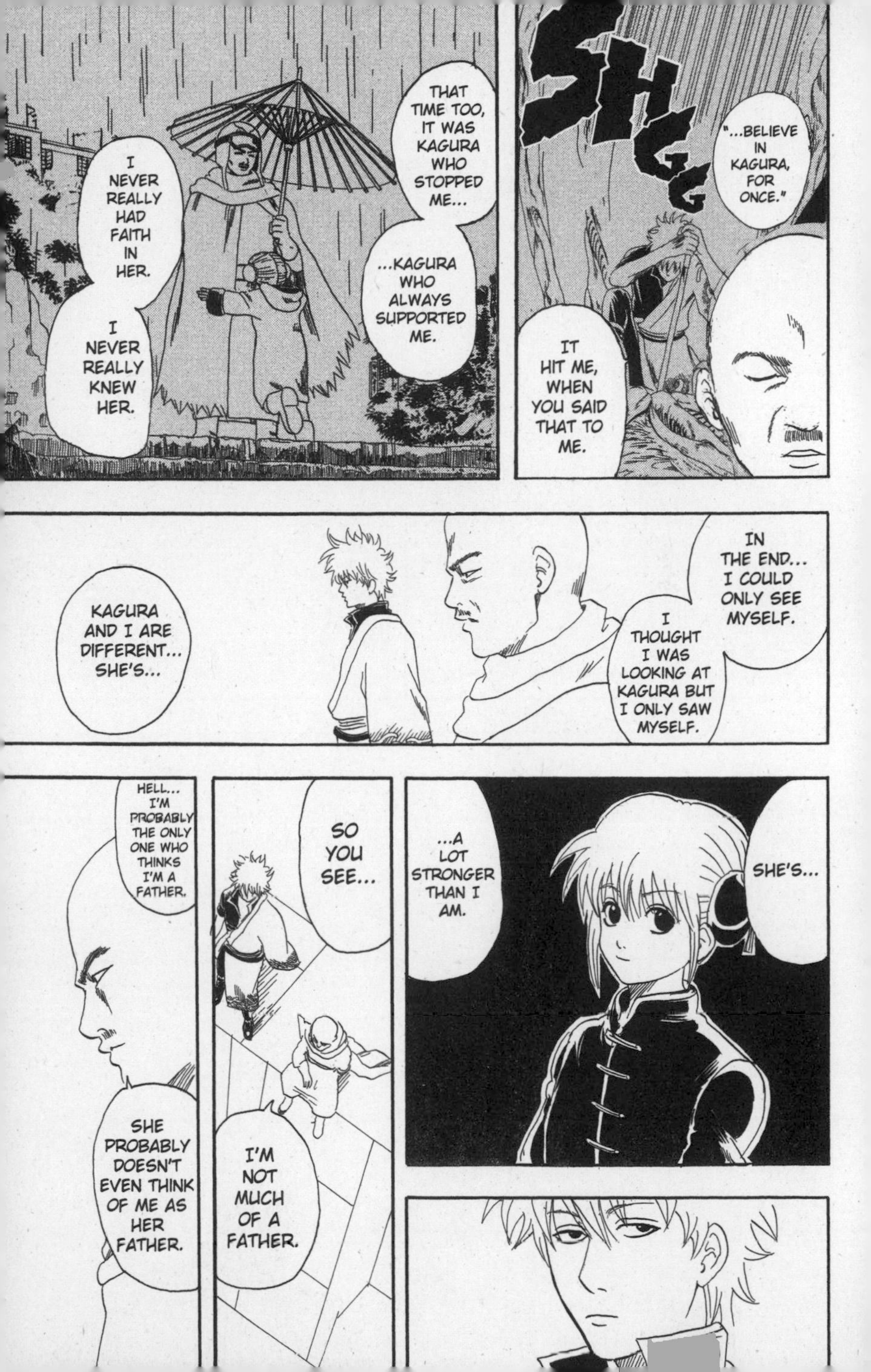
SHGG
"...BELIEVE IN KAGURA, FOR ONCE."
IT HIT ME, WHEN YOU SAID THAT TO ME.
THAT TIME TOO, IT WAS KAGURA WHO STOPPED ME...
...KAGURA WHO ALWAYS SUPPORTED ME.
I NEVER REALLY HAD FAITH IN HER.
I NEVER REALLY KNEW HER.
IN THE END... I COULD ONLY SEE MYSELF.
I THOUGHT I WAS LOOKING AT KAGURA BUT I ONLY SAW MYSELF.
KAGURA AND I ARE DIFFERENT... SHE'S...
SHE'S...
...A LOT STRONGER THAN I AM.
SO YOU SEE...
I'M NOT MUCH OF A FATHER.
HELL... I'M PROBABLY THE ONLY ONE WHO THINKS I'M A FATHER.
SHE PROBABLY DOESN'T EVEN THINK OF ME AS HER FATHER.

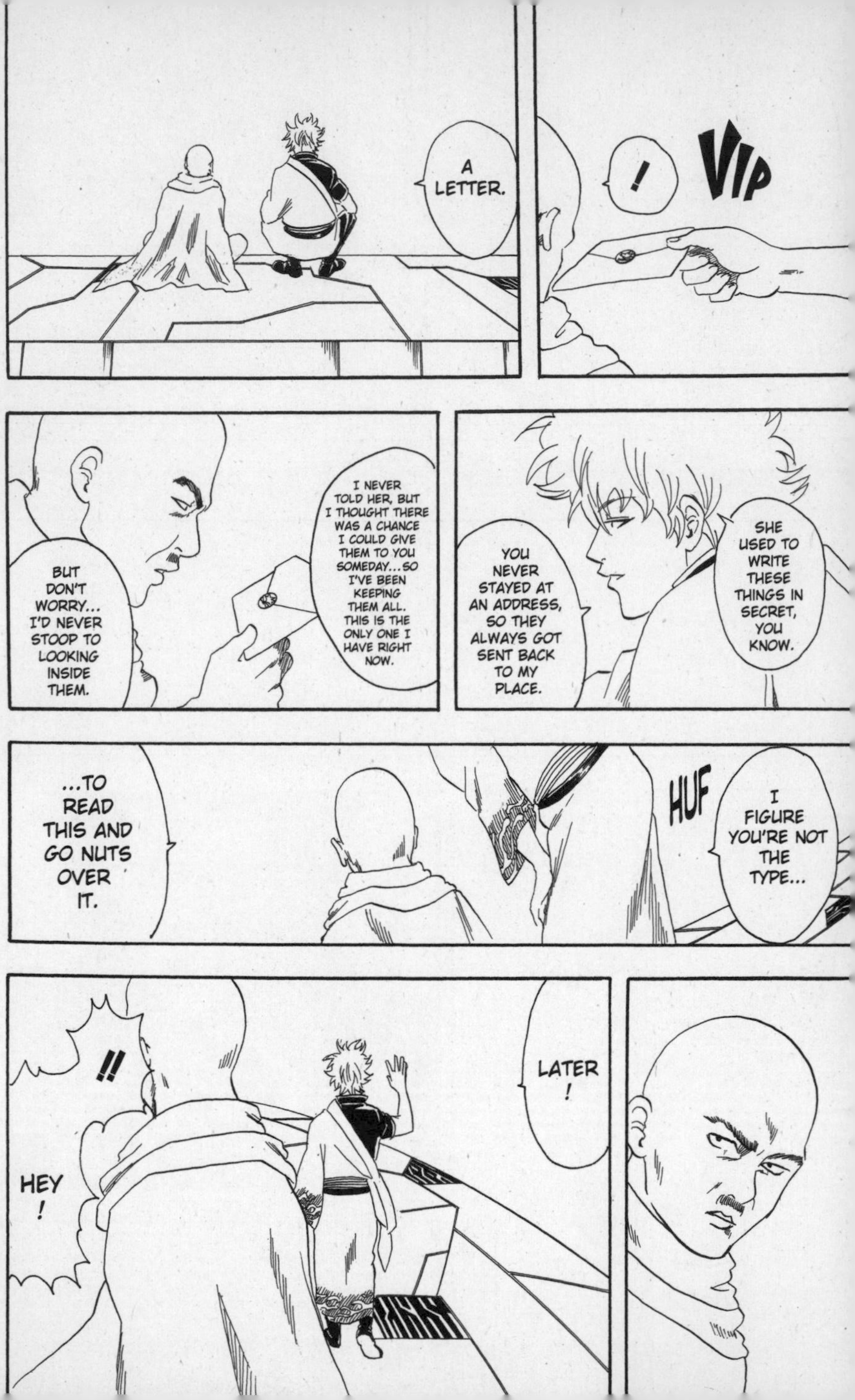
!
VIP
A LETTER.
SHE USED TO WRITE THESE THINGS IN SECRET, YOU KNOW.
YOU NEVER STAYED AT AN ADDRESS, SO THEY ALWAYS GOT SENT BACK TO MY PLACE.
I NEVER TOLD HER, BUT I THOUGHT THERE WAS A CHANCE I COULD GIVE THEM TO YOU SOMEDAY...SO I'VE BEEN KEEPING THEM ALL. THIS IS THE ONLY ONE I HAVE RIGHT NOW.
BUT DON'T WORRY... I'D NEVER STOOP TO LOOKING INSIDE THEM.
I FIGURE YOU'RE NOT THE TYPE...
HUF
...TO READ THIS AND GO NUTS OVER IT.
LATER!
!!
HEY!

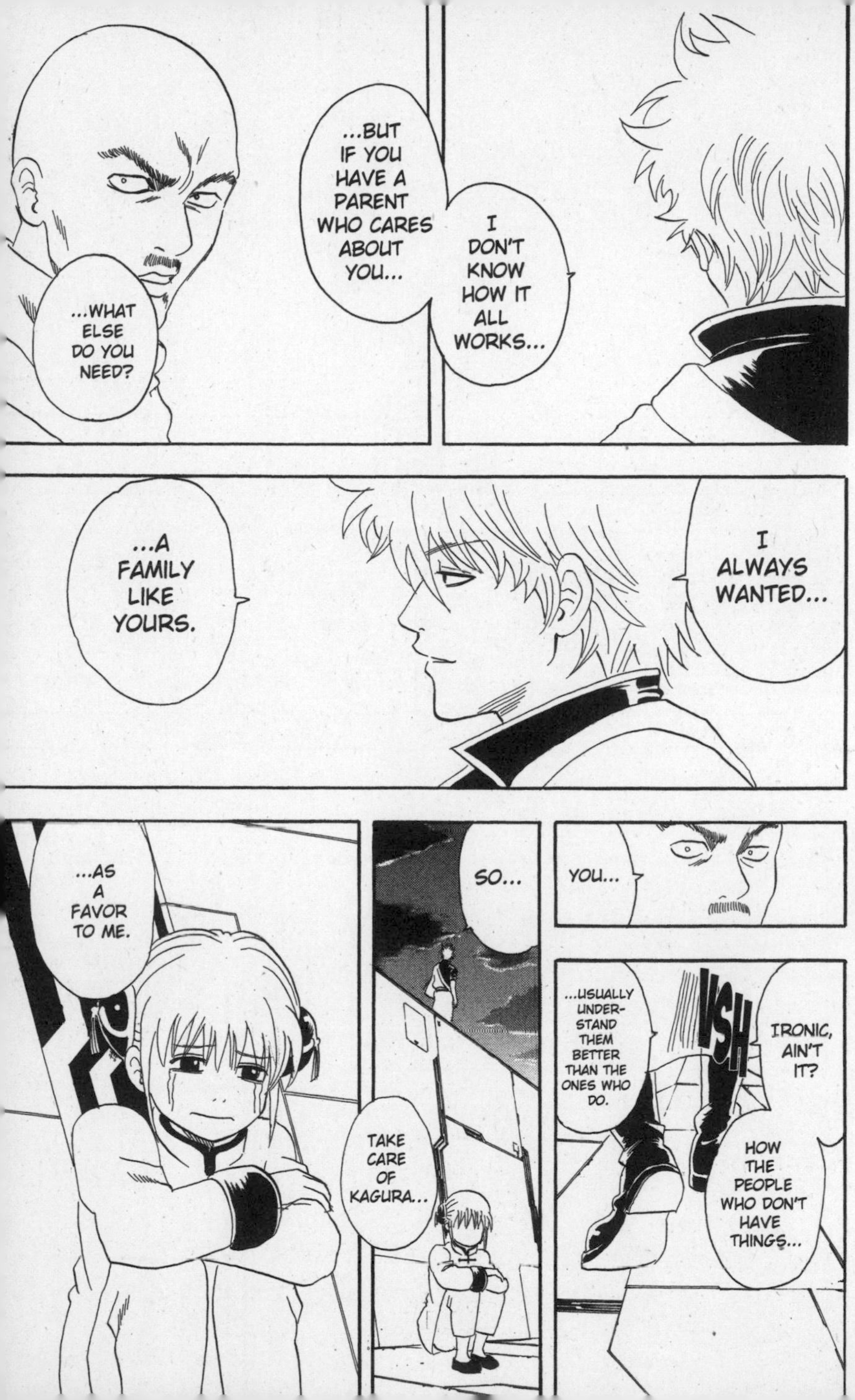
I DON'T KNOW HOW IT ALL WORKS...
...BUT IF YOU HAVE A PARENT WHO CARES ABOUT YOU...
...WHAT ELSE DO YOU NEED?
I ALWAYS WANTED...
...A FAMILY LIKE YOURS.
YOU...
IRONIC, AIN'T IT?
VSH
HOW THE PEOPLE WHO DON'T HAVE THINGS...
...USUALLY UNDER-STAND THEM BETTER THAN THE ONES WHO DO.
SO...
TAKE CARE OF KAGURA...
...AS A FAVOR TO ME.

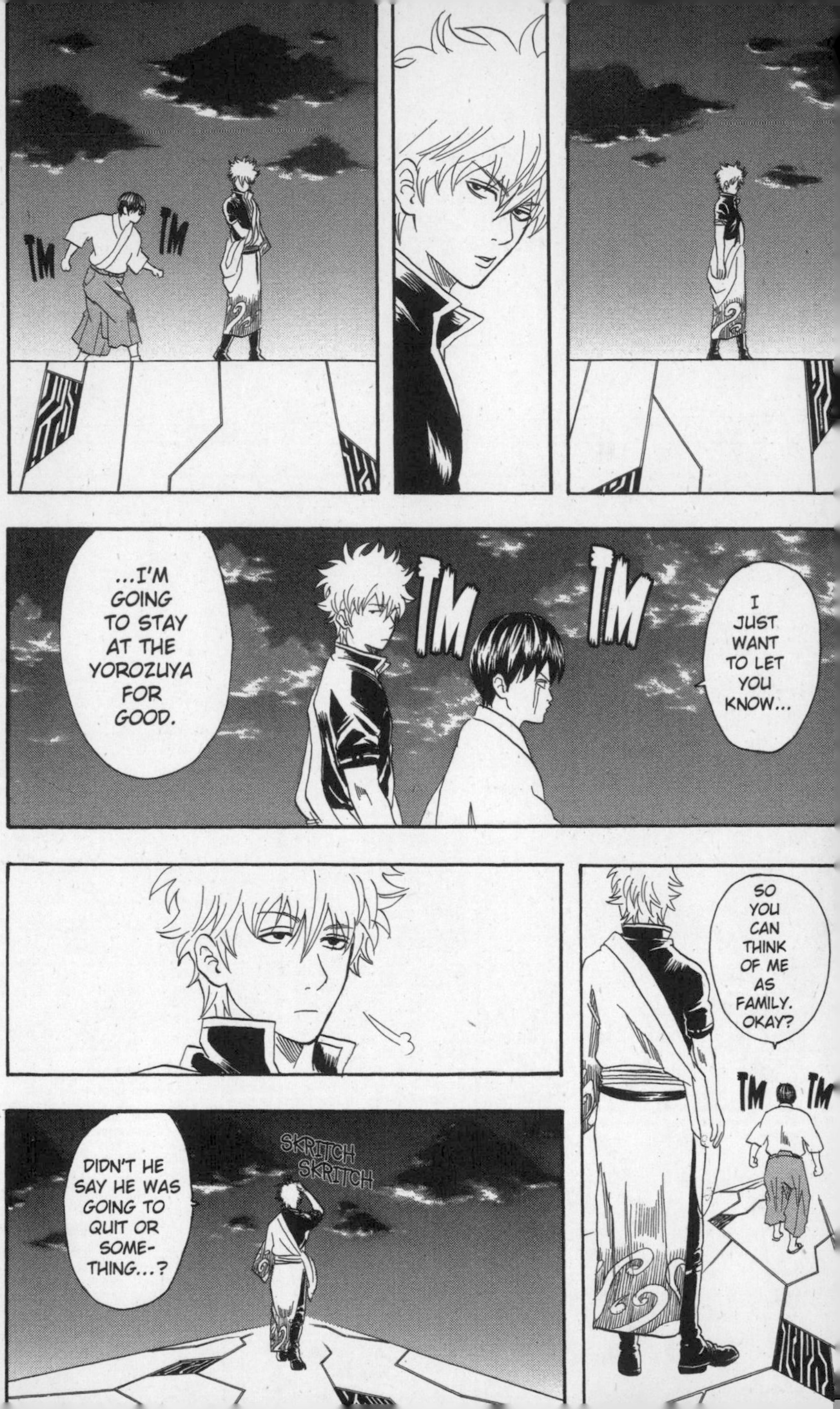
TM TM
I JUST WANT TO LET YOU KNOW...
TM TM
...I'M GOING TO STAY AT THE YOROZUYA FOR GOOD.
SO YOU CAN THINK OF ME AS FAMILY. OKAY?
TM TM
SKRITCH SKRITCH
DIDN'T HE SAY HE WAS GOING TO QUIT OR SOME-THING...?

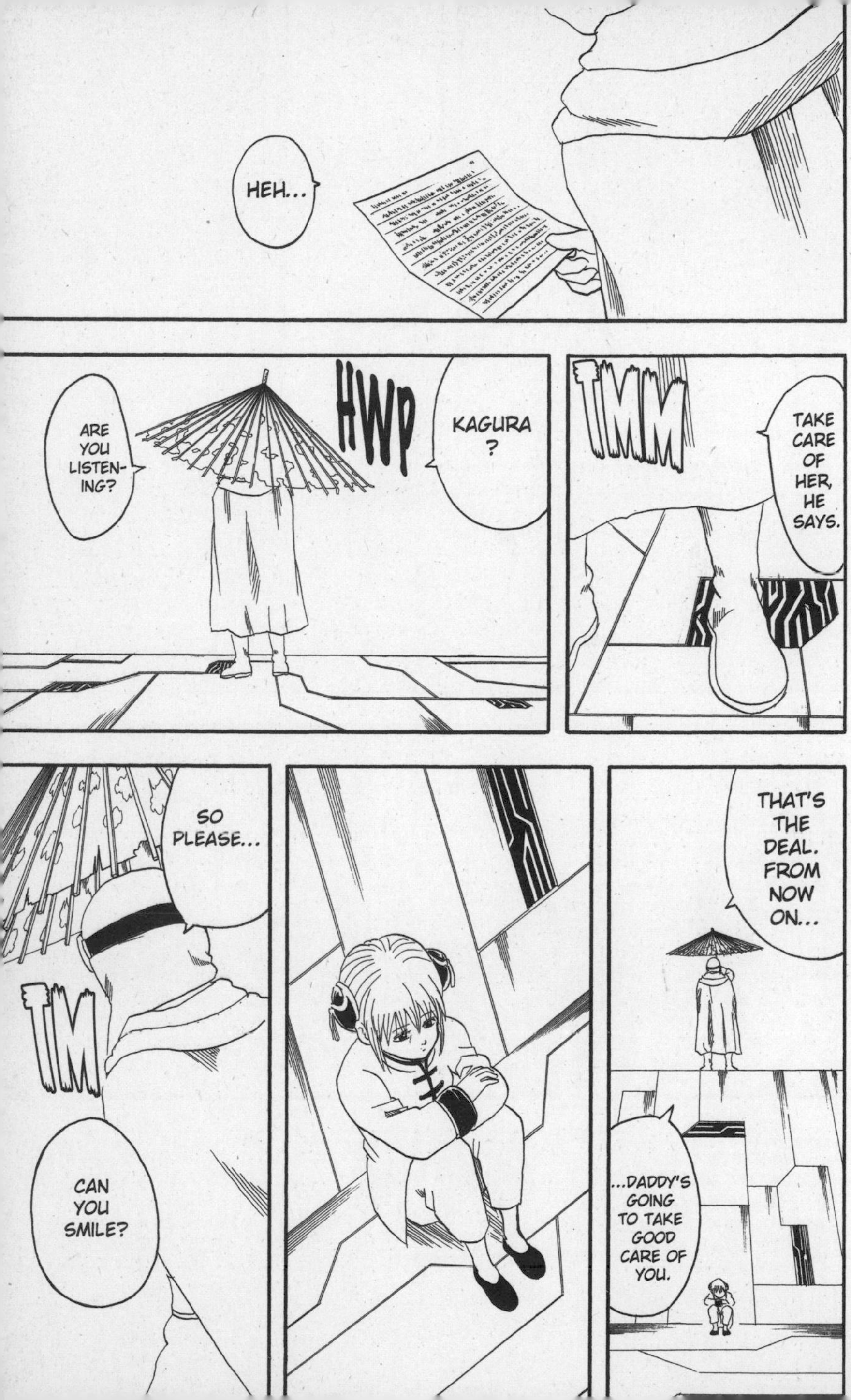
HEH...
TMM
TAKE CARE OF HER, HE SAYS.
HWP
KAGURA?
ARE YOU LISTENING?
THAT'S THE DEAL. FROM NOW ON...
...DADDY'S GOING TO TAKE GOOD CARE OF YOU.
SO PLEASE...
TM
CAN YOU SMILE?

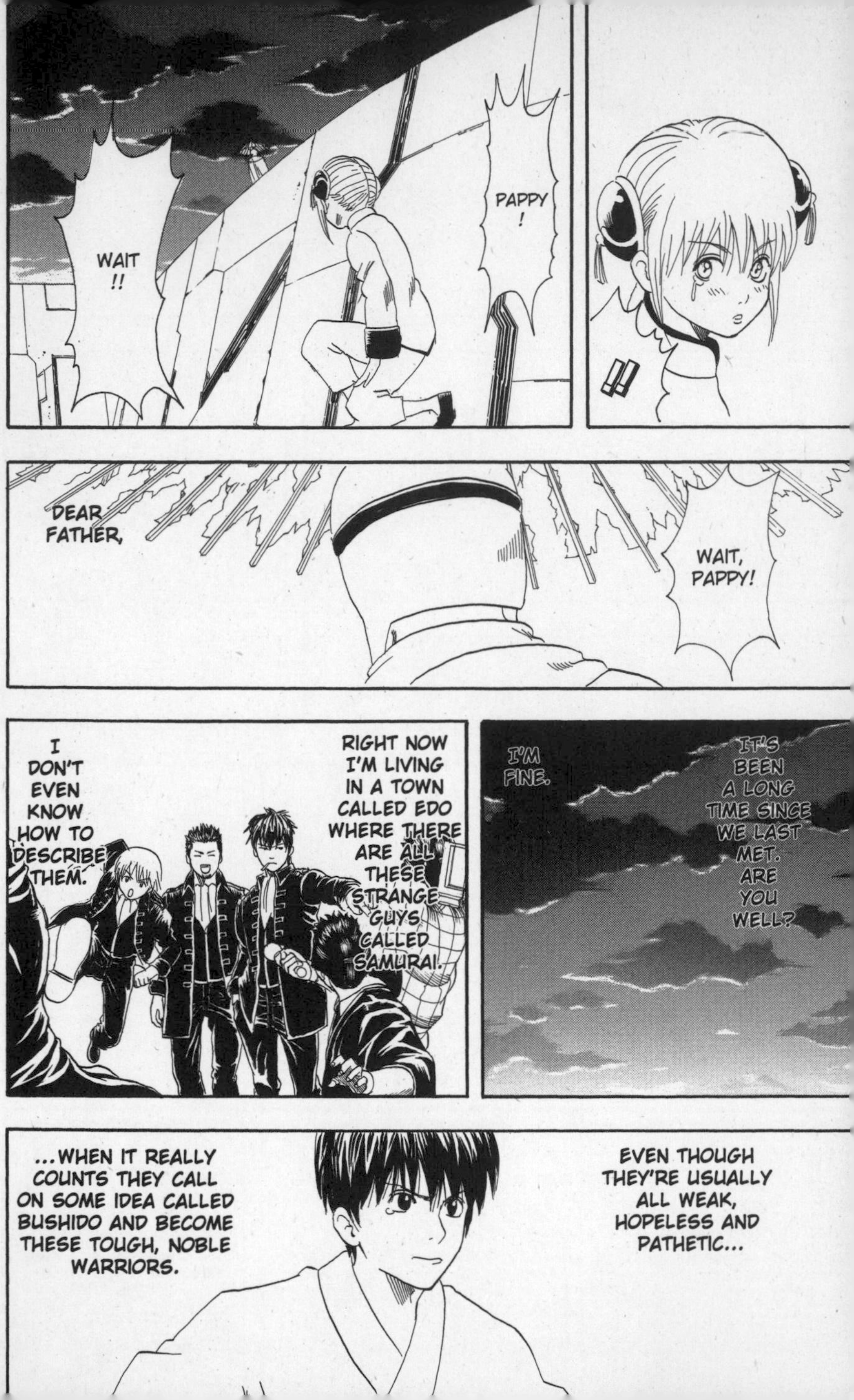
!!
PAPPY!
WAIT!!
WAIT, PAPPY!
DEAR FATHER,
IT'S BEEN A LONG TIME SINCE WE LAST MET. ARE YOU WELL?
I'M FINE.
RIGHT NOW I'M LIVING IN A TOWN CALLED EDO WHERE THERE ARE ALL THESE STRANGE GUYS CALLED SAMURAI.
I DON'T EVEN KNOW HOW TO DESCRIBE THEM.
EVEN THOUGH THEY'RE USUALLY ALL WEAK, HOPELESS AND PATHETIC...
...WHEN IT REALLY COUNTS THEY CALL ON SOME IDEA CALLED BUSHIDO AND BECOME THESE TOUGH, NOBLE WARRIORS.

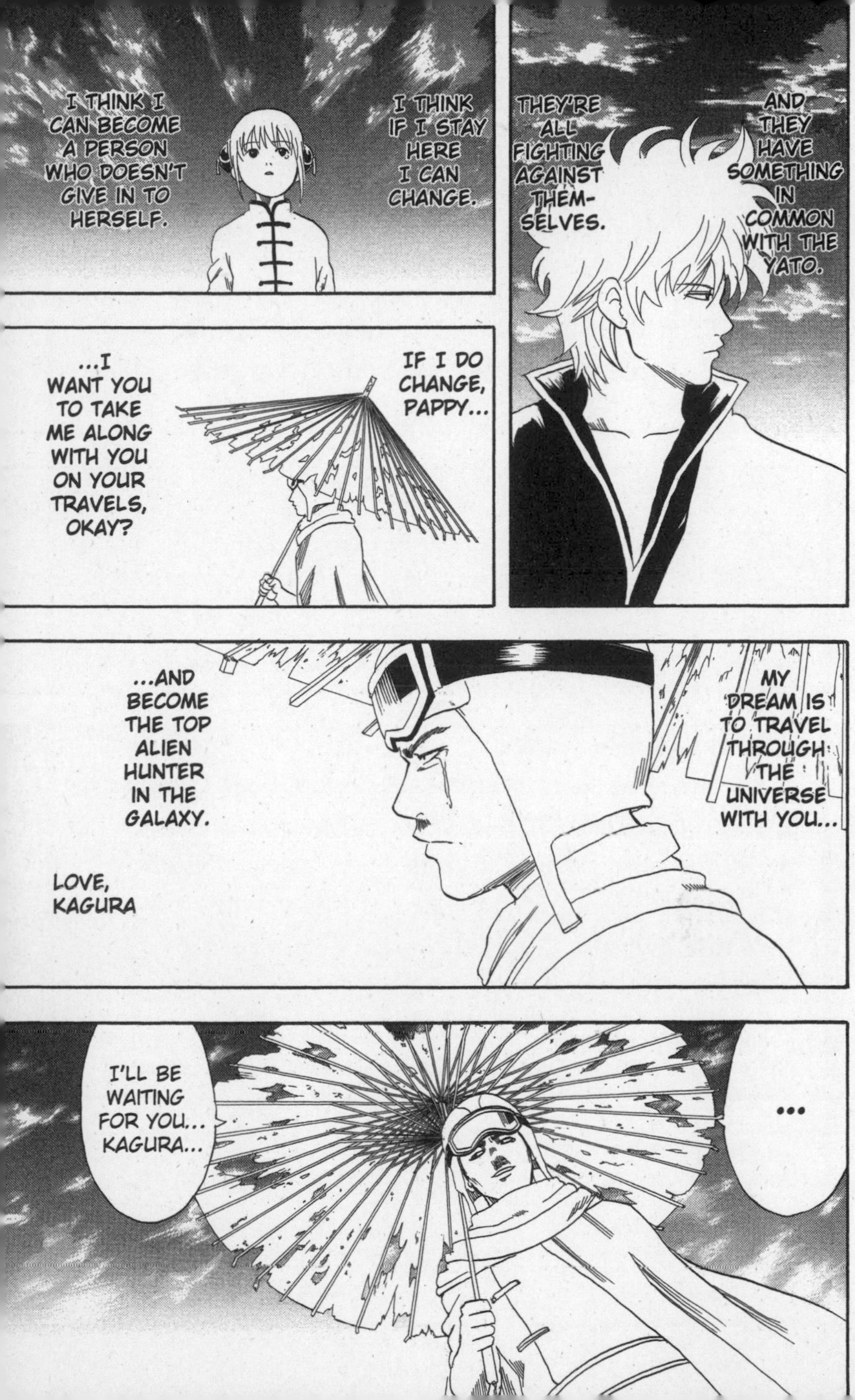
AND THEY HAVE SOMETHING IN COMMON WITH THE YATO.
THEY'RE ALL FIGHTING AGAINST THEMSELVES.
I THINK IF I STAY HERE I CAN CHANGE.
I THINK I CAN BECOME A PERSON WHO DOESN'T GIVE IN TO HERSELF.
IF I DO CHANGE, PAPPY...
...I WANT YOU TO TAKE ME ALONG WITH YOU ON YOUR TRAVELS, OKAY?
MY DREAM IS TO TRAVEL THROUGH THE UNIVERSE WITH YOU...
...AND BECOME THE TOP ALIEN HUNTER IN THE GALAXY.
LOVE, KAGURA
...
I'LL BE WAITING FOR YOU... KAGURA...

Sorachi's Q&A Corner #16

<From "Nonmii-san" of Niigata Prefecture>

Sorachi-sensei, how much butt hair do you have? If possible please provide a sketch.

<Answer>

It's impossible to provide a sketch unless this manga gets an "adults only" rating.

And when did Sorachi become famous for his butt-hair, anyway? Should I be suing somebody?!

I mean, yeah, people sometimes say, "Hey, Sorachi! Did you shove a wig in your underwear?" But...oh, never mind! Why am I writing about this? My parents read this comic, for God's sake! My grandma has a copy in the family altar in the living room!

So lay off already, will you? And don't think I'm writing about this because I want to, either! Cheez...

(Q&A #17 is on page 128)

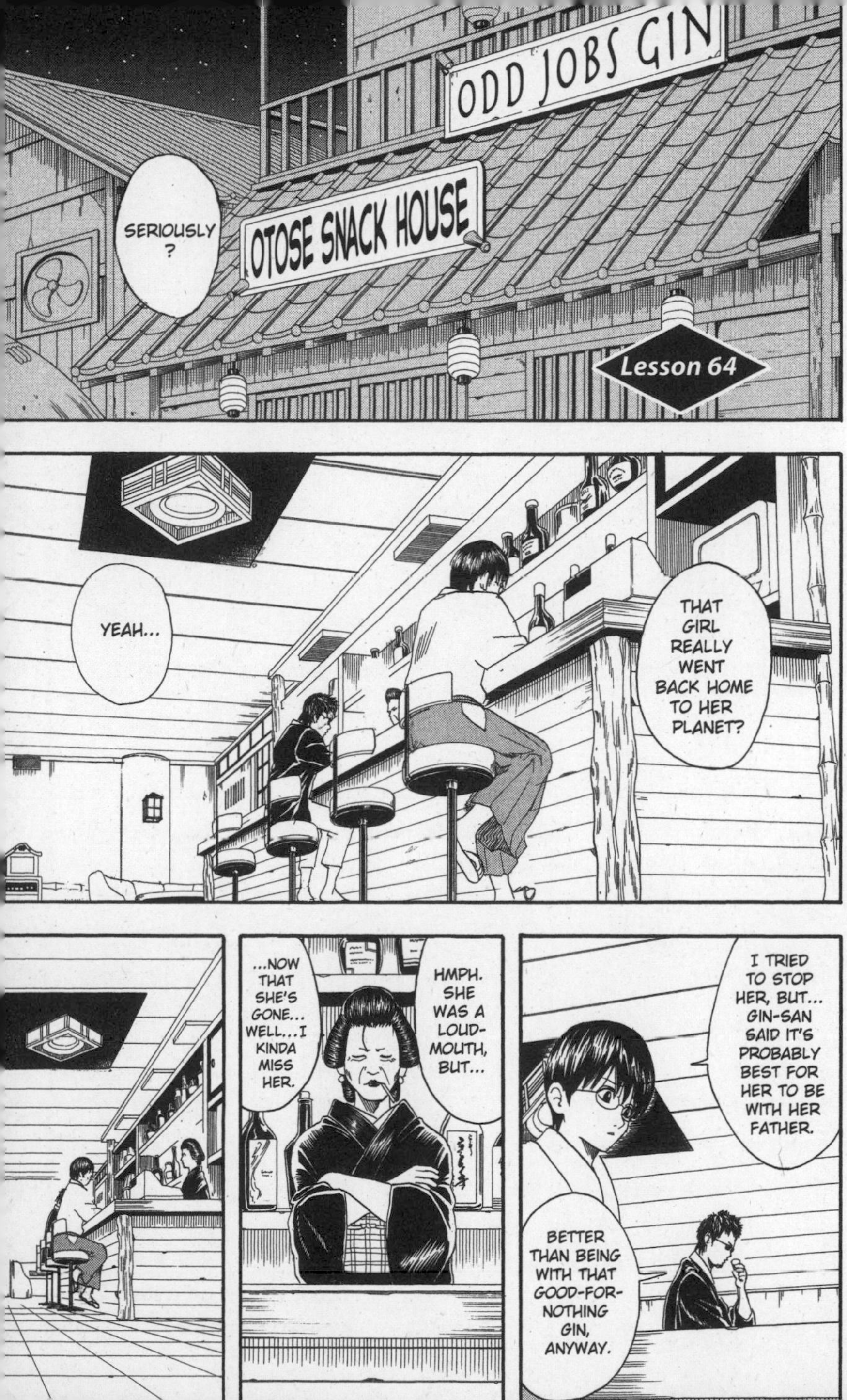
ODD JOBS GIN
OTOSE SNACK HOUSE
SERIOUSLY?
Lesson 64
THAT GIRL REALLY WENT BACK HOME TO HER PLANET?
YEAH...
I TRIED TO STOP HER, BUT... GIN-SAN SAID IT'S PROBABLY BEST FOR HER TO BE WITH HER FATHER.
BETTER THAN BEING WITH THAT GOOD-FOR-NOTHING GIN, ANYWAY.
HMPH. SHE WAS A LOUD-MOUTH, BUT...
...NOW THAT SHE'S GONE... WELL...I KINDA MISS HER.

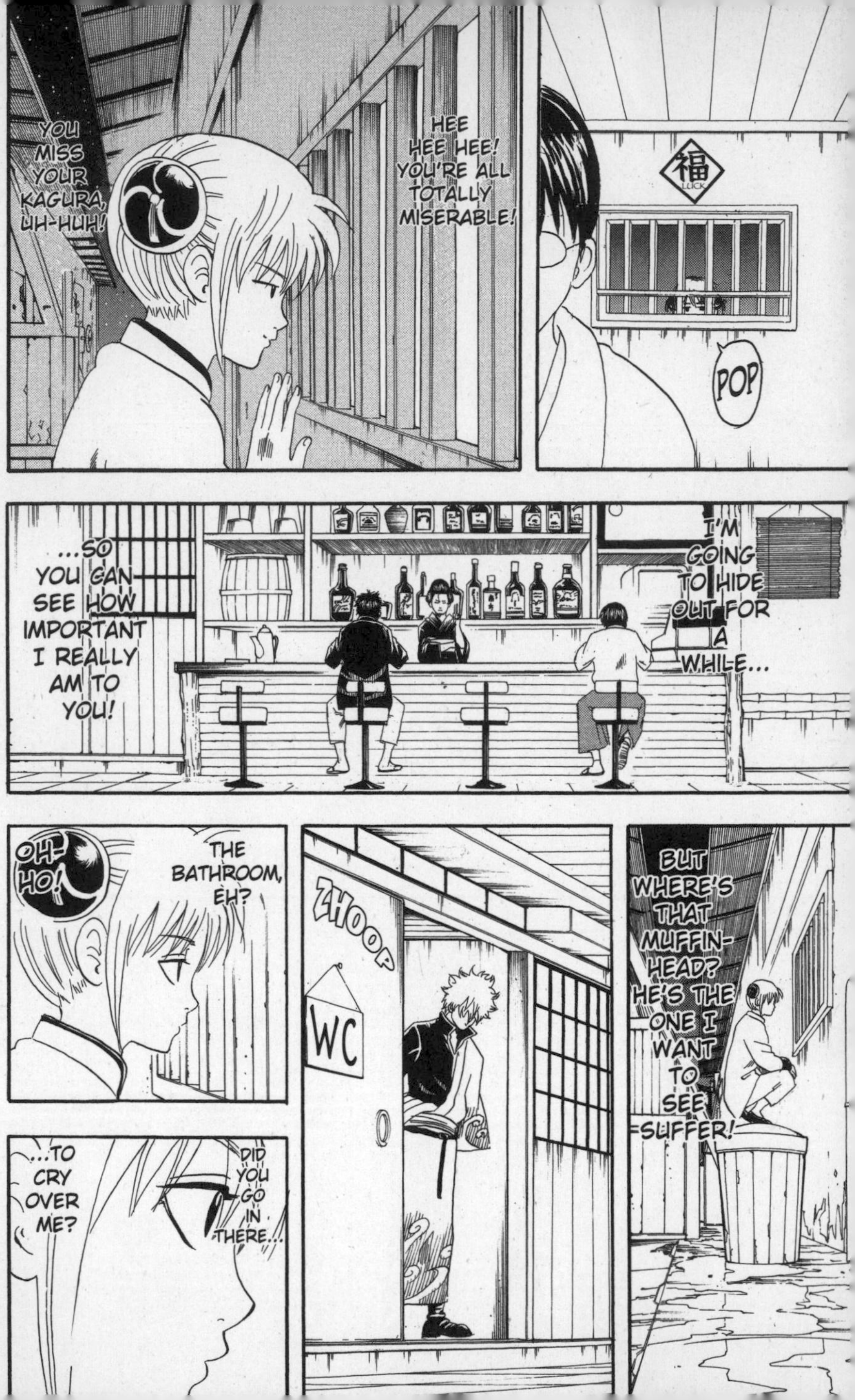
福
LUCK
POP
HEE HEE HEE! YOU'RE ALL TOTALLY MISERABLE!
YOU MISS YOUR KAGURA, UH-HUH!
I'M GOING TO HIDE OUT FOR A WHILE...
...SO YOU CAN SEE HOW IMPORTANT I REALLY AM TO YOU!
BUT WHERE'S THAT MUFFIN-HEAD? HE'S THE ONE I WANT TO SEE SUFFER!
ZHOOP
WC
THE BATHROOM, EH?
OH-HO!
DID YOU GO IN THERE...
...TO CRY OVER ME?

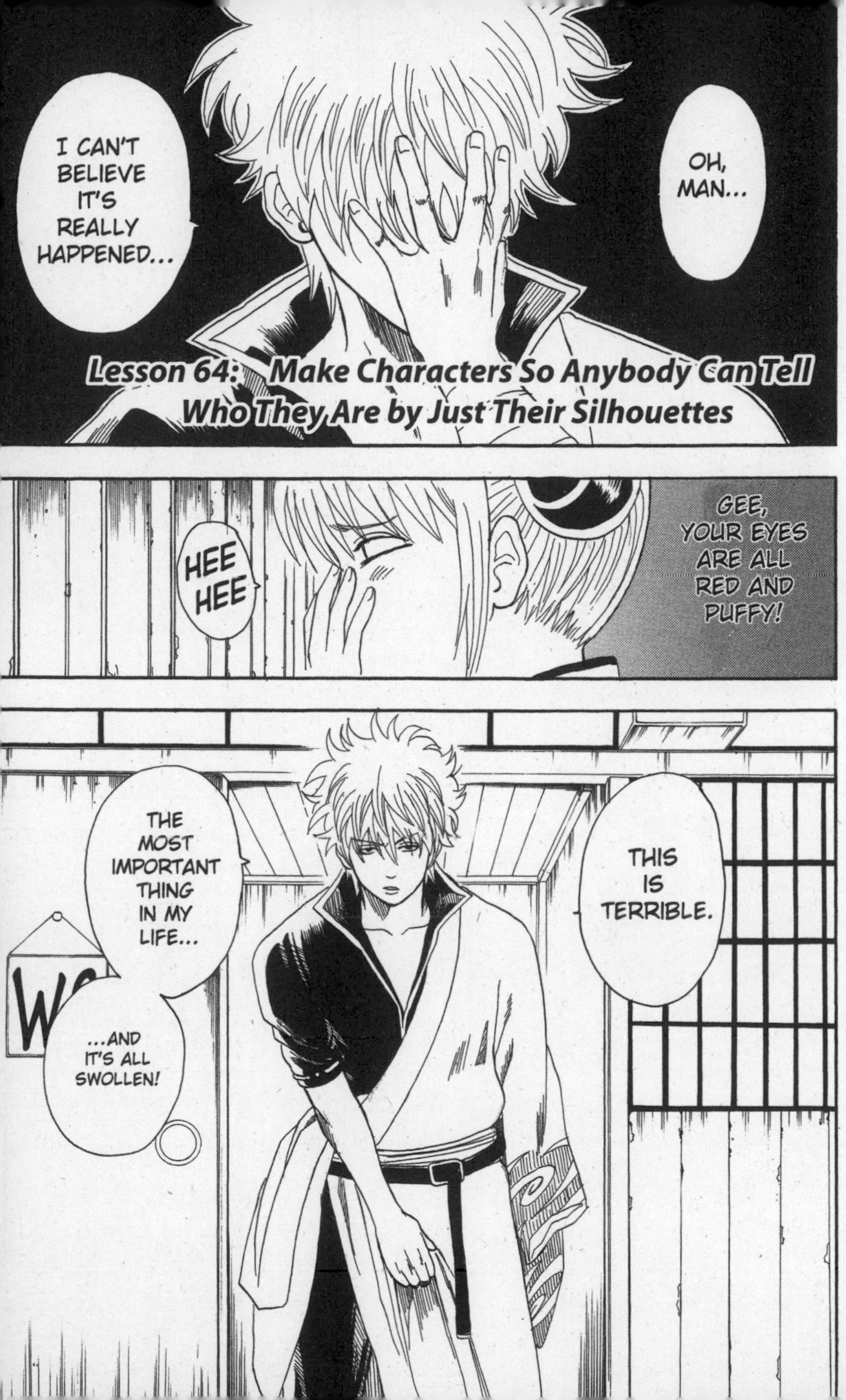
OH, MAN...
I CAN'T BELIEVE IT'S REALLY HAPPENED...
Lesson 64: Make Characters So Anybody Can Tell Who They Are by Just Their Silhouettes
GEE, YOUR EYES ARE ALL RED AND PUFFY!
HEE HEE
THIS IS TERRIBLE.
THE MOST IMPORTANT THING IN MY LIFE...
...AND IT'S ALL SWOLLEN!

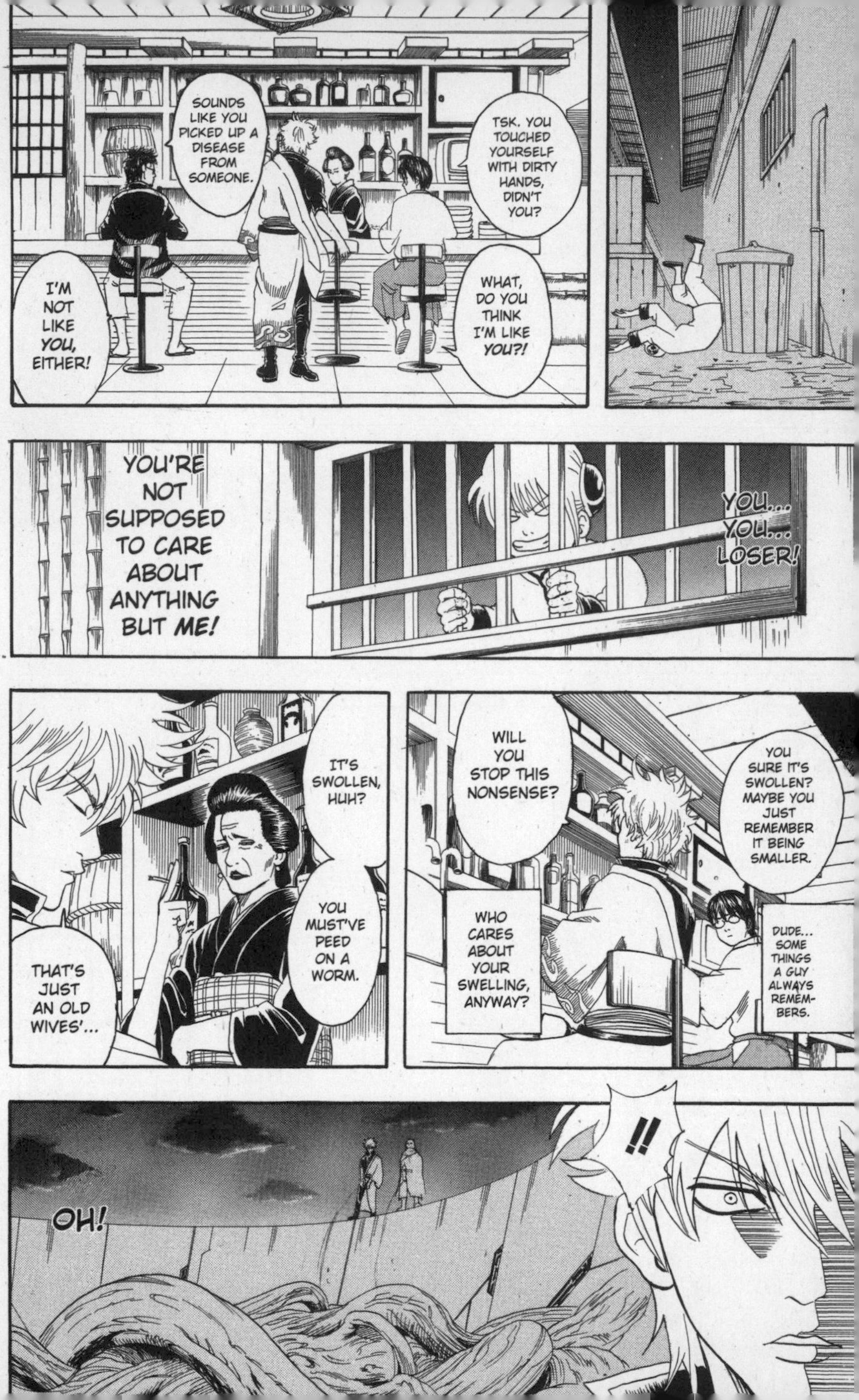

TSK. YOU TOUCHED YOURSELF WITH DIRTY HANDS, DIDN'T YOU?
SOUNDS LIKE YOU PICKED UP A DISEASE FROM SOMEONE.
WHAT, DO YOU THINK I'M LIKE YOU?!
I'M NOT LIKE YOU, EITHER!
YOU... YOU... LOSER!
YOU'RE NOT SUPPOSED TO CARE ABOUT ANYTHING BUT ME!
YOU SURE IT'S SWOLLEN? MAYBE YOU JUST REMEMBER IT BEING SMALLER.
WILL YOU STOP THIS NONSENSE?
DUDE... SOME THINGS A GUY ALWAYS REMEM-BERS.
WHO CARES ABOUT YOUR SWELLING, ANYWAY?
IT'S SWOLLEN, HUH?
YOU MUST'VE PEED ON A WORM.
THAT'S JUST AN OLD WIVES'...
!!
OH!

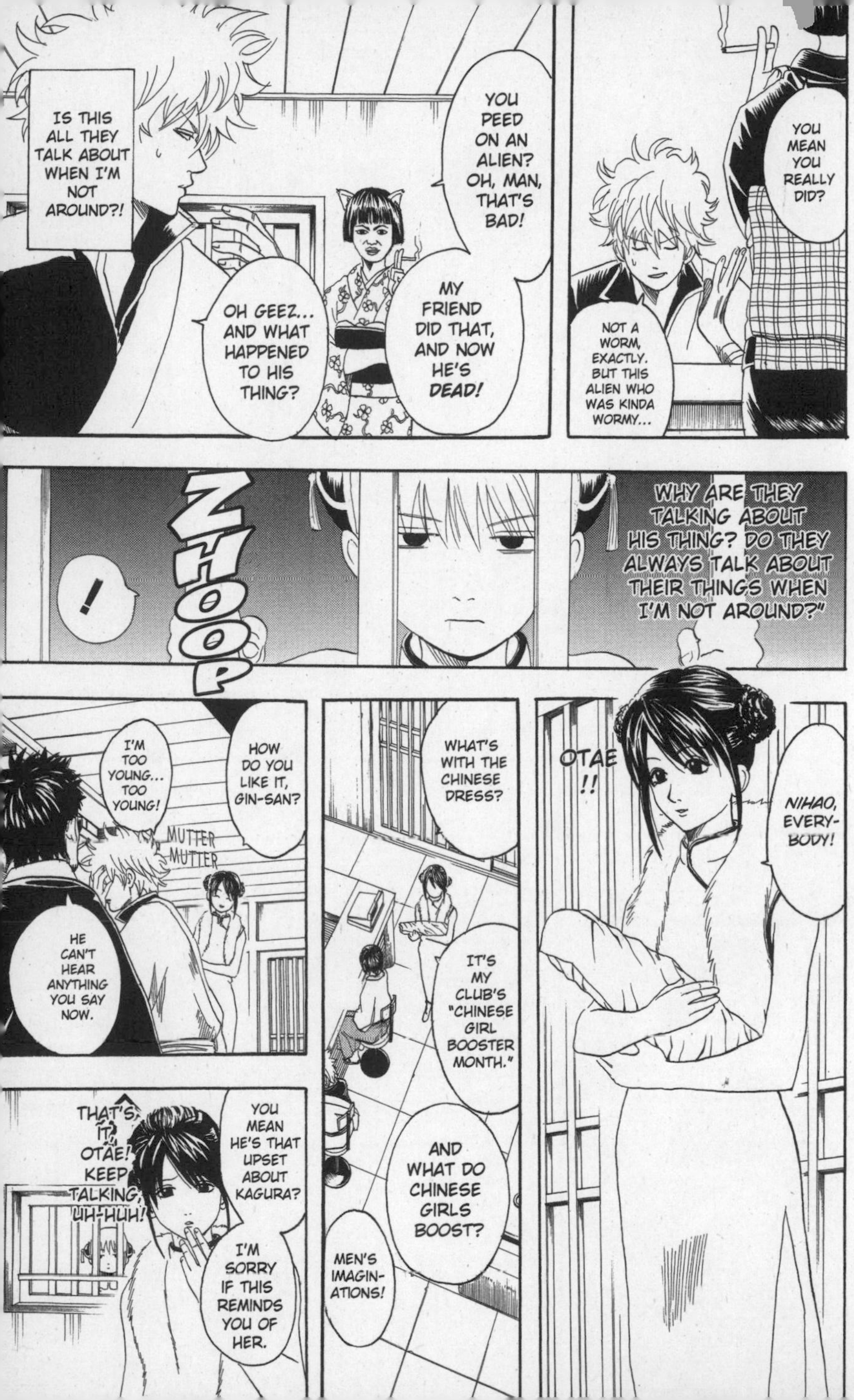
YOU MEAN YOU REALLY DID?
NOT A WORM, EXACTLY. BUT THIS ALIEN WHO WAS KINDA WORMY...
YOU PEED ON AN ALIEN? OH, MAN, THAT'S BAD!
MY FRIEND DID THAT, AND NOW HE'S DEAD!
OH GEEZ... AND WHAT HAPPENED TO HIS THING?
IS THIS ALL THEY TALK ABOUT WHEN I'M NOT AROUND?!
WHY ARE THEY TALKING ABOUT HIS THING? DO THEY ALWAYS TALK ABOUT THEIR THINGS WHEN I'M NOT AROUND?"
ZHOOOP
!
NIHAO, EVERY-BODY!
OTAE!!
WHAT'S WITH THE CHINESE DRESS?
IT'S MY CLUB'S "CHINESE GIRL BOOSTER MONTH."
AND WHAT DO CHINESE GIRLS BOOST?
MEN'S IMAGIN-ATIONS!
HOW DO YOU LIKE IT, GIN-SAN?
I'M TOO YOUNG... TOO YOUNG!
MUTTER MUTTER
HE CAN'T HEAR ANYTHING YOU SAY NOW.
YOU MEAN HE'S THAT UPSET ABOUT KAGURA?
I'M SORRY IF THIS REMINDS YOU OF HER.
THAT'S IT, OTAE! KEEP TALKING, UH-HUH!

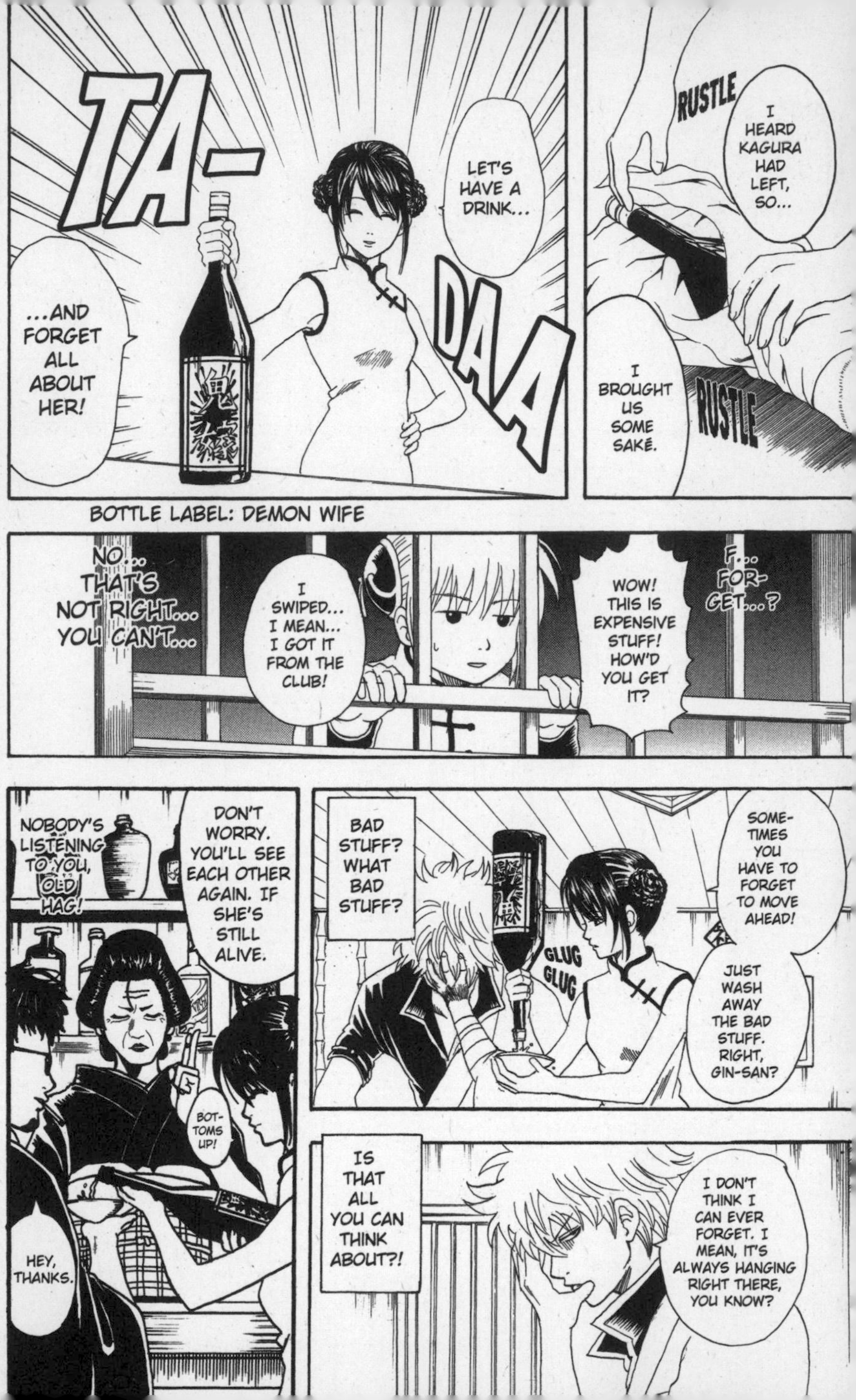
RUSTLE
I HEARD KAGURA HAD LEFT, SO...
I BROUGHT US SOME SAKE.
RUSTLE
TA-DAA
LET'S HAVE A DRINK...
...AND FORGET ALL ABOUT HER!
BOTTLE LABEL: DEMON WIFE
F... FOR-GET...?
WOW! THIS IS EXPENSIVE STUFF! HOW'D YOU GET IT?
I SWIPED... I MEAN... I GOT IT FROM THE CLUB!
NO... THAT'S NOT RIGHT... YOU CAN'T...
SOME-TIMES YOU HAVE TO FORGET TO MOVE AHEAD!
JUST WASH AWAY THE BAD STUFF. RIGHT, GIN-SAN?
BAD STUFF? WHAT BAD STUFF?
GLUG GLUG
I DON'T THINK I CAN EVER FORGET. I MEAN, IT'S ALWAYS HANGING RIGHT THERE, YOU KNOW?
IS THAT ALL YOU CAN THINK ABOUT?!
DON'T WORRY. YOU'LL SEE EACH OTHER AGAIN. IF SHE'S STILL ALIVE.
NOBODY'S LISTENING TO YOU, OLD HAG!
BOT-TOMS UP!
HEY, THANKS.

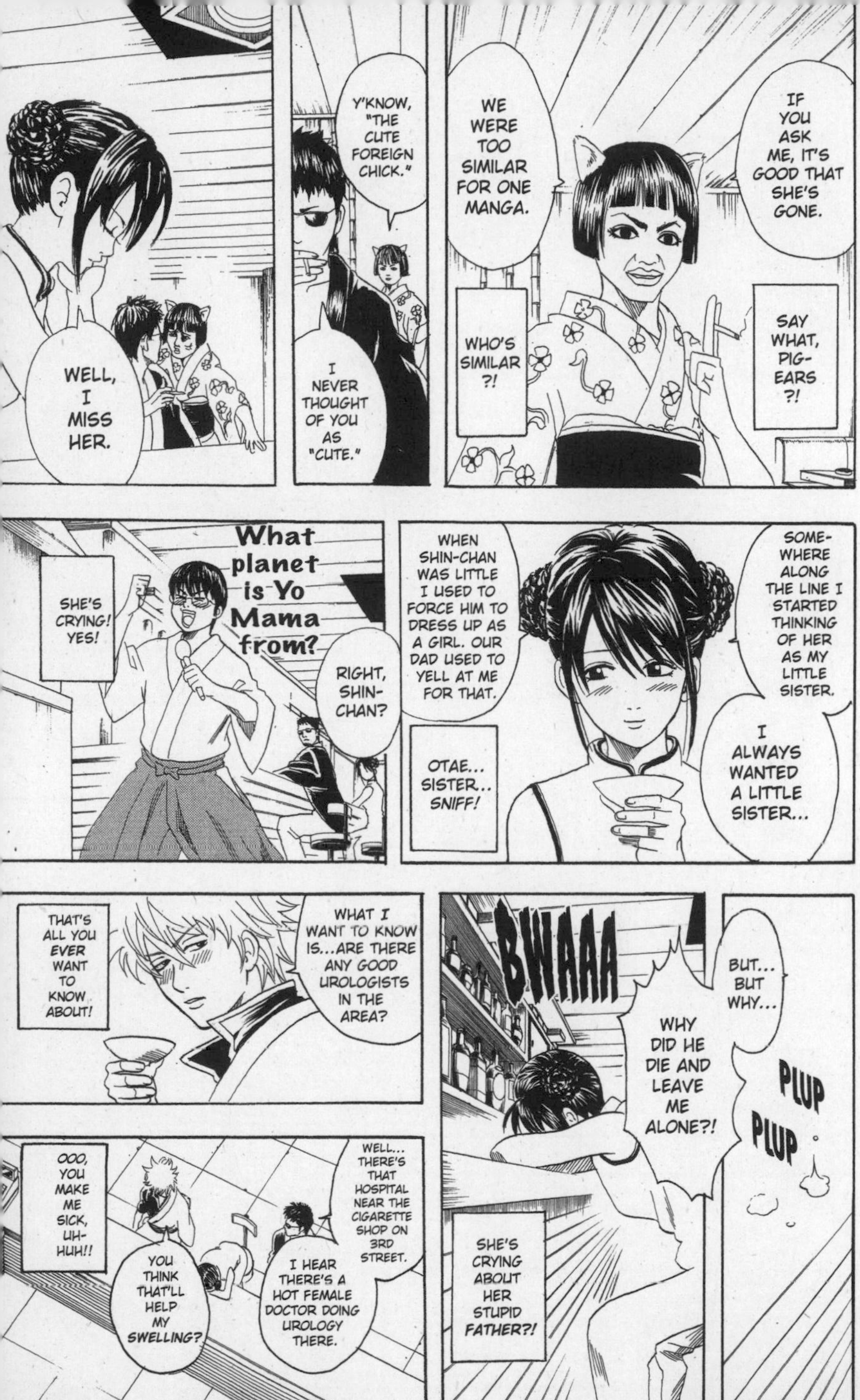
IF YOU ASK ME, IT'S GOOD THAT SHE'S GONE.
WE WERE TOO SIMILAR FOR ONE MANGA.
SAY WHAT, PIG-EARS?!
WHO'S SIMILAR?!
Y'KNOW, "THE CUTE FOREIGN CHICK."
I NEVER THOUGHT OF YOU AS "CUTE."
WELL, I MISS HER.
SOME-WHERE ALONG THE LINE I STARTED THINKING OF HER AS MY LITTLE SISTER.
WHEN SHIN-CHAN WAS LITTLE I USED TO FORCE HIM TO DRESS UP AS A GIRL. OUR DAD USED TO YELL AT ME FOR THAT.
I ALWAYS WANTED A LITTLE SISTER...
OTAE... SISTER... SNIFF!
What planet is Yo Mama from?
RIGHT, SHIN-CHAN?
SHE'S CRYING! YES!
BUT... BUT WHY...
BWAAA
WHY DID HE DIE AND LEAVE ME ALONE?!
PLUP
PLUP
SHE'S CRYING ABOUT HER STUPID FATHER?!
WHAT I WANT TO KNOW IS...ARE THERE ANY GOOD UROLOGISTS IN THE AREA?
THAT'S ALL YOU EVER WANT TO KNOW ABOUT!
WELL... THERE'S THAT HOSPITAL NEAR THE CIGARETTE SHOP ON 3RD STREET.
I HEAR THERE'S A HOT FEMALE DOCTOR DOING UROLOGY THERE.
OOO, YOU MAKE ME SICK, UH-HUH!!
YOU THINK THAT'LL HELP MY SWELLING?

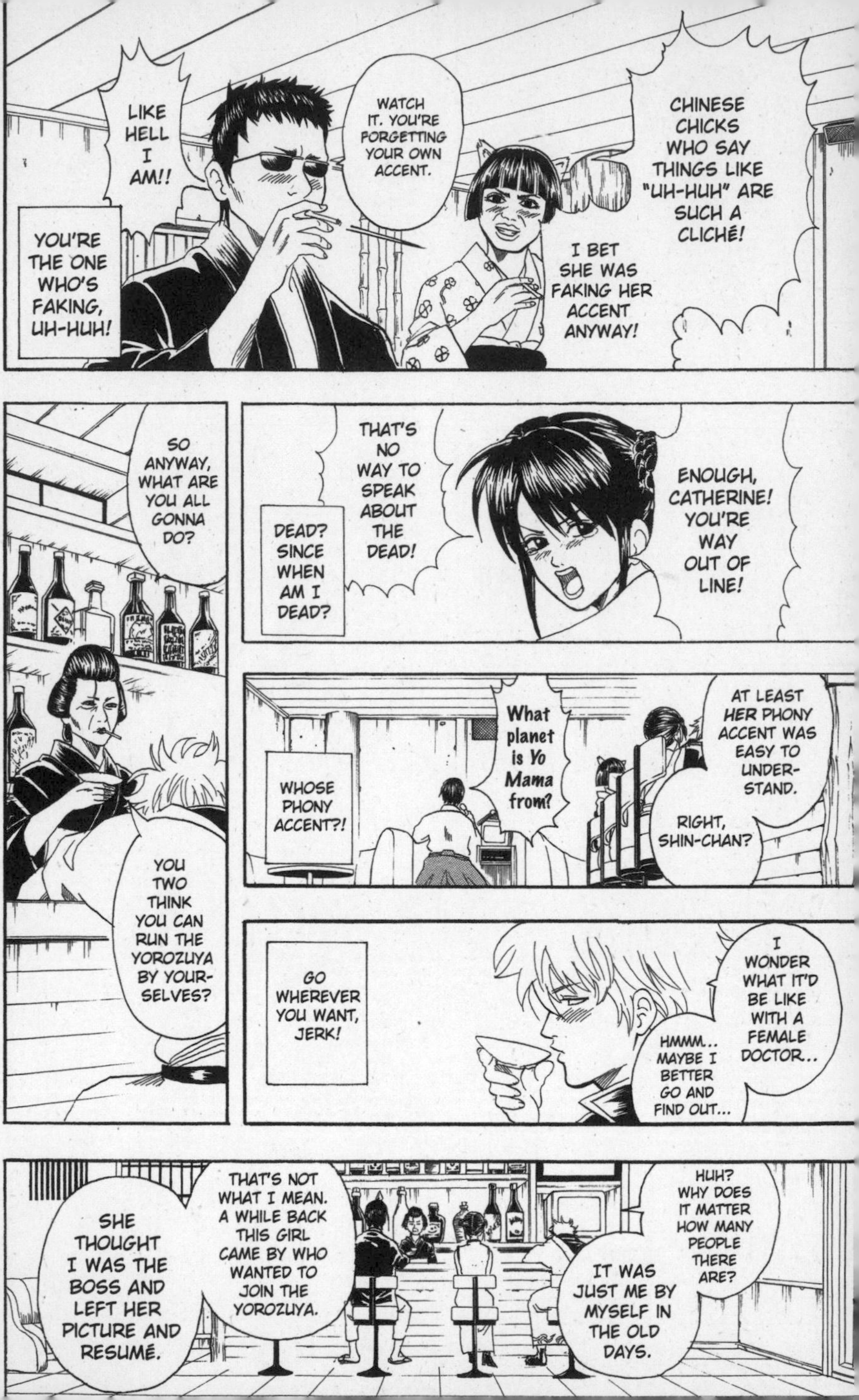
CHINESE CHICKS WHO SAY THINGS LIKE "UH-HUH" ARE SUCH A CLICHÉ!
I BET SHE WAS FAKING HER ACCENT ANYWAY!
WATCH IT. YOU'RE FORGETTING YOUR OWN ACCENT.
LIKE HELL I AM!!
YOU'RE THE ONE WHO'S FAKING, UH-HUH!
ENOUGH, CATHERINE! YOU'RE WAY OUT OF LINE!
THAT'S NO WAY TO SPEAK ABOUT THE DEAD!
DEAD? SINCE WHEN AM I DEAD?
AT LEAST HER PHONY ACCENT WAS EASY TO UNDER-STAND.
RIGHT, SHIN-CHAN?
What planet is Yo Mama from?
WHOSE PHONY ACCENT?!
I WONDER WHAT IT'D BE LIKE WITH A FEMALE DOCTOR...
HMMM... MAYBE I BETTER GO AND FIND OUT...
GO WHEREVER YOU WANT, JERK!
SO ANYWAY, WHAT ARE YOU ALL GONNA DO?
YOU TWO THINK YOU CAN RUN THE YOROZUYA BY YOUR-SELVES?
HUH? WHY DOES IT MATTER HOW MANY PEOPLE THERE ARE?
IT WAS JUST ME BY MYSELF IN THE OLD DAYS.
THAT'S NOT WHAT I MEAN. A WHILE BACK THIS GIRL CAME BY WHO WANTED TO JOIN THE YOROZUYA.
SHE THOUGHT I WAS THE BOSS AND LEFT HER PICTURE AND RESUMÉ.

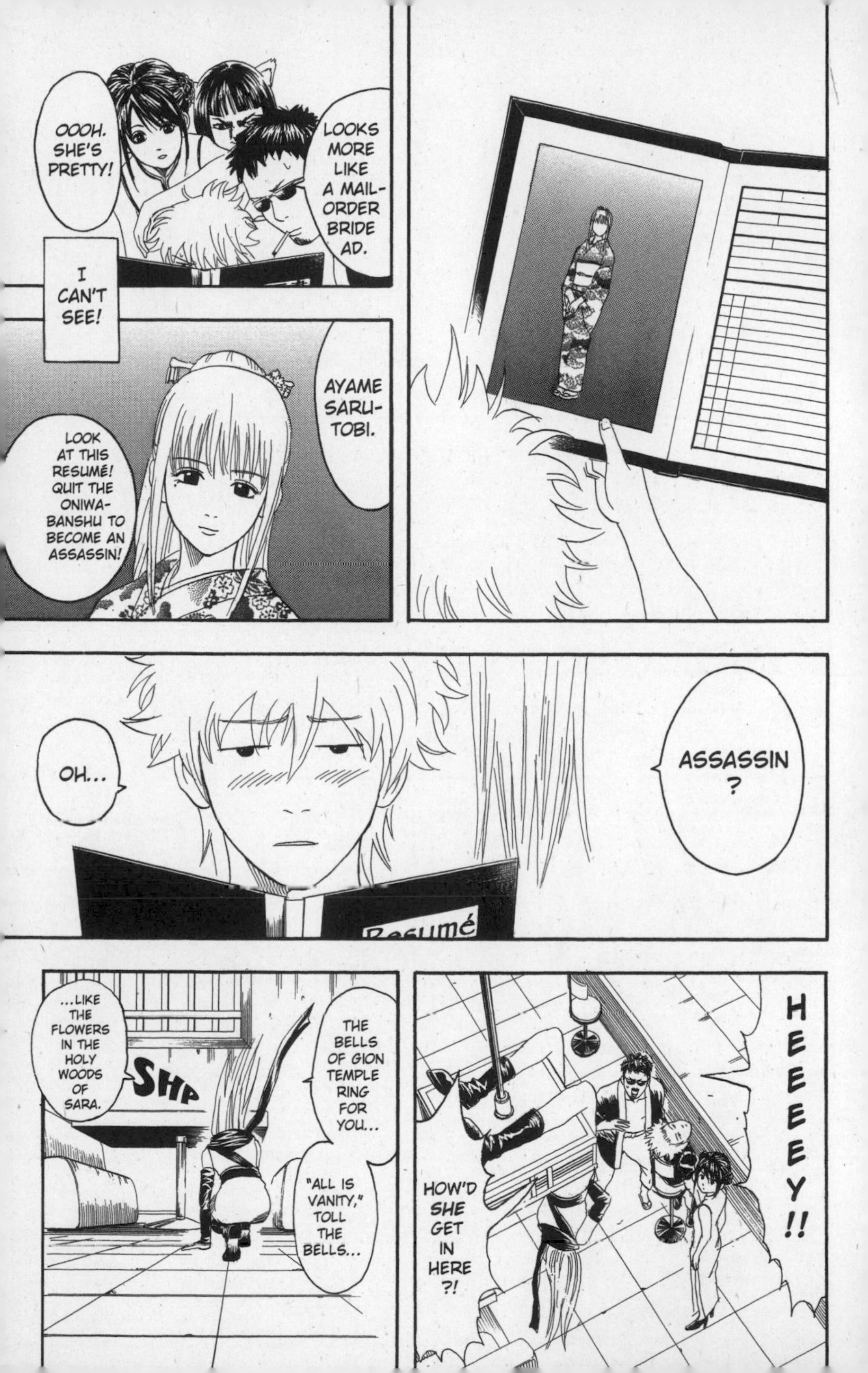
LOOKS MORE LIKE A MAIL-ORDER BRIDE AD.
OOOH. SHE'S PRETTY!
I CAN'T SEE!
AYAME SARUTOBI.
LOOK AT THIS RESUMÉ! QUIT THE ONIWABANSHU TO BECOME AN ASSASSIN!
ASSASSIN ?
OH...
Resumé
HEEEEEY!!
HOW'D SHE GET IN HERE ?!
THE BELLS OF GION TEMPLE RING FOR YOU...
...LIKE THE FLOWERS IN THE HOLY WOODS OF SARA.
SHP
"ALL IS VANITY," TOLL THE BELLS...

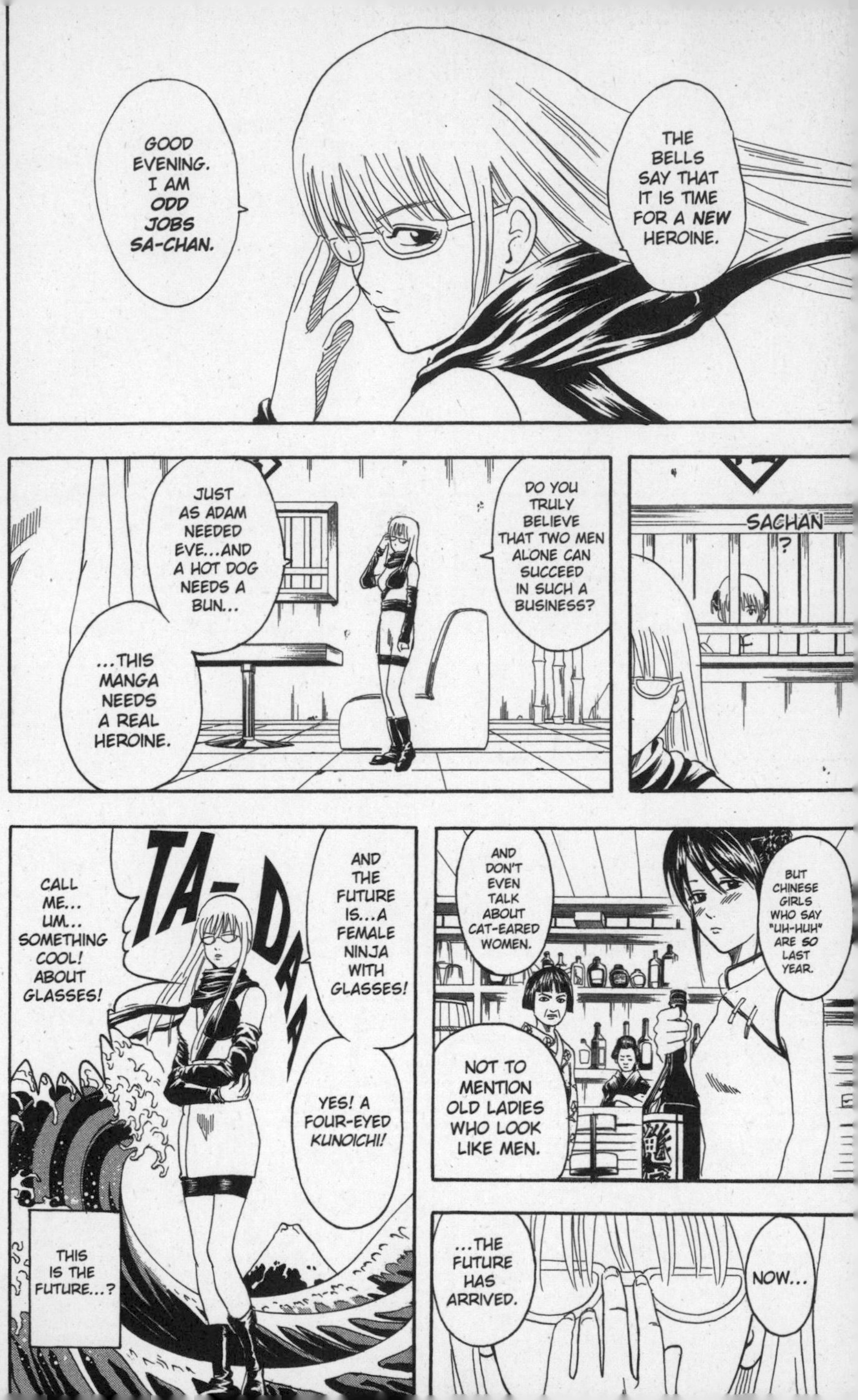
THE BELLS SAY THAT IT IS TIME FOR A NEW HEROINE.
GOOD EVENING. I AM ODD JOBS SA-CHAN.
SACHAN ?
DO YOU TRULY BELIEVE THAT TWO MEN ALONE CAN SUCCEED IN SUCH A BUSINESS?
JUST AS ADAM NEEDED EVE...AND A HOT DOG NEEDS A BUN...
...THIS MANGA NEEDS A REAL HEROINE.
BUT CHINESE GIRLS WHO SAY "UH-HUH" ARE SO LAST YEAR.
AND DON'T EVEN TALK ABOUT CAT-EARED WOMEN.
NOT TO MENTION OLD LADIES WHO LOOK LIKE MEN.
NOW...
...THE FUTURE HAS ARRIVED.
AND THE FUTURE IS...A FEMALE NINJA WITH GLASSES!
TA-DAA
YES! A FOUR-EYED KUNOICHI!
CALL ME... UM.. SOMETHING COOL! ABOUT GLASSES!
THIS IS THE FUTURE...?

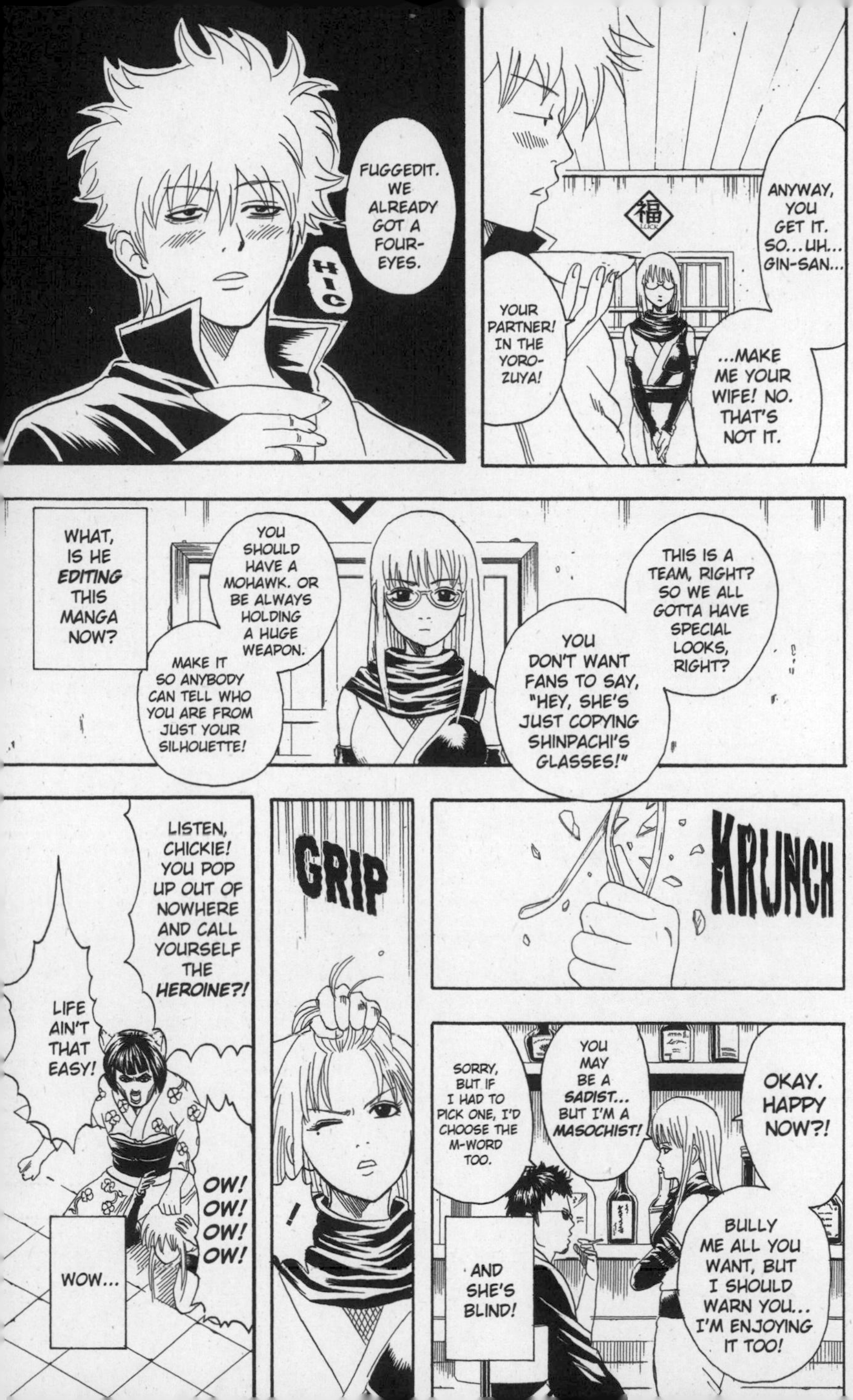
ANYWAY, YOU GET IT. SO...UH... GIN-SAN...
...MAKE ME YOUR WIFE! NO. THAT'S NOT IT.
YOUR PARTNER! IN THE YORO-ZUYA!
FUGGEDIT. WE ALREADY GOT A FOUR-EYES.
HIC
THIS IS A TEAM, RIGHT? SO WE ALL GOTTA HAVE SPECIAL LOOKS, RIGHT?
YOU DON'T WANT FANS TO SAY, "HEY, SHE'S JUST COPYING SHINPACHI'S GLASSES!"
YOU SHOULD HAVE A MOHAWK. OR BE ALWAYS HOLDING A HUGE WEAPON.
MAKE IT SO ANYBODY CAN TELL WHO YOU ARE FROM JUST YOUR SILHOUETTE!
WHAT, IS HE EDITING THIS MANGA NOW?
KRUNCH
OKAY. HAPPY NOW?!
BULLY ME ALL YOU WANT, BUT I SHOULD WARN YOU... I'M ENJOYING IT TOO!
YOU MAY BE A SADIST... BUT I'M A MASOCHIST!
SORRY, BUT IF I HAD TO PICK ONE, I'D CHOOSE THE M-WORD TOO.
AND SHE'S BLIND!
GRIP
!
LISTEN, CHICKIE! YOU POP UP OUT OF NOWHERE AND CALL YOURSELF THE HEROINE?!
LIFE AIN'T THAT EASY!
OW! OW! OW! OW!
WOW...

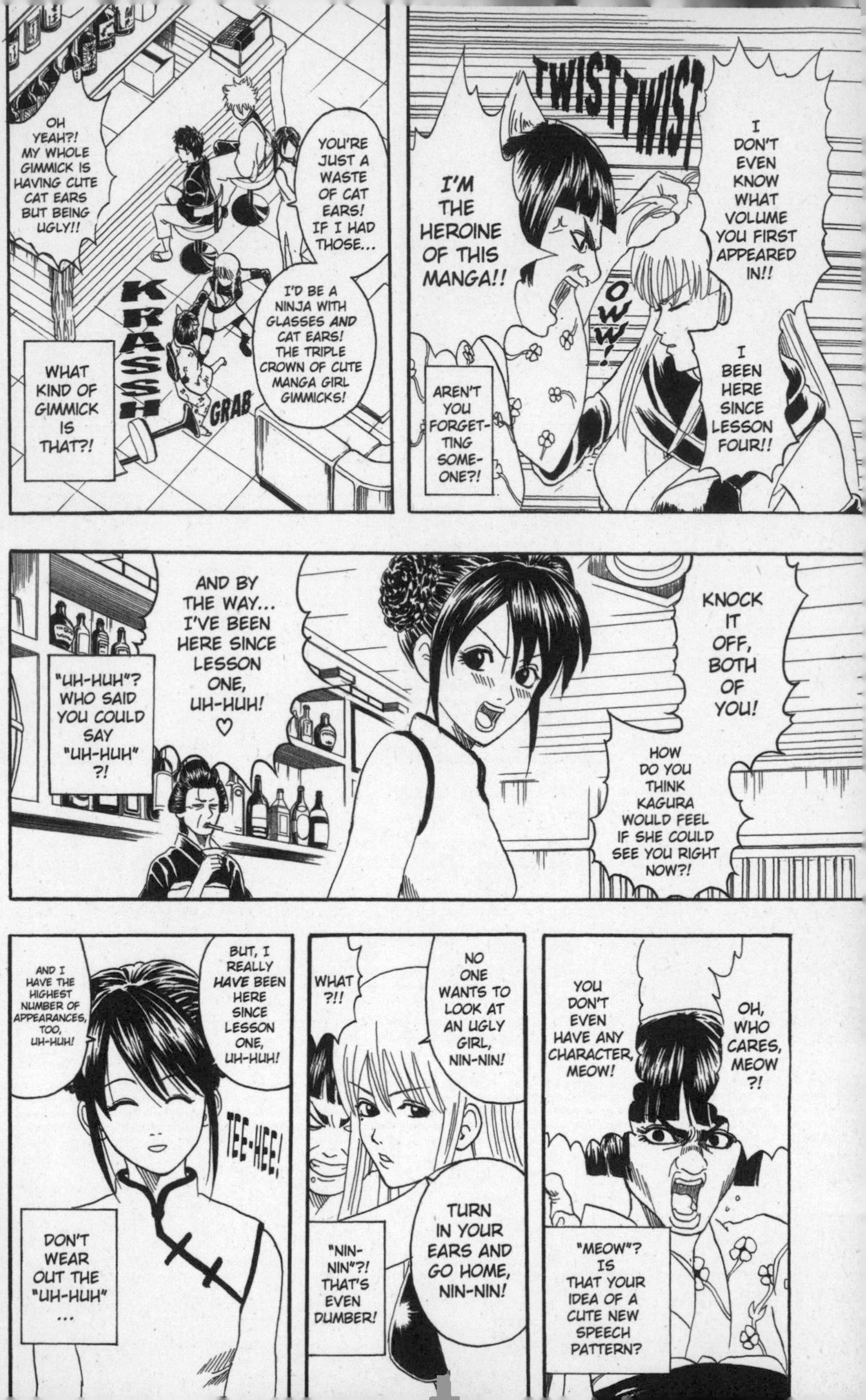
I DON'T EVEN KNOW WHAT VOLUME YOU FIRST APPEARED IN!!
TWIST TWIST
I'M THE HEROINE OF THIS MANGA!!
OWW!
I BEEN HERE SINCE LESSON FOUR!!
AREN'T YOU FORGETTING SOMEONE?!
YOU'RE JUST A WASTE OF CAT EARS! IF I HAD THOSE...
I'D BE A NINJA WITH GLASSES AND CAT EARS! THE TRIPLE CROWN OF CUTE MANGA GIRL GIMMICKS!
OH YEAH?! MY WHOLE GIMMICK IS HAVING CUTE CAT EARS BUT BEING UGLY!!
KRASSH
GRAB
WHAT KIND OF GIMMICK IS THAT?!
KNOCK IT OFF, BOTH OF YOU!
HOW DO YOU THINK KAGURA WOULD FEEL IF SHE COULD SEE YOU RIGHT NOW?!
AND BY THE WAY... I'VE BEEN HERE SINCE LESSON ONE, UH-HUH! ♡
"UH-HUH"? WHO SAID YOU COULD SAY "UH-HUH"?!
OH, WHO CARES, MEOW?!
YOU DON'T EVEN HAVE ANY CHARACTER, MEOW!
"MEOW"? IS THAT YOUR IDEA OF A CUTE NEW SPEECH PATTERN?
NO ONE WANTS TO LOOK AT AN UGLY GIRL, NIN-NIN!
WHAT?!!
TURN IN YOUR EARS AND GO HOME, NIN-NIN!
"NIN-NIN"?! THAT'S EVEN DUMBER!
BUT, I REALLY HAVE BEEN HERE SINCE LESSON ONE, UH-HUH!
AND I HAVE THE HIGHEST NUMBER OF APPEARANCES, TOO, UH-HUH!
TEE-HEE!
DON'T WEAR OUT THE "UH-HUH"...

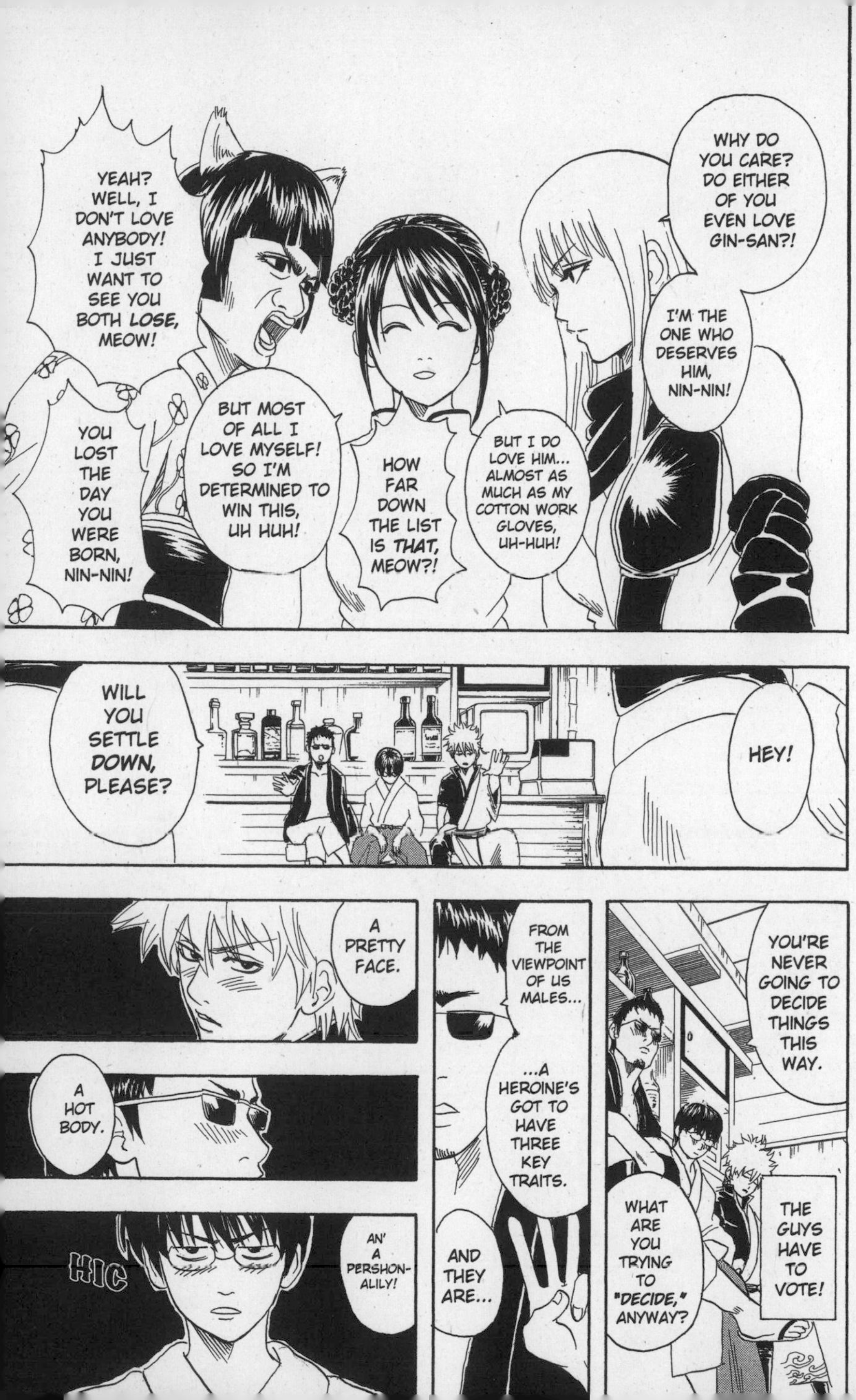
WHY DO YOU CARE? DO EITHER OF YOU EVEN LOVE GIN-SAN?!
I'M THE ONE WHO DESERVES HIM, NIN-NIN!
BUT I DO LOVE HIM... ALMOST AS MUCH AS MY COTTON WORK GLOVES, UH-HUH!
HOW FAR DOWN THE LIST IS THAT, MEOW?!
BUT MOST OF ALL I LOVE MYSELF! SO I'M DETERMINED TO WIN THIS, UH HUH!
YEAH? WELL, I DON'T LOVE ANYBODY! I JUST WANT TO SEE YOU BOTH LOSE, MEOW!
YOU LOST THE DAY YOU WERE BORN, NIN-NIN!
HEY!
WILL YOU SETTLE DOWN, PLEASE?
YOU'RE NEVER GOING TO DECIDE THINGS THIS WAY.
THE GUYS HAVE TO VOTE!
WHAT ARE YOU TRYING TO "DECIDE," ANYWAY?
FROM THE VIEWPOINT OF US MALES...
...A HEROINE'S GOT TO HAVE THREE KEY TRAITS.
AND THEY ARE...
A PRETTY FACE.
A HOT BODY.
AN' A PERSHON-ALILY!
HIC

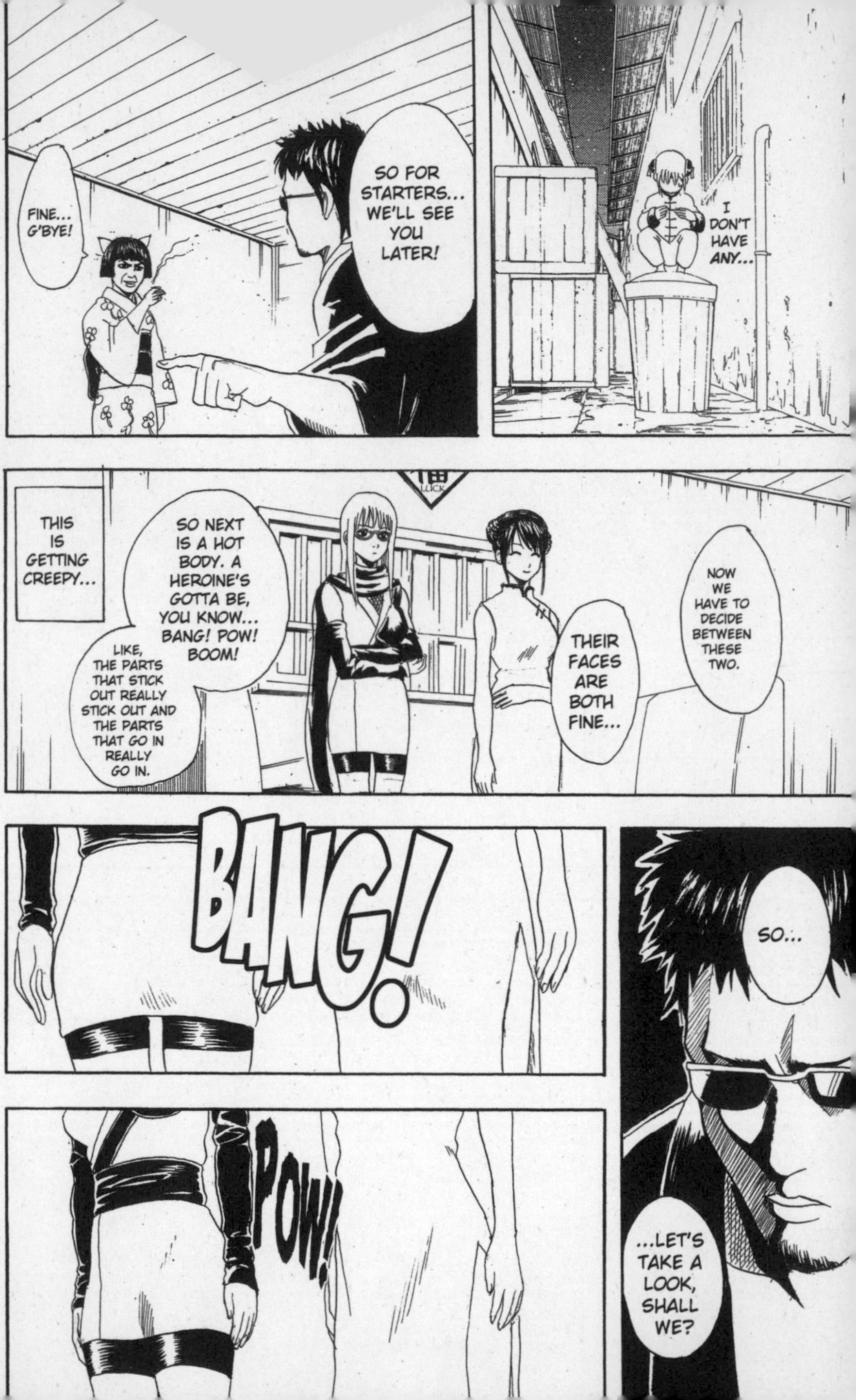
I DON'T HAVE ANY...
SO FOR STARTERS... WE'LL SEE YOU LATER!
FINE... G'BYE!
NOW WE HAVE TO DECIDE BETWEEN THESE TWO.
THEIR FACES ARE BOTH FINE...
SO NEXT IS A HOT BODY. A HEROINE'S GOTTA BE, YOU KNOW... BANG! POW! BOOM!
LIKE, THE PARTS THAT STICK OUT REALLY STICK OUT AND THE PARTS THAT GO IN REALLY GO IN.
THIS IS GETTING CREEPY...
SO...
...LET'S TAKE A LOOK, SHALL WE?
BANG!
POW!

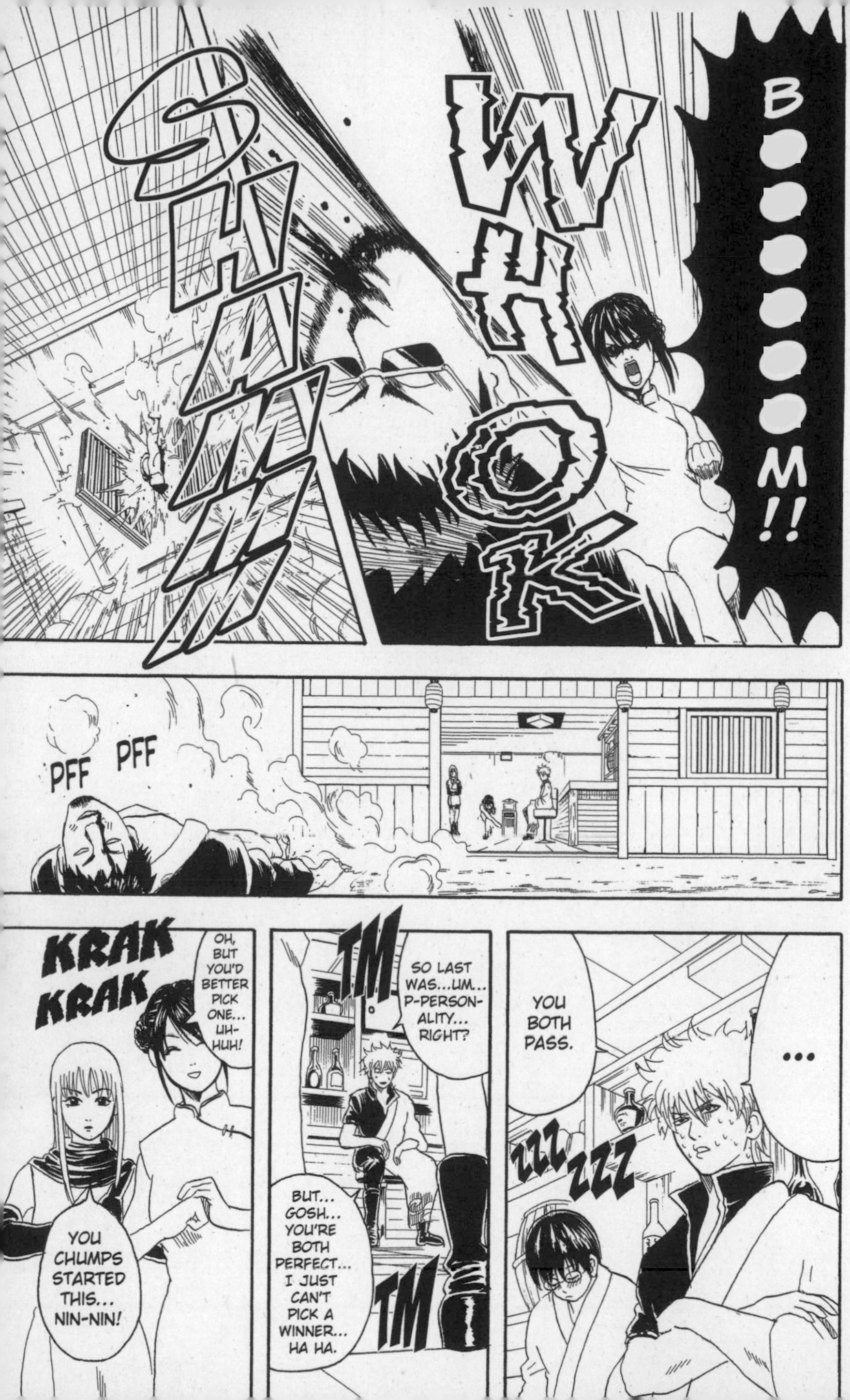
BOOOOOOOM!!
WHOK
SHAM!!
PFF PFF
...
YOU BOTH PASS.
ZZZ ZZZ
TM
SO LAST WAS...UM... P-PERSONALITY... RIGHT?
BUT... GOSH... YOU'RE BOTH PERFECT... I JUST CAN'T PICK A WINNER... HA HA.
TM
OH, BUT YOU'D BETTER PICK ONE... UH-HUH!
KRAK KRAK
YOU CHUMPS STARTED THIS... NIN-NIN!

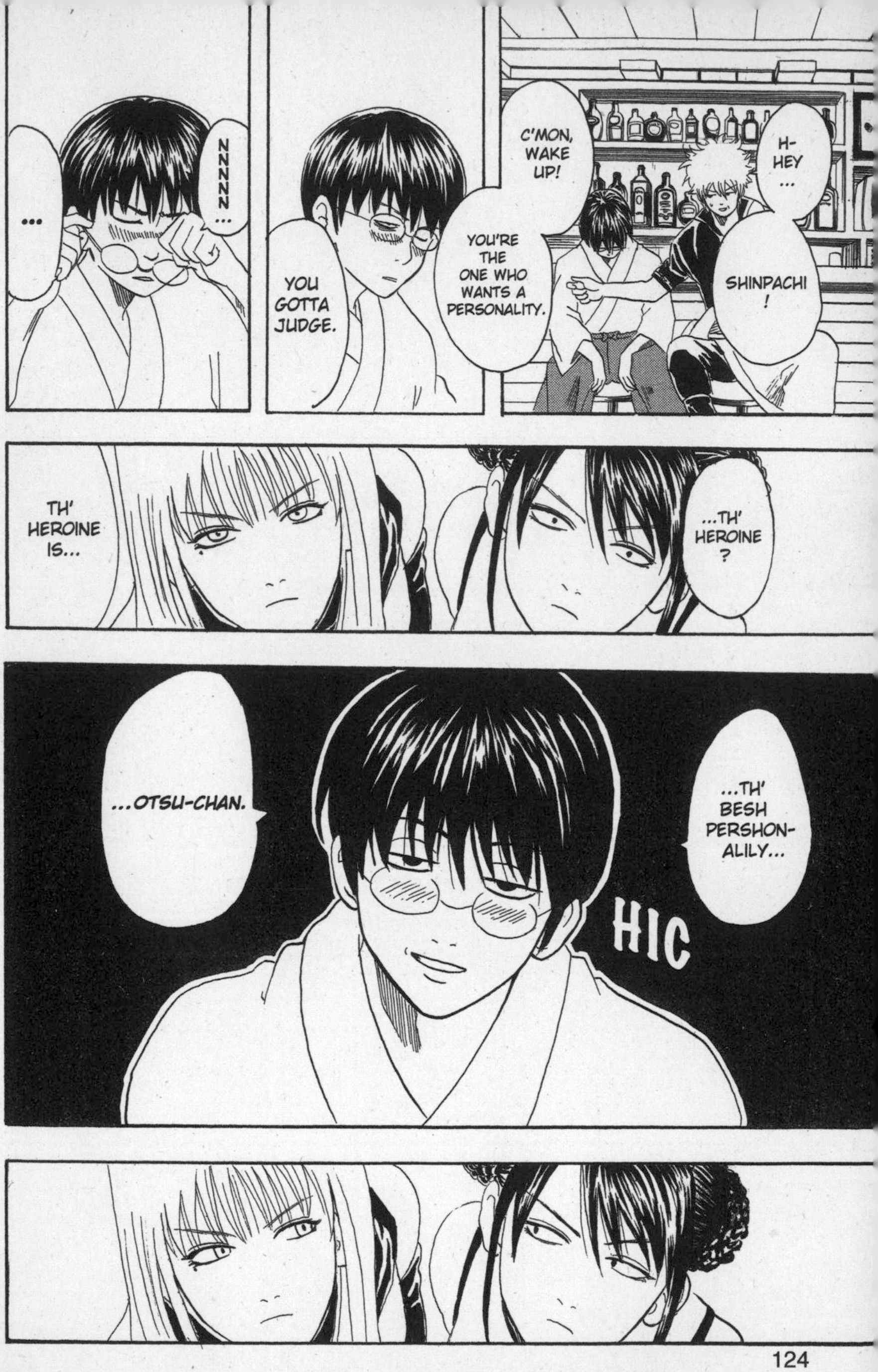
H-HEY...
SHINPACHI!
C'MON, WAKE UP!
YOU'RE THE ONE WHO WANTS A PERSONALITY.
YOU GOTTA JUDGE.
NNNNN...
...
...TH' HEROINE?
TH' HEROINE IS...
...TH' BESH PERSHON-ALILY...
...OTSU-CHAN.
HIC

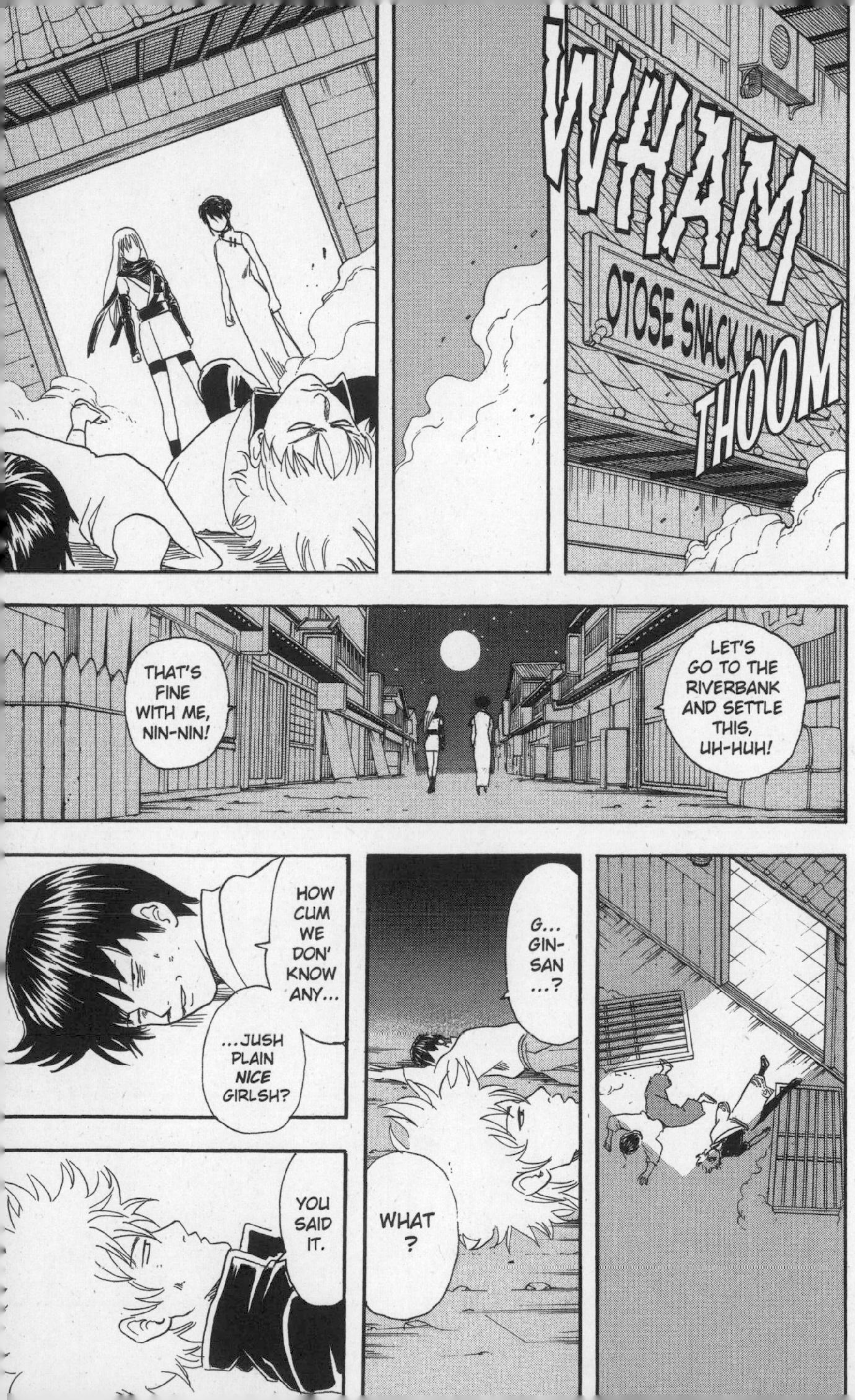
WHAM
OTOSE SNACK HOU
THOOM
LET'S GO TO THE RIVERBANK AND SETTLE THIS, UH-HUH!
THAT'S FINE WITH ME, NIN-NIN!
G... GIN-SAN ...?
WHAT ?
HOW CUM WE DON' KNOW ANY...
...JUSH PLAIN NICE GIRLSH?
YOU SAID IT.

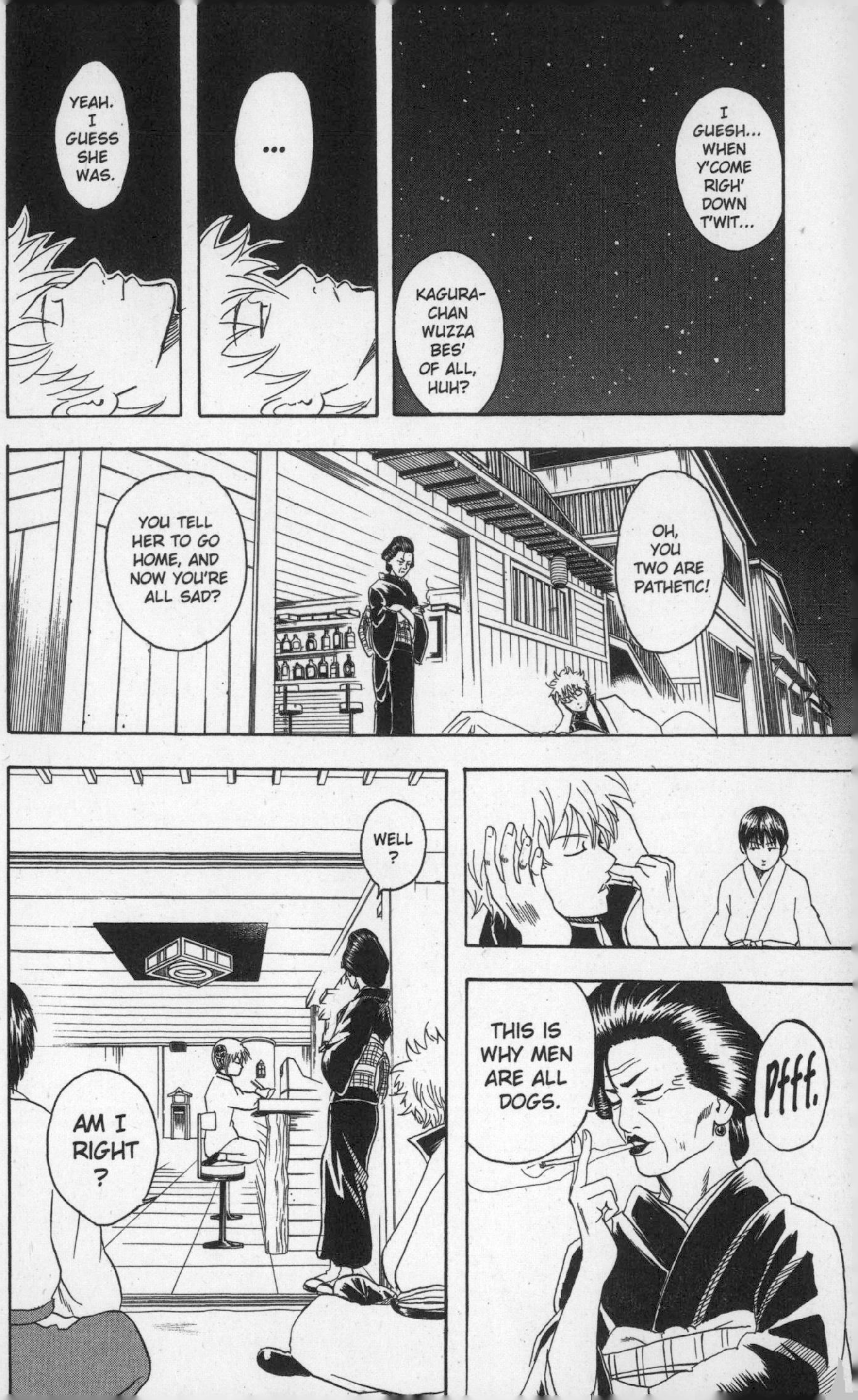
I GUESH... WHEN Y'COME RIGH' DOWN T'WIT...
KAGURA-CHAN WUZZA BES' OF ALL, HUH?
...
YEAH. I GUESS SHE WAS.
OH, YOU TWO ARE PATHETIC!
YOU TELL HER TO GO HOME, AND NOW YOU'RE ALL SAD?
Pfff.
THIS IS WHY MEN ARE ALL DOGS.
WELL ?
AM I RIGHT ?

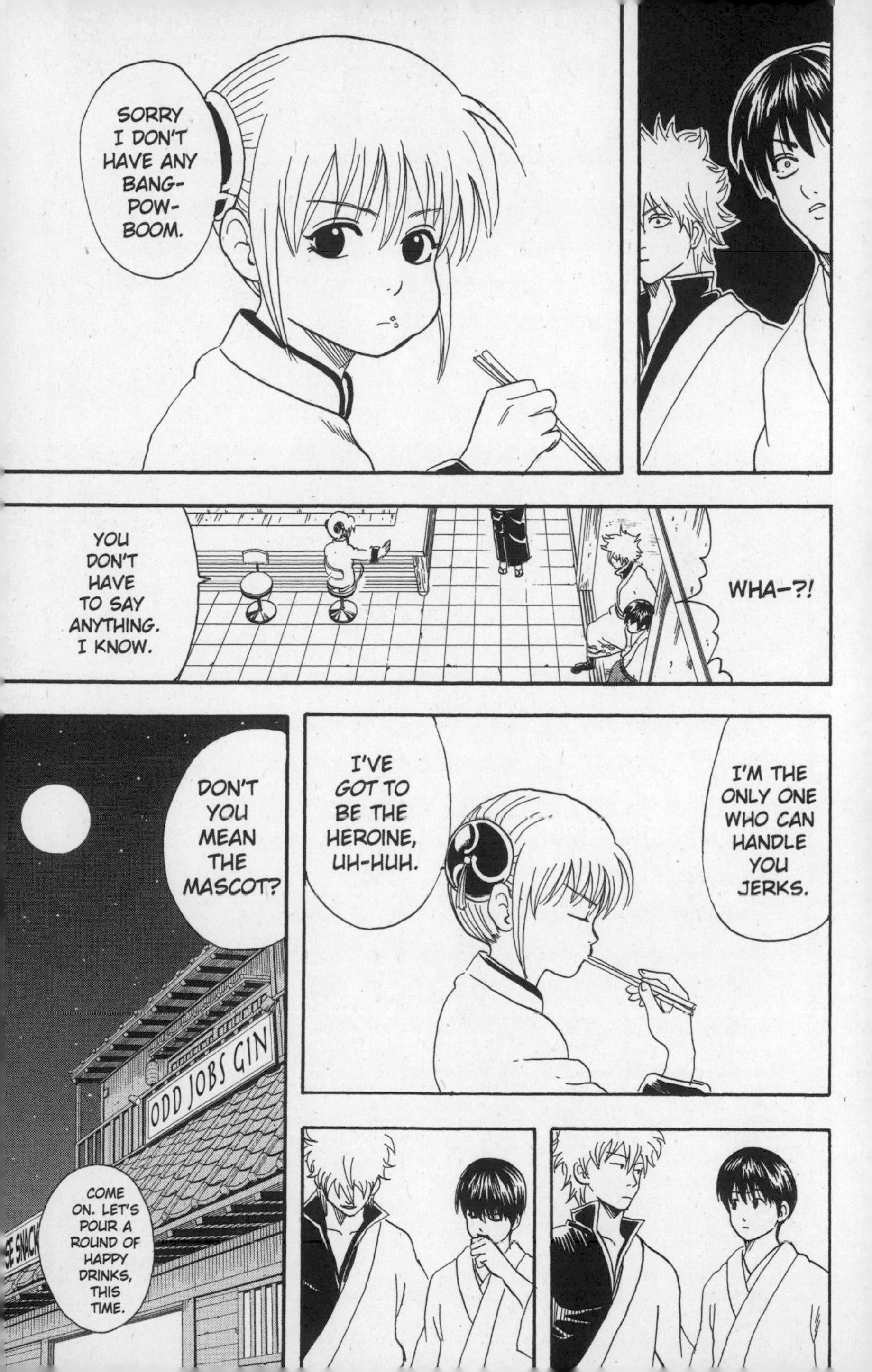
SORRY I DON'T HAVE ANY BANG-POW-BOOM.
WHA-?!
YOU DON'T HAVE TO SAY ANYTHING. I KNOW.
I'M THE ONLY ONE WHO CAN HANDLE YOU JERKS.
I'VE GOT TO BE THE HEROINE, UH-HUH.
DON'T YOU MEAN THE MASCOT?
ODD JOBS GIN
SE SNACK
COME ON. LET'S POUR A ROUND OF HAPPY DRINKS, THIS TIME.

Sorachi's Q&A Corner #17

<From "Down-pointing eyelashes are supposed to protect the eyeball but are hurting it instead which is just proof that the person's DNA sucks!" -san of Saitama prefecture>

I have a question. Lord Zura's cosplay: is that really his hobby? It keeps going through my mind. It goes through my mind so much I'm going to fail my exams.

<Answer>

The rebel Zura is modeled after Katsura Kogoro, who was called "Runaway Kogoro" because he used all kinds of tricks and disguises to elude the Shinsengumi. Even though a lot of the rebels from that era died from assassination or in battle, Kogoro lived on for years afterward. Samurai are obsessed with appearances. They're the kind of guys who'll walk right up and go, "You Shinsengumi are losers," and get killed, so I fell in love with the image of a special case who, when he runs away, would do it single-mindedly, giving it his all. So that's how Zura turned out like that. Though with Zura it's not camouflage. He seems to be having fun doing it too, doesn't he?

(Q&A #18 is on page 148)

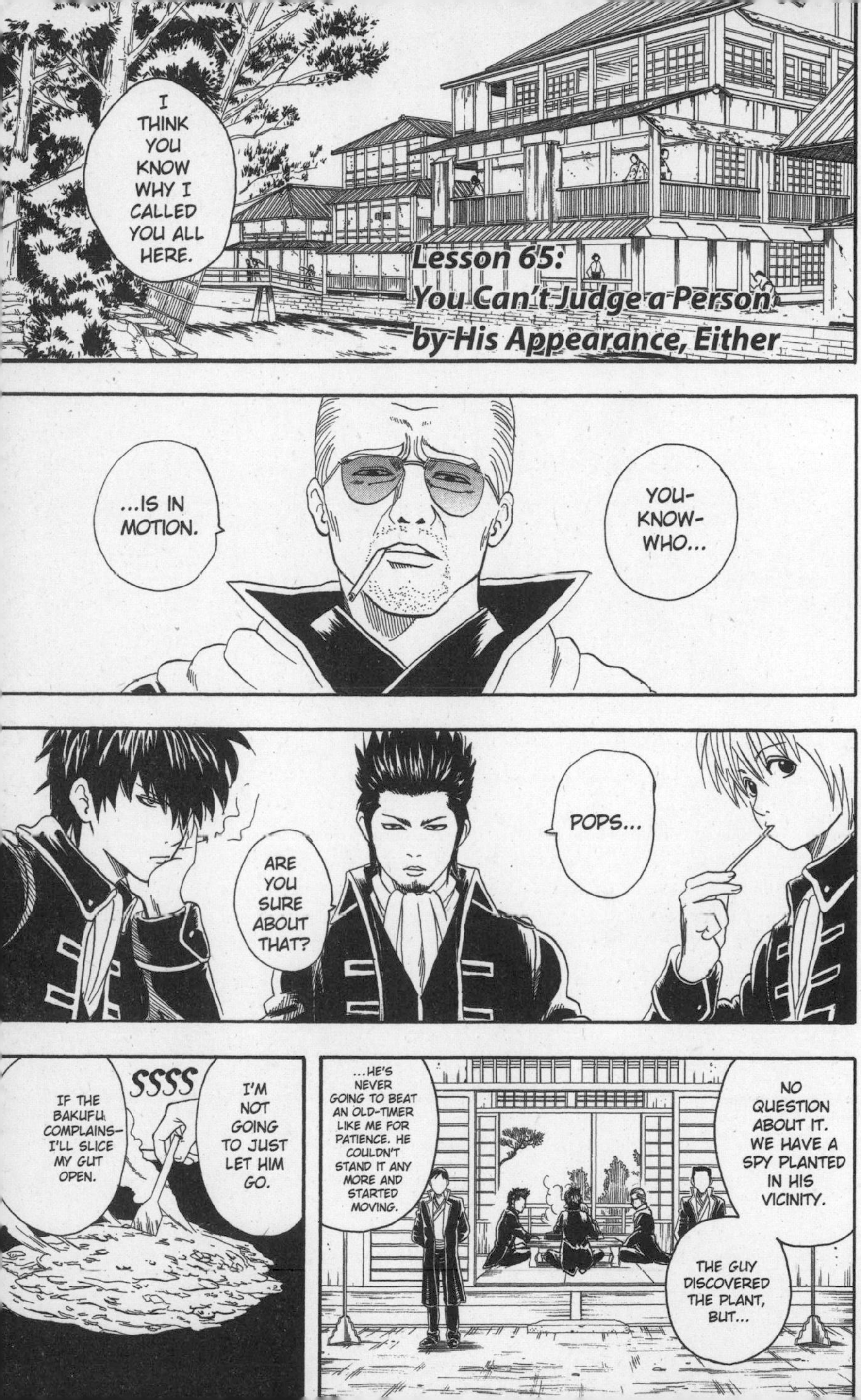
Lesson 65: You Can't Judge a Person by His Appearance, Either
I THINK YOU KNOW WHY I CALLED YOU ALL HERE.
YOU-KNOW-WHO...
...IS IN MOTION.
POPS...
ARE YOU SURE ABOUT THAT?
NO QUESTION ABOUT IT. WE HAVE A SPY PLANTED IN HIS VICINITY.
THE GUY DISCOVERED THE PLANT, BUT...
...HE'S NEVER GOING TO BEAT AN OLD-TIMER LIKE ME FOR PATIENCE. HE COULDN'T STAND IT ANY MORE AND STARTED MOVING.
SSSS
I'M NOT GOING TO JUST LET HIM GO.
IF THE BAKUFU COMPLAINS— I'LL SLICE MY GUT OPEN.

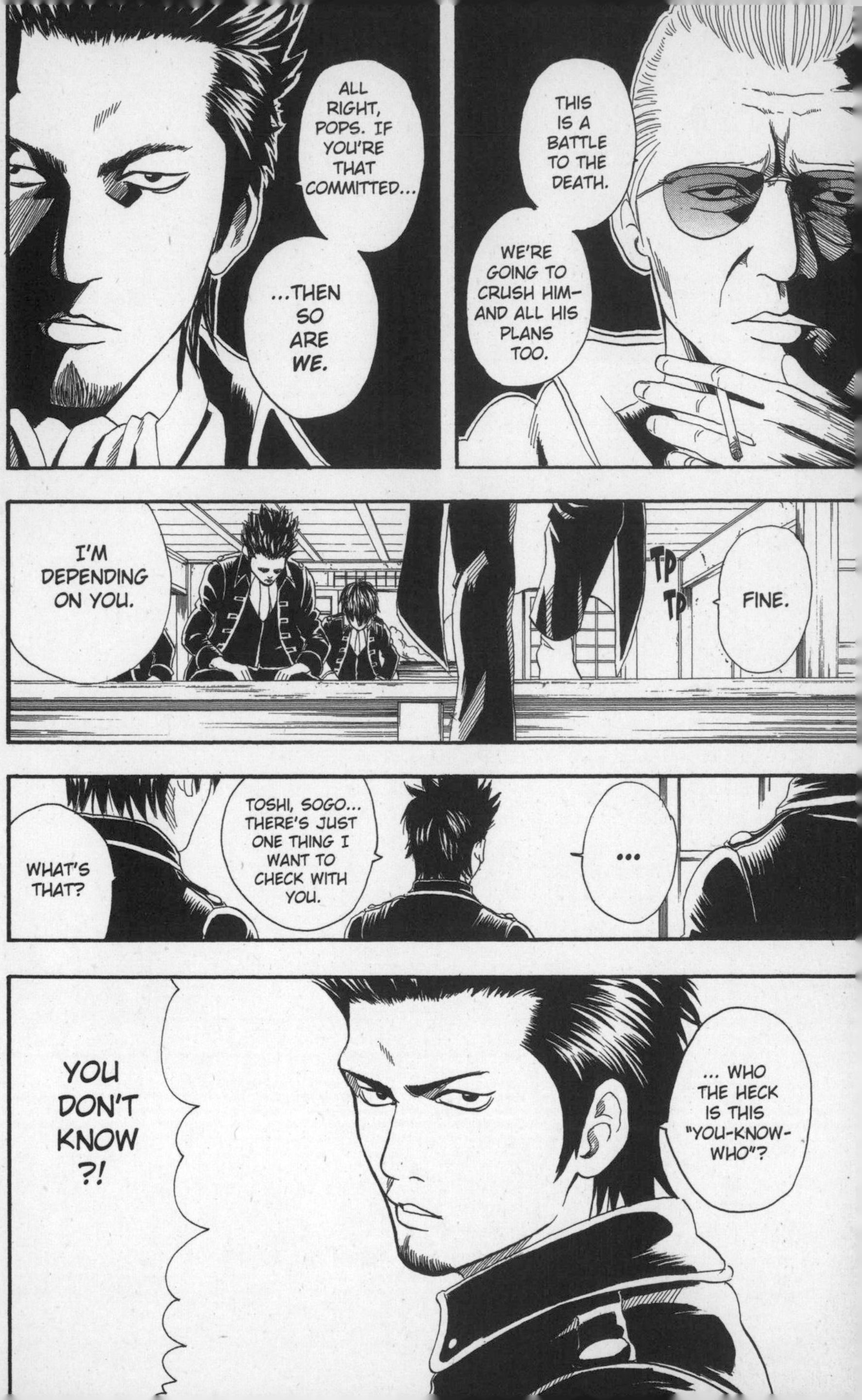
THIS IS A BATTLE TO THE DEATH.
WE'RE GOING TO CRUSH HIM—AND ALL HIS PLANS TOO.
ALL RIGHT, POPS. IF YOU'RE THAT COMMITTED...
...THEN SO ARE WE.
TP TP
FINE.
I'M DEPENDING ON YOU.
...
TOSHI, SOGO... THERE'S JUST ONE THING I WANT TO CHECK WITH YOU.
WHAT'S THAT?
... WHO THE HECK IS THIS "YOU-KNOW-WHO"?
YOU DON'T KNOW ?!

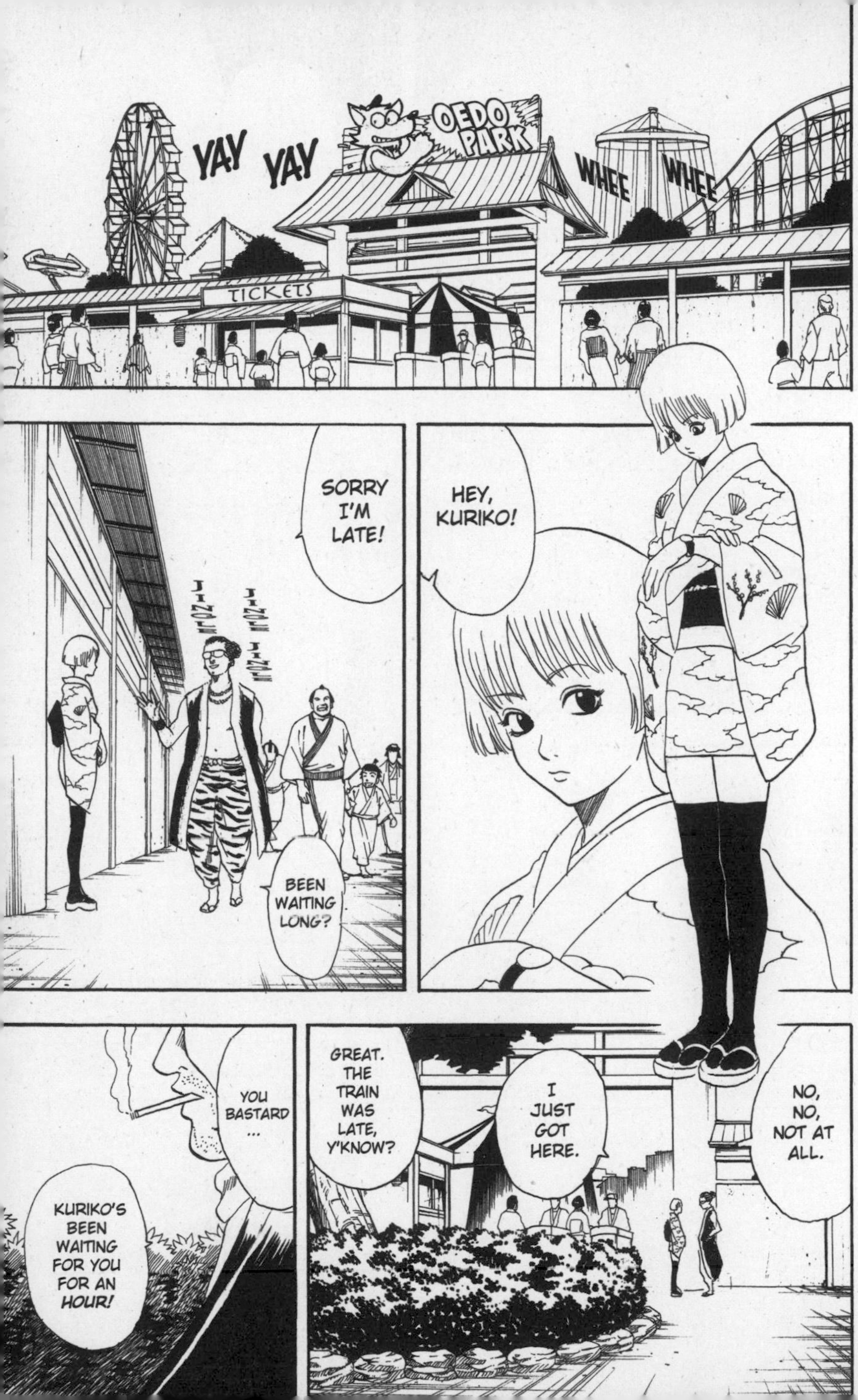
WHEE WHEE
OEDO PARK
YAY YAY
TICKETS
HEY, KURIKO!
SORRY I'M LATE!
JINGLE JINGLE JINGLE
BEEN WAITING LONG?
NO, NO, NOT AT ALL.
I JUST GOT HERE.
GREAT. THE TRAIN WAS LATE, Y'KNOW?
YOU BASTARD...
KURIKO'S BEEN WAITING FOR YOU FOR AN HOUR!

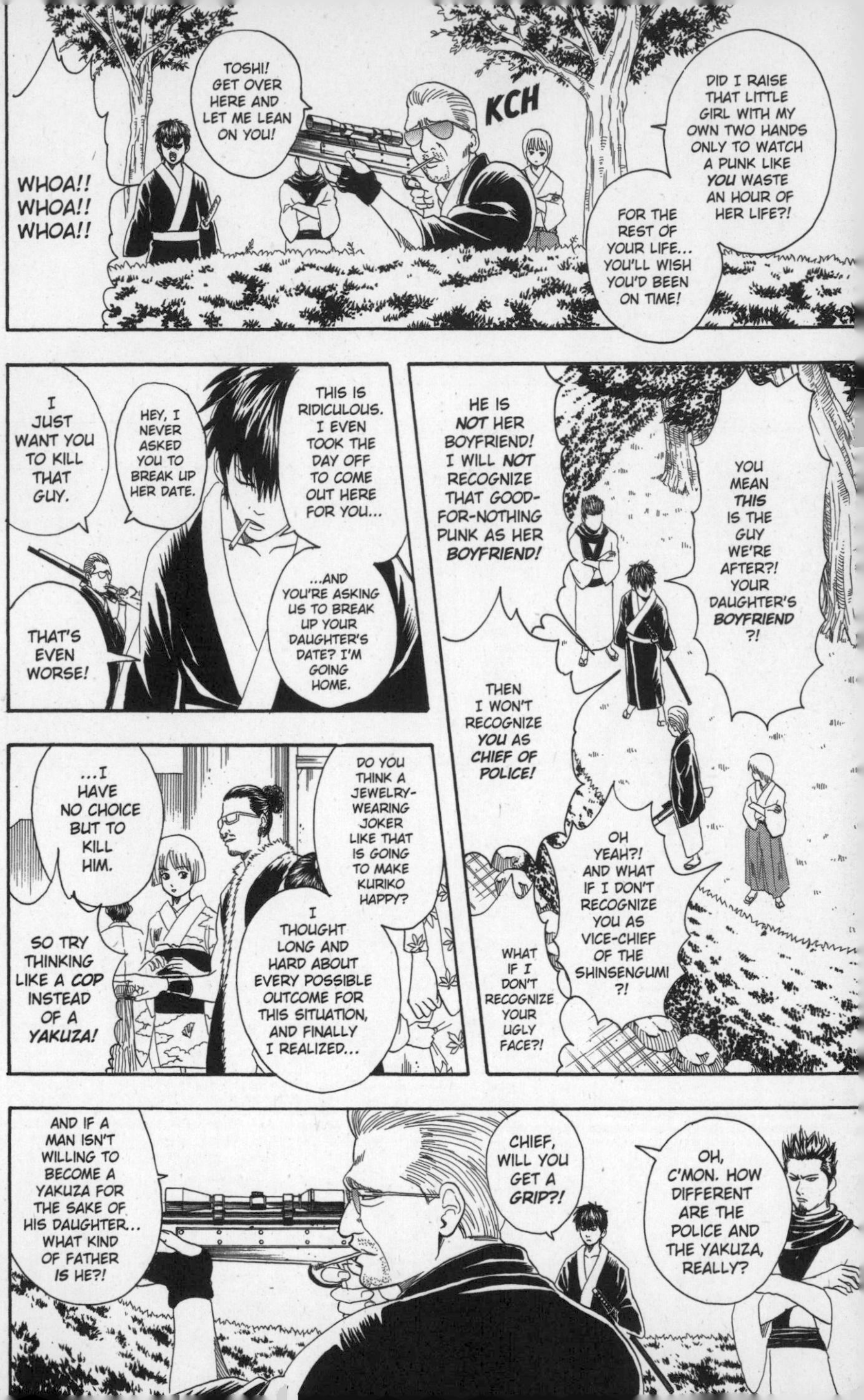
DID I RAISE THAT LITTLE GIRL WITH MY OWN TWO HANDS ONLY TO WATCH A PUNK LIKE *YOU* WASTE AN HOUR OF HER LIFE?!
FOR THE REST OF YOUR LIFE... YOU'LL WISH YOU'D BEEN ON TIME!
KCH
TOSHI! GET OVER HERE AND LET ME LEAN ON YOU!
WHOA!! WHOA!! WHOA!!
YOU MEAN *THIS* IS THE GUY WE'RE AFTER?! YOUR DAUGHTER'S *BOYFRIEND* ?!
HE IS *NOT* HER BOYFRIEND! I WILL *NOT* RECOGNIZE THAT GOOD-FOR-NOTHING PUNK AS HER *BOYFRIEND!*
THEN I WON'T RECOGNIZE *YOU* AS *CHIEF OF POLICE!*
OH YEAH?! AND WHAT IF I DON'T RECOGNIZE YOU AS VICE-CHIEF OF THE SHINSENGUMI ?!
WHAT IF I DON'T RECOGNIZE YOUR UGLY FACE?!
THIS IS RIDICULOUS. I EVEN TOOK THE DAY OFF TO COME OUT HERE FOR YOU...
...AND YOU'RE ASKING US TO BREAK UP YOUR DAUGHTER'S DATE? I'M GOING HOME.
HEY, I NEVER ASKED YOU TO BREAK UP HER DATE.
I JUST WANT YOU TO KILL THAT GUY.
THAT'S EVEN WORSE!
DO YOU THINK A JEWELRY-WEARING JOKER LIKE THAT IS GOING TO MAKE KURIKO HAPPY?
I THOUGHT LONG AND HARD ABOUT EVERY POSSIBLE OUTCOME FOR THIS SITUATION, AND FINALLY I REALIZED...
...I HAVE NO CHOICE BUT TO KILL HIM.
SO TRY THINKING LIKE A *COP* INSTEAD OF A *YAKUZA!*
AND IF A MAN ISN'T WILLING TO BECOME A YAKUZA FOR THE SAKE OF HIS DAUGHTER... WHAT KIND OF FATHER *IS* HE?!
CHIEF, WILL YOU GET A *GRIP?!*
OH, C'MON. HOW DIFFERENT ARE THE POLICE AND THE YAKUZA, REALLY?

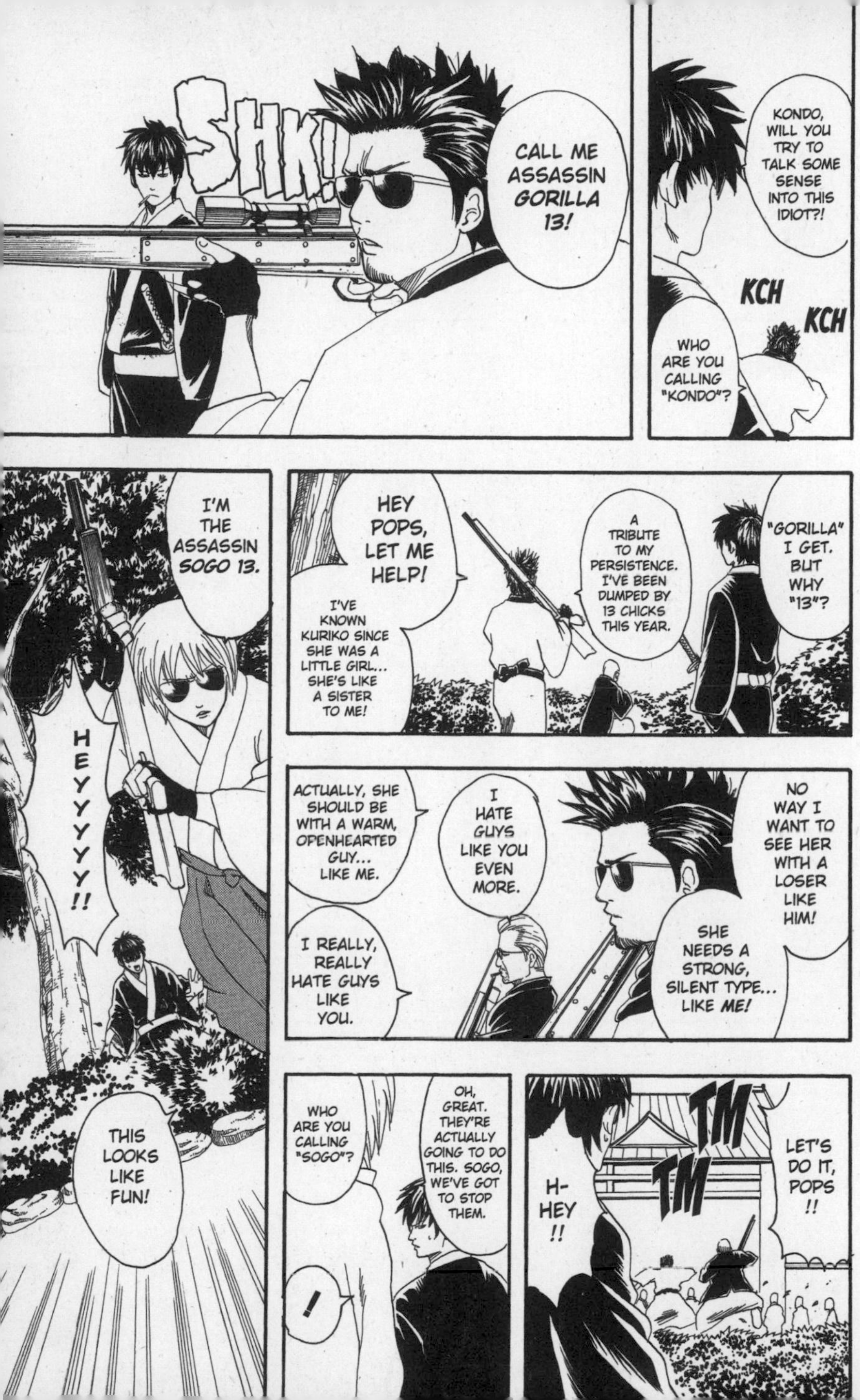
KONDO, WILL YOU TRY TO TALK SOME SENSE INTO THIS IDIOT?!
KCH
KCH
WHO ARE YOU CALLING "KONDO"?
CALL ME ASSASSIN GORILLA 13!
SHK!
"GORILLA" I GET. BUT WHY "13"?
A TRIBUTE TO MY PERSISTENCE. I'VE BEEN DUMPED BY 13 CHICKS THIS YEAR.
HEY POPS, LET ME HELP!
I'VE KNOWN KURIKO SINCE SHE WAS A LITTLE GIRL... SHE'S LIKE A SISTER TO ME!
NO WAY I WANT TO SEE HER WITH A LOSER LIKE HIM!
SHE NEEDS A STRONG, SILENT TYPE... LIKE ME!
I HATE GUYS LIKE YOU EVEN MORE.
ACTUALLY, SHE SHOULD BE WITH A WARM, OPENHEARTED GUY... LIKE ME.
I REALLY, REALLY HATE GUYS LIKE YOU.
I'M THE ASSASSIN SOGO 13.
HEYYYYYY!!
THIS LOOKS LIKE FUN!
TM
TM
LET'S DO IT, POPS!!
H-HEY!!
OH, GREAT. THEY'RE ACTUALLY GOING TO DO THIS. SOGO, WE'VE GOT TO STOP THEM.
WHO ARE YOU CALLING "SOGO"?
!

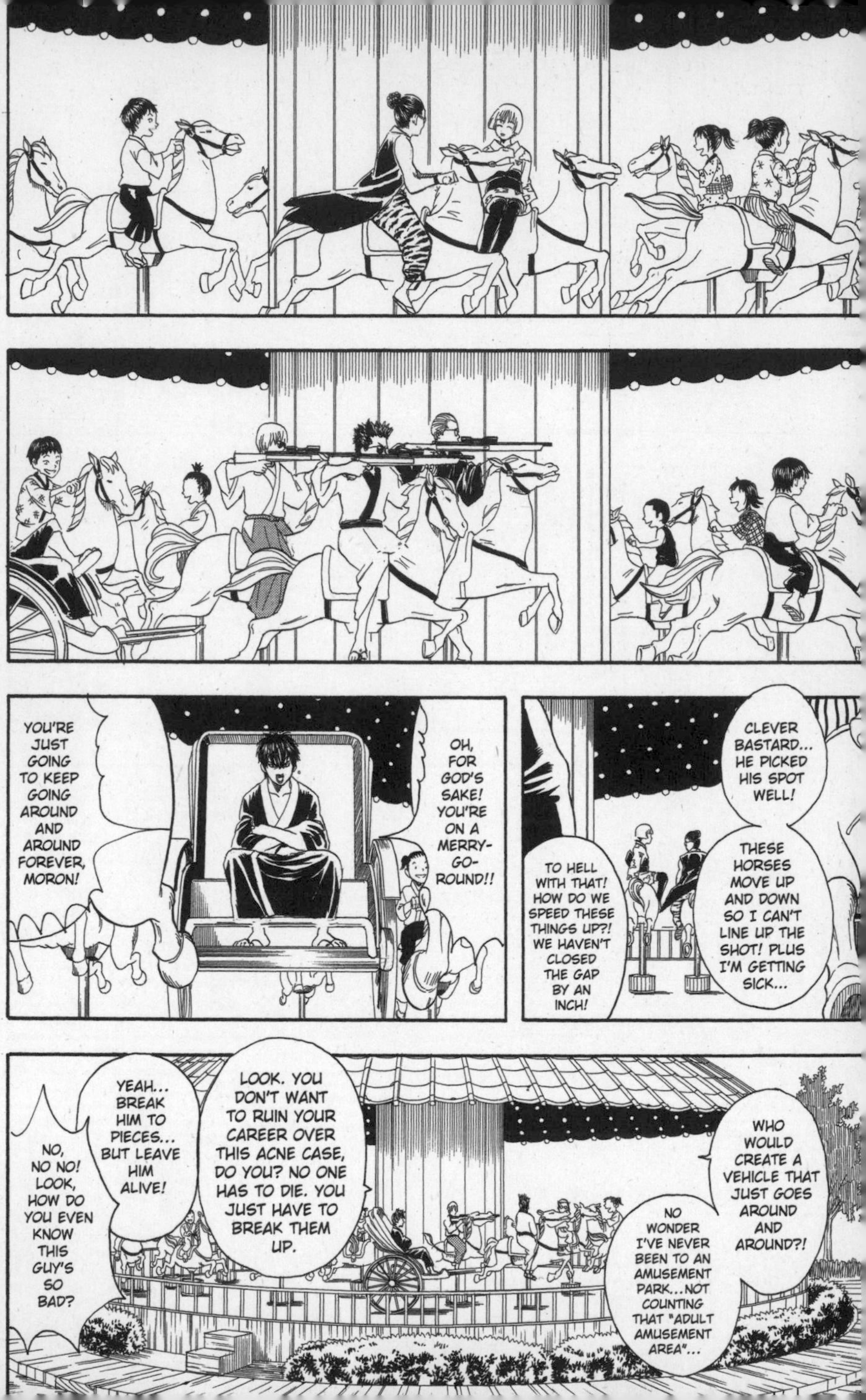
CLEVER BASTARD... HE PICKED HIS SPOT WELL!
THESE HORSES MOVE UP AND DOWN SO I CAN'T LINE UP THE SHOT! PLUS I'M GETTING SICK...
TO HELL WITH THAT! HOW DO WE SPEED THESE THINGS UP?! WE HAVEN'T CLOSED THE GAP BY AN INCH!
OH, FOR GOD'S SAKE! YOU'RE ON A MERRY-GO-ROUND!!
YOU'RE JUST GOING TO KEEP GOING AROUND AND AROUND FOREVER, MORON!
WHO WOULD CREATE A VEHICLE THAT JUST GOES AROUND AND AROUND?!
NO WONDER I'VE NEVER BEEN TO AN AMUSEMENT PARK...NOT COUNTING THAT "ADULT AMUSEMENT AREA"...
LOOK. YOU DON'T WANT TO RUIN YOUR CAREER OVER THIS ACNE CASE, DO YOU? NO ONE HAS TO DIE. YOU JUST HAVE TO BREAK THEM UP.
YEAH... BREAK HIM TO PIECES... BUT LEAVE HIM ALIVE!
NO, NO NO! LOOK, HOW DO YOU EVEN KNOW THIS GUY'S SO BAD?

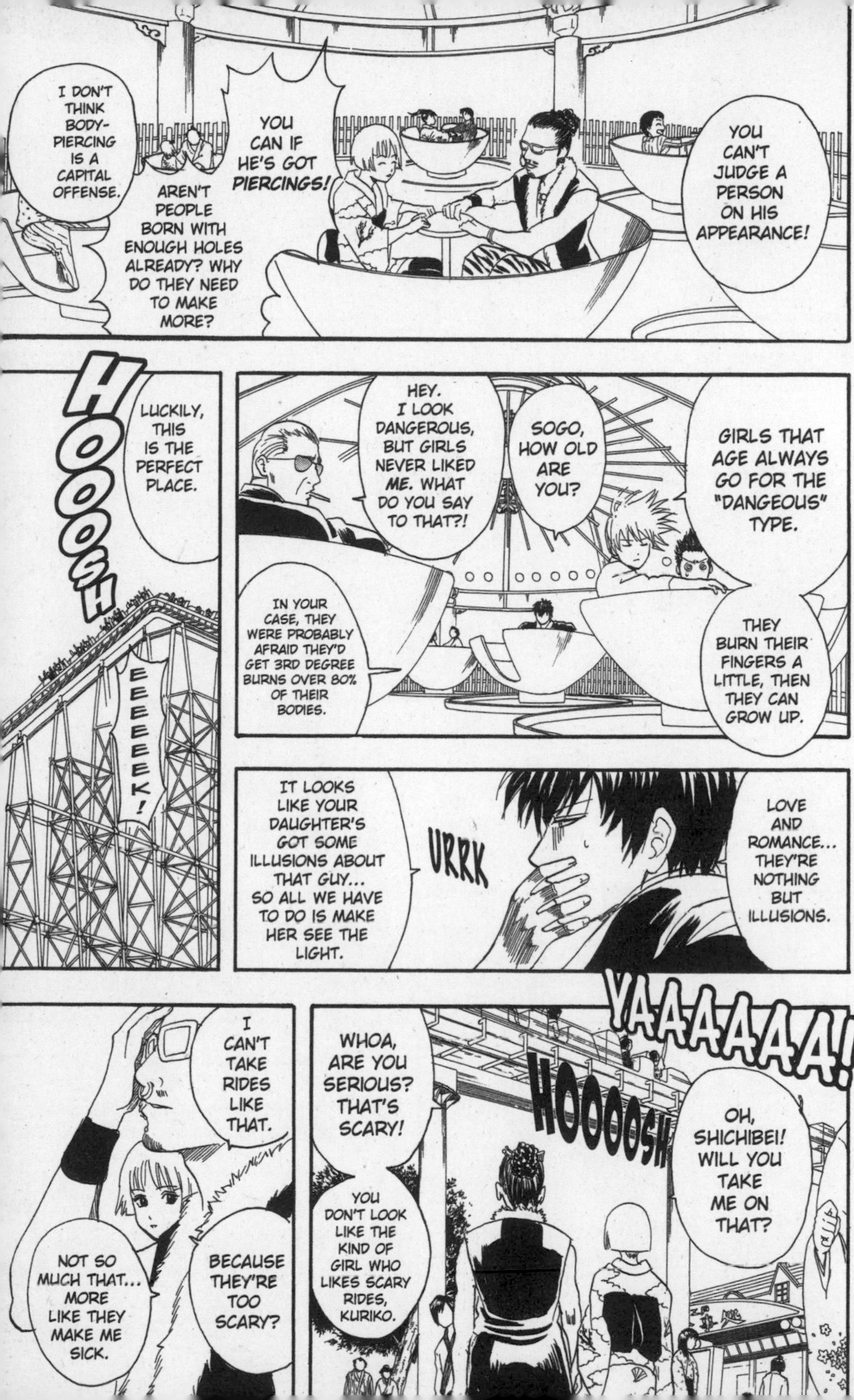
YOU CAN'T JUDGE A PERSON ON HIS APPEARANCE!
YOU CAN IF HE'S GOT PIERCINGS!
I DON'T THINK BODY-PIERCING IS A CAPITAL OFFENSE.
AREN'T PEOPLE BORN WITH ENOUGH HOLES ALREADY? WHY DO THEY NEED TO MAKE MORE?
GIRLS THAT AGE ALWAYS GO FOR THE "DANGEOUS" TYPE.
SOGO, HOW OLD ARE YOU?
HEY. I LOOK DANGEROUS, BUT GIRLS NEVER LIKED ME. WHAT DO YOU SAY TO THAT?!
THEY BURN THEIR FINGERS A LITTLE, THEN THEY CAN GROW UP.
IN YOUR CASE, THEY WERE PROBABLY AFRAID THEY'D GET 3RD DEGREE BURNS OVER 80% OF THEIR BODIES.
LOVE AND ROMANCE... THEY'RE NOTHING BUT ILLUSIONS.
URRK
IT LOOKS LIKE YOUR DAUGHTER'S GOT SOME ILLUSIONS ABOUT THAT GUY... SO ALL WE HAVE TO DO IS MAKE HER SEE THE LIGHT.
HOOOOSH
LUCKILY, THIS IS THE PERFECT PLACE.
EEEEEEEK!
YAAAAAAA!
HOOOOSH
OH, SHICHIBEI! WILL YOU TAKE ME ON THAT?
WHOA, ARE YOU SERIOUS? THAT'S SCARY!
YOU DON'T LOOK LIKE THE KIND OF GIRL WHO LIKES SCARY RIDES, KURIKO.
I CAN'T TAKE RIDES LIKE THAT.
BECAUSE THEY'RE TOO SCARY?
NOT SO MUCH THAT... MORE LIKE THEY MAKE ME SICK.

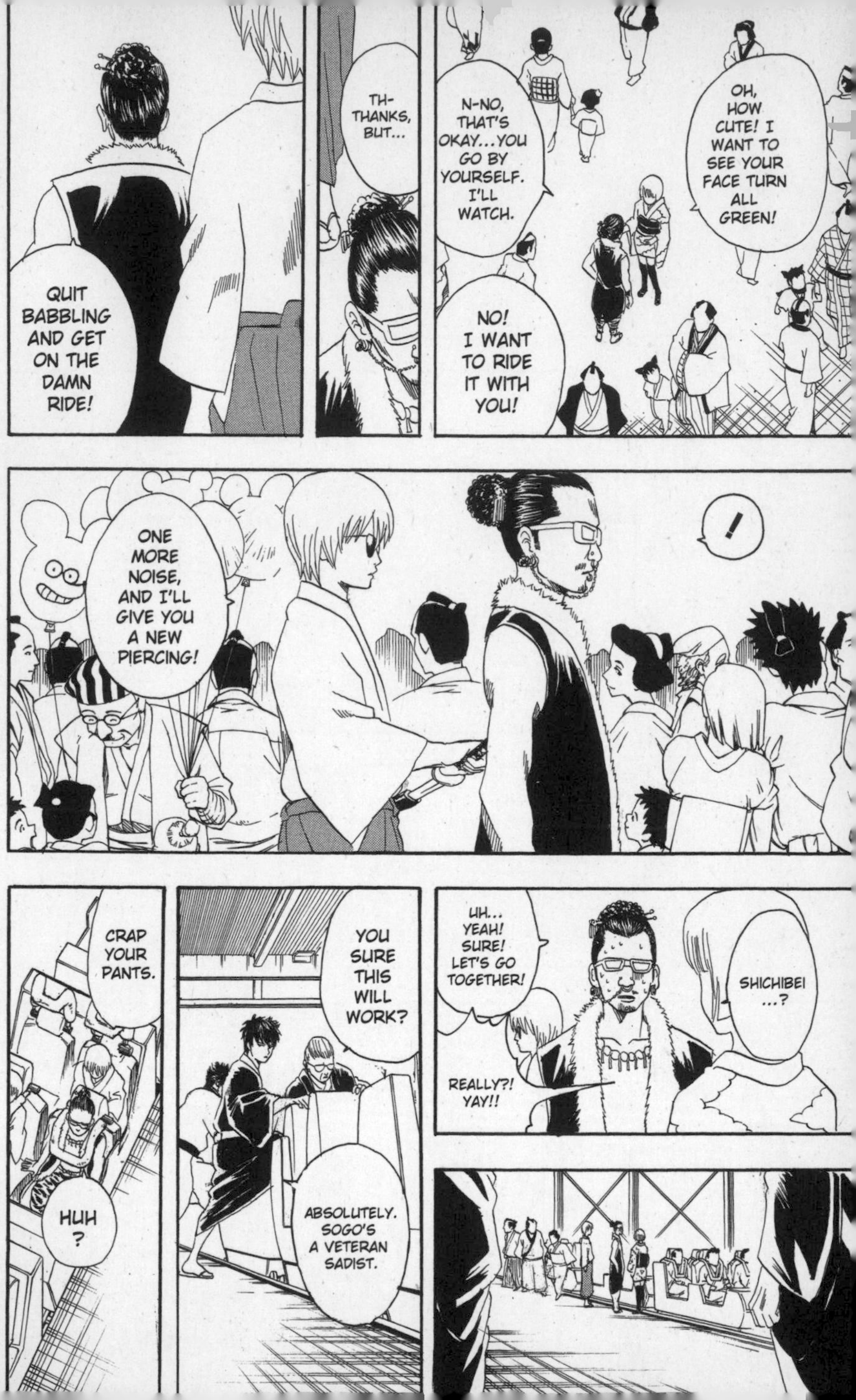
OH, HOW CUTE! I WANT TO SEE YOUR FACE TURN ALL GREEN!
N-NO, THAT'S OKAY...YOU GO BY YOURSELF. I'LL WATCH.
NO! I WANT TO RIDE IT WITH YOU!
TH-THANKS, BUT...
QUIT BABBLING AND GET ON THE DAMN RIDE!
!
ONE MORE NOISE, AND I'LL GIVE YOU A NEW PIERCING!
SHICHIBEI ...?
UH... YEAH! SURE! LET'S GO TOGETHER!
REALLY?! YAY!!
YOU SURE THIS WILL WORK?
ABSOLUTELY. SOGO'S A VETERAN SADIST.
CRAP YOUR PANTS.
HUH ?

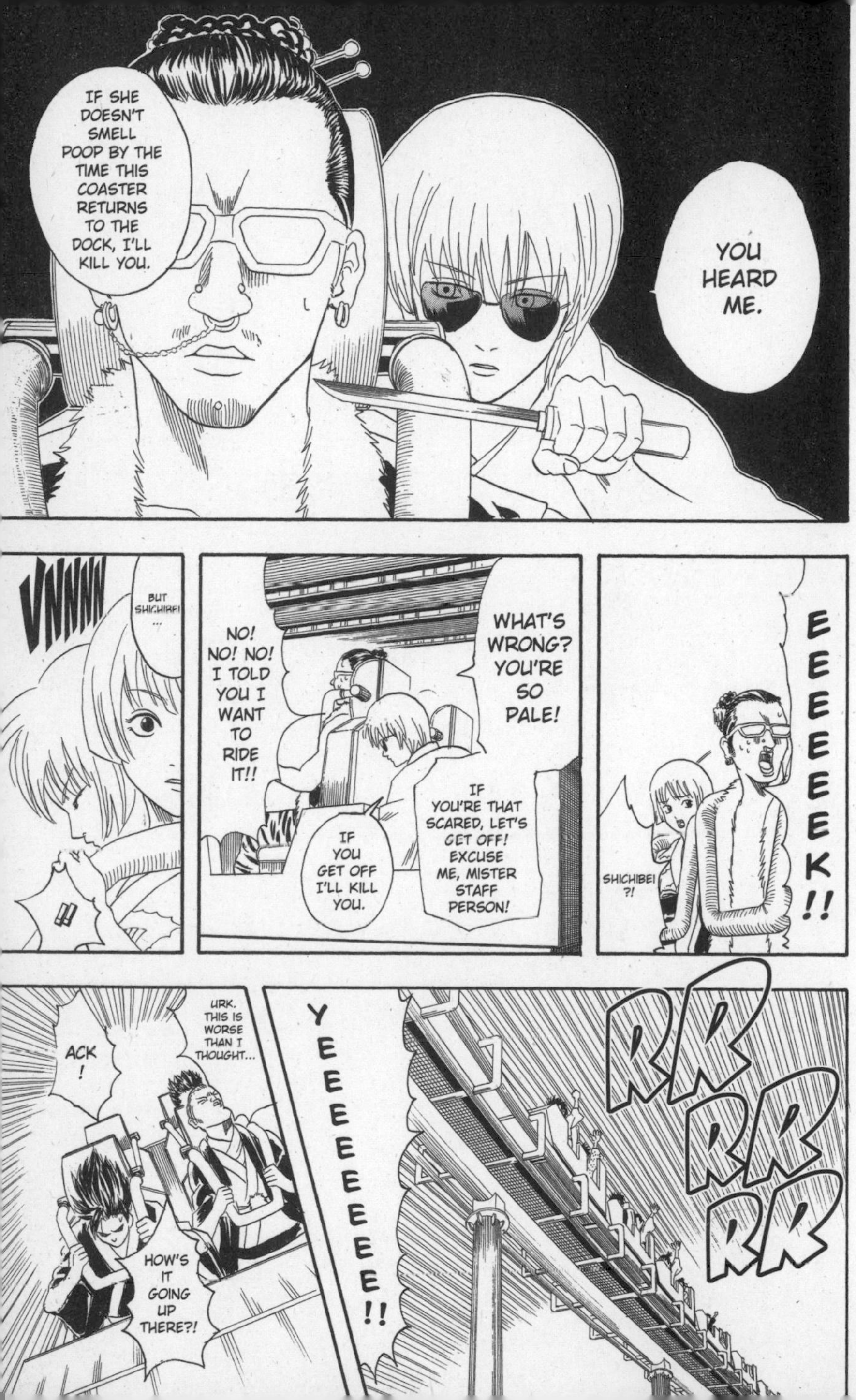
IF SHE DOESN'T SMELL POOP BY THE TIME THIS COASTER RETURNS TO THE DOCK, I'LL KILL YOU.
YOU HEARD ME.
EEEEEEEK!!
SHICHIBEI ?!
WHAT'S WRONG? YOU'RE SO PALE!
NO! NO! NO! I TOLD YOU I WANT TO RIDE IT!!
IF YOU'RE THAT SCARED, LET'S GET OFF! EXCUSE ME, MISTER STAFF PERSON!
IF YOU GET OFF I'LL KILL YOU.
VNNNN
BUT SHICHIBEI ...
!!
RRRRRR
YEEEEEEEE!!
URK. THIS IS WORSE THAN I THOUGHT...
ACK!
HOW'S IT GOING UP THERE?!

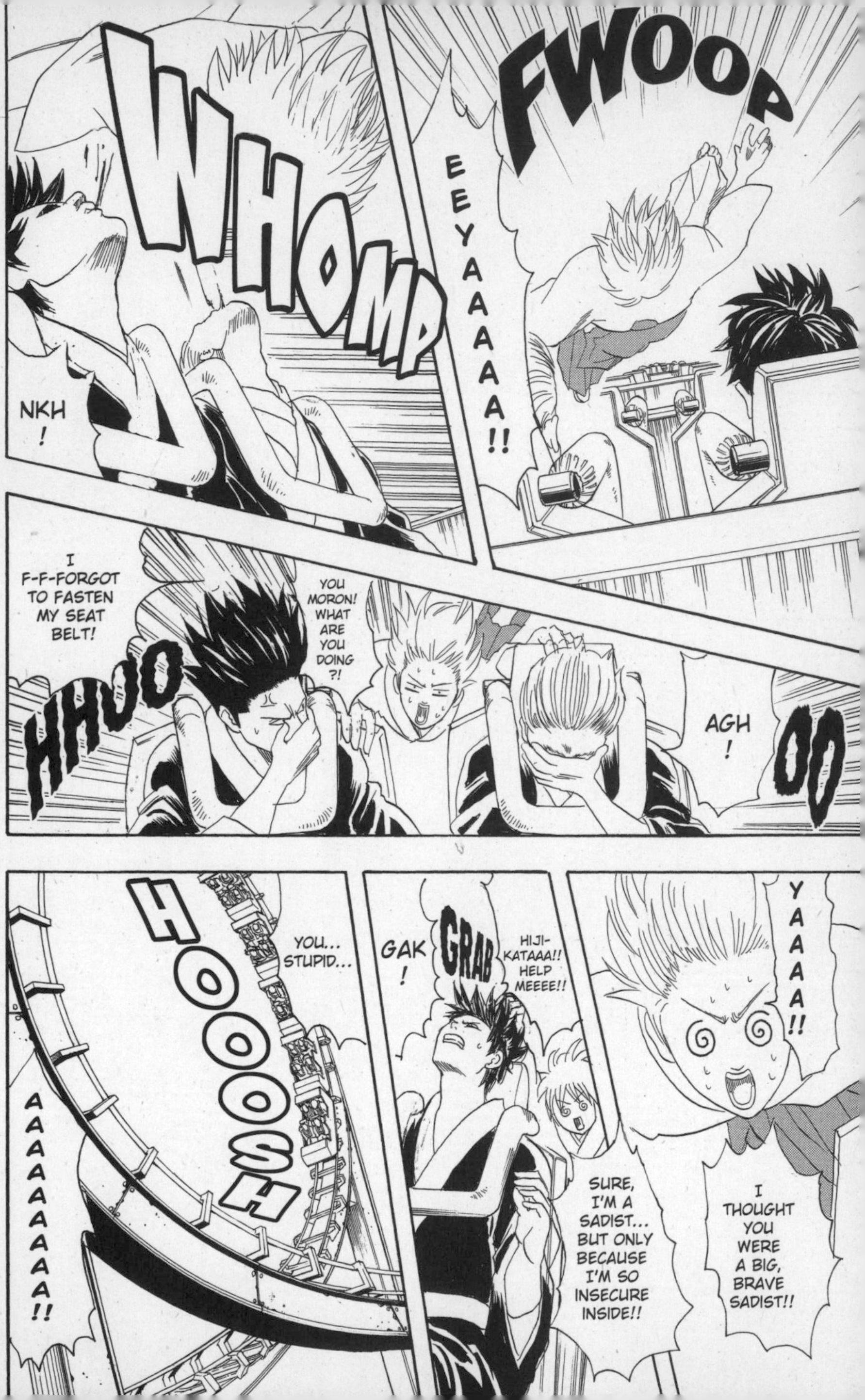
FWOOP
EEYAAAAAA!!
WHOMP
NKH!
AGH!
HHUOO
YOU MORON! WHAT ARE YOU DOING?!
I F-F-FORGOT TO FASTEN MY SEAT BELT!
YAAAAA!!
I THOUGHT YOU WERE A BIG, BRAVE SADIST!!
HIJI-KATAAA!! HELP MEEEE!!
GRAB
GAK!
SURE, I'M A SADIST... BUT ONLY BECAUSE I'M SO INSECURE INSIDE!!
YOU... STUPID...
WHOOOOSH
AAAAAAAAAAA!!

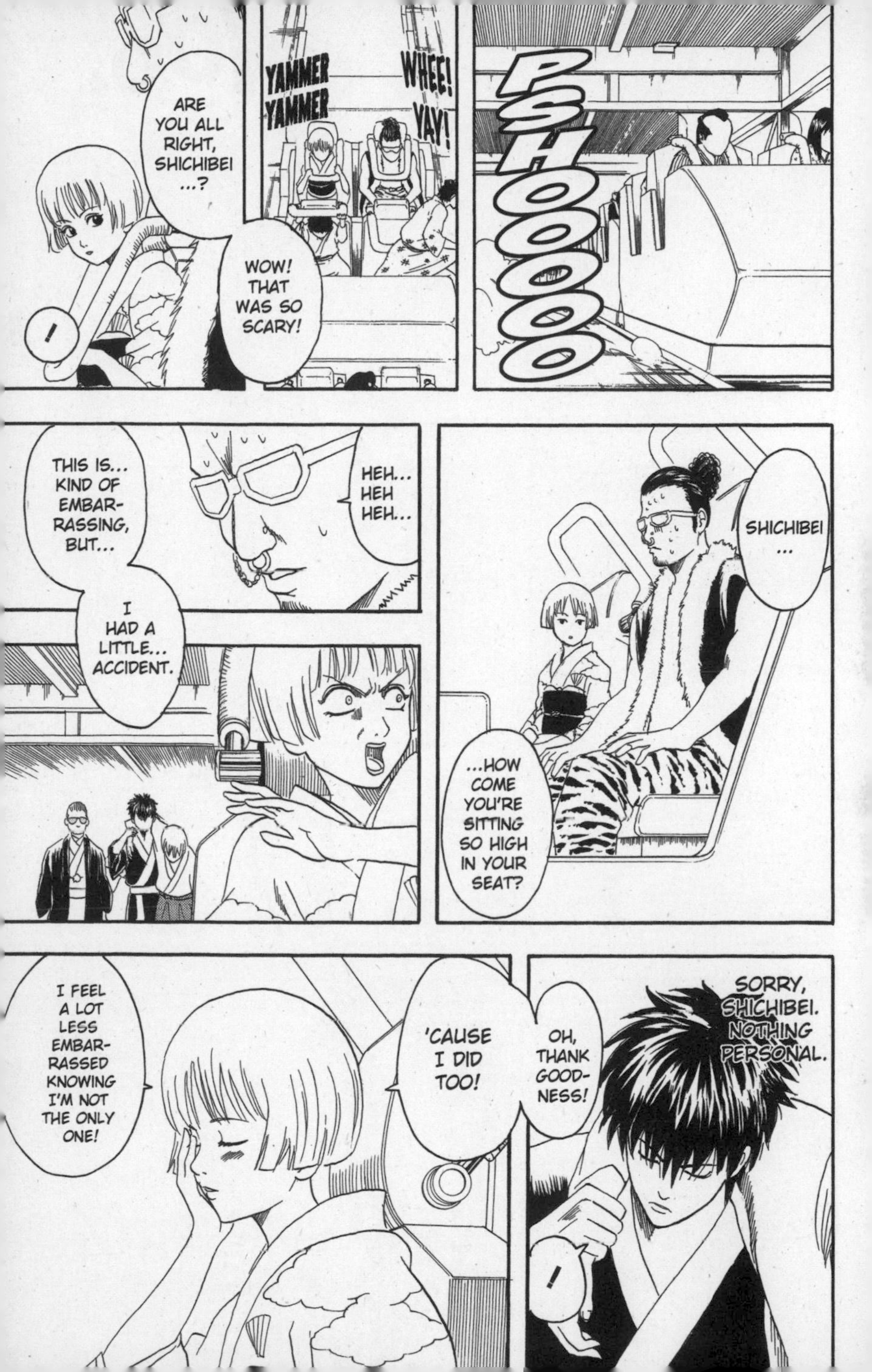
PSHOOOOOO
WHEE! YAY!
YAMMER YAMMER
WOW! THAT WAS SO SCARY!
ARE YOU ALL RIGHT, SHICHIBEI ...?
!
SHICHIBEI ...
...HOW COME YOU'RE SITTING SO HIGH IN YOUR SEAT?
HEH... HEH HEH...
THIS IS... KIND OF EMBARRASSING, BUT...
I HAD A LITTLE... ACCIDENT.
SORRY, SHICHIBEI. NOTHING PERSONAL.
!
OH, THANK GOODNESS!
'CAUSE I DID TOO!
I FEEL A LOT LESS EMBARRASSED KNOWING I'M NOT THE ONLY ONE!

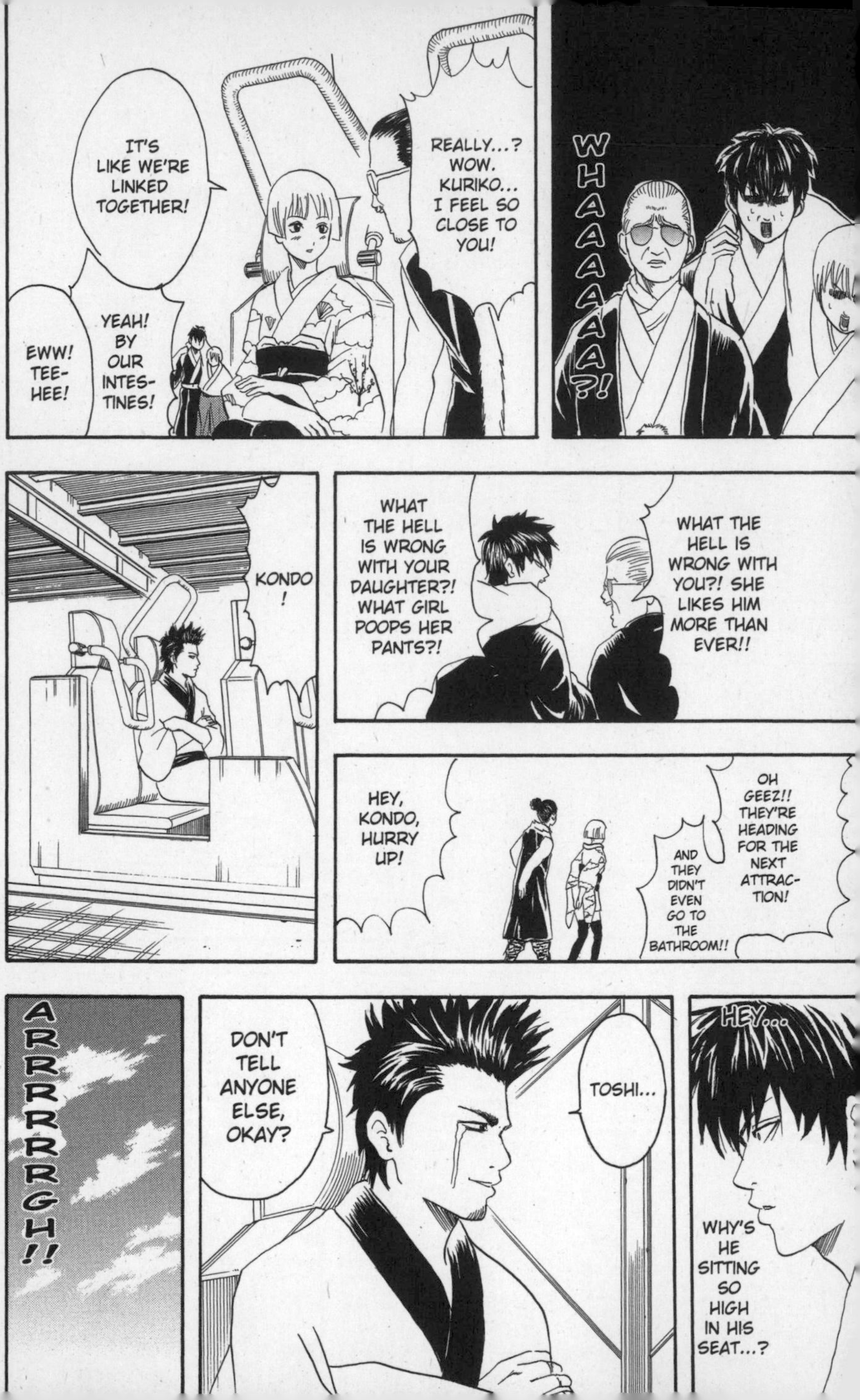
WHAAAAAAA?!
REALLY...? WOW. KURIKO... I FEEL SO CLOSE TO YOU!
IT'S LIKE WE'RE LINKED TOGETHER!
YEAH! BY OUR INTESTINES!
EWW! TEE-HEE!
WHAT THE HELL IS WRONG WITH YOU?! SHE LIKES HIM MORE THAN EVER!!
WHAT THE HELL IS WRONG WITH YOUR DAUGHTER?! WHAT GIRL POOPS HER PANTS?!
OH GEEZ!! THEY'RE HEADING FOR THE NEXT ATTRACTION!
AND THEY DIDN'T EVEN GO TO THE BATHROOM!!
HEY, KONDO, HURRY UP!
KONDO!
HEY...
WHY'S HE SITTING SO HIGH IN HIS SEAT...?
TOSHI...
DON'T TELL ANYONE ELSE, OKAY?
ARRRRRGH!!

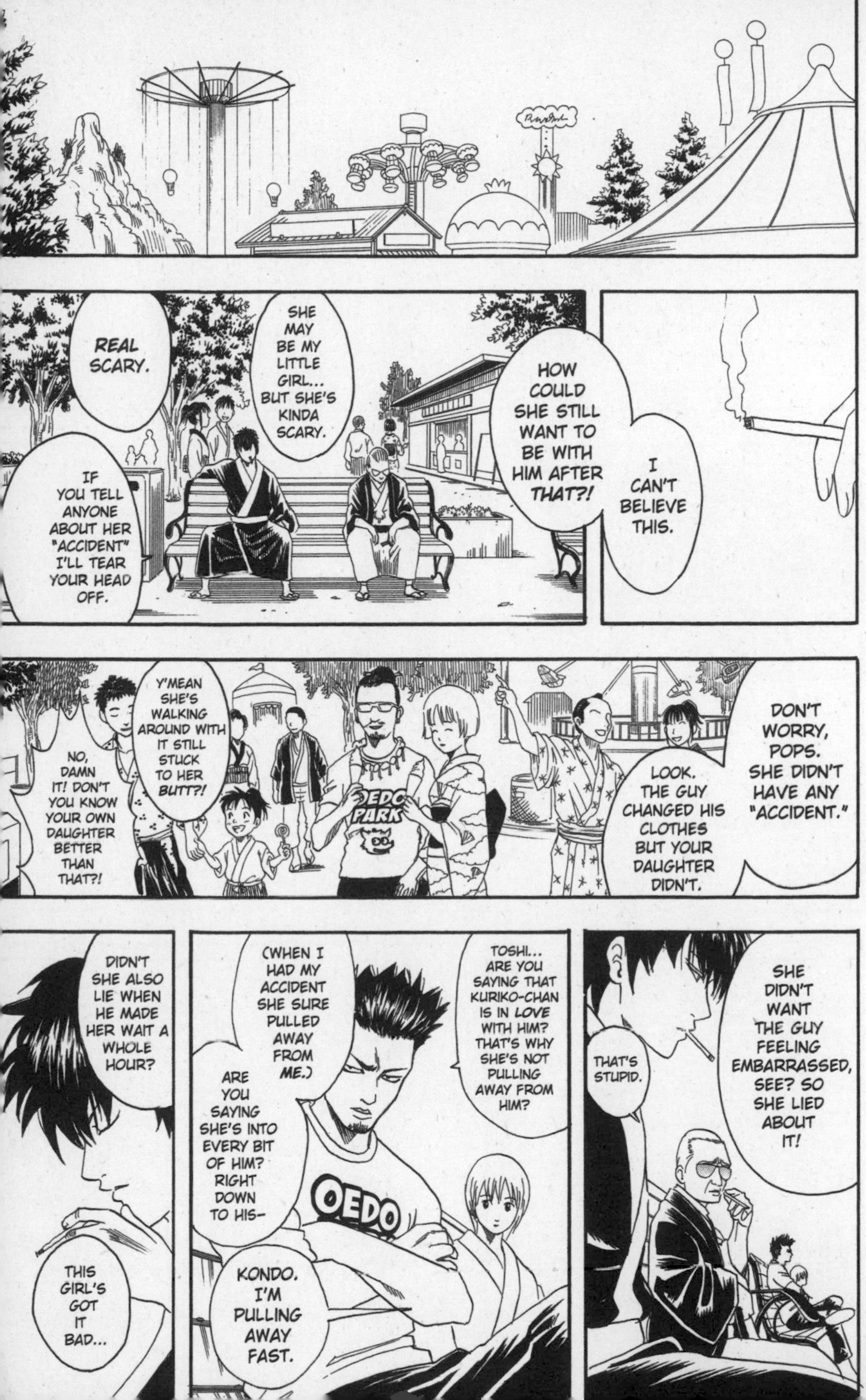
I CAN'T BELIEVE THIS.
HOW COULD SHE STILL WANT TO BE WITH HIM AFTER *THAT*?!
SHE MAY BE MY LITTLE GIRL... BUT SHE'S KINDA SCARY.
REAL SCARY.
IF YOU TELL ANYONE ABOUT HER "ACCIDENT" I'LL TEAR YOUR HEAD OFF.
DON'T WORRY, POPS. SHE DIDN'T HAVE ANY "ACCIDENT."
LOOK. THE GUY CHANGED HIS CLOTHES BUT YOUR DAUGHTER DIDN'T.
OEDO PARK
Y'MEAN SHE'S WALKING AROUND WITH IT STILL STUCK TO HER *BUTT*?!
NO, DAMN IT! DON'T YOU KNOW YOUR OWN DAUGHTER BETTER THAN THAT?!
SHE DIDN'T WANT THE GUY FEELING EMBARRASSED, SEE? SO SHE LIED ABOUT IT!
THAT'S STUPID.
TOSHI... ARE YOU SAYING THAT KURIKO-CHAN IS IN *LOVE* WITH HIM? THAT'S WHY SHE'S NOT PULLING AWAY FROM HIM?
(WHEN I HAD MY ACCIDENT SHE SURE PULLED AWAY FROM *ME*.)
ARE YOU SAYING SHE'S INTO EVERY BIT OF HIM? RIGHT DOWN TO HIS-
OEDO
KONDO. I'M PULLING AWAY FAST.
DIDN'T SHE ALSO LIE WHEN HE MADE HER WAIT A WHOLE HOUR?
THIS GIRL'S GOT IT BAD...

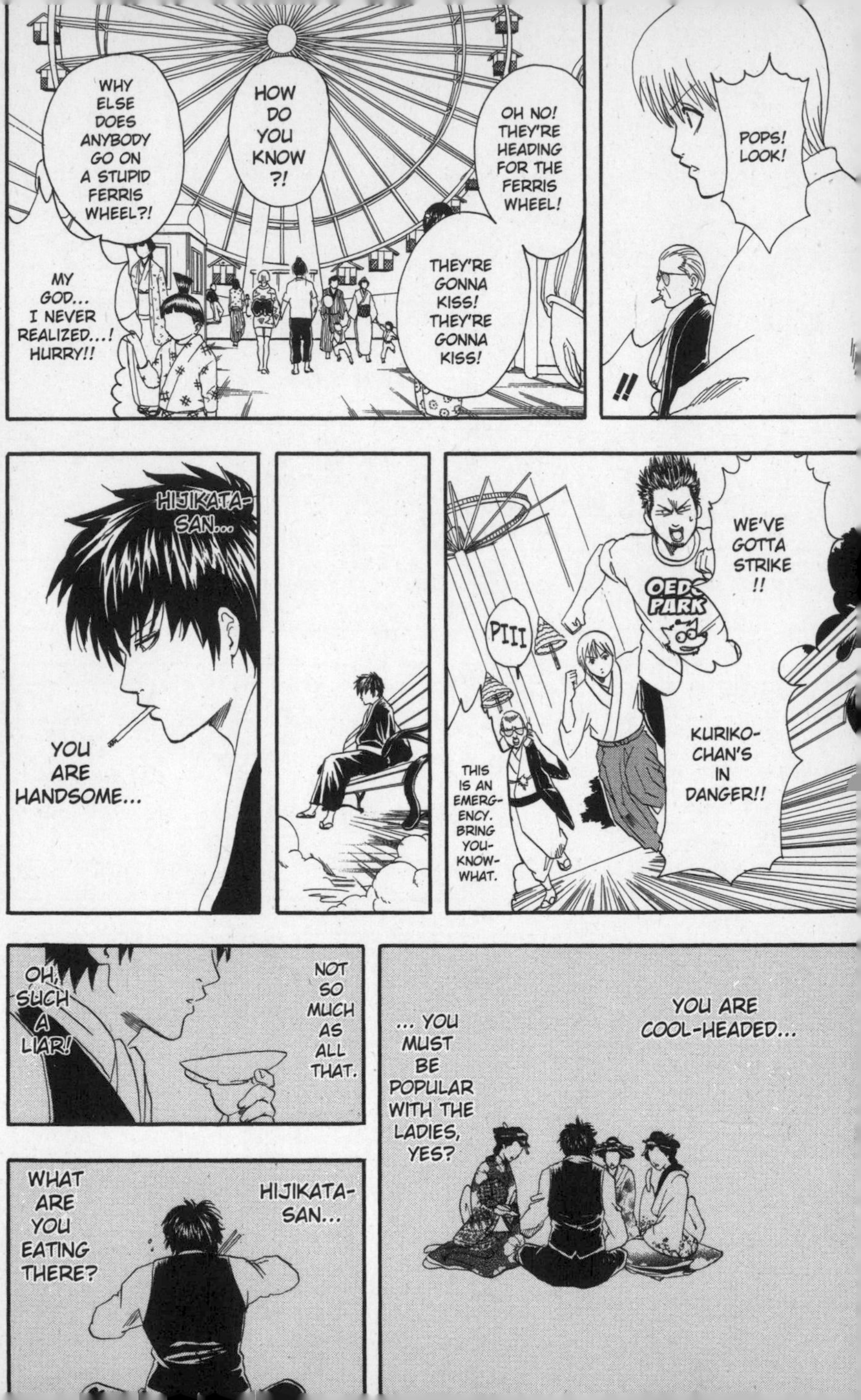
POPS! LOOK!
!!
OH NO! THEY'RE HEADING FOR THE FERRIS WHEEL!
HOW DO YOU KNOW?!
WHY ELSE DOES ANYBODY GO ON A STUPID FERRIS WHEEL?!
THEY'RE GONNA KISS! THEY'RE GONNA KISS!
MY GOD... I NEVER REALIZED...! HURRY!!
WE'VE GOTTA STRIKE!!
PIII
KURIKO-CHAN'S IN DANGER!!
THIS IS AN EMERG-ENCY. BRING YOU-KNOW-WHAT.
HIJIKATA-SAN...
YOU ARE HANDSOME...
YOU ARE COOL-HEADED...
... YOU MUST BE POPULAR WITH THE LADIES, YES?
NOT SO MUCH AS ALL THAT.
OH, SUCH A LIAR!
HIJIKATA-SAN...
WHAT ARE YOU EATING THERE?

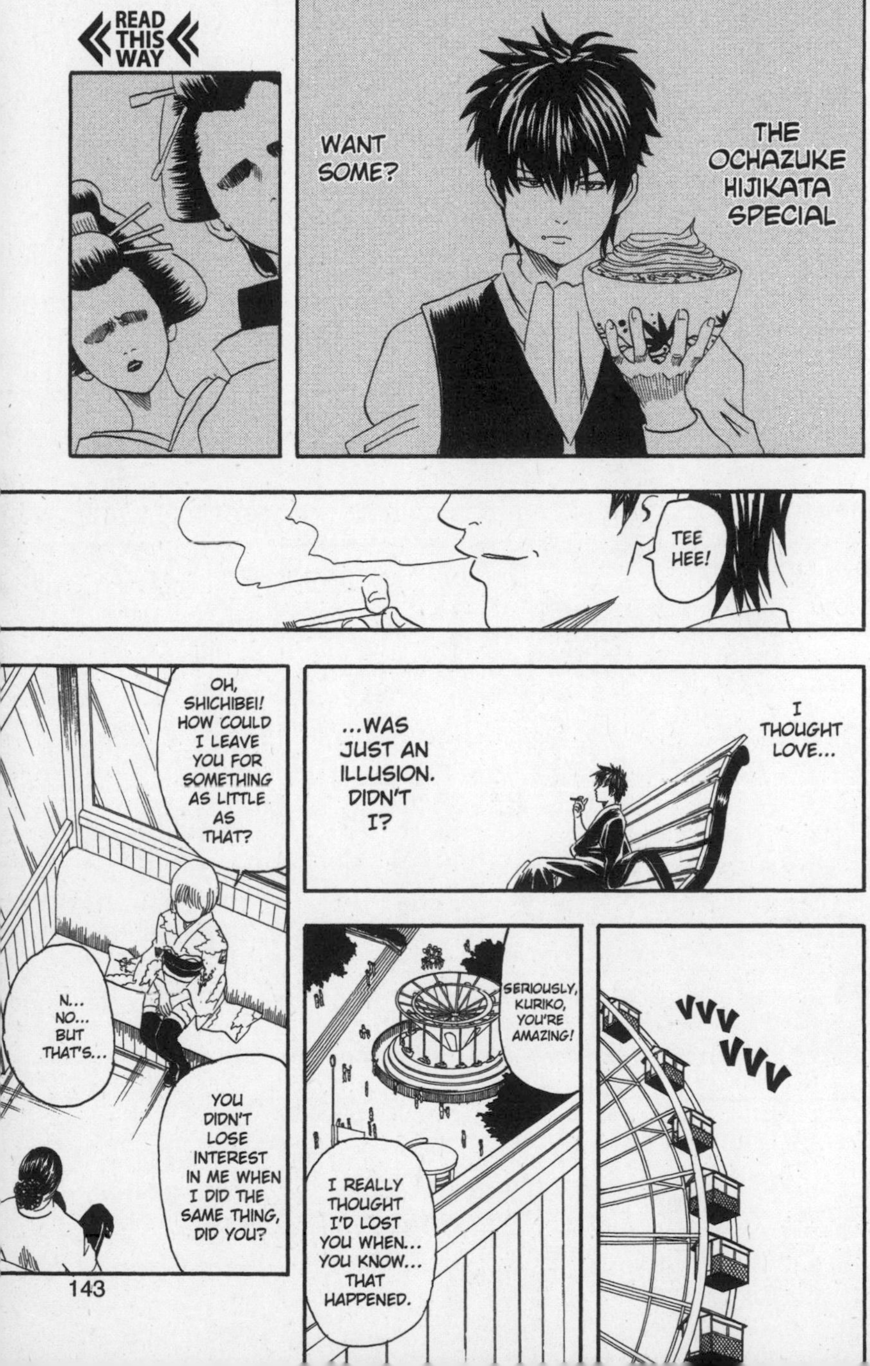
READ THIS WAY
THE OCHAZUKE HIJIKATA SPECIAL
WANT SOME?
TEE HEE!
I THOUGHT LOVE...
...WAS JUST AN ILLUSION. DIDN'T I?
VVV VVV
SERIOUSLY, KURIKO, YOU'RE AMAZING!
I REALLY THOUGHT I'D LOST YOU WHEN... YOU KNOW... THAT HAPPENED.
OH, SHICHIBEI! HOW COULD I LEAVE YOU FOR SOMETHING AS LITTLE AS THAT?
N... NO... BUT THAT'S...
YOU DIDN'T LOSE INTEREST IN ME WHEN I DID THE SAME THING, DID YOU?

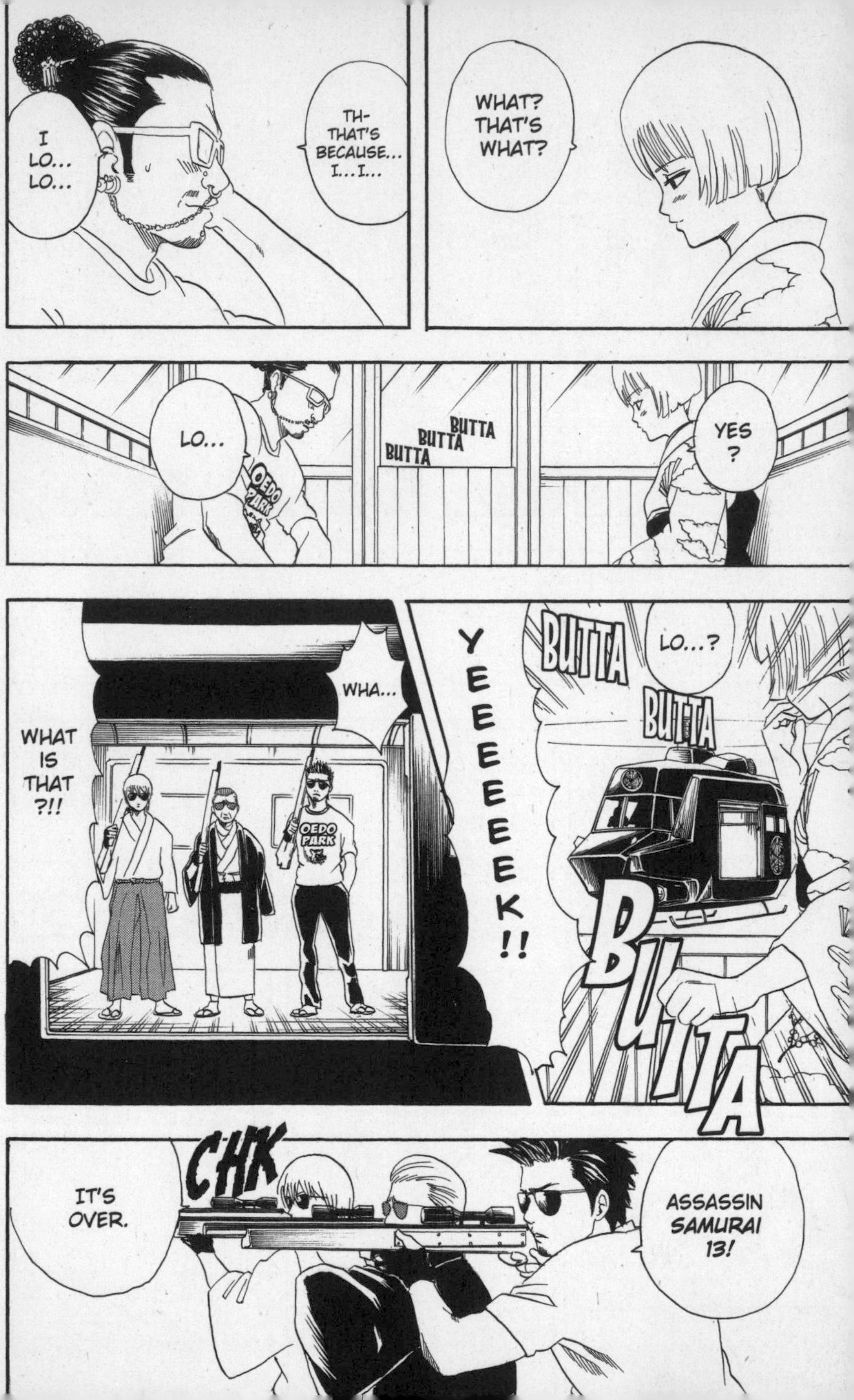
WHAT? THAT'S WHAT?
TH- THAT'S BECAUSE... I...I...
I LO... LO...
YES ?
BUTTA
BUTTA
BUTTA
LO...
LO...?
BUTTA
BUTTA
BUTTA
YEEEEEEEK!!
WHA...
WHAT IS THAT ?!!
OEDO PARK
ASSASSIN SAMURAI 13!
CHK
IT'S OVER.

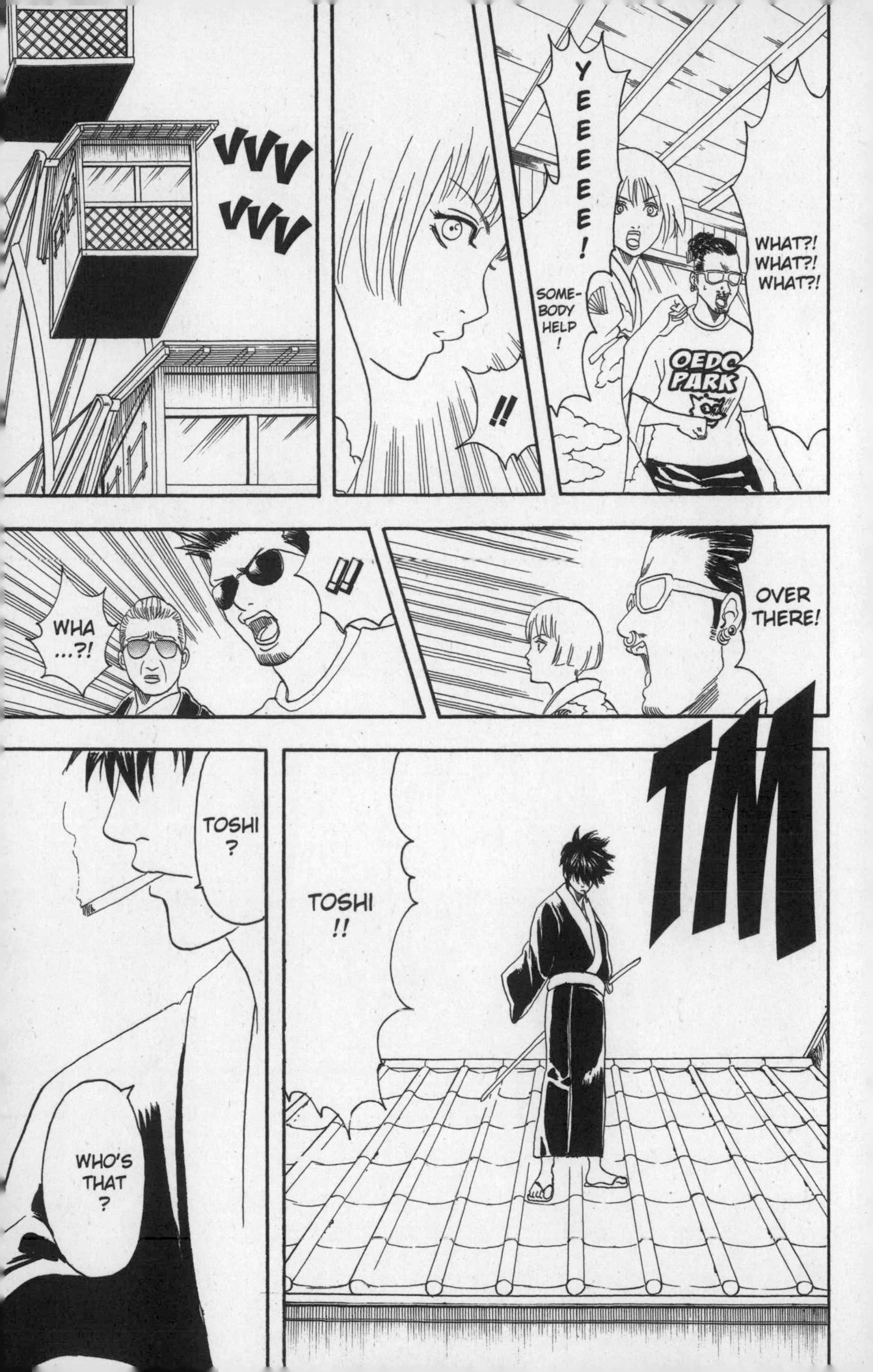
YEEEEEE!
WHAT?! WHAT?! WHAT?!
SOMEBODY HELP!
!!
VVV VVV
OVER THERE!
!!
WHA...?!
TM
TOSHI!!
TOSHI?
WHO'S THAT?

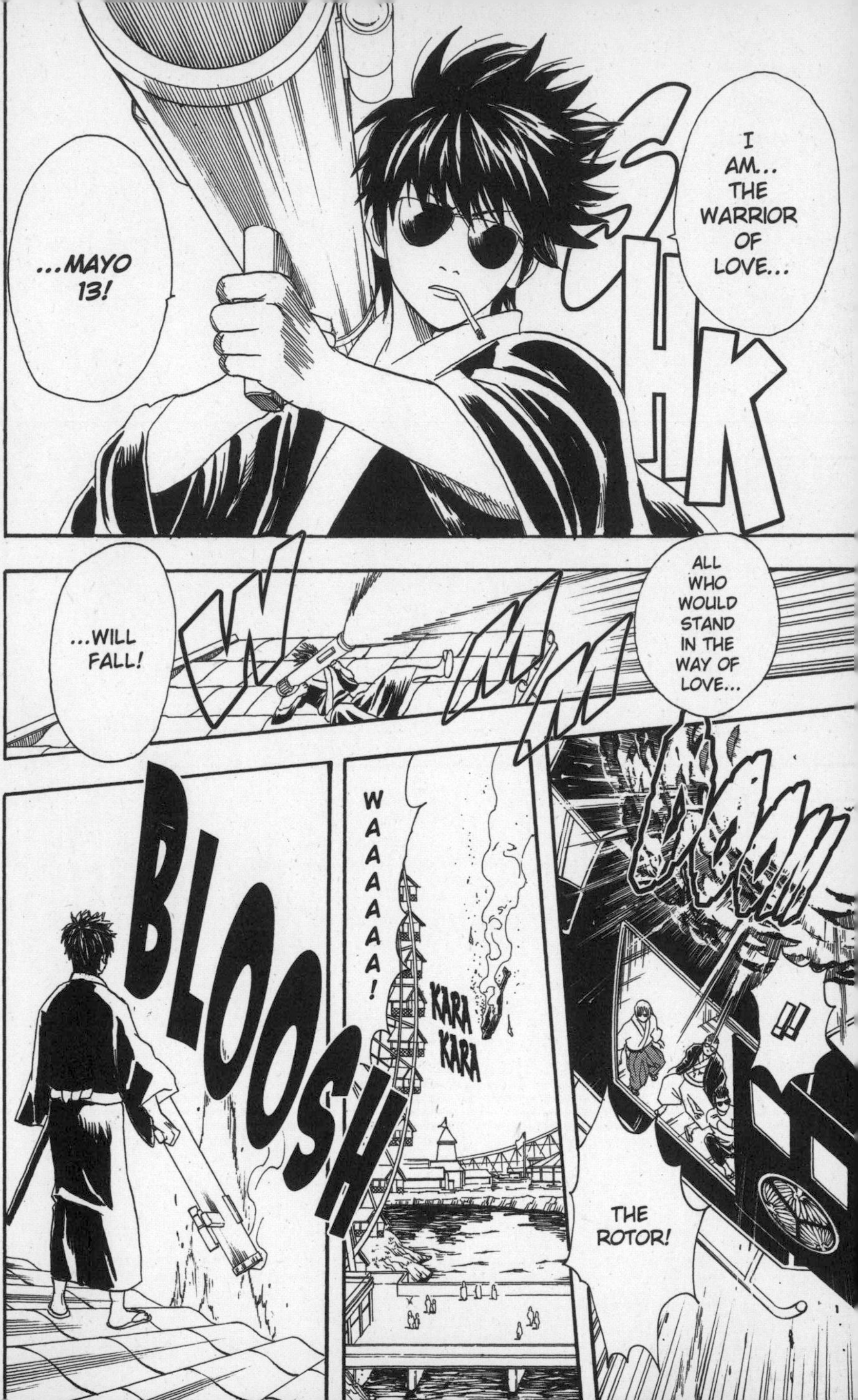
I AM... THE WARRIOR OF LOVE...
...MAYO 13!
ALL WHO WOULD STAND IN THE WAY OF LOVE...
...WILL FALL!
THE ROTOR!
!!
WAAAAAAA!
KARA KARA
BLOOSH

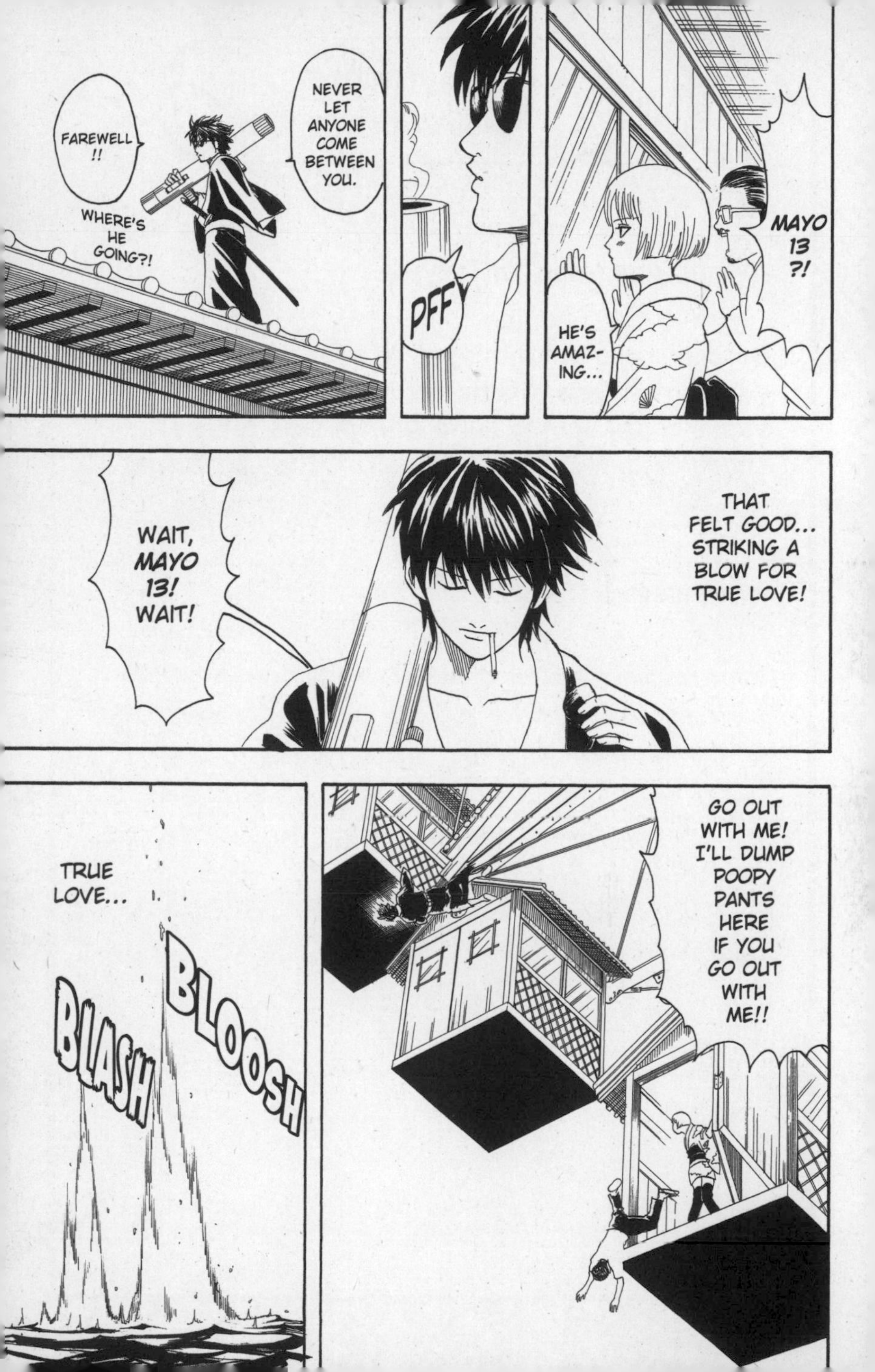
MAYO 13?!
HE'S AMAZ-ING...
PFF
NEVER LET ANYONE COME BETWEEN YOU.
FAREWELL!!
WHERE'S HE GOING?!
THAT FELT GOOD... STRIKING A BLOW FOR TRUE LOVE!
WAIT, MAYO 13! WAIT!
GO OUT WITH ME! I'LL DUMP POOPY PANTS HERE IF YOU GO OUT WITH ME!!
TRUE LOVE...
BLOOSH
BLASH

Sorachi's Q&A Corner #18

<From "Aaaa-san" of Tokyo>

Sorachi-sensei, I think you're a loser, because you don't have a nickname that would make it easier for people to bond with you. So please choose either "Sorachintama" or "Hideakintama."

<Answer>

You're right. I'm a loser. Not like you, writing fan letters calling people "losers." Not like your mother, who raised a child with no manners. I was still all excited about the *Gin Tama* anime when I got this letter...which is a good thing. I'd hate to see how my usual cranky self would have reacted!

Sincerely, "Sorachintama."

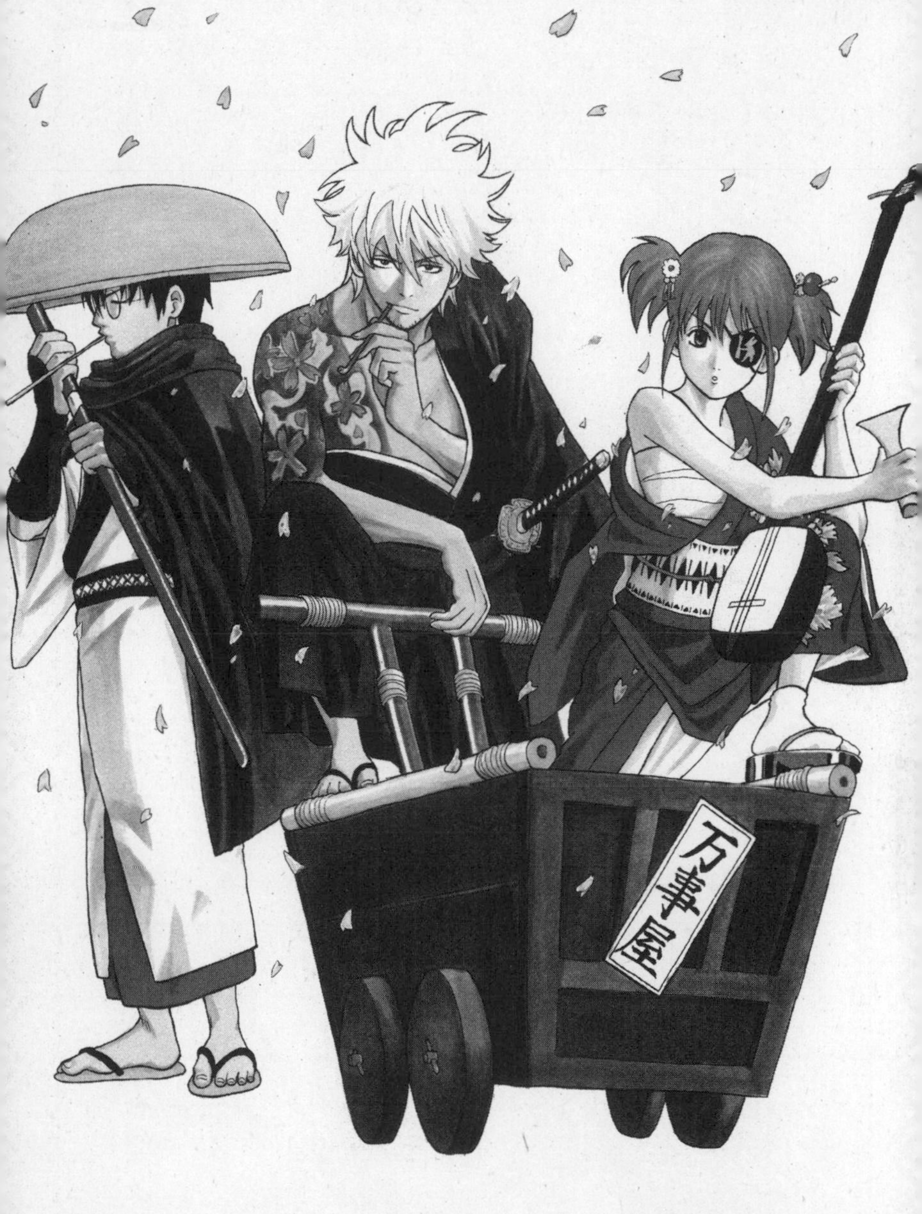
万事屋

Lesson 66: Do Cherries Come from Cherry Trees?

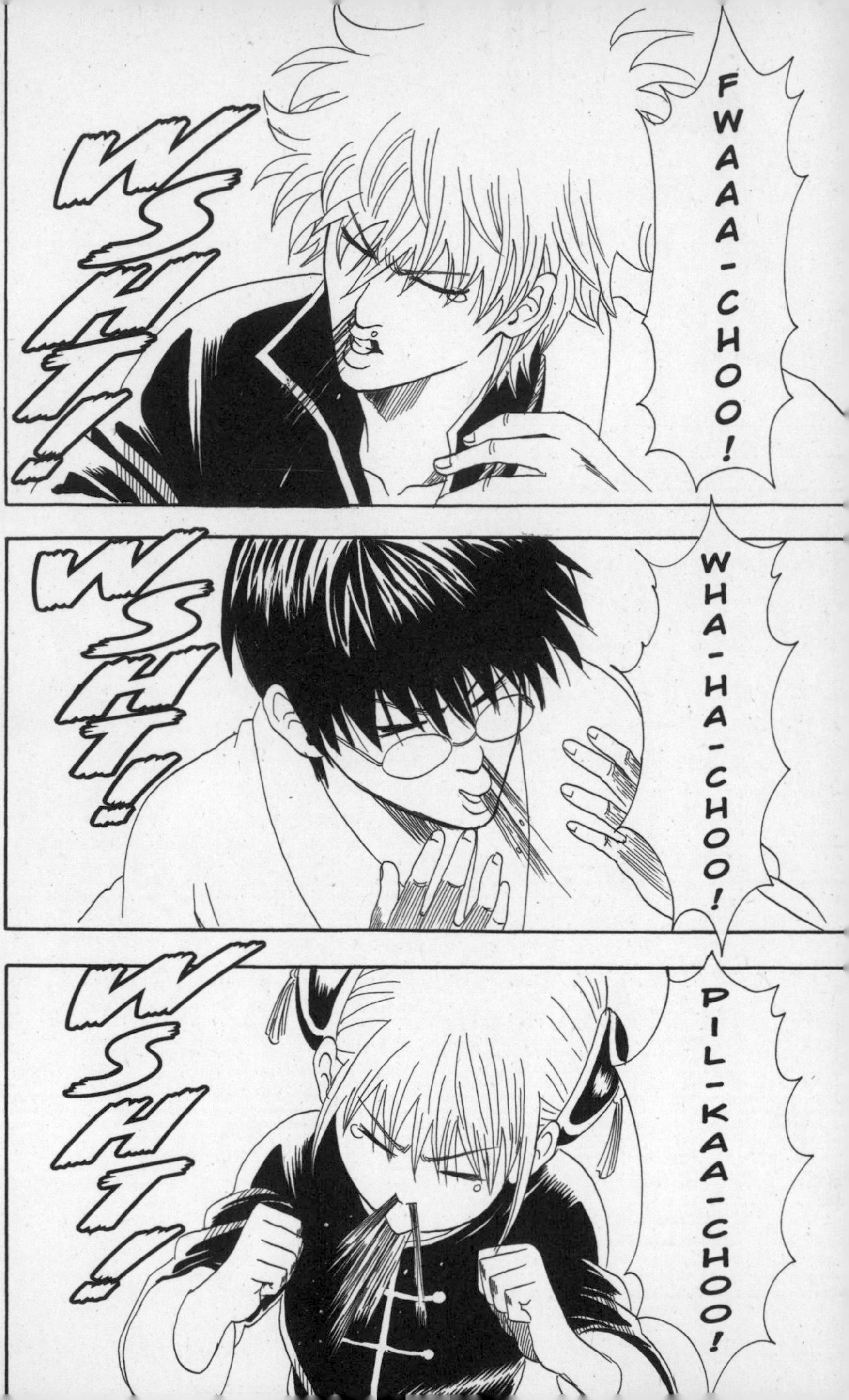
FWAAA-CHOO!
WSHH!!
WHA-HA-CHOO!
WSHH!
PIL-KAA-CHOO!
WSHH!!

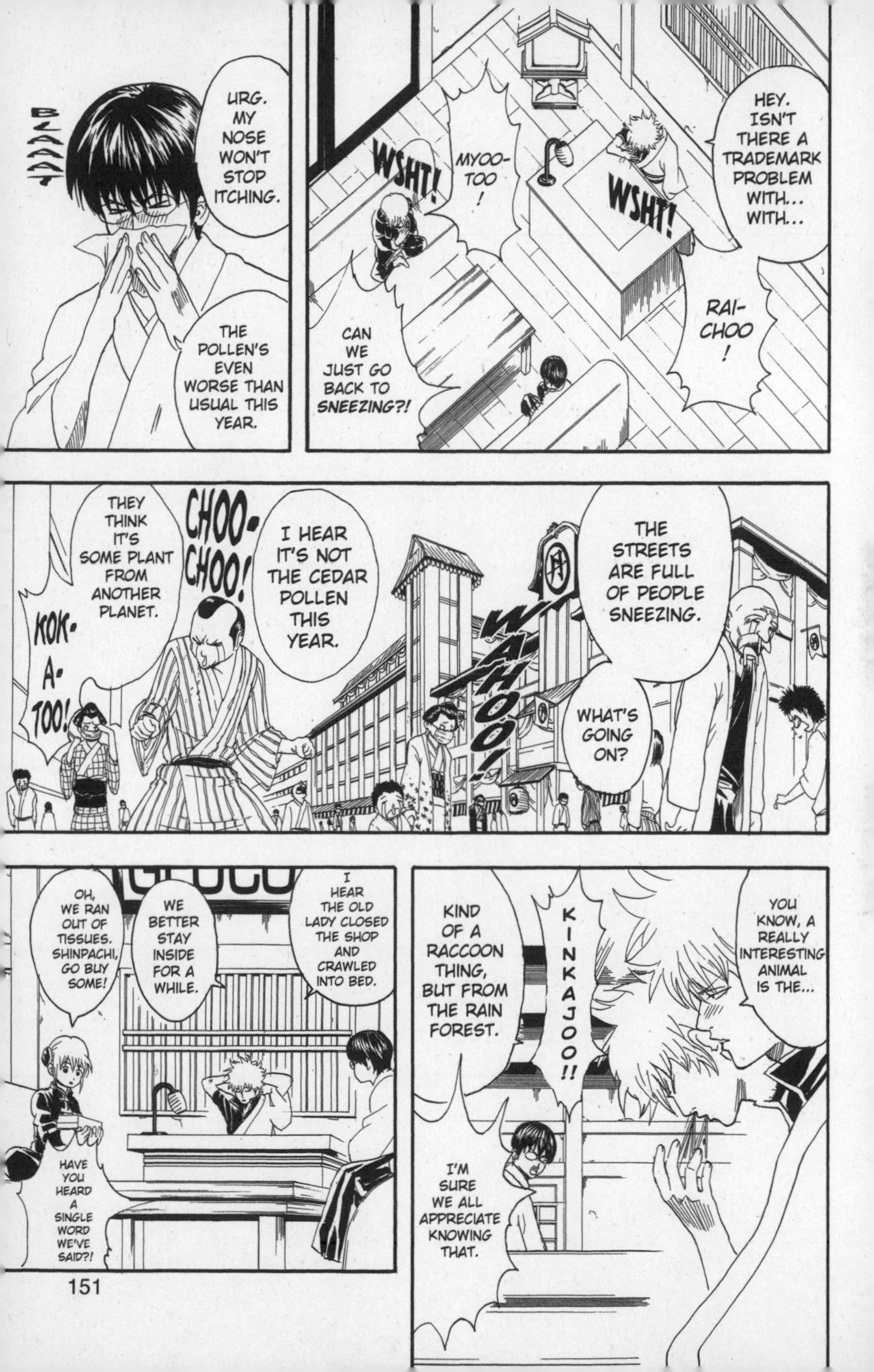
HEY. ISN'T THERE A TRADEMARK PROBLEM WITH... WITH...
RAI-CHOO!
WSHT!
MYOO-TOO!
WSHT!
CAN WE JUST GO BACK TO SNEEZING?!
BLAAAT
URG. MY NOSE WON'T STOP ITCHING.
THE POLLEN'S EVEN WORSE THAN USUAL THIS YEAR.
THE STREETS ARE FULL OF PEOPLE SNEEZING.
WHAT'S GOING ON?
WAHOO!!
I HEAR IT'S NOT THE CEDAR POLLEN THIS YEAR.
CHOO-CHOO!
THEY THINK IT'S SOME PLANT FROM ANOTHER PLANET.
KOK-A-TOO!
YOU KNOW, A REALLY INTERESTING ANIMAL IS THE...
KINKAJOO!!
KIND OF A RACCOON THING, BUT FROM THE RAIN FOREST.
I'M SURE WE ALL APPRECIATE KNOWING THAT.
I HEAR THE OLD LADY CLOSED THE SHOP AND CRAWLED INTO BED.
WE BETTER STAY INSIDE FOR A WHILE.
OH, WE RAN OUT OF TISSUES. SHINPACHI, GO BUY SOME!
HAVE YOU HEARD A SINGLE WORD WE'VE SAID?!

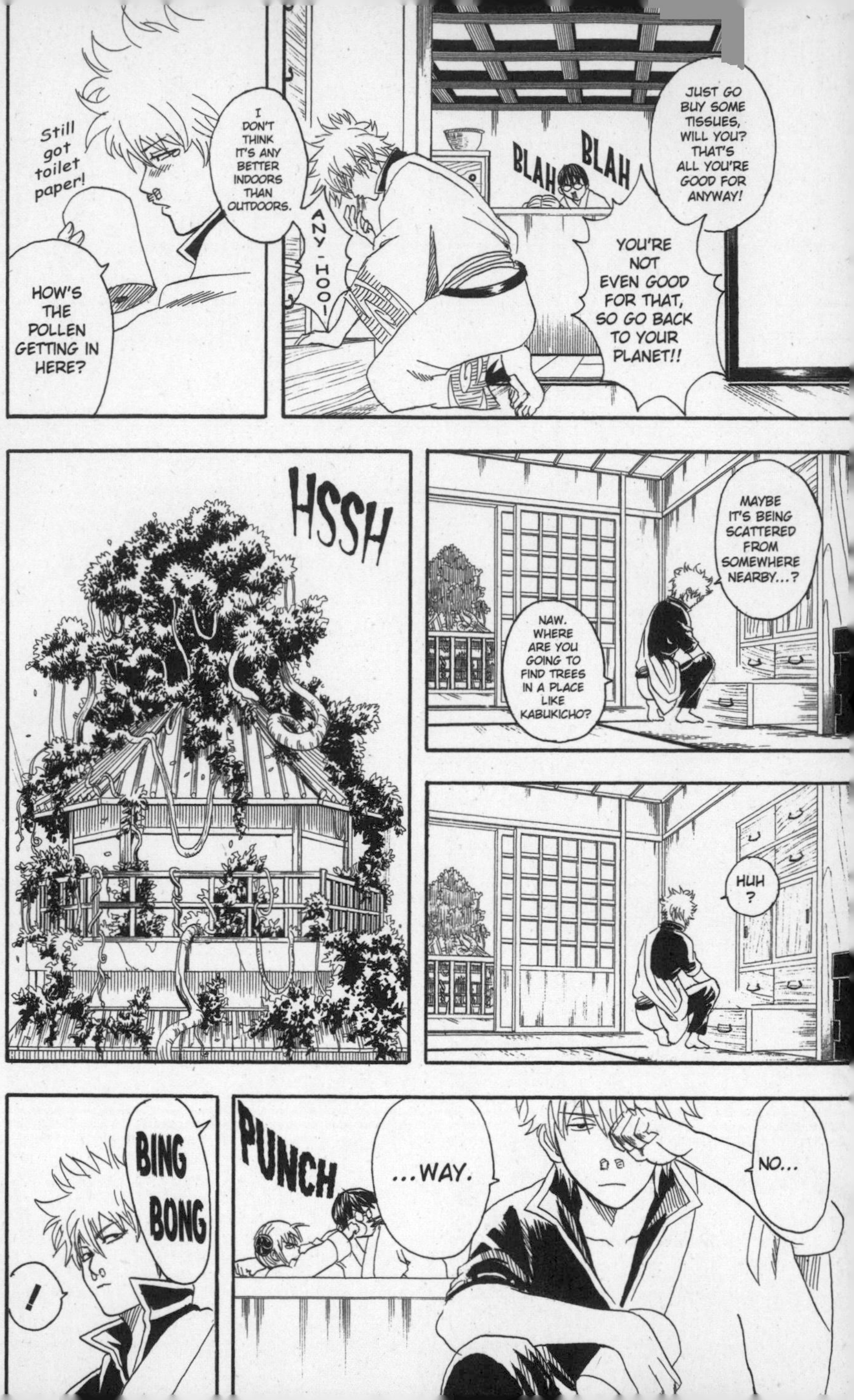

JUST GO BUY SOME TISSUES, WILL YOU? THAT'S ALL YOU'RE GOOD FOR ANYWAY!
BLAH BLAH
YOU'RE NOT EVEN GOOD FOR THAT, SO GO BACK TO YOUR PLANET!!
ANY-HOO!
I DON'T THINK IT'S ANY BETTER INDOORS THAN OUTDOORS.
Still got toilet paper!
HOW'S THE POLLEN GETTING IN HERE?
MAYBE IT'S BEING SCATTERED FROM SOMEWHERE NEARBY...?
NAW. WHERE ARE YOU GOING TO FIND TREES IN A PLACE LIKE KABUKICHO?
HUH?
HSSH
NO...
...WAY.
PUNCH
BING BONG
!

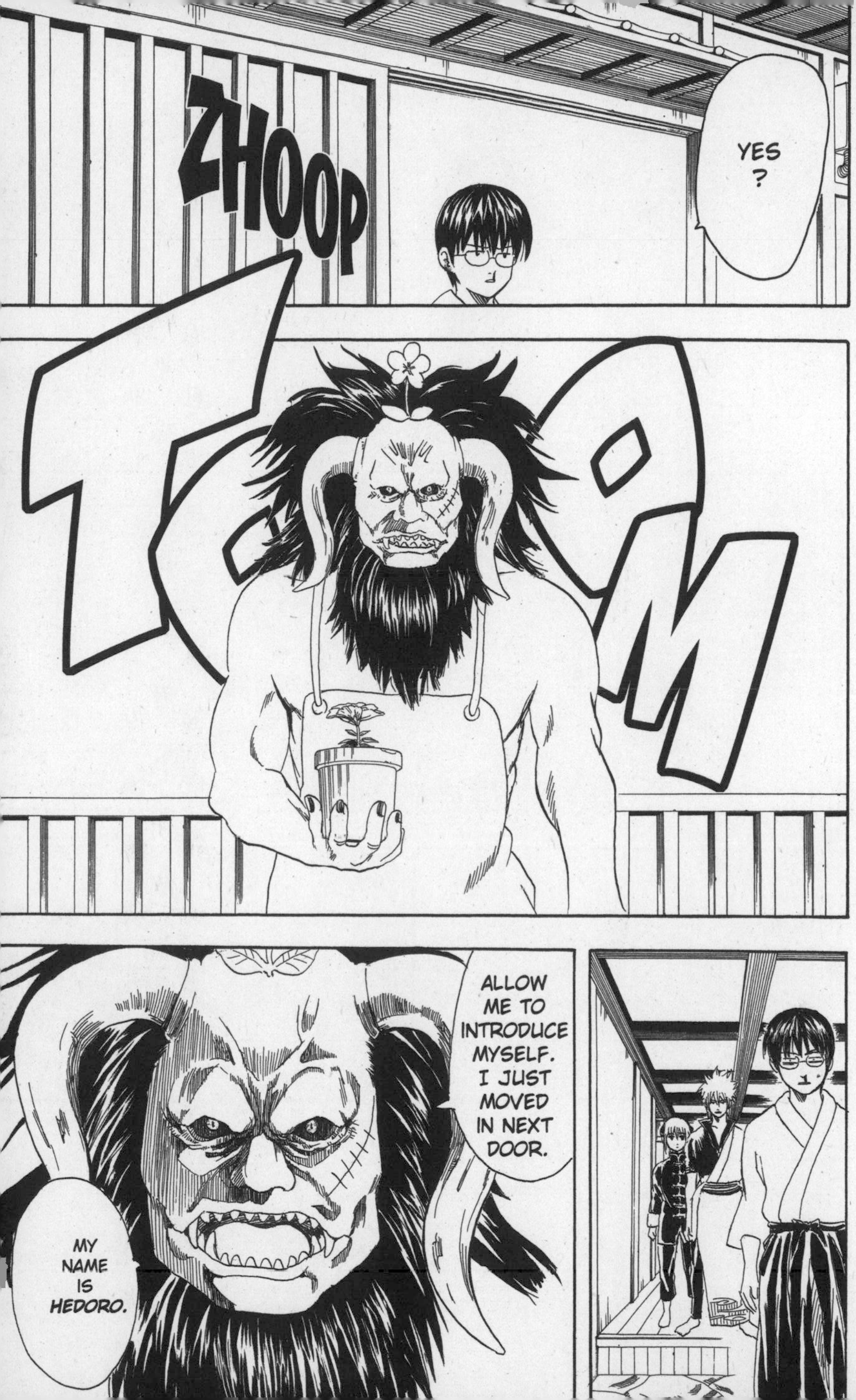
YES ?
ZHOOP
TOM
ALLOW ME TO INTRODUCE MYSELF. I JUST MOVED IN NEXT DOOR.
MY NAME IS HEDORO.

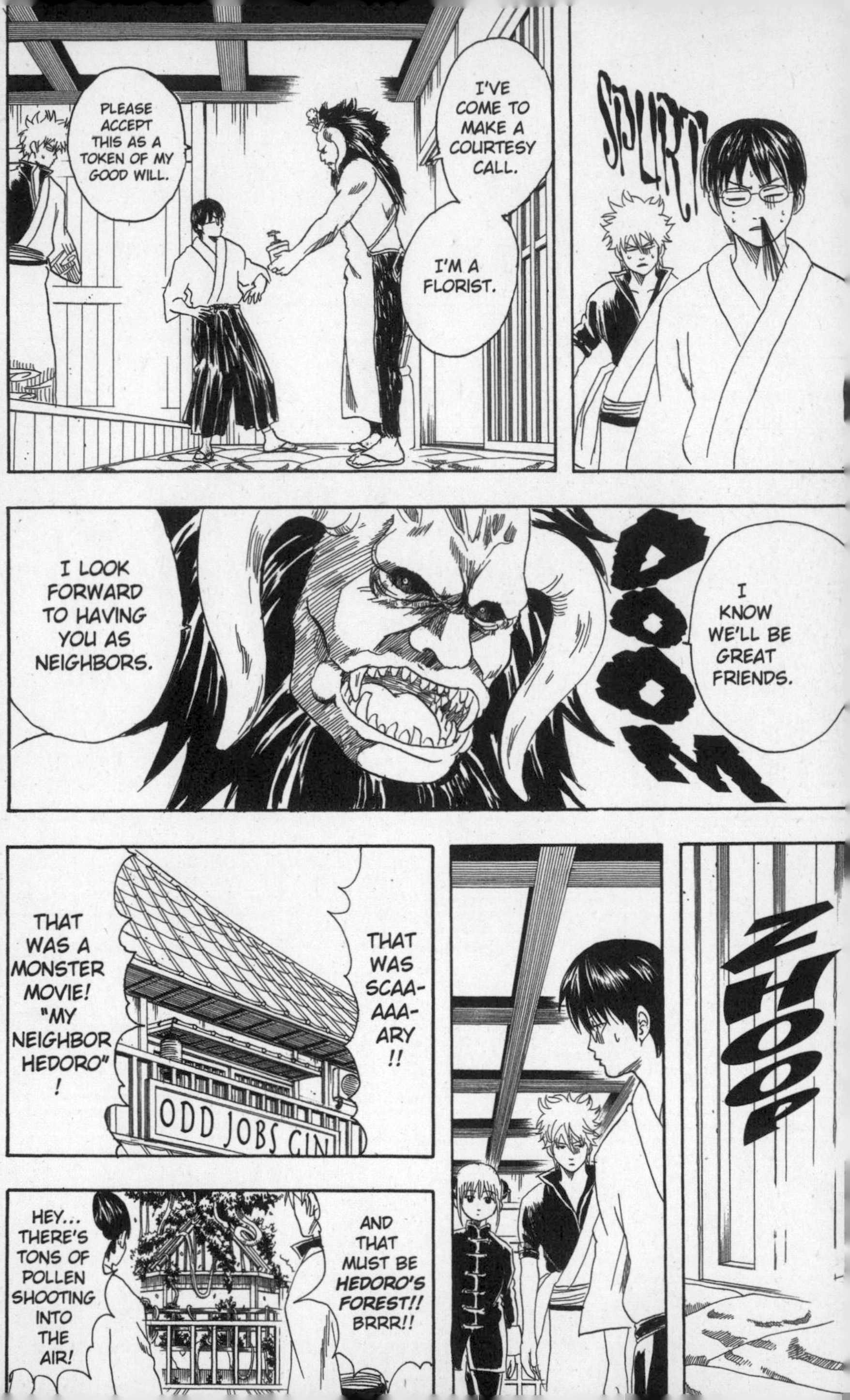
SPLURT
I'VE COME TO MAKE A COURTESY CALL.
I'M A FLORIST.
PLEASE ACCEPT THIS AS A TOKEN OF MY GOOD WILL.
I KNOW WE'LL BE GREAT FRIENDS.
DOOM
I LOOK FORWARD TO HAVING YOU AS NEIGHBORS.
ZHOOP
THAT WAS SCAA-AAA-ARY!!
THAT WAS A MONSTER MOVIE! "MY NEIGHBOR HEDORO"!
ODD JOBS GIN
AND THAT MUST BE HEDORO'S FOREST!! BRRR!!
HEY... THERE'S TONS OF POLLEN SHOOTING INTO THE AIR!

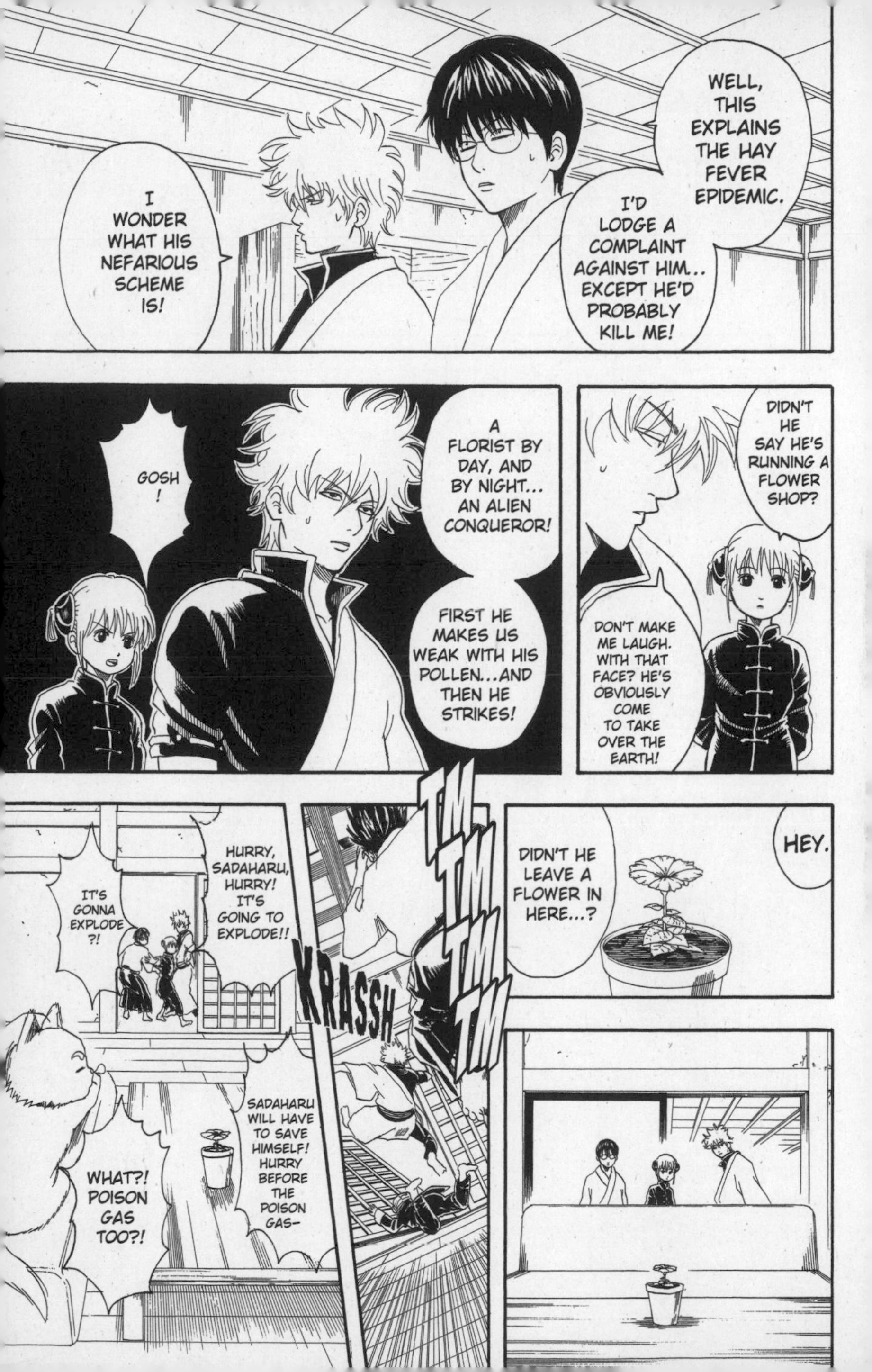
WELL, THIS EXPLAINS THE HAY FEVER EPIDEMIC.
I'D LODGE A COMPLAINT AGAINST HIM... EXCEPT HE'D PROBABLY KILL ME!
I WONDER WHAT HIS NEFARIOUS SCHEME IS!
DIDN'T HE SAY HE'S RUNNING A FLOWER SHOP?
DON'T MAKE ME LAUGH. WITH THAT FACE? HE'S OBVIOUSLY COME TO TAKE OVER THE EARTH!
A FLORIST BY DAY, AND BY NIGHT... AN ALIEN CONQUEROR!
FIRST HE MAKES US WEAK WITH HIS POLLEN...AND THEN HE STRIKES!
GOSH!
HEY.
DIDN'T HE LEAVE A FLOWER IN HERE...?
TMTMTMTMTM
KRASSH
SADAHARU WILL HAVE TO SAVE HIMSELF! HURRY BEFORE THE POISON GAS-
HURRY, SADAHARU, HURRY! IT'S GOING TO EXPLODE!!
IT'S GONNA EXPLODE?!
WHAT?! POISON GAS TOO?!

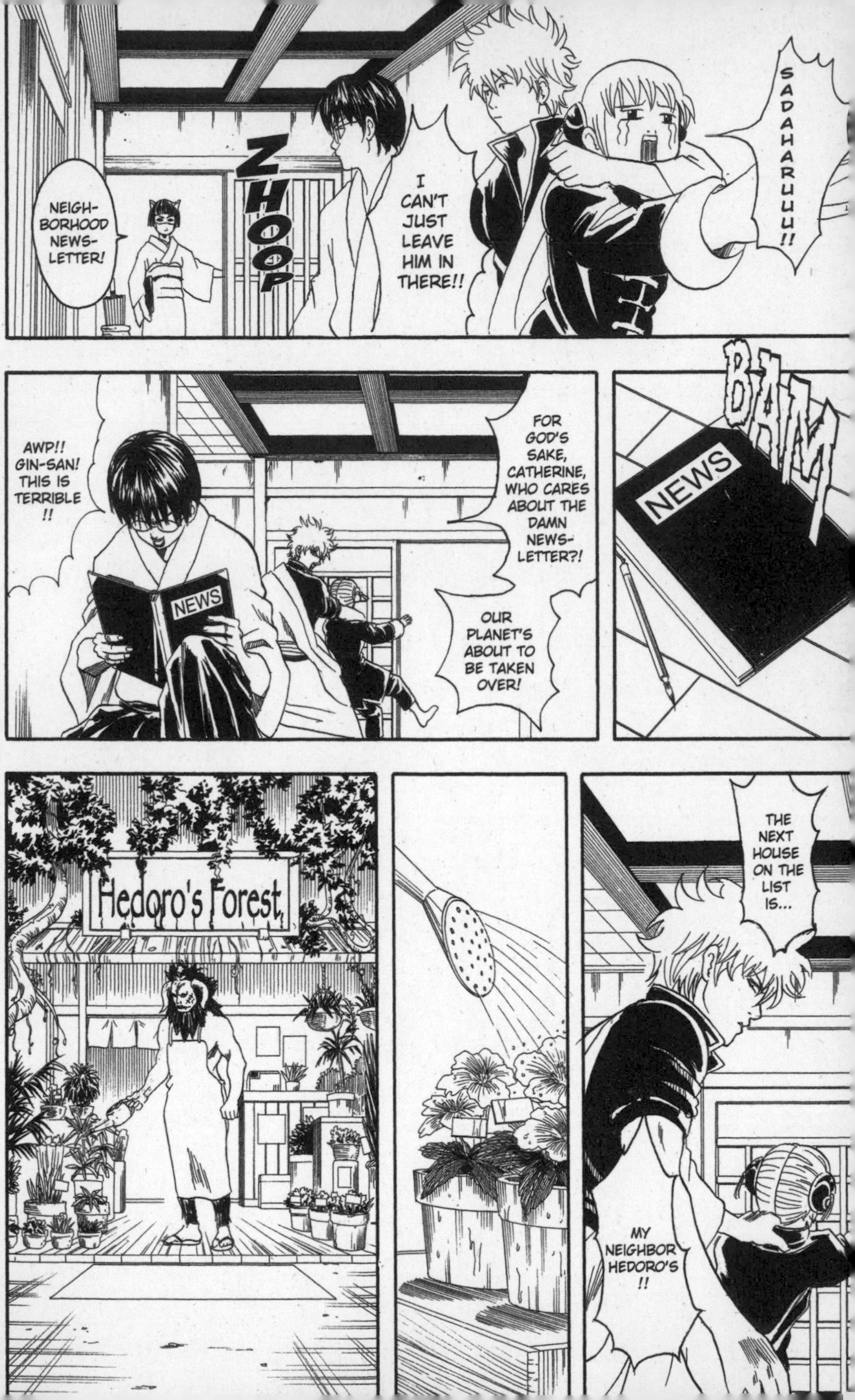

SADAHARUUU!!
I CAN'T JUST LEAVE HIM IN THERE!!
ZHOOP
NEIGH-BORHOOD NEWS-LETTER!
BAM
NEWS
FOR GOD'S SAKE, CATHERINE, WHO CARES ABOUT THE DAMN NEWS-LETTER?!
OUR PLANET'S ABOUT TO BE TAKEN OVER!
AWP!! GIN-SAN! THIS IS TERRIBLE!!
NEWS
THE NEXT HOUSE ON THE LIST IS...
MY NEIGHBOR HEDORO'S!!
Hedoro's Forest

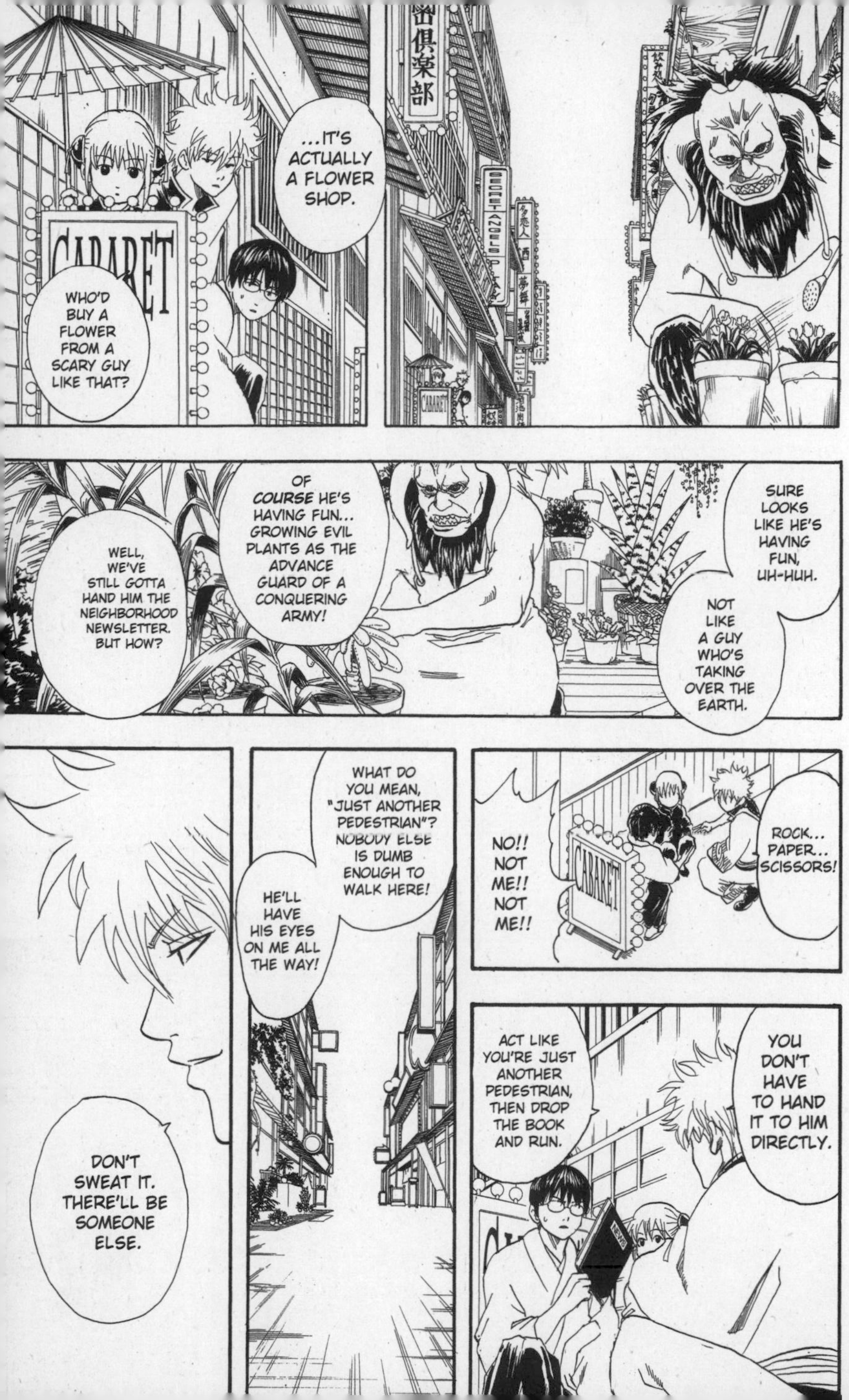
SECRET ANGELS
CABARET
...IT'S ACTUALLY A FLOWER SHOP.
CABARET
WHO'D BUY A FLOWER FROM A SCARY GUY LIKE THAT?
SURE LOOKS LIKE HE'S HAVING FUN, UH-HUH.
NOT LIKE A GUY WHO'S TAKING OVER THE EARTH.
OF COURSE HE'S HAVING FUN... GROWING EVIL PLANTS AS THE ADVANCE GUARD OF A CONQUERING ARMY!
WELL, WE'VE STILL GOTTA HAND HIM THE NEIGHBORHOOD NEWSLETTER. BUT HOW?
ROCK... PAPER... SCISSORS!
NO!! NOT ME!! NOT ME!!
CABARET
YOU DON'T HAVE TO HAND IT TO HIM DIRECTLY.
ACT LIKE YOU'RE JUST ANOTHER PEDESTRIAN, THEN DROP THE BOOK AND RUN.
WHAT DO YOU MEAN, "JUST ANOTHER PEDESTRIAN"? NOBODY ELSE IS DUMB ENOUGH TO WALK HERE!
HE'LL HAVE HIS EYES ON ME ALL THE WAY!
DON'T SWEAT IT. THERE'LL BE SOMEONE ELSE.

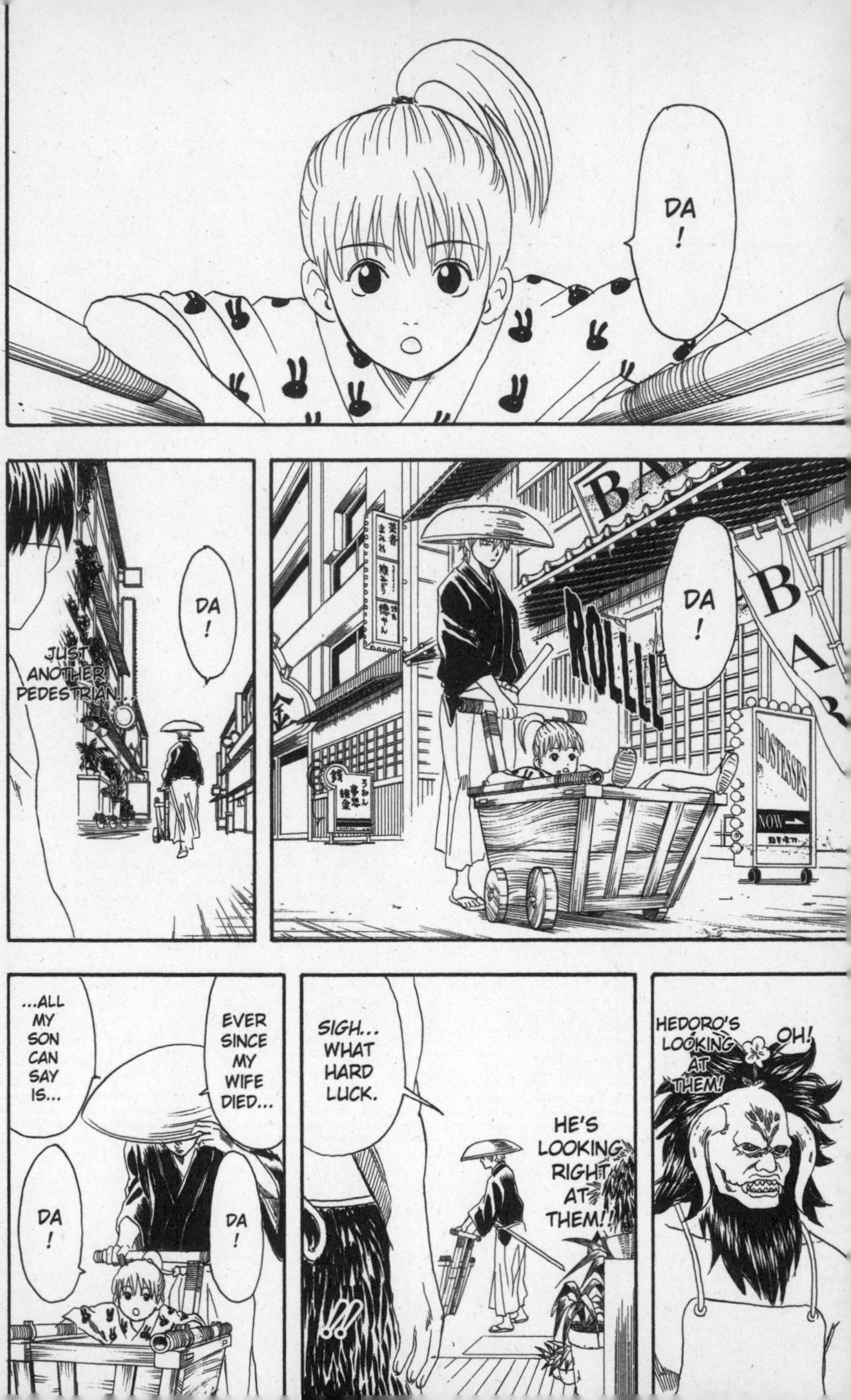
DA !
DA !
ROLLLL
DA !
JUST ANOTHER PEDESTRIAN...
OH!
HEDORO'S LOOKING AT THEM!
SIGH... WHAT HARD LUCK.
HE'S LOOKING RIGHT AT THEM!!
!!
EVER SINCE MY WIFE DIED...
...ALL MY SON CAN SAY IS...
DA !
DA !

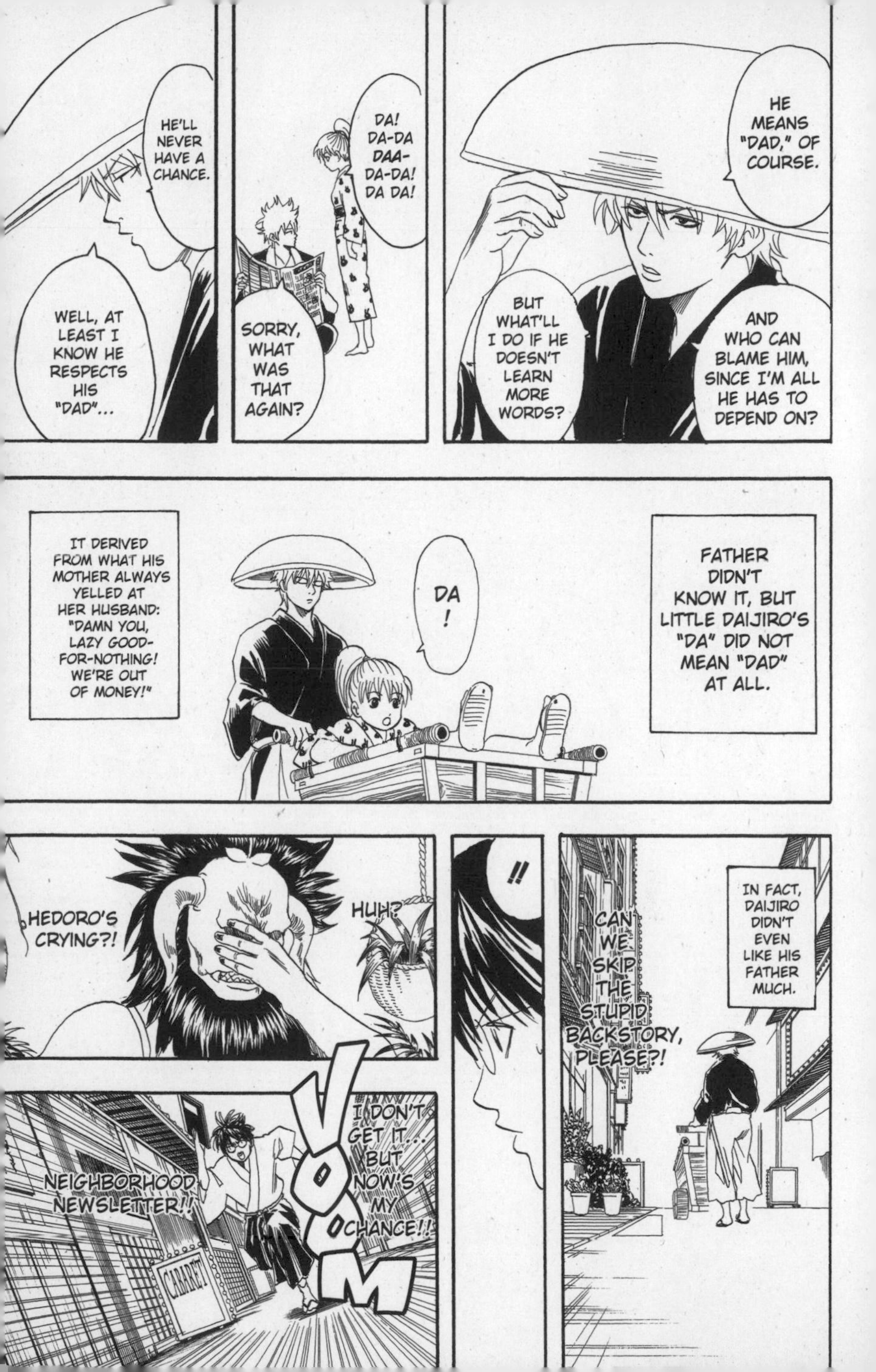
HE MEANS "DAD," OF COURSE.
AND WHO CAN BLAME HIM, SINCE I'M ALL HE HAS TO DEPEND ON?
BUT WHAT'LL I DO IF HE DOESN'T LEARN MORE WORDS?
DA! DA-DA DAA-DA-DA! DA DA!
SORRY, WHAT WAS THAT AGAIN?
HE'LL NEVER HAVE A CHANCE.
WELL, AT LEAST I KNOW HE RESPECTS HIS "DAD"...
FATHER DIDN'T KNOW IT, BUT LITTLE DAIJIRO'S "DA" DID NOT MEAN "DAD" AT ALL.
DA!
IT DERIVED FROM WHAT HIS MOTHER ALWAYS YELLED AT HER HUSBAND: "DAMN YOU, LAZY GOOD-FOR-NOTHING! WE'RE OUT OF MONEY!"
IN FACT, DAIJIRO DIDN'T EVEN LIKE HIS FATHER MUCH.
CAN WE SKIP THE STUPID BACKSTORY, PLEASE?!
!!
HUH?
HEDORO'S CRYING?!
I DON'T GET IT... BUT NOW'S MY CHANCE!!
VOOM
NEIGHBORHOOD NEWSLETTER!!
CABARET

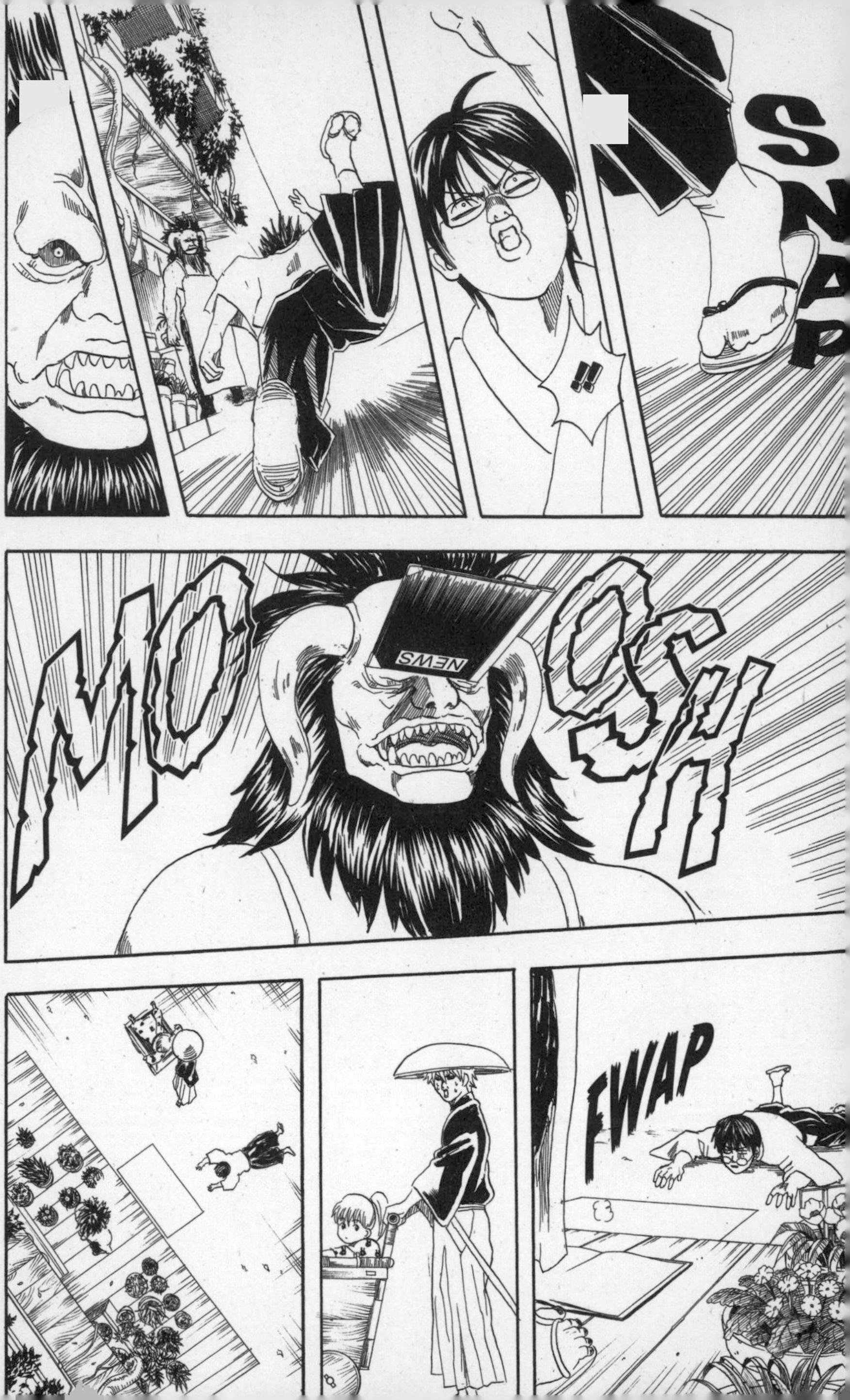
SNAP
!!
MOGSH
NEWS
FWAP

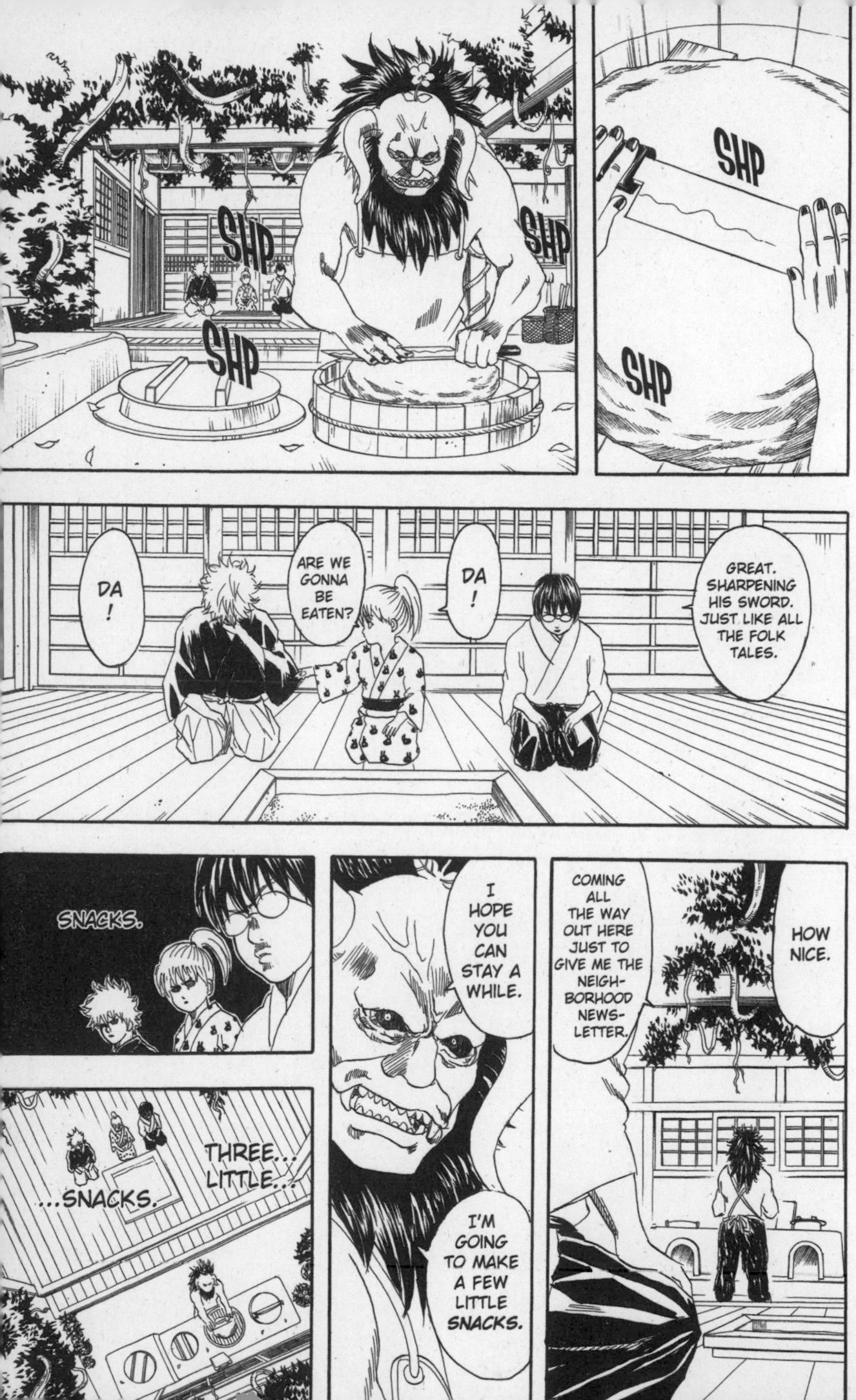
SHP
SHP
SHP
SHP
SHP
GREAT. SHARPENING HIS SWORD. JUST LIKE ALL THE FOLK TALES.
DA !
ARE WE GONNA BE EATEN?
DA !
HOW NICE.
COMING ALL THE WAY OUT HERE JUST TO GIVE ME THE NEIGHBORHOOD NEWSLETTER.
I HOPE YOU CAN STAY A WHILE.
I'M GOING TO MAKE A FEW LITTLE SNACKS.
SNACKS.
THREE... LITTLE...
...SNACKS.

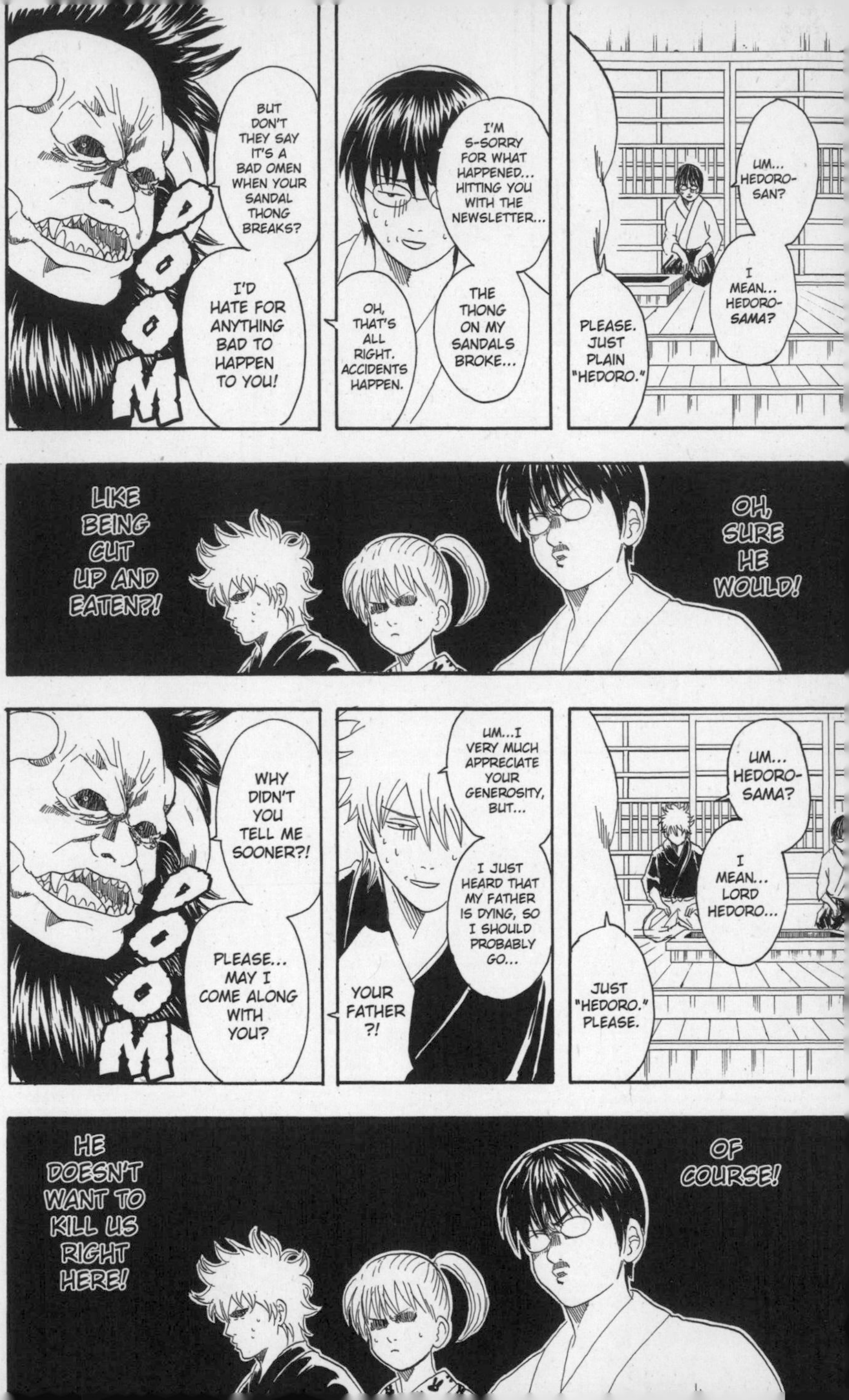
UM... HEDORO-SAN?
I MEAN... HEDORO-SAMA?
PLEASE. JUST PLAIN "HEDORO."
I'M S-SORRY FOR WHAT HAPPENED... HITTING YOU WITH THE NEWSLETTER...
THE THONG ON MY SANDALS BROKE...
OH, THAT'S ALL RIGHT. ACCIDENTS HAPPEN.
BUT DON'T THEY SAY IT'S A BAD OMEN WHEN YOUR SANDAL THONG BREAKS?
I'D HATE FOR ANYTHING BAD TO HAPPEN TO YOU!
DOOOM
OH, SURE HE WOULD!
LIKE BEING CUT UP AND EATEN?!
UM... HEDORO-SAMA?
I MEAN... LORD HEDORO...
JUST "HEDORO." PLEASE.
UM...I VERY MUCH APPRECIATE YOUR GENEROSITY, BUT...
I JUST HEARD THAT MY FATHER IS DYING, SO I SHOULD PROBABLY GO...
YOUR FATHER?!
WHY DIDN'T YOU TELL ME SOONER?!
PLEASE... MAY I COME ALONG WITH YOU?
DOOOM
OF COURSE!
HE DOESN'T WANT TO KILL US RIGHT HERE!

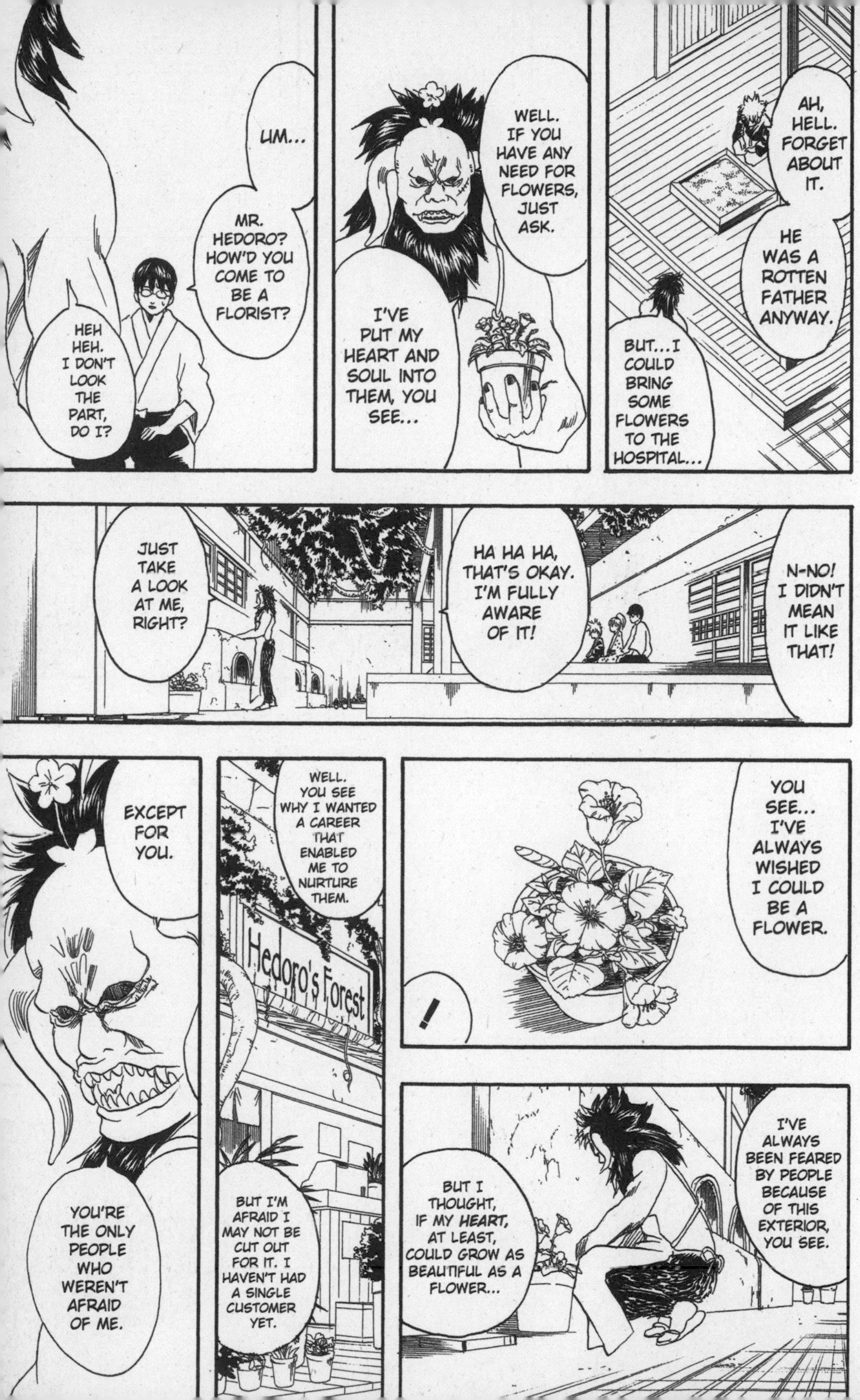
AH, HELL. FORGET ABOUT IT.
HE WAS A ROTTEN FATHER ANYWAY.
BUT...I COULD BRING SOME FLOWERS TO THE HOSPITAL...
WELL. IF YOU HAVE ANY NEED FOR FLOWERS, JUST ASK.
I'VE PUT MY HEART AND SOUL INTO THEM, YOU SEE...
UM...
MR. HEDORO? HOW'D YOU COME TO BE A FLORIST?
HEH HEH. I DON'T LOOK THE PART, DO I?
N-NO! I DIDN'T MEAN IT LIKE THAT!
HA HA HA, THAT'S OKAY. I'M FULLY AWARE OF IT!
JUST TAKE A LOOK AT ME, RIGHT?
YOU SEE... I'VE ALWAYS WISHED I COULD BE A FLOWER.
!
I'VE ALWAYS BEEN FEARED BY PEOPLE BECAUSE OF THIS EXTERIOR, YOU SEE.
BUT I THOUGHT, IF MY HEART, AT LEAST, COULD GROW AS BEAUTIFUL AS A FLOWER...
WELL. YOU SEE WHY I WANTED A CAREER THAT ENABLED ME TO NURTURE THEM.
Hedoro's Forest
BUT I'M AFRAID I MAY NOT BE CUT OUT FOR IT. I HAVEN'T HAD A SINGLE CUSTOMER YET.
EXCEPT FOR YOU.
YOU'RE THE ONLY PEOPLE WHO WEREN'T AFRAID OF ME.

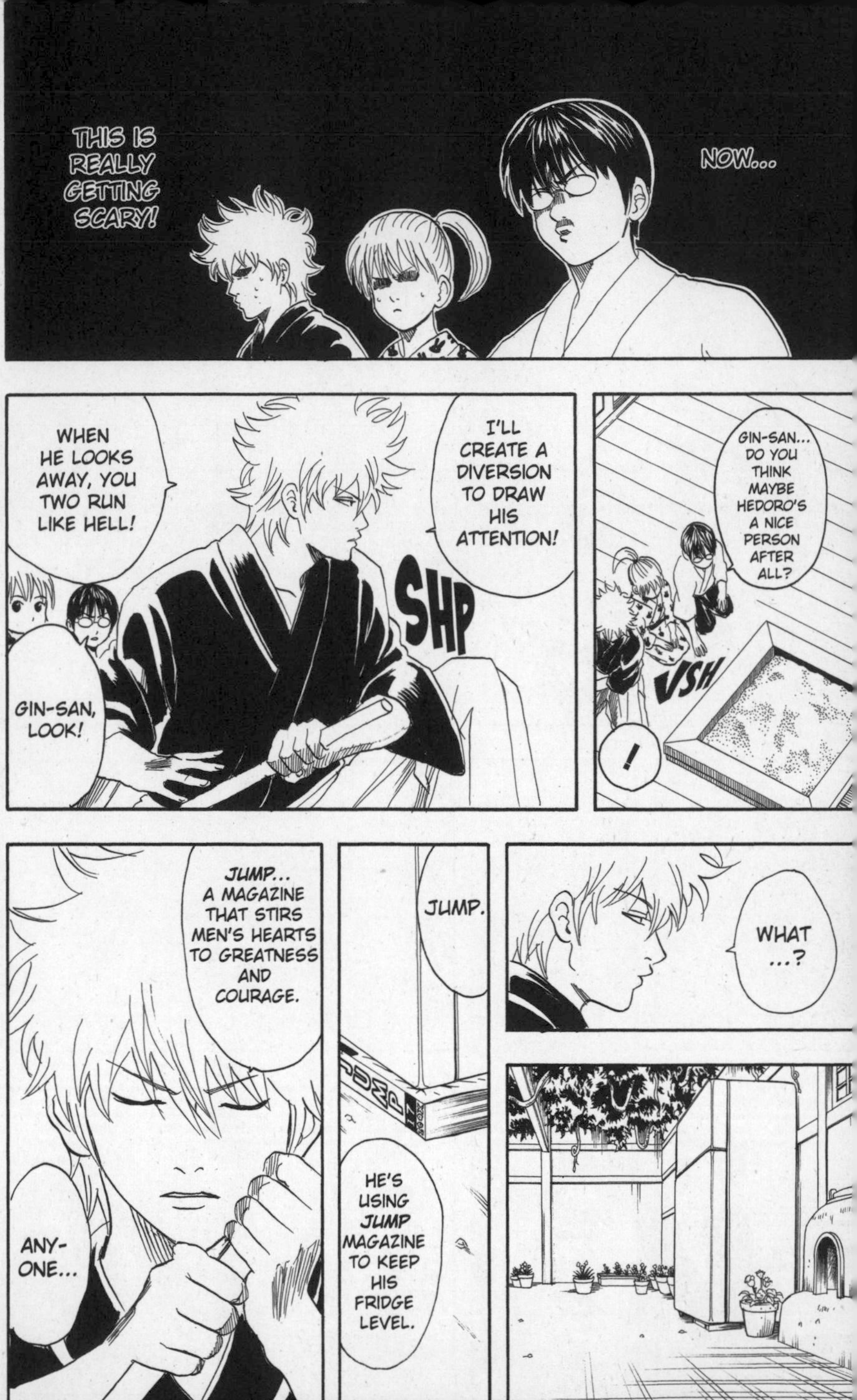
NOW...
THIS IS REALLY GETTING SCARY!
GIN-SAN... DO YOU THINK MAYBE HEDORO'S A NICE PERSON AFTER ALL?
VSH
!
I'LL CREATE A DIVERSION TO DRAW HIS ATTENTION!
WHEN HE LOOKS AWAY, YOU TWO RUN LIKE HELL!
SHP
GIN-SAN, LOOK!
WHAT ...?
JUMP.
HE'S USING *JUMP* MAGAZINE TO KEEP HIS FRIDGE LEVEL.
JUMP... A MAGAZINE THAT STIRS MEN'S HEARTS TO GREATNESS AND COURAGE.
ANY-ONE...

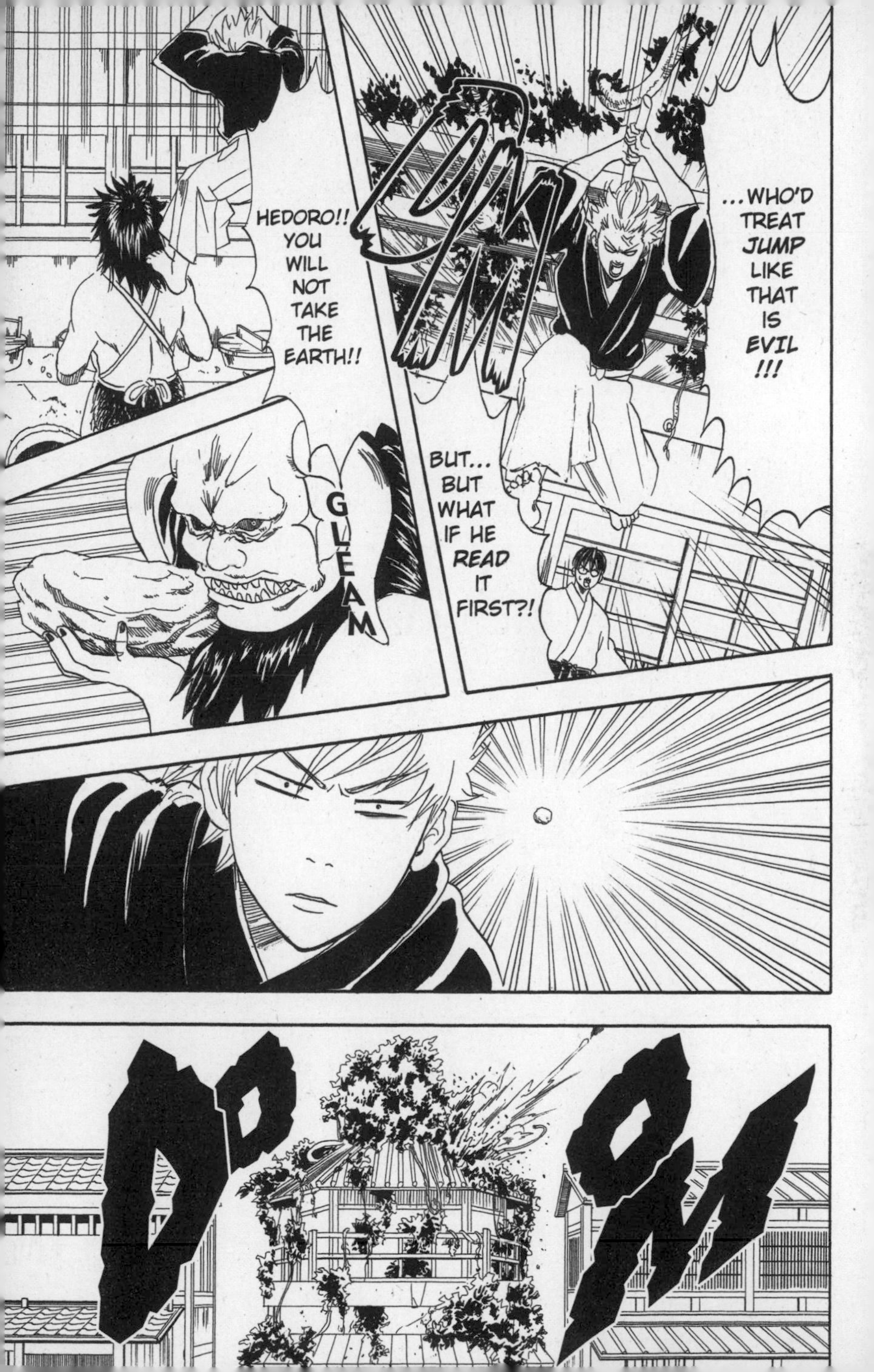
...WHO'D TREAT JUMP LIKE THAT IS EVIL!!!
BUT... BUT WHAT IF HE READ IT FIRST?!
HEDORO!! YOU WILL NOT TAKE THE EARTH!!
GLEAM

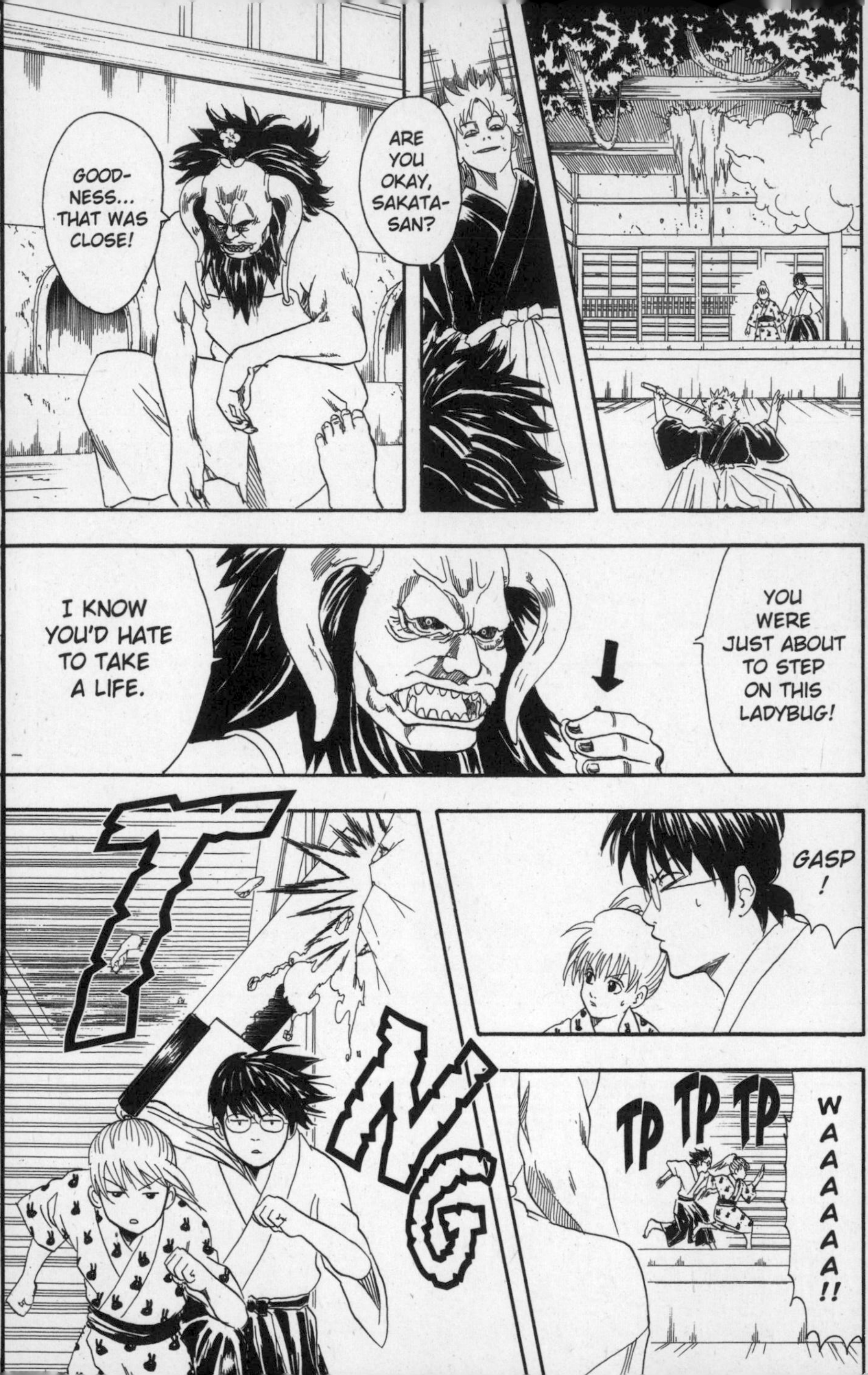
ARE YOU OKAY, SAKATA-SAN?
GOOD-NESS... THAT WAS CLOSE!
YOU WERE JUST ABOUT TO STEP ON THIS LADYBUG!
I KNOW YOU'D HATE TO TAKE A LIFE.
GASP!
TP TP TP
WAAAAAAA!!
TING

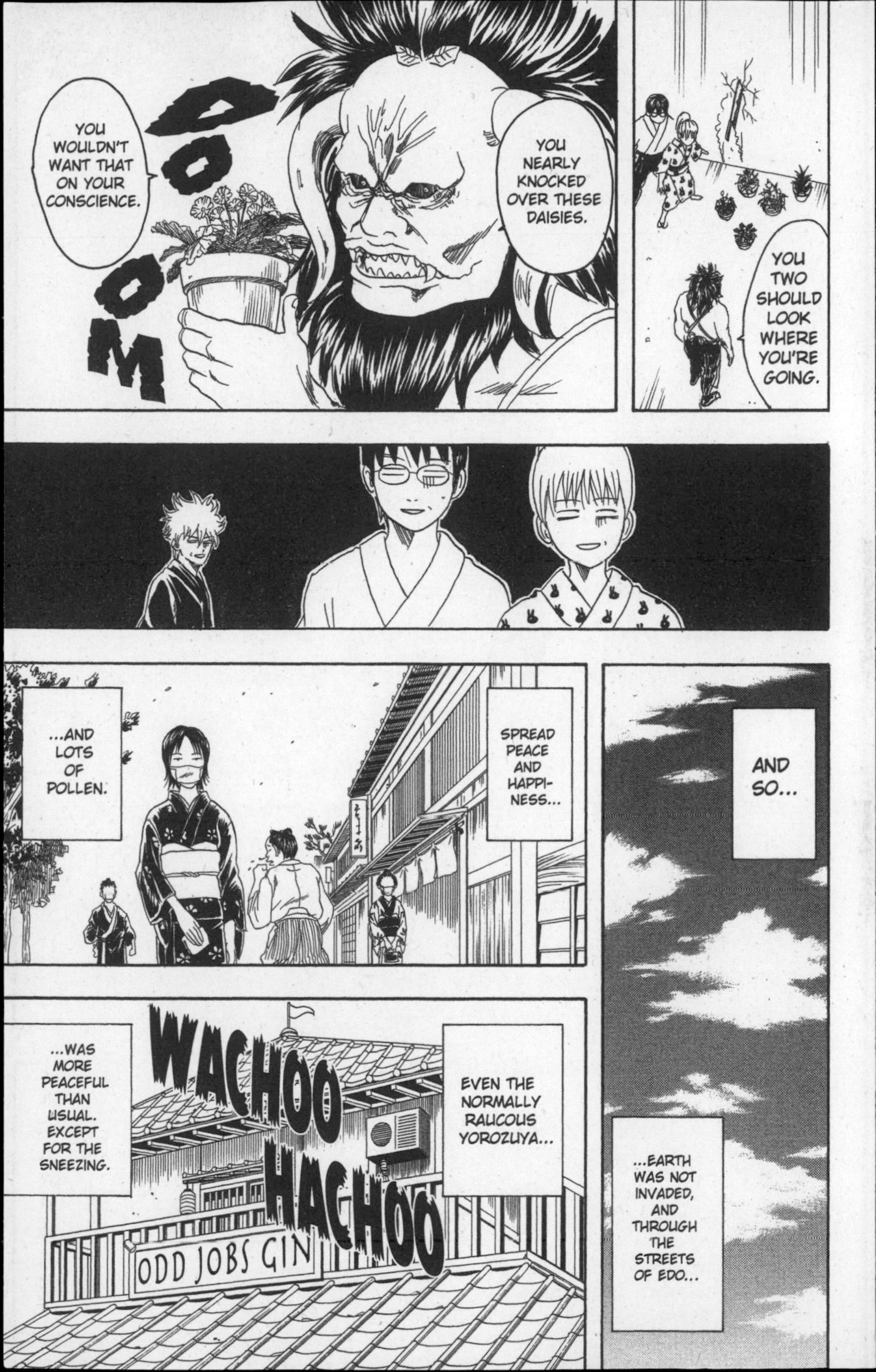
YOU TWO SHOULD LOOK WHERE YOU'RE GOING.
YOU NEARLY KNOCKED OVER THESE DAISIES.
DOOOM
YOU WOULDN'T WANT THAT ON YOUR CONSCIENCE.
AND SO...
...EARTH WAS NOT INVADED, AND THROUGH THE STREETS OF EDO...
SPREAD PEACE AND HAPPINESS...
...AND LOTS OF POLLEN.
EVEN THE NORMALLY RAUCOUS YOROZUYA...
WACHOO
HACHOO
...WAS MORE PEACEFUL THAN USUAL. EXCEPT FOR THE SNEEZING.
ODD JOBS GIN

Well, I went into these freebie pages planning to write mostly about the anime, but somewhere along the way this turned into a special feature on Katsura. And butt-hair. Sorry.

By the way, a lot more postcards came in than I expected about the "Think about the Amanto" contest last volume, and next time I'll announce the results. We're still open for submissions, so please send them on in for both this and the Q&A corner too.

Also, please go see the animated movie! It's free too. Why is it free? Because their real goal is to lure in customers and then make them buy all the collectibles being sold on the side, see. So don't be fooled, just go watch the free anime, and then sneak home.

Alrighty...see you next volume!

Sayo-nara-

Send your letters and fan art to:
VIZ Media
Attn: Mike Montesa, Editor
P.O. Box 77010
San Francisco, CA. 94107

Editor's note: Sorachi-sensei is referring to a contest held in the Japanese edition of *Shonen Jump* that has now ended. You might still see your art published in these pages of *Gin Tama*, but only if a) it's awesome and b) you include a signed release form available here: http://www.shonenjump.com/fanart/Fan_Art_Release.pdf
Good luck!

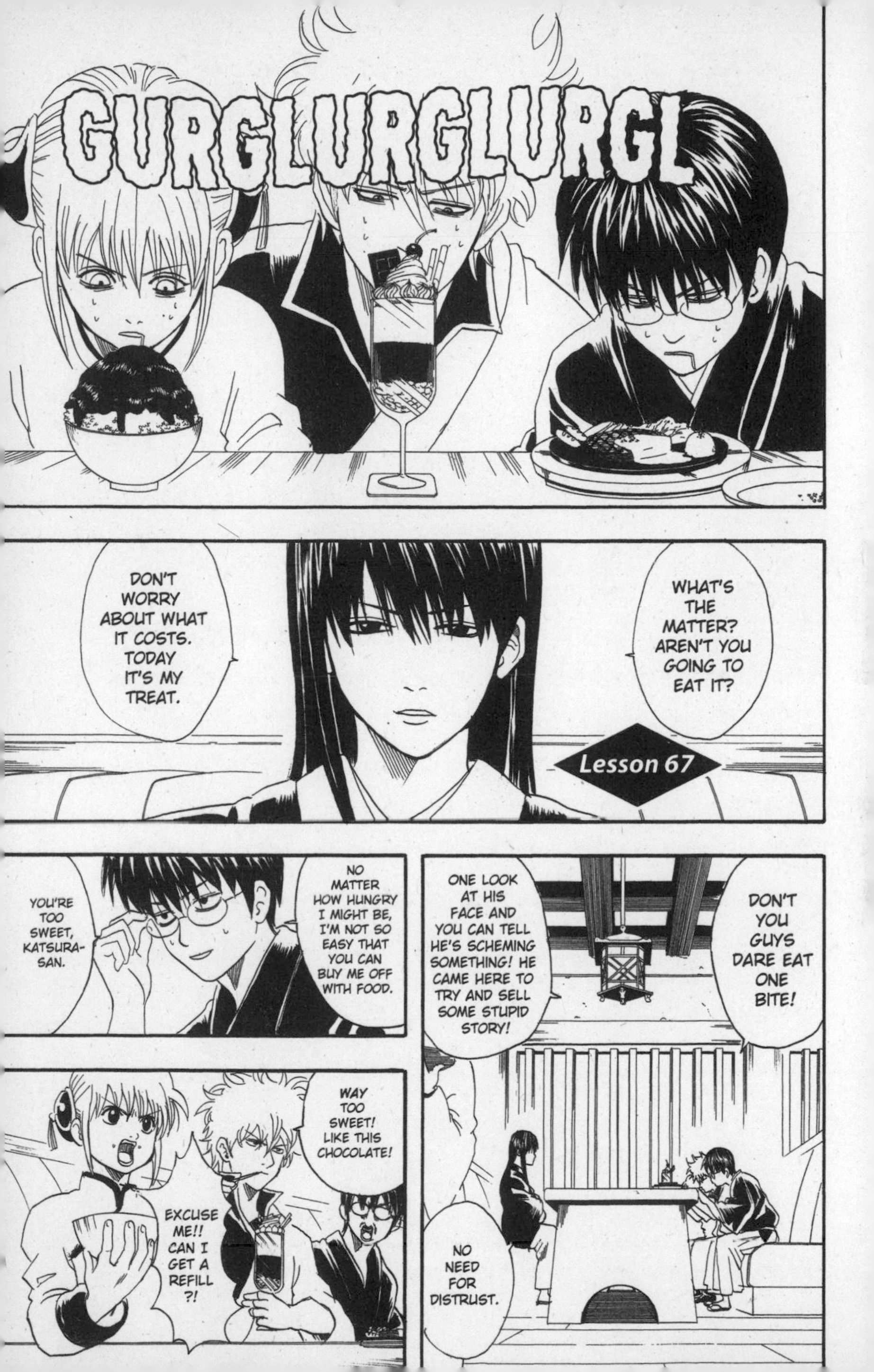
GURGLURGLURGL
WHAT'S THE MATTER? AREN'T YOU GOING TO EAT IT?
DON'T WORRY ABOUT WHAT IT COSTS. TODAY IT'S MY TREAT.
Lesson 67
DON'T YOU GUYS DARE EAT ONE BITE!
ONE LOOK AT HIS FACE AND YOU CAN TELL HE'S SCHEMING SOMETHING! HE CAME HERE TO TRY AND SELL SOME STUPID STORY!
NO NEED FOR DISTRUST.
NO MATTER HOW HUNGRY I MIGHT BE, I'M NOT SO EASY THAT YOU CAN BUY ME OFF WITH FOOD.
YOU'RE TOO SWEET, KATSURA-SAN.
WAY TOO SWEET! LIKE THIS CHOCOLATE!
EXCUSE ME!! CAN I GET A REFILL ?!

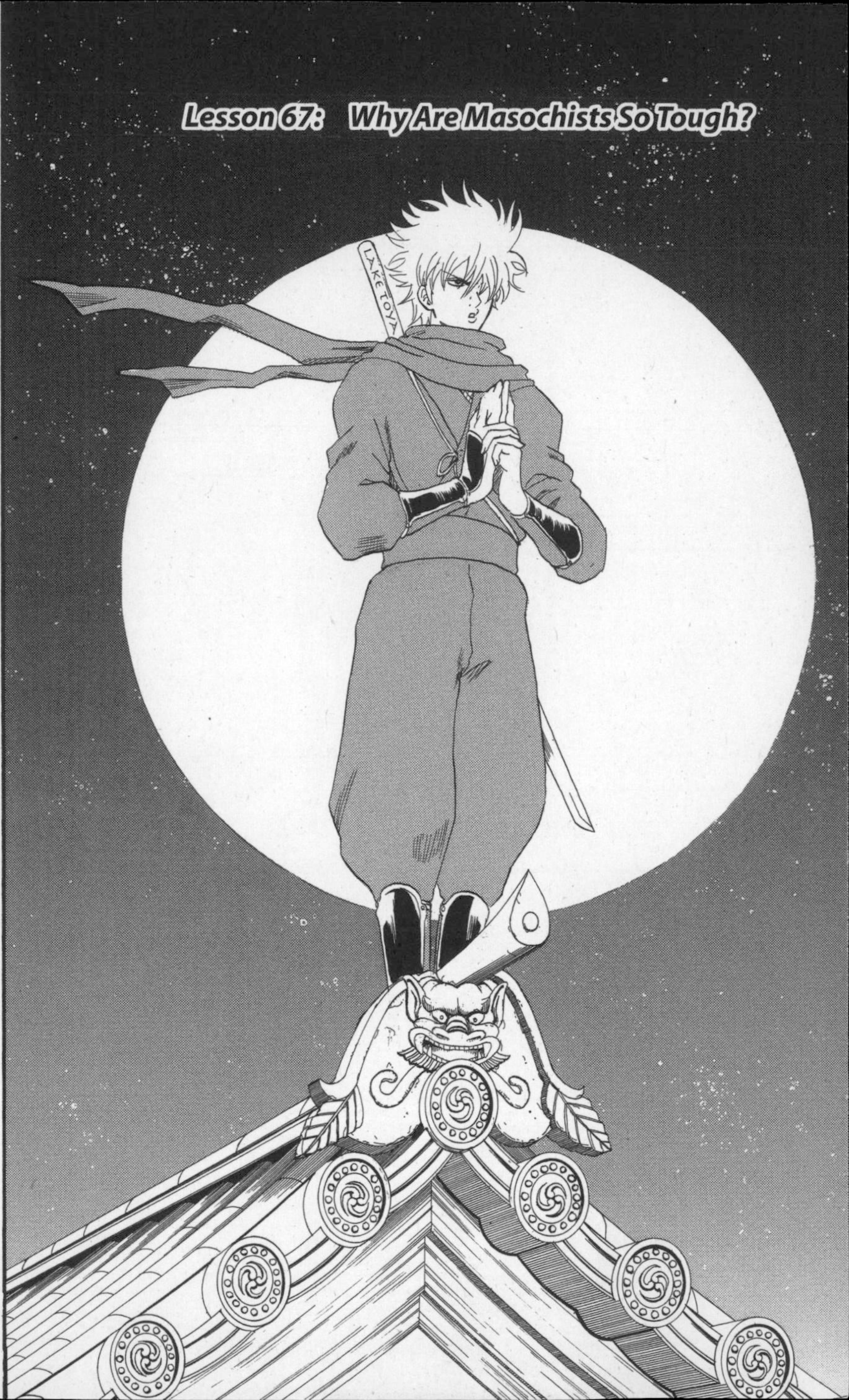
Lesson 67: Why Are Masochists So Tough?
LAKE TOYA

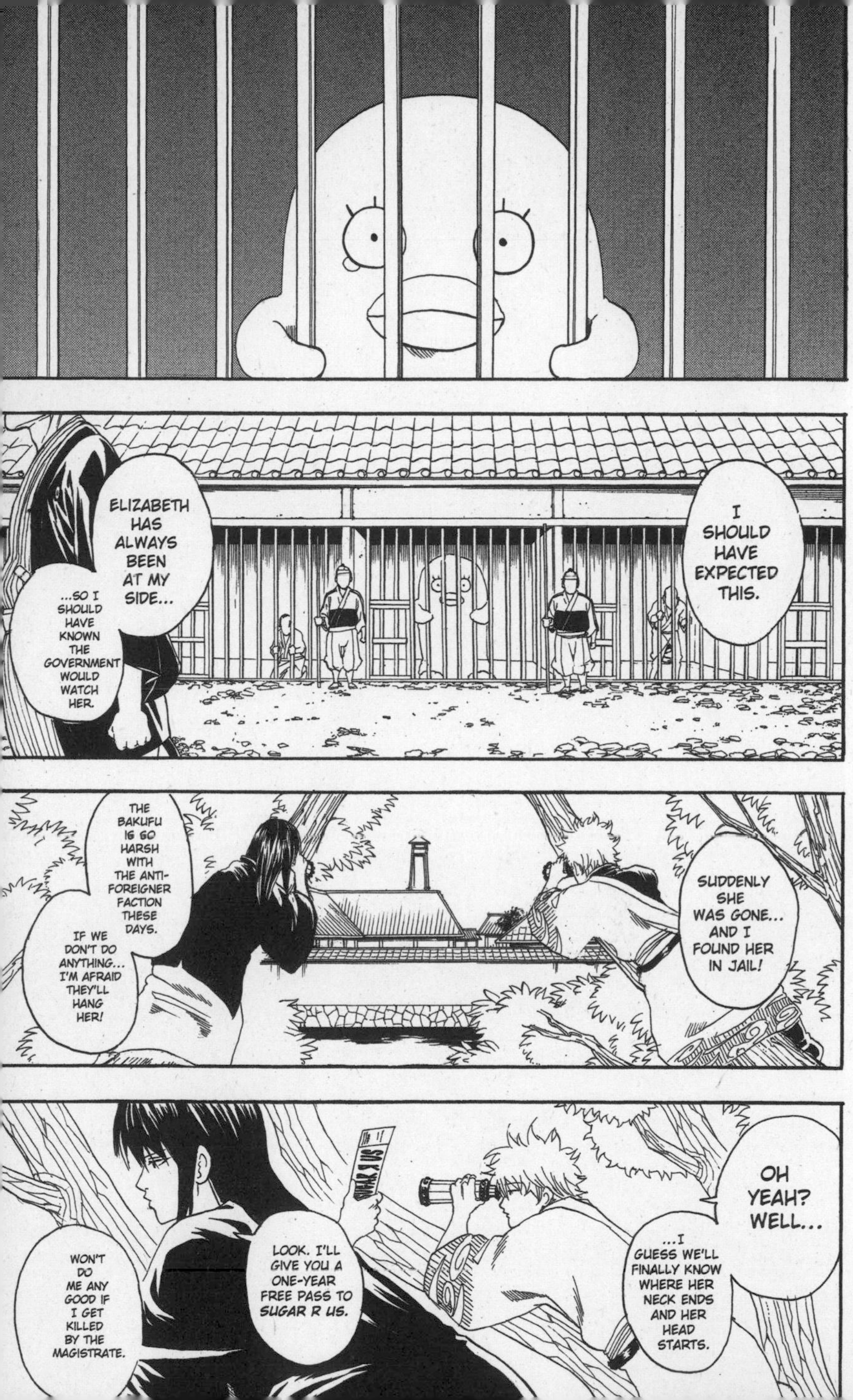
I SHOULD HAVE EXPECTED THIS.
ELIZABETH HAS ALWAYS BEEN AT MY SIDE...
...SO I SHOULD HAVE KNOWN THE GOVERNMENT WOULD WATCH HER.
SUDDENLY SHE WAS GONE... AND I FOUND HER IN JAIL!
THE BAKUFU IS SO HARSH WITH THE ANTI-FOREIGNER FACTION THESE DAYS.
IF WE DON'T DO ANYTHING... I'M AFRAID THEY'LL HANG HER!
OH YEAH? WELL...
...I GUESS WE'LL FINALLY KNOW WHERE HER NECK ENDS AND HER HEAD STARTS.
SUGAR R US
LOOK. I'LL GIVE YOU A ONE-YEAR FREE PASS TO SUGAR R US.
WON'T DO ME ANY GOOD IF I GET KILLED BY THE MAGISTRATE.

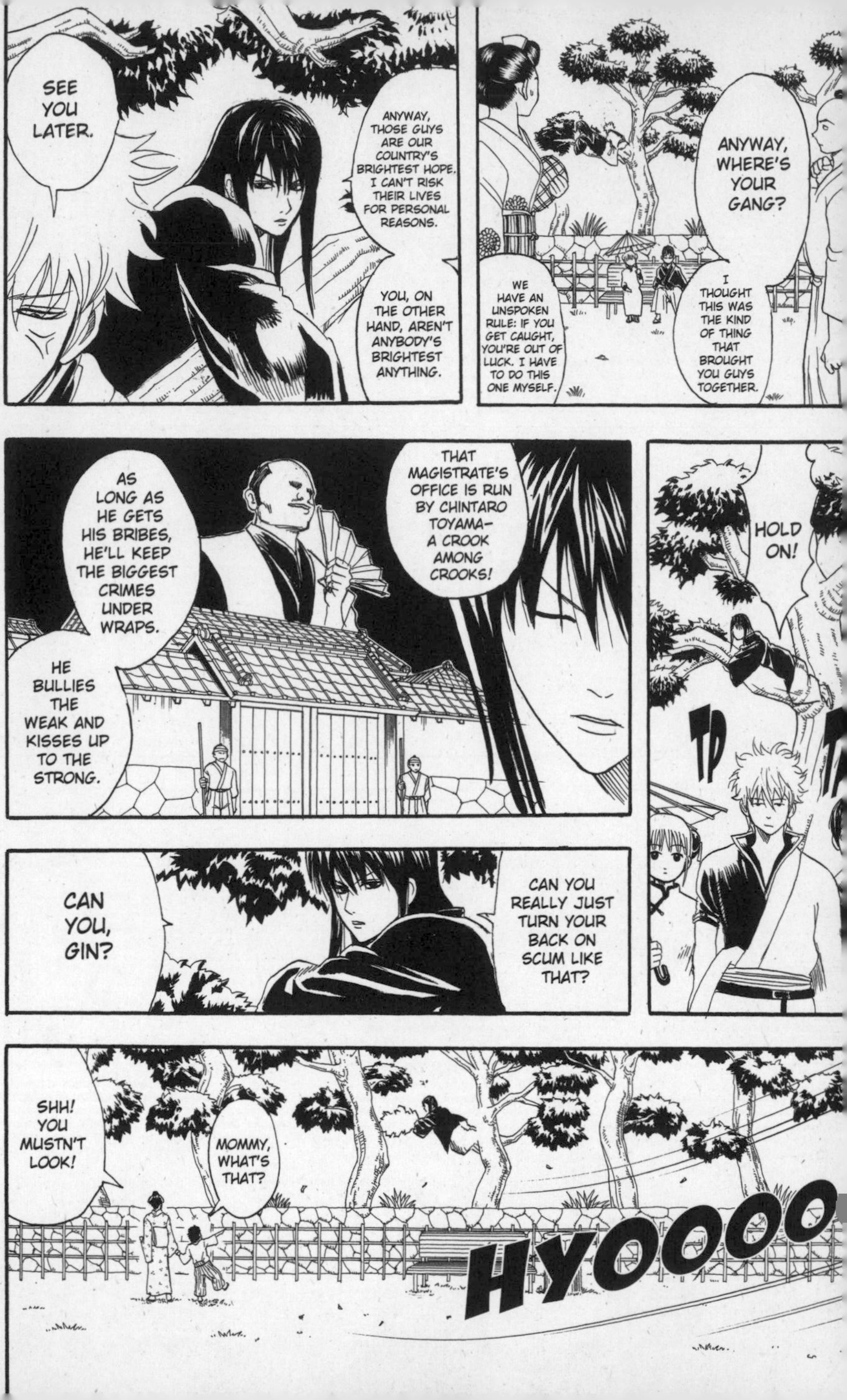
ANYWAY, WHERE'S YOUR GANG?
I THOUGHT THIS WAS THE KIND OF THING THAT BROUGHT YOU GUYS TOGETHER.
WE HAVE AN UNSPOKEN RULE: IF YOU GET CAUGHT, YOU'RE OUT OF LUCK. I HAVE TO DO THIS ONE MYSELF.
ANYWAY, THOSE GUYS ARE OUR COUNTRY'S BRIGHTEST HOPE. I CAN'T RISK THEIR LIVES FOR PERSONAL REASONS.
YOU, ON THE OTHER HAND, AREN'T ANYBODY'S BRIGHTEST ANYTHING.
SEE YOU LATER.
HOLD ON!
TD
THAT MAGISTRATE'S OFFICE IS RUN BY CHINTARO TOYAMA- A CROOK AMONG CROOKS!
AS LONG AS HE GETS HIS BRIBES, HE'LL KEEP THE BIGGEST CRIMES UNDER WRAPS.
HE BULLIES THE WEAK AND KISSES UP TO THE STRONG.
CAN YOU REALLY JUST TURN YOUR BACK ON SCUM LIKE THAT?
CAN YOU, GIN?
HYOOOOO
MOMMY, WHAT'S THAT?
SHH! YOU MUSTN'T LOOK!

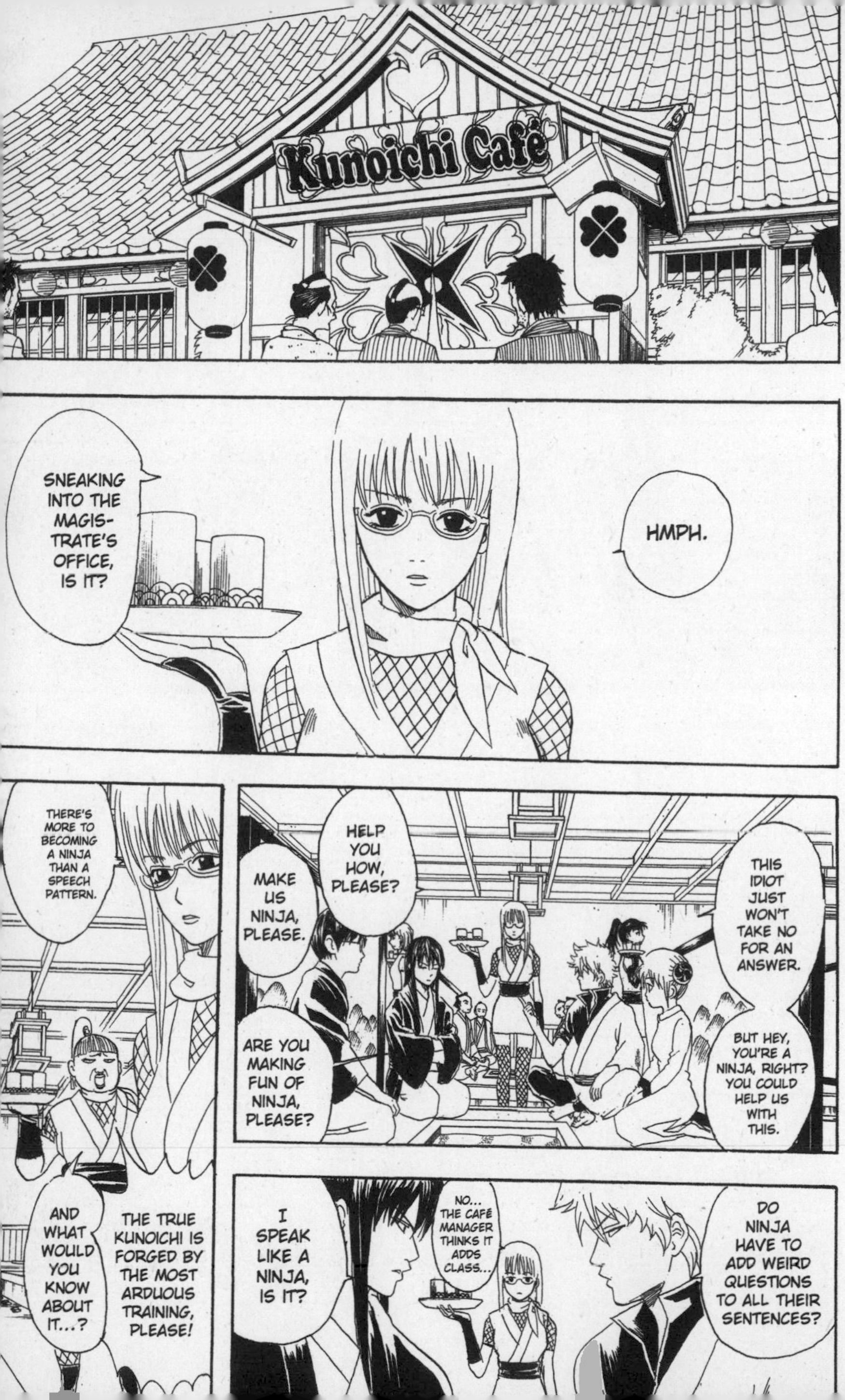
Kunoichi Café
HMPH.
SNEAKING INTO THE MAGISTRATE'S OFFICE, IS IT?
THIS IDIOT JUST WON'T TAKE NO FOR AN ANSWER.
BUT HEY, YOU'RE A NINJA, RIGHT? YOU COULD HELP US WITH THIS.
HELP YOU HOW, PLEASE?
MAKE US NINJA, PLEASE.
ARE YOU MAKING FUN OF NINJA, PLEASE?
DO NINJA HAVE TO ADD WEIRD QUESTIONS TO ALL THEIR SENTENCES?
NO... THE CAFÉ MANAGER THINKS IT ADDS CLASS...
I SPEAK LIKE A NINJA, IS IT?
THERE'S MORE TO BECOMING A NINJA THAN A SPEECH PATTERN.
THE TRUE KUNOICHI IS FORGED BY THE MOST ARDUOUS TRAINING, PLEASE!
AND WHAT WOULD YOU KNOW ABOUT IT...?

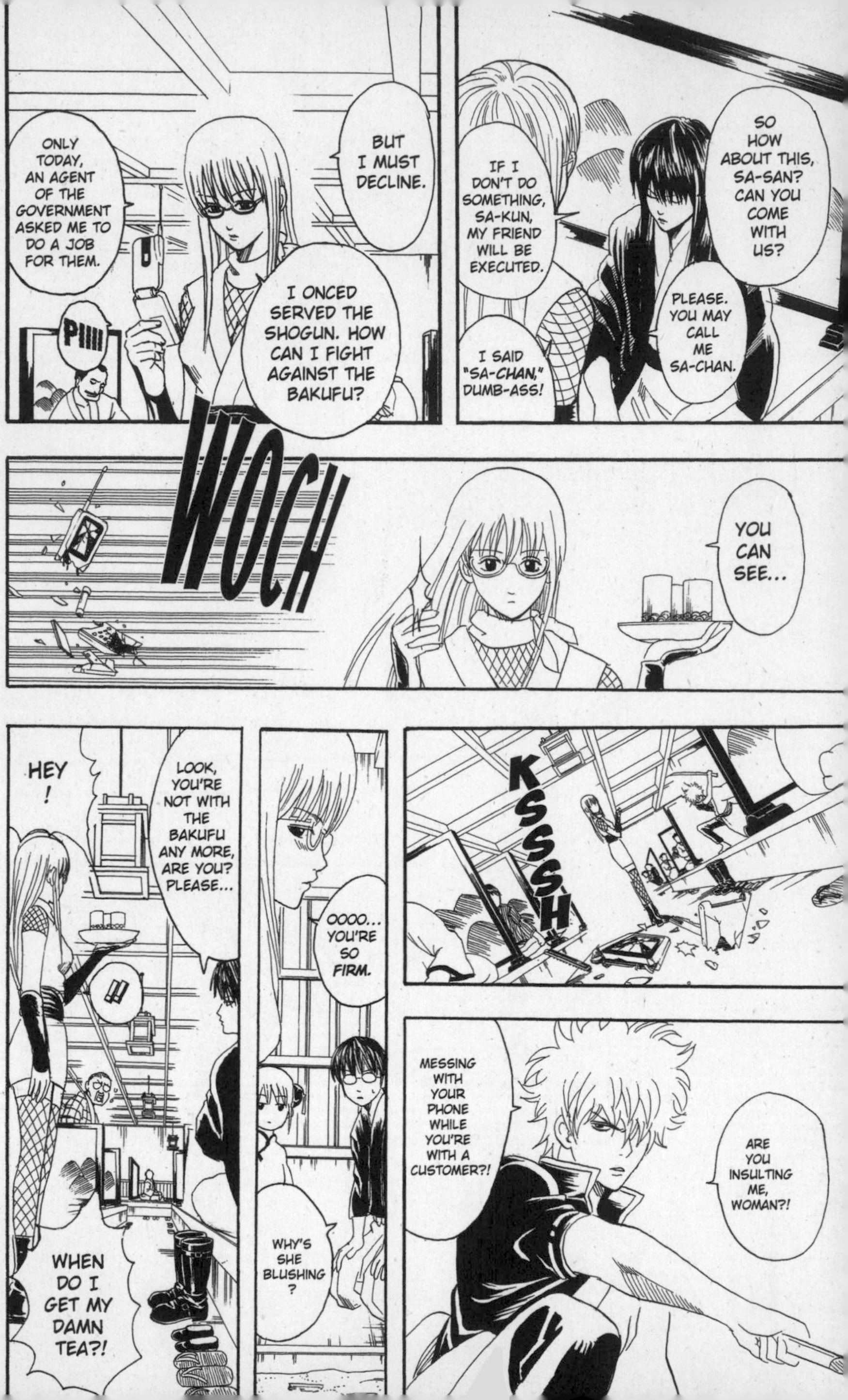
SO HOW ABOUT THIS, SA-SAN? CAN YOU COME WITH US?
IF I DON'T DO SOMETHING, SA-KUN, MY FRIEND WILL BE EXECUTED.
PLEASE. YOU MAY CALL ME SA-CHAN.
I SAID "SA-CHAN," DUMB-ASS!
BUT I MUST DECLINE.
ONLY TODAY, AN AGENT OF THE GOVERNMENT ASKED ME TO DO A JOB FOR THEM.
I ONCED SERVED THE SHOGUN. HOW CAN I FIGHT AGAINST THE BAKUFU?
PIIII
WOCH
YOU CAN SEE...
KSSSH
MESSING WITH YOUR PHONE WHILE YOU'RE WITH A CUSTOMER?!
ARE YOU INSULTING ME, WOMAN?!
OOOO... YOU'RE SO FIRM.
WHY'S SHE BLUSHING?
HEY!
LOOK, YOU'RE NOT WITH THE BAKUFU ANY MORE, ARE YOU? PLEASE...
!!
WHEN DO I GET MY DAMN TEA?!

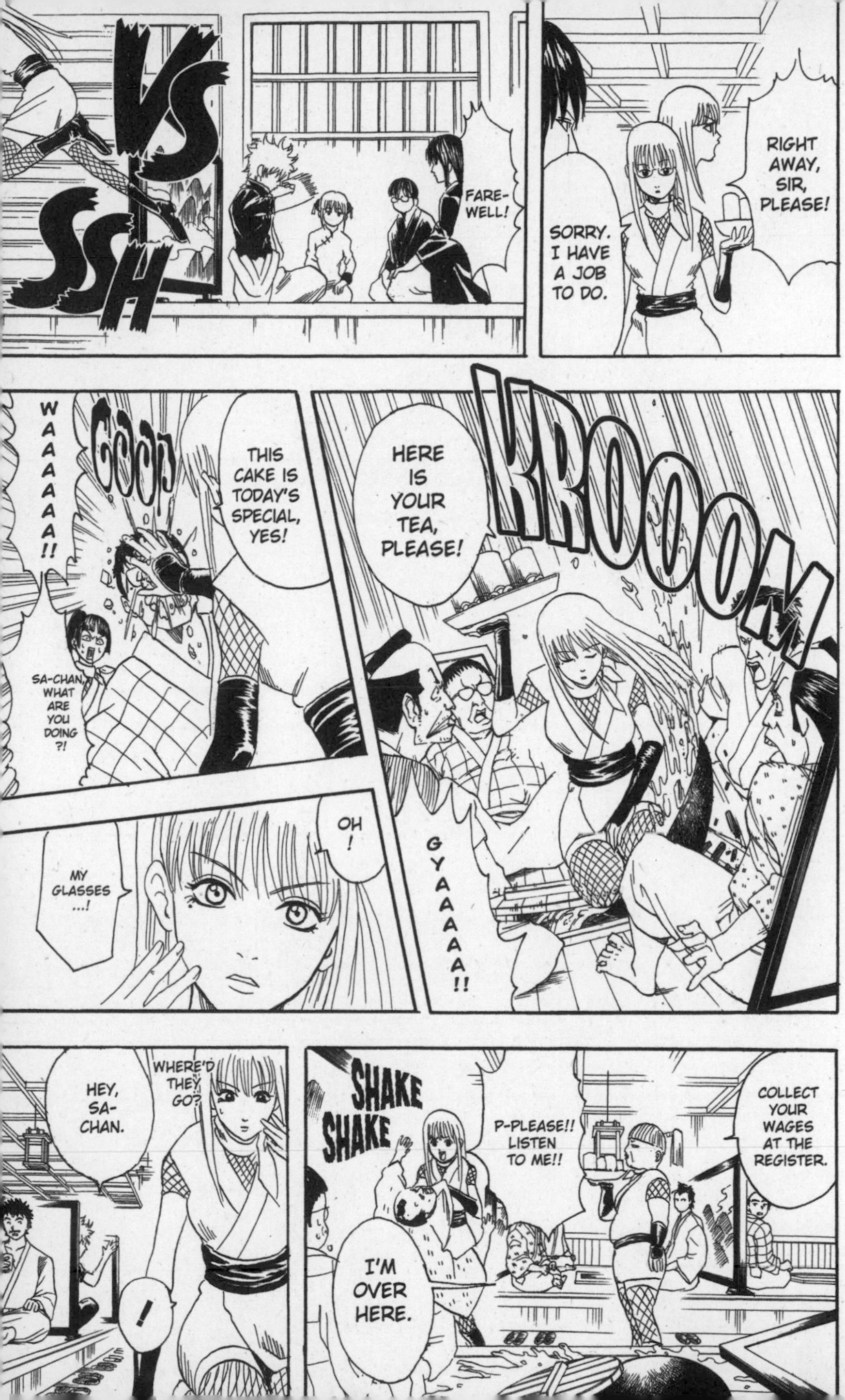
RIGHT AWAY, SIR, PLEASE!
SORRY. I HAVE A JOB TO DO.
FAREWELL!
VSSH
KROOOOM
HERE IS YOUR TEA, PLEASE!
GYAAAAAA!!
THIS CAKE IS TODAY'S SPECIAL, YES!
GOOP
WAAAAAAA!!
SA-CHAN, WHAT ARE YOU DOING?!
OH!
MY GLASSES ...!
COLLECT YOUR WAGES AT THE REGISTER.
P-PLEASE!! LISTEN TO ME!!
SHAKE SHAKE
I'M OVER HERE.
HEY, SA-CHAN.
WHERE'D THEY GO?
!

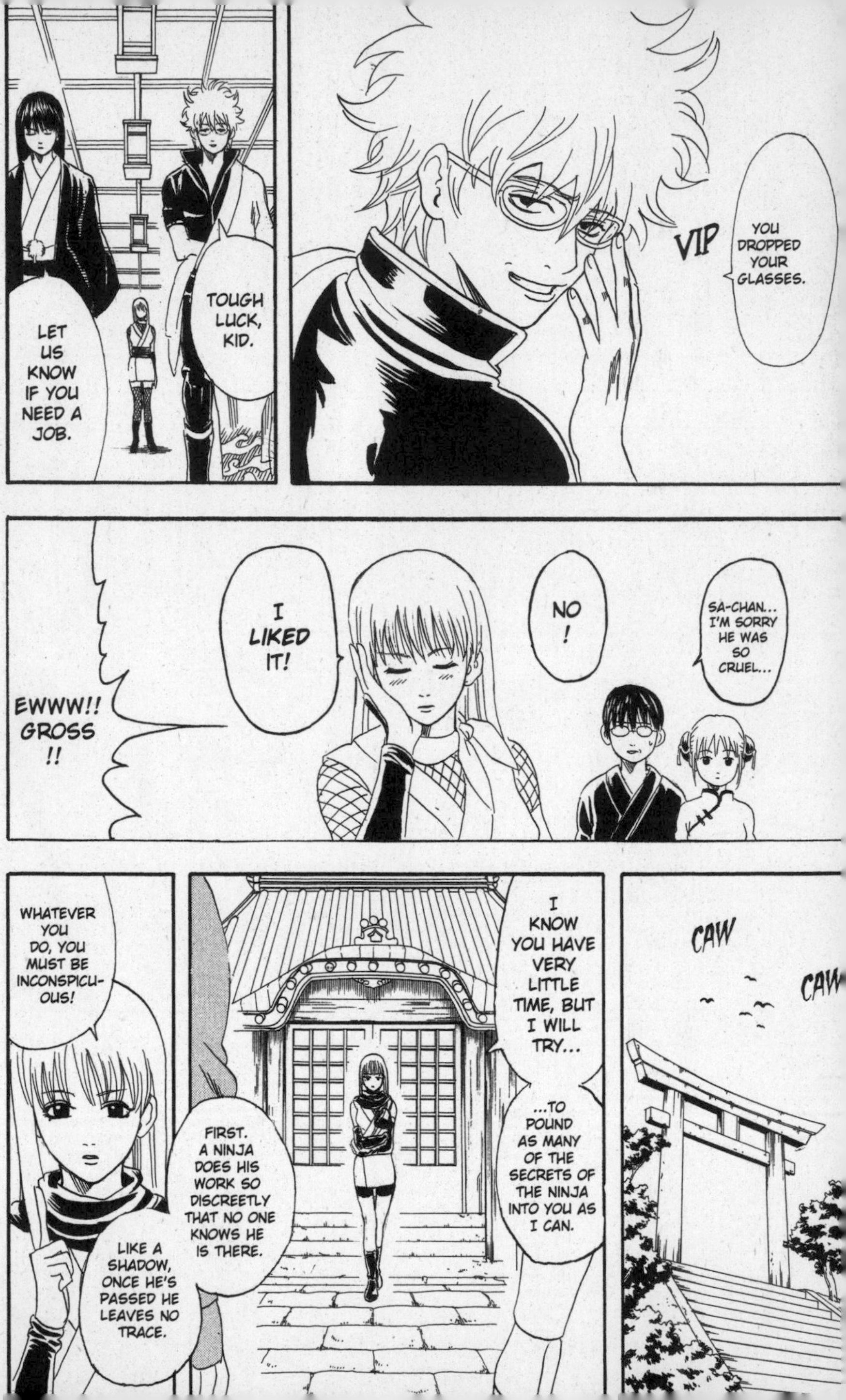
VIP
YOU DROPPED YOUR GLASSES.
TOUGH LUCK, KID.
LET US KNOW IF YOU NEED A JOB.
SA-CHAN... I'M SORRY HE WAS SO CRUEL...
NO!
I LIKED IT!
EWWW!! GROSS!!
CAW
CAW
I KNOW YOU HAVE VERY LITTLE TIME, BUT I WILL TRY...
...TO POUND AS MANY OF THE SECRETS OF THE NINJA INTO YOU AS I CAN.
FIRST. A NINJA DOES HIS WORK SO DISCREETLY THAT NO ONE KNOWS HE IS THERE.
WHATEVER YOU DO, YOU MUST BE INCONSPICU-OUS!
LIKE A SHADOW, ONCE HE'S PASSED HE LEAVES NO TRACE.

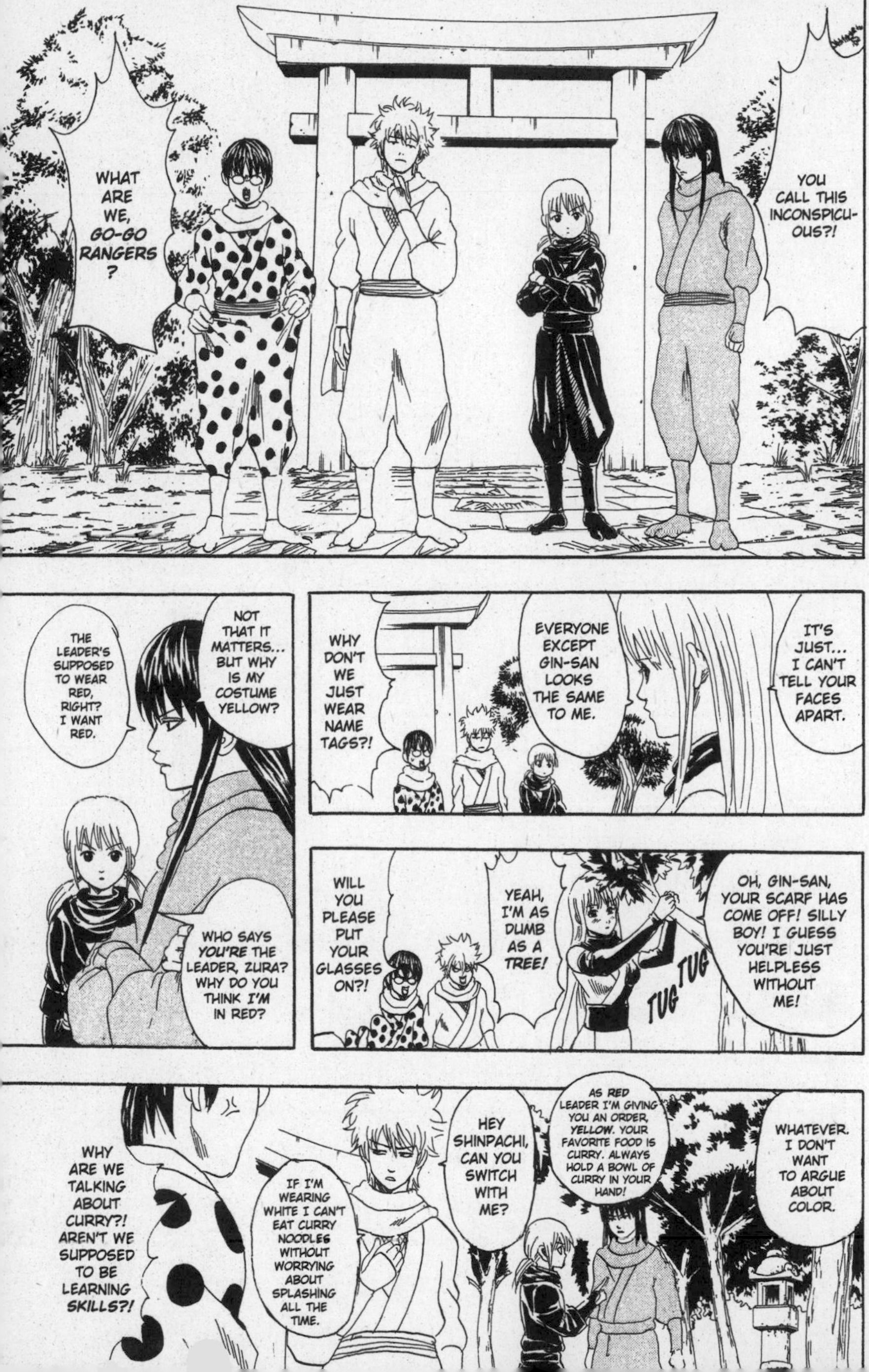
YOU CALL THIS INCONSPICUOUS?!
WHAT ARE WE, GO-GO RANGERS?
IT'S JUST... I CAN'T TELL YOUR FACES APART.
EVERYONE EXCEPT GIN-SAN LOOKS THE SAME TO ME.
WHY DON'T WE JUST WEAR NAME TAGS?!
OH, GIN-SAN, YOUR SCARF HAS COME OFF! SILLY BOY! I GUESS YOU'RE JUST HELPLESS WITHOUT ME!
TUG TUG
YEAH, I'M AS DUMB AS A TREE!
WILL YOU PLEASE PUT YOUR GLASSES ON?!
NOT THAT IT MATTERS... BUT WHY IS MY COSTUME YELLOW?
THE LEADER'S SUPPOSED TO WEAR RED, RIGHT? I WANT RED.
WHO SAYS *YOU'RE* THE LEADER, ZURA? WHY DO YOU THINK *I'M* IN RED?
WHATEVER. I DON'T WANT TO ARGUE ABOUT COLOR.
AS RED LEADER I'M GIVING YOU AN ORDER, YELLOW. YOUR FAVORITE FOOD IS CURRY. ALWAYS HOLD A BOWL OF CURRY IN YOUR HAND!
HEY SHINPACHI, CAN YOU SWITCH WITH ME?
IF I'M WEARING WHITE I CAN'T EAT CURRY NOODLES WITHOUT WORRYING ABOUT SPLASHING ALL THE TIME.
WHY ARE WE TALKING ABOUT CURRY?! AREN'T WE SUPPOSED TO BE LEARNING **SKILLS?!**

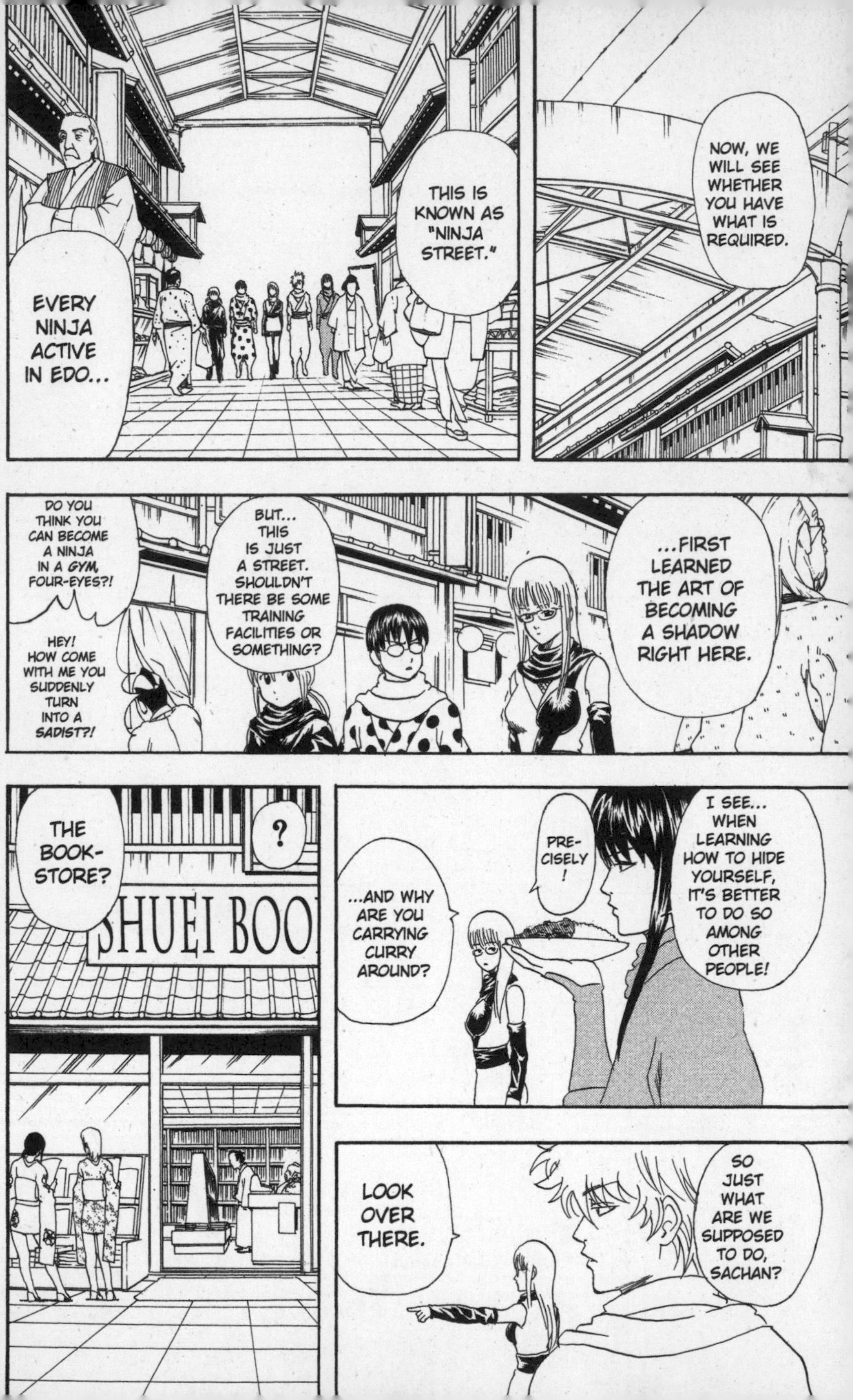
NOW, WE WILL SEE WHETHER YOU HAVE WHAT IS REQUIRED.
THIS IS KNOWN AS "NINJA STREET."
EVERY NINJA ACTIVE IN EDO...
...FIRST LEARNED THE ART OF BECOMING A SHADOW RIGHT HERE.
BUT... THIS IS JUST A STREET. SHOULDN'T THERE BE SOME TRAINING FACILITIES OR SOMETHING?
DO YOU THINK YOU CAN BECOME A NINJA IN A *GYM*, FOUR-EYES?!
HEY! HOW COME WITH ME YOU SUDDENLY TURN INTO A SADIST?!
I SEE... WHEN LEARNING HOW TO HIDE YOURSELF, IT'S BETTER TO DO SO AMONG OTHER PEOPLE!
PRE-CISELY!
...AND WHY ARE YOU CARRYING CURRY AROUND?
SO JUST WHAT ARE WE SUPPOSED TO DO, SACHAN?
LOOK OVER THERE.
?
THE BOOK-STORE?
SHUEI BOO

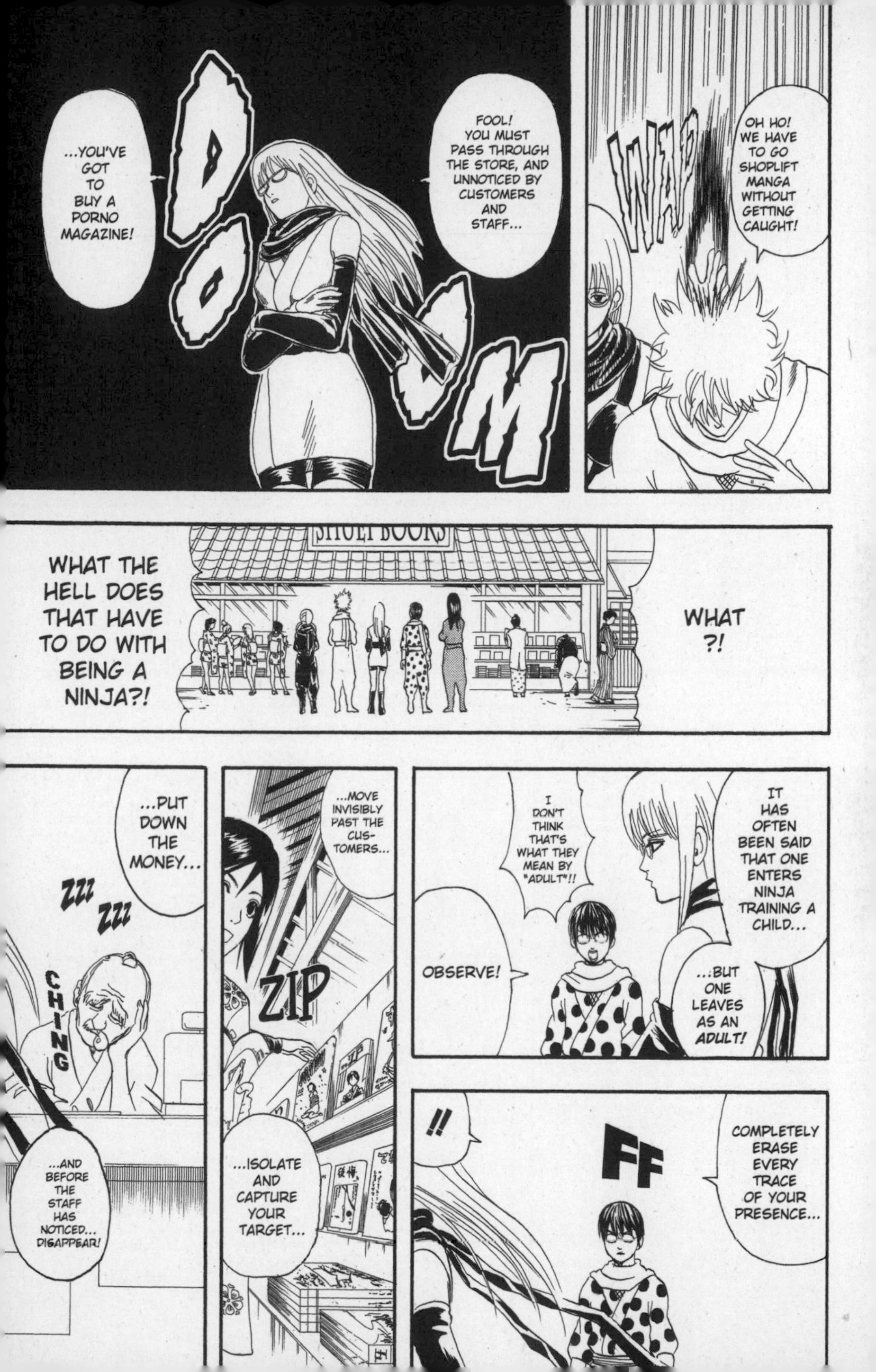
OH HO! WE HAVE TO GO SHOPLIFT MANGA WITHOUT GETTING CAUGHT!
WAP
FOOL! YOU MUST PASS THROUGH THE STORE, AND UNNOTICED BY CUSTOMERS AND STAFF...
...YOU'VE GOT TO BUY A PORNO MAGAZINE!
DOOM
WHAT ?!
WHAT THE HELL DOES THAT HAVE TO DO WITH BEING A NINJA?!
IT HAS OFTEN BEEN SAID THAT ONE ENTERS NINJA TRAINING A CHILD...
...BUT ONE LEAVES AS AN ADULT!
I DON'T THINK THAT'S WHAT THEY MEAN BY "ADULT"!!
OBSERVE!
COMPLETELY ERASE EVERY TRACE OF YOUR PRESENCE...
FF
!!
...MOVE INVISIBLY PAST THE CUS-TOMERS...
ZIP
...ISOLATE AND CAPTURE YOUR TARGET...
...PUT DOWN THE MONEY...
ZZZ ZZZ
CHING
...AND BEFORE THE STAFF HAS NOTICED... DISAPPEAR!

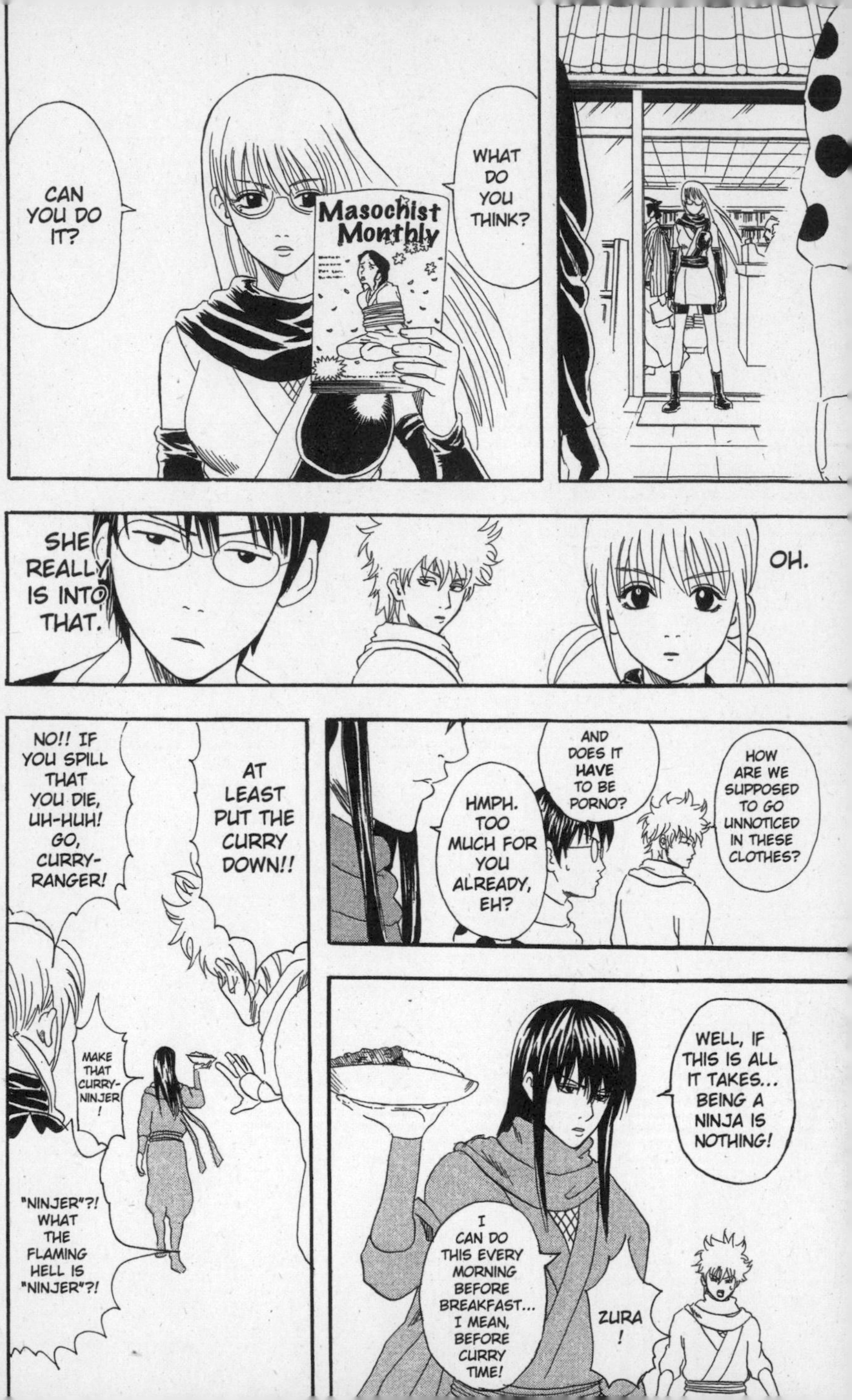
WHAT DO YOU THINK?
Masochist Monthly
CAN YOU DO IT?
OH.
SHE REALLY IS INTO THAT.
HOW ARE WE SUPPOSED TO GO UNNOTICED IN THESE CLOTHES?
AND DOES IT HAVE TO BE PORNO?
HMPH. TOO MUCH FOR YOU ALREADY, EH?
WELL, IF THIS IS ALL IT TAKES... BEING A NINJA IS NOTHING!
I CAN DO THIS EVERY MORNING BEFORE BREAKFAST... I MEAN, BEFORE CURRY TIME!
ZURA!
AT LEAST PUT THE CURRY DOWN!!
NO!! IF YOU SPILL THAT YOU DIE, UH-HUH! GO, CURRY-RANGER!
MAKE THAT CURRY-NINJER!
"NINJER"?! WHAT THE FLAMING HELL IS "NINJER"?!

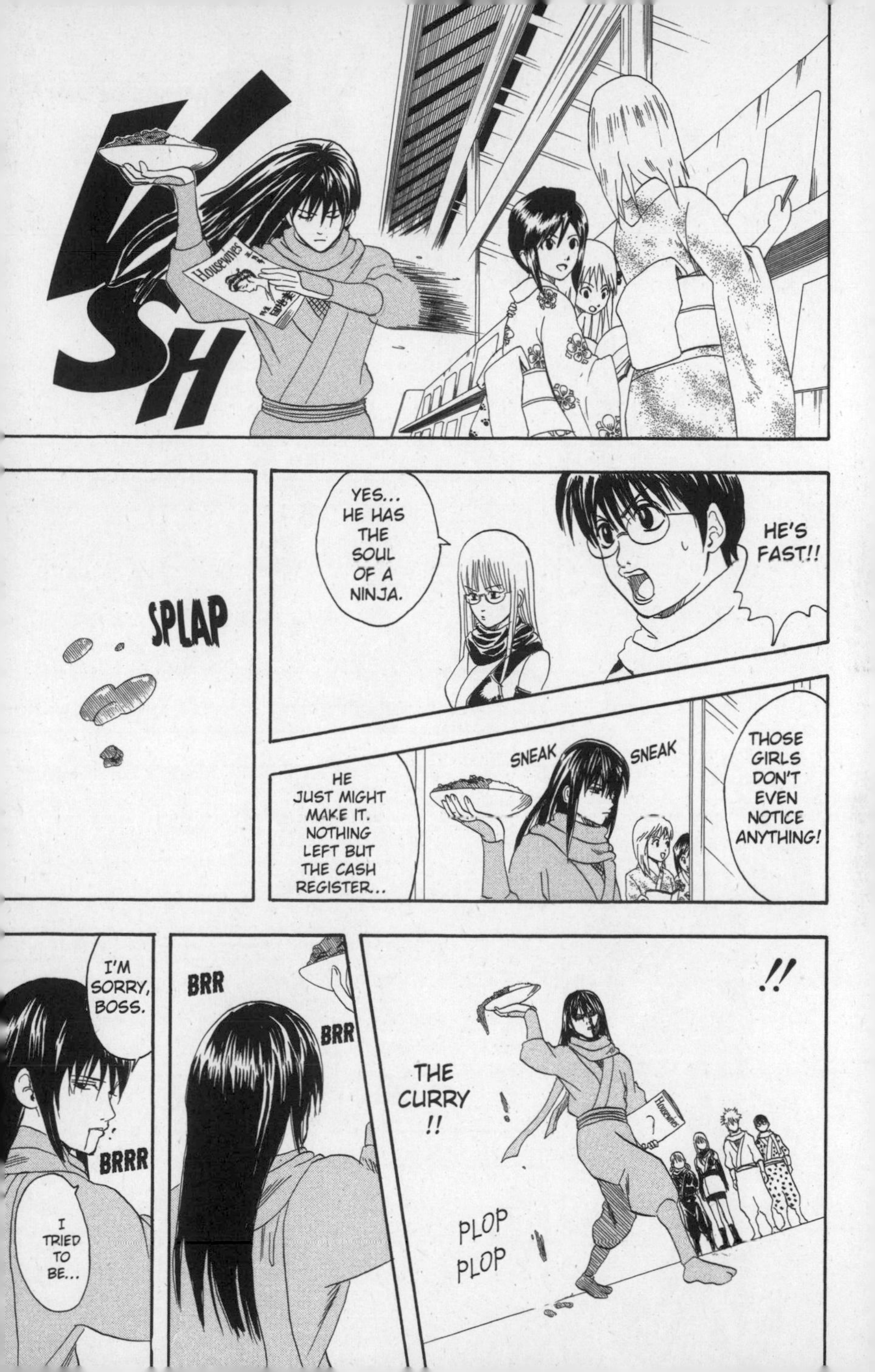
SH
Housewives
HE'S FAST!!
YES... HE HAS THE SOUL OF A NINJA.
THOSE GIRLS DON'T EVEN NOTICE ANYTHING!
SNEAK
SNEAK
HE JUST MIGHT MAKE IT. NOTHING LEFT BUT THE CASH REGISTER...
SPLAP
!!
THE CURRY !!
Housewives
PLOP PLOP
BRR
BRR
I'M SORRY, BOSS.
BRRR
I TRIED TO BE...

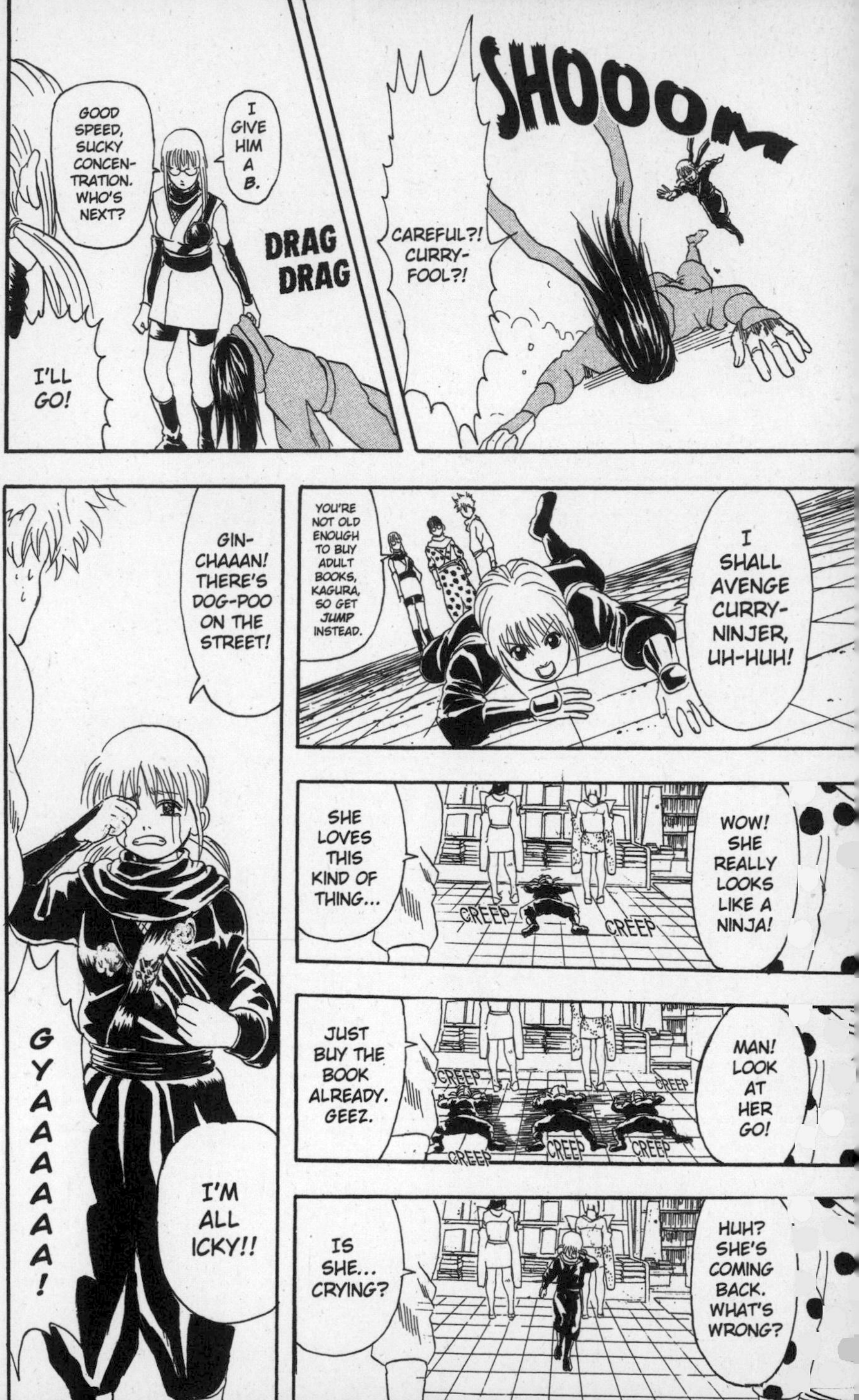
SHOOOM
CAREFUL?! CURRY-FOOL?!
I GIVE HIM A B.
GOOD SPEED, SUCKY CONCEN-TRATION. WHO'S NEXT?
DRAG DRAG
I'LL GO!
I SHALL AVENGE CURRY-NINJER, UH-HUH!
YOU'RE NOT OLD ENOUGH TO BUY ADULT BOOKS, KAGURA, SO GET JUMP INSTEAD.
WOW! SHE REALLY LOOKS LIKE A NINJA!
SHE LOVES THIS KIND OF THING...
CREEP
CREEP
MAN! LOOK AT HER GO!
JUST BUY THE BOOK ALREADY. GEEZ.
CREEP
CREEP
CREEP
CREEP
CREEP
HUH? SHE'S COMING BACK. WHAT'S WRONG?
IS SHE... CRYING?
GIN-CHAAAN! THERE'S DOG-POO ON THE STREET!
I'M ALL ICKY!!
GYAAAAAAA!

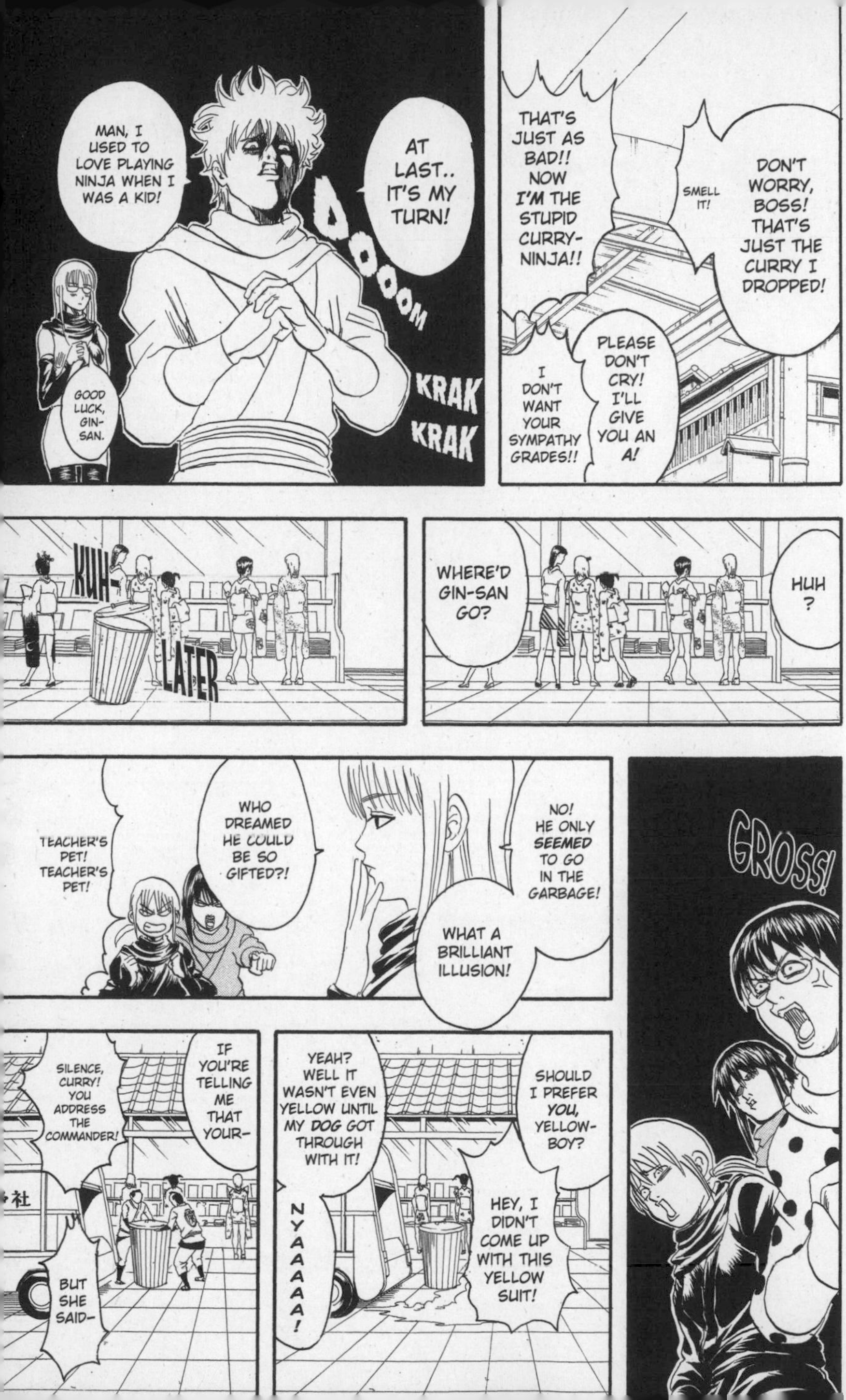
DON'T WORRY, BOSS! THAT'S JUST THE CURRY I DROPPED!
SMELL IT!
THAT'S JUST AS BAD!! NOW I'M THE STUPID CURRY-NINJA!!
PLEASE DON'T CRY! I'LL GIVE YOU AN A!
I DON'T WANT YOUR SYMPATHY GRADES!!
AT LAST.. IT'S MY TURN!
DOOOOM
KRAK KRAK
MAN, I USED TO LOVE PLAYING NINJA WHEN I WAS A KID!
GOOD LUCK, GIN-SAN.
HUH?
WHERE'D GIN-SAN GO?
KUH-
LATER
GROSS!
NO! HE ONLY SEEMED TO GO IN THE GARBAGE!
WHAT A BRILLIANT ILLUSION!
WHO DREAMED HE COULD BE SO GIFTED?!
TEACHER'S PET! TEACHER'S PET!
SHOULD I PREFER YOU, YELLOW-BOY?
YEAH? WELL IT WASN'T EVEN YELLOW UNTIL MY DOG GOT THROUGH WITH IT!
HEY, I DIDN'T COME UP WITH THIS YELLOW SUIT!
NYAAAAAA!
IF YOU'RE TELLING ME THAT YOUR-
SILENCE, CURRY! YOU ADDRESS THE COMMANDER!
BUT SHE SAID-

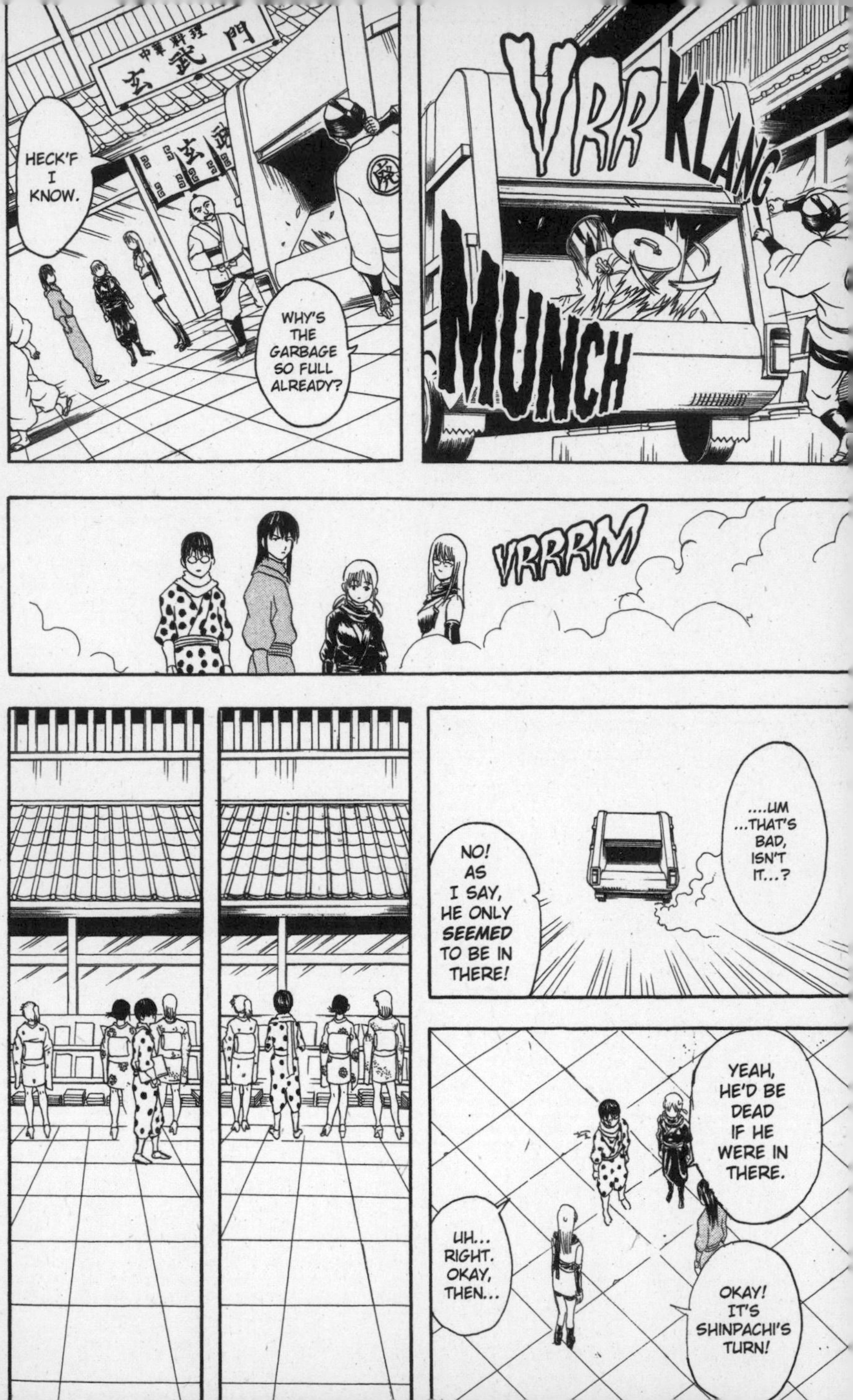
VRR
KLANG
MUNCH
WHY'S THE GARBAGE SO FULL ALREADY?
HECK'F I KNOW.
VRRRM
...UM ...THAT'S BAD, ISN'T IT...?
NO! AS I SAY, HE ONLY SEEMED TO BE IN THERE!
YEAH, HE'D BE DEAD IF HE WERE IN THERE.
UH... RIGHT. OKAY, THEN...
OKAY! IT'S SHINPACHI'S TURN!

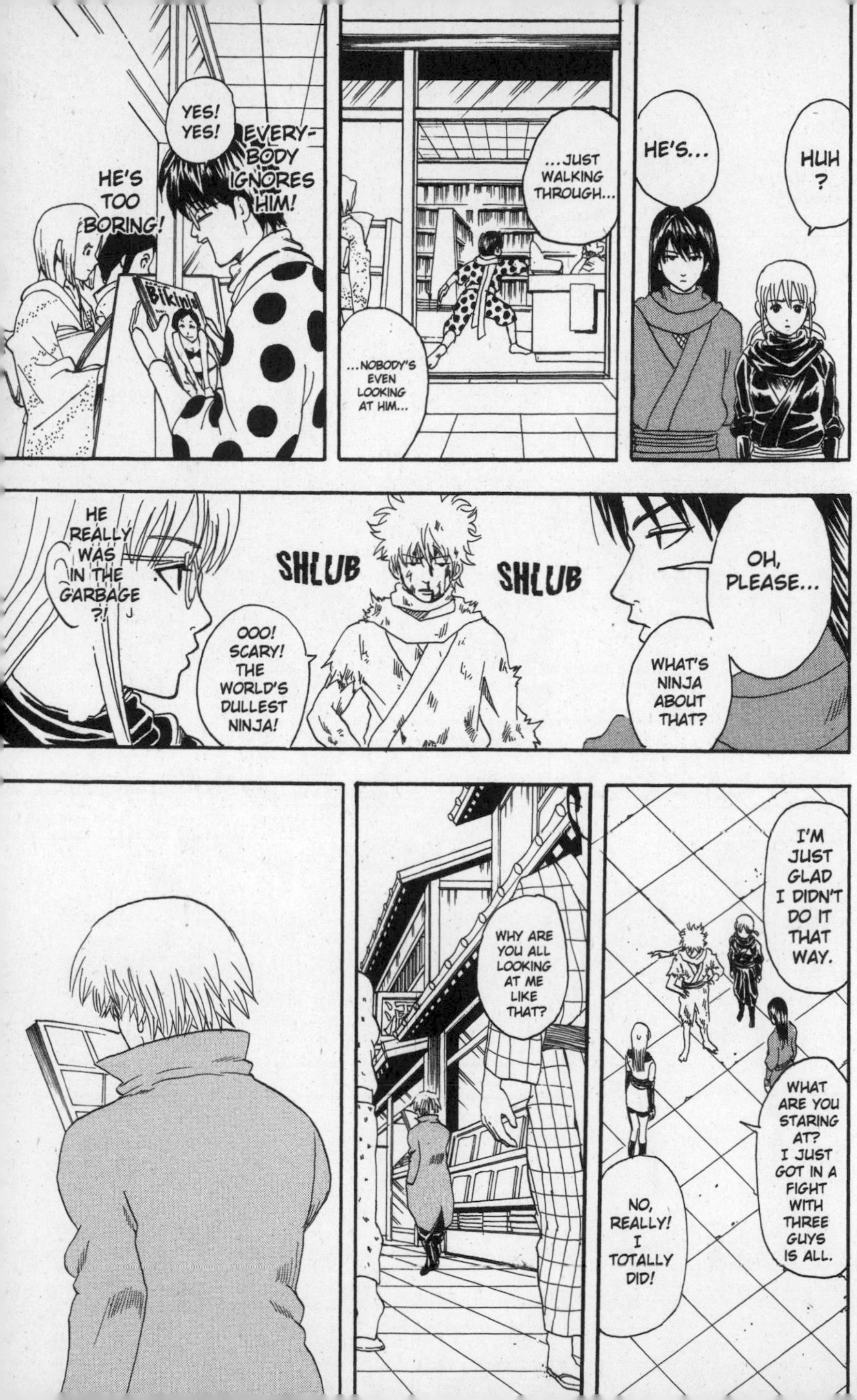
HUH?
HE'S...
...JUST WALKING THROUGH...
...NOBODY'S EVEN LOOKING AT HIM...
YES! YES!
EVERYBODY IGNORES HIM!
HE'S TOO BORING!
OH, PLEASE...
WHAT'S NINJA ABOUT THAT?
SHLUB
SHLUB
OOO! SCARY! THE WORLD'S DULLEST NINJA!
HE REALLY WAS IN THE GARBAGE?!
I'M JUST GLAD I DIDN'T DO IT THAT WAY.
WHAT ARE YOU STARING AT? I JUST GOT IN A FIGHT WITH THREE GUYS IS ALL.
NO, REALLY! I TOTALLY DID!
WHY ARE YOU ALL LOOKING AT ME LIKE THAT?

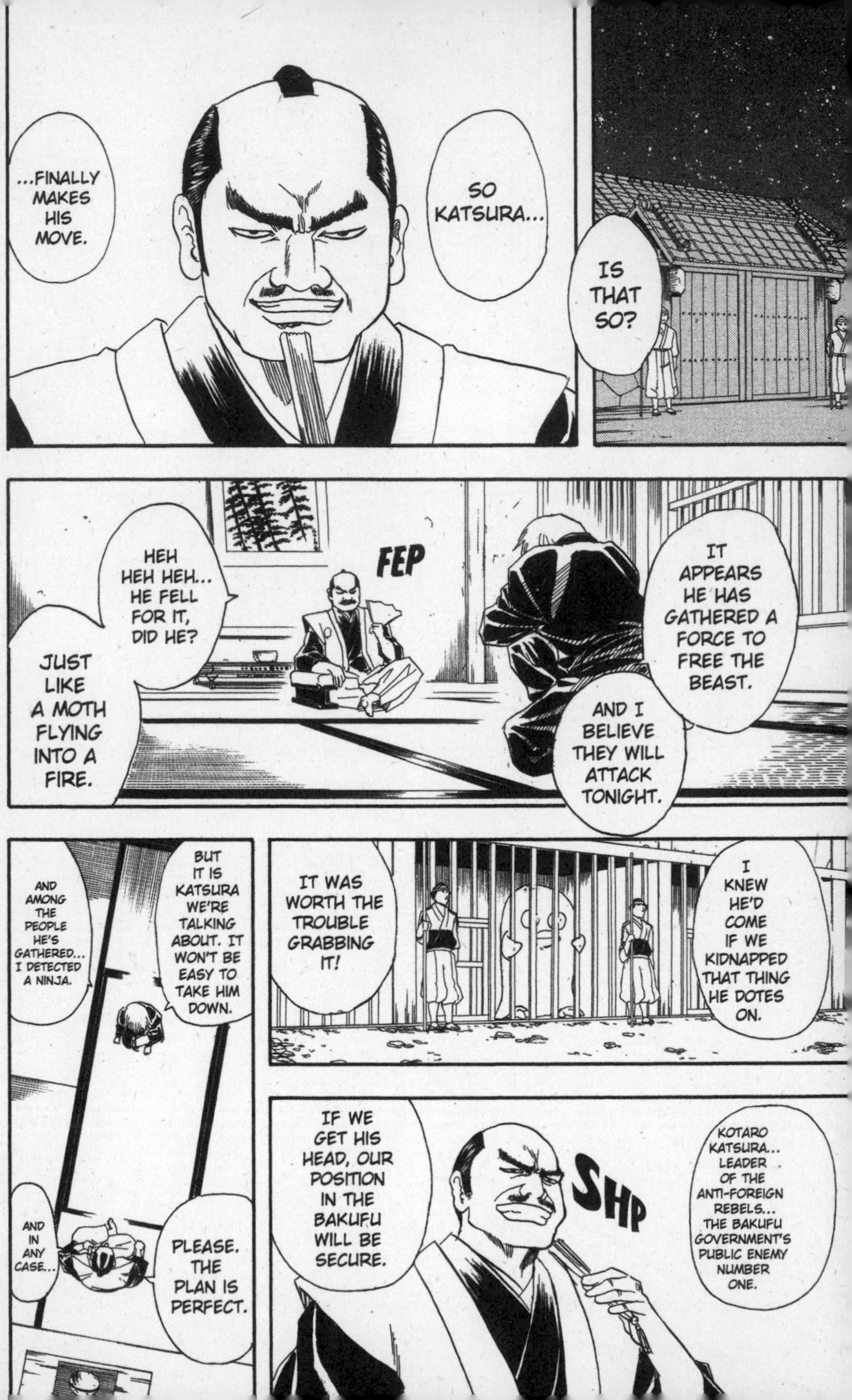
IS THAT SO?
SO KATSURA...
...FINALLY MAKES HIS MOVE.
IT APPEARS HE HAS GATHERED A FORCE TO FREE THE BEAST.
AND I BELIEVE THEY WILL ATTACK TONIGHT.
FEP
HEH HEH HEH... HE FELL FOR IT, DID HE?
JUST LIKE A MOTH FLYING INTO A FIRE.
I KNEW HE'D COME IF WE KIDNAPPED THAT THING HE DOTES ON.
IT WAS WORTH THE TROUBLE GRABBING IT!
KOTARO KATSURA... LEADER OF THE ANTI-FOREIGN REBELS... THE BAKUFU GOVERNMENT'S PUBLIC ENEMY NUMBER ONE.
SHP
IF WE GET HIS HEAD, OUR POSITION IN THE BAKUFU WILL BE SECURE.
BUT IT IS KATSURA WE'RE TALKING ABOUT. IT WON'T BE EASY TO TAKE HIM DOWN.
AND AMONG THE PEOPLE HE'S GATHERED... I DETECTED A NINJA.
PLEASE. THE PLAN IS PERFECT.
AND IN ANY CASE...

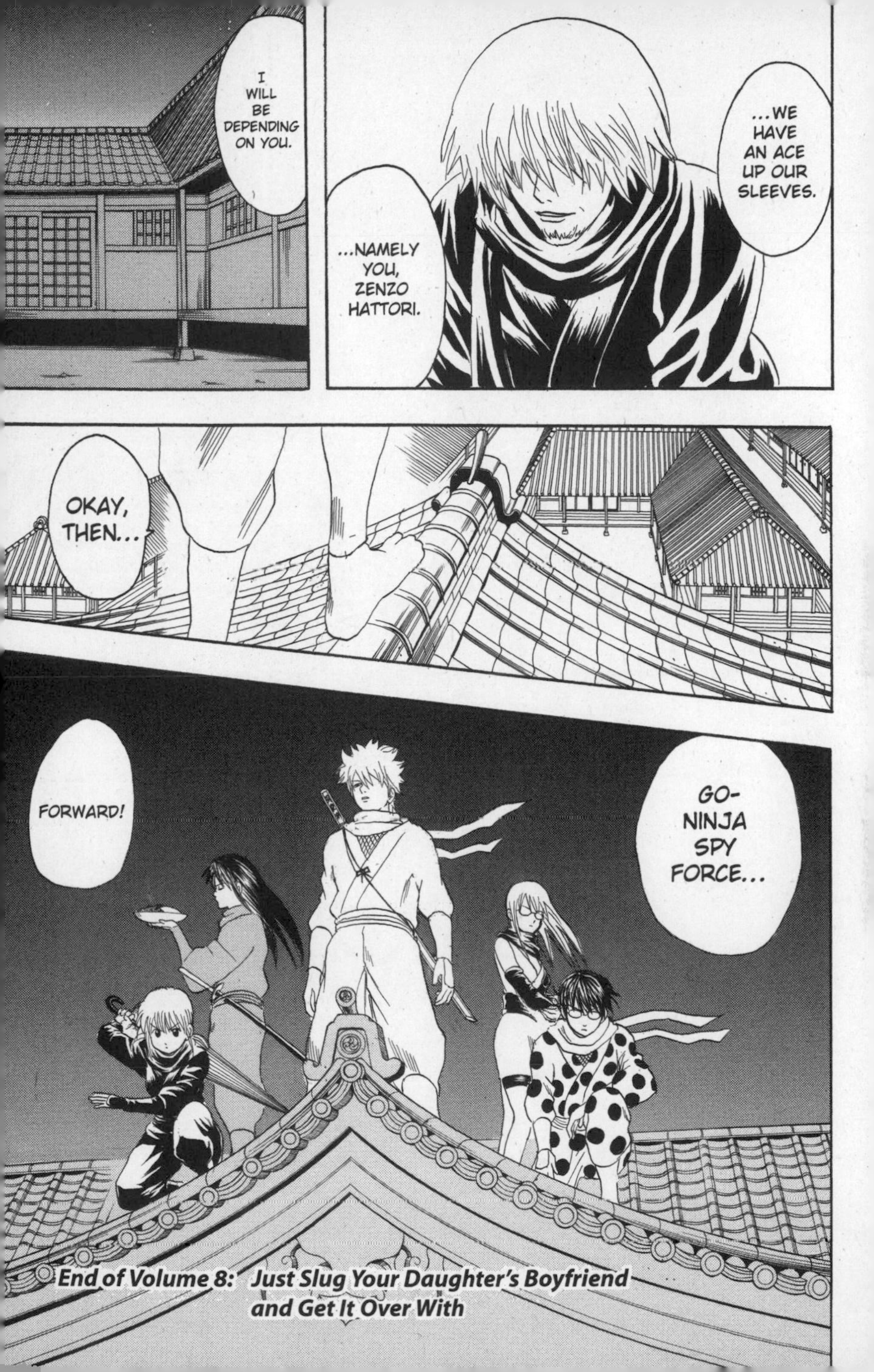
...WE HAVE AN ACE UP OUR SLEEVES.
...NAMELY YOU, ZENZO HATTORI.
I WILL BE DEPENDING ON YOU.
OKAY, THEN...
GO-NINJA SPY FORCE...
FORWARD!

End of Volume 8: Just Slug Your Daughter's Boyfriend and Get It Over With

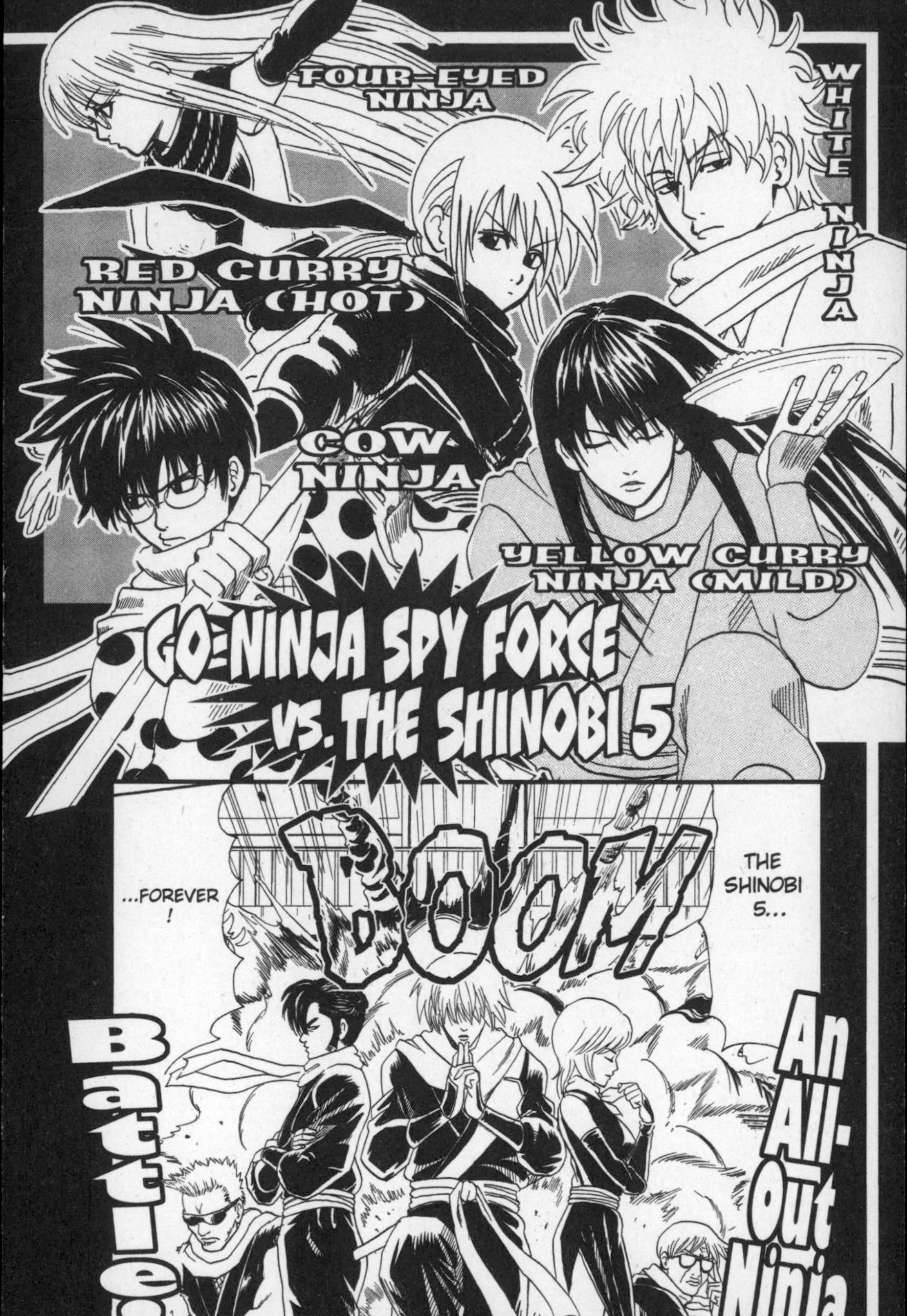
WHITE NINJA
FOUR-EYED NINJA
RED CURRY NINJA (HOT)
COW NINJA
YELLOW CURRY NINJA (MILD)
GO: NINJA SPY FORCE VS. THE SHINOBI 5
THE SHINOBI 5...
BOOM
...FOREVER!
An All-Out Ninja
Battle!

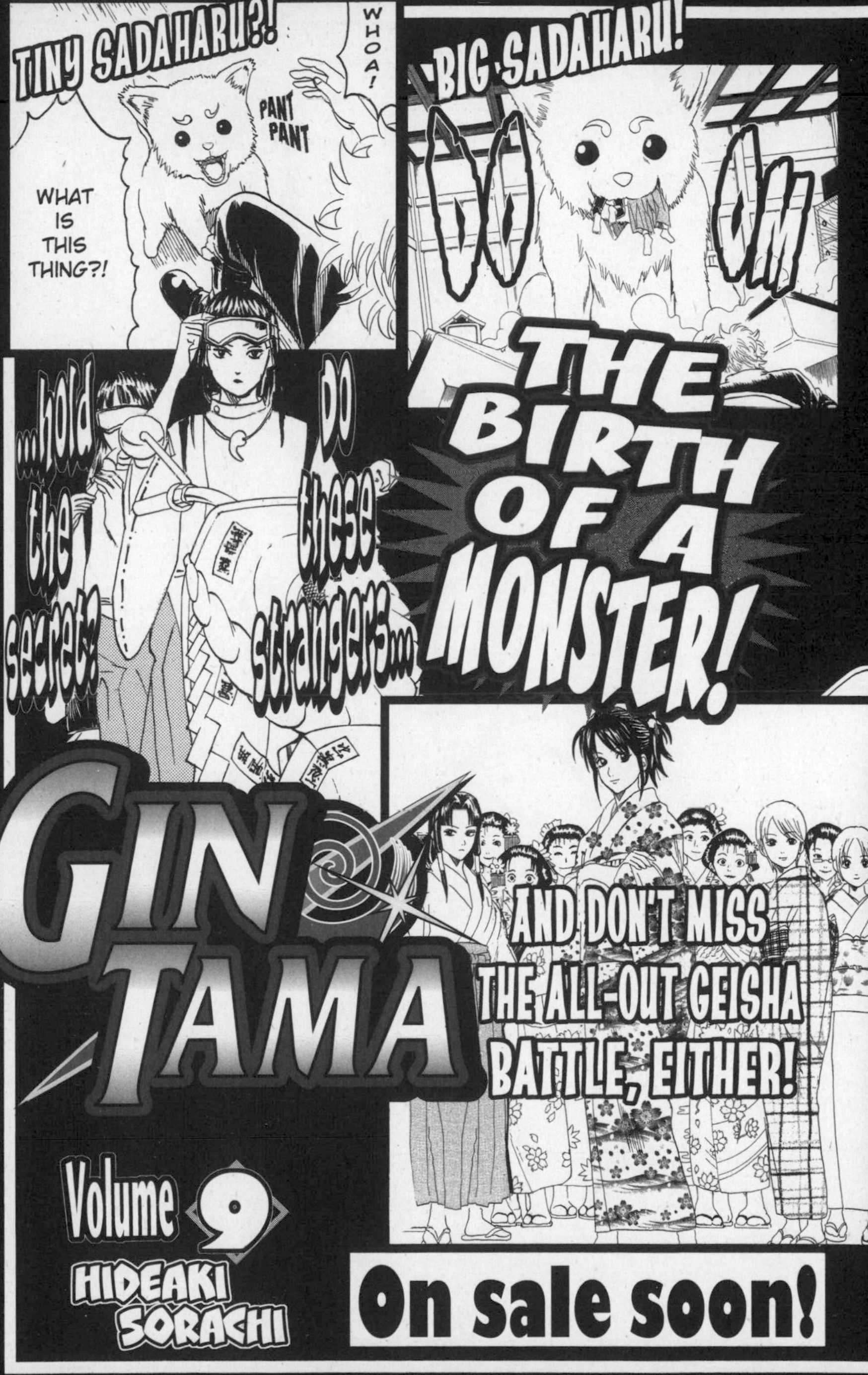
TINY SADAHARU?!
WHOA!
PANT PANT
WHAT IS THIS THING?!
BIG SADAHARU!
DOOM
THE BIRTH OF A MONSTER!
...hold the secret?
Do these strangers...
GIN TAMA
AND DON'T MISS THE ALL-OUT GEISHA BATTLE, EITHER!
Volume 9
HIDEAKI SORACHI
On sale soon!

Ninja Food-Fight!!

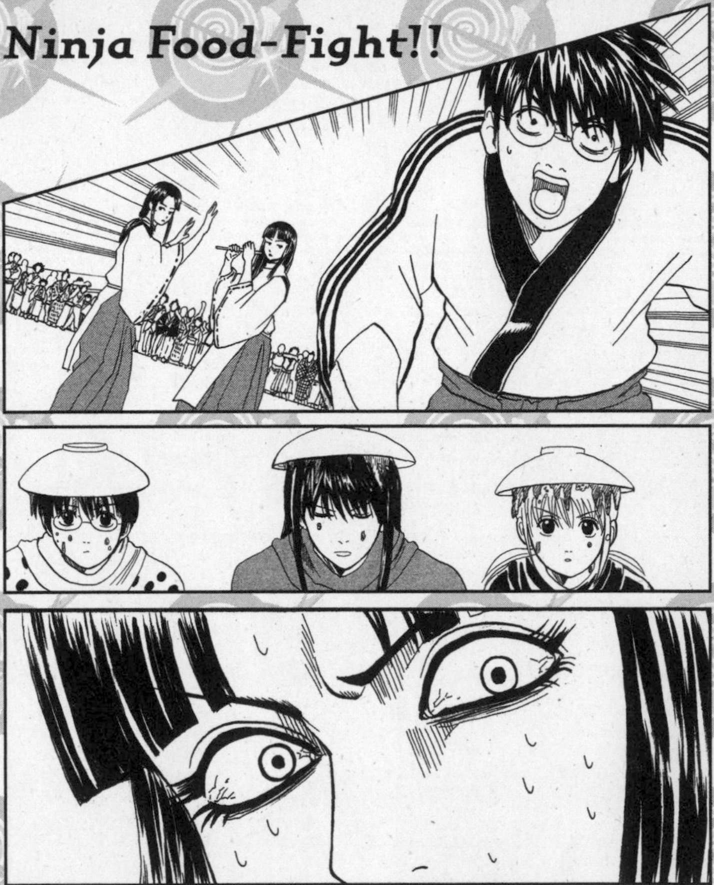

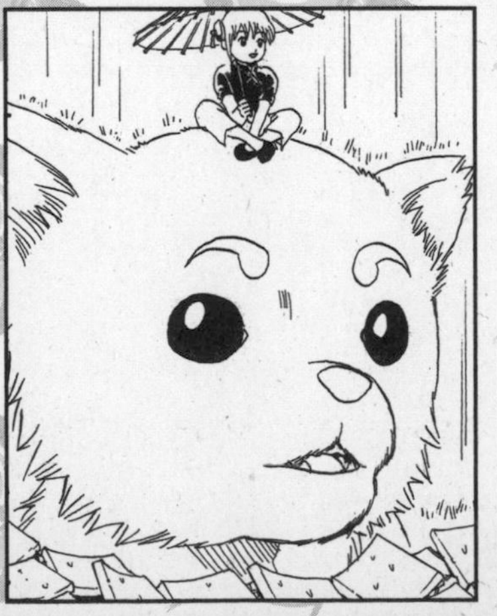

Gin's Ho-Hum Weekend To-Do List

1. Stock up on paper napkins and stain remover.
2. Think of a good excuse not to buy Hasegawa a new shirt.
3. Find out what kind of monster would swipe my strawberry milk from the fridge.
4. Get tickets to the game at Edo Dome while it's still standing.
5. Tell Shinpachi, Kondo and Matsudaira they're buying if they want me to go for drinks with them.

COMING NOVEMBER 2008